Echoes from the Boys of Company H

Echoes from the Boys of Company H

A chronicle through letters, diaries, and speeches of Civil War soldiers from Company H of the 100th Regiment, New York State Volunteers, of their experiences in the Siege of Charleston, SC, the Virginia Campaigns of Bermuda Hundred, Petersburg, Richmond, and Andersonville Prison.

Neal E. Wixson, Editor

iUniverse, Inc.
New York   Bloomington

Echoes from the Boys of Company 'H'
The Seige of Charleston, the Assault on Fort Wagner, the
Virginia Campaigns for Petersburg and Richmond, and prison
life in Andersonville as chronicled by Civil War Soldiers
from the 100th New York State Regiment, Company H

iUniverse books may be ordered through booksellers or by contacting:

iUniverse
1663 Liberty Drive
Bloomington, IN 47403
www.iuniverse.com
1-800-Authors (1-800-288-4677)

Because of the dynamic nature of the Internet, any Web addresses or links contained in this book
may have changed since publication and may no longer be valid. The views expressed in this work
are solely those of the author and do not necessarily reflect the views of the publisher, and the
publisher hereby disclaims any responsibility for them.

ISBN: 978-1-4401-2243-9 (pbk)
ISBN: 978-1-4401-2244-6 (ebk)

Printed in the United States of America

iUniverse rev. date: 2/20/2009

Contents

ILLUSTRATIONS
Harper's Weekly

Birdseye View of Charleston, South Carolina Harbor
Harper's Weekly – August 15, 1863

Pictures of Morris Island, South Carolina
Harper's Weekly – August 22, 1863

Bombardment of Fort Wagner
Harper's Weekly – August 29, 1863

Pictures of Morris Island, South Carolina
Harper's Weekly – September 5, 1863

Charleston Campaign
Harper's Weekly – September 12, 1863

Union Troops Occupying Petersburg, Virginia
Harper's Weekly – April 22, 1865

Reception of Exchanged Prisoners from Andersonville Prison
Harper's Weekly – December 10, 1864

Fall of Richmond, Virginia
Harper's Weekly – April 22, 1865

Andersonville Prison Scenes
September 16, 1865

Edward Cook Letter dated January 19, 1863

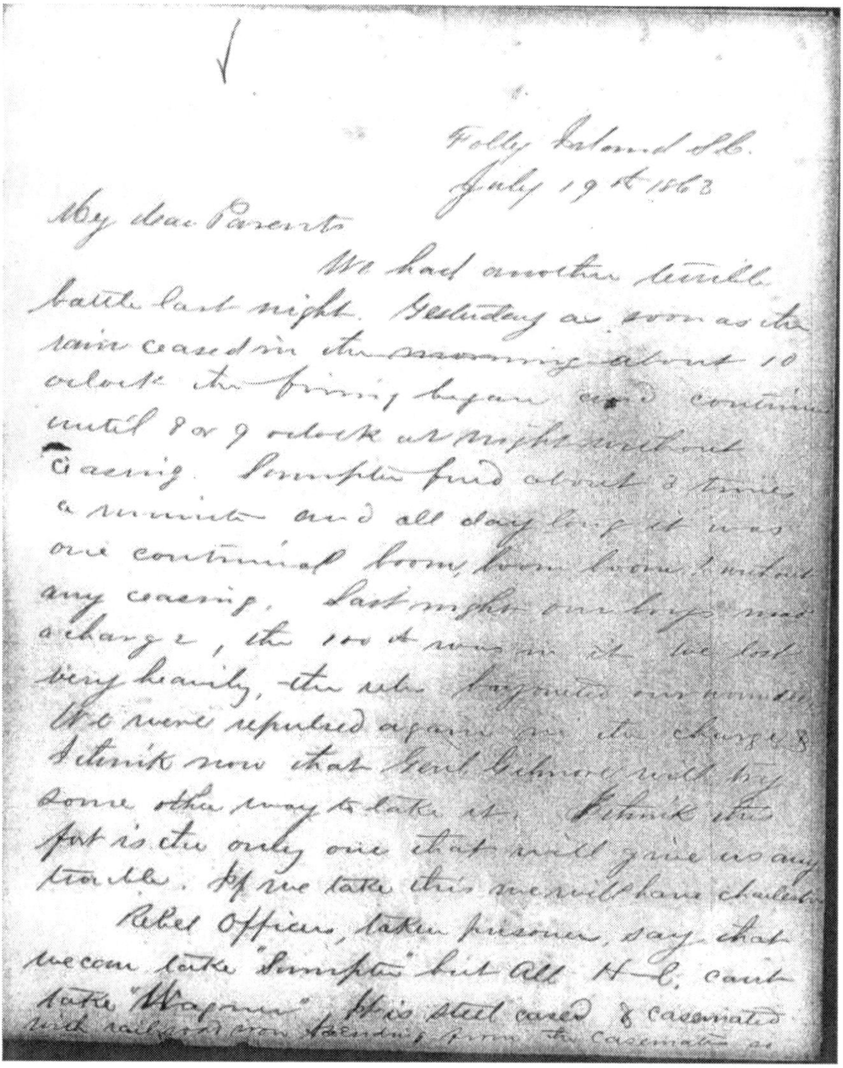

Folly Island S.C.
July 19th 1863

My dear Parents

We had another terrible battle last night. Yesterday as soon as the rain ceased in the morning about 10 o'clock the firing began and continued until 8 or 9 o'clock at night without ceasing. Sumpter fired about 3 times a minute and all day long it was one continual boom, boom boom, without any ceasing. Last night our boys made a charge, the 100th was in it. We lost very heavily, the rebs bayoneted our wounded. We were repulsed again in the charge & I think now that Genl Gilmore will try some other way to take it. I think the fort is the only one that will give us any trouble. If we take this we will have Charleston.

Rebel Officers, taken prisoner, say that we can take "Sumpter" but All H—l can't take "Wagner". It is steel cased & casemated with railroad iron standing from the casemates as that it is perfectly Boom proof.

I think we will take within a fortnight
our loss is terrible. One regiment lost all
their field officers all the line officers
but five. Our Major was wounded.
Genls. Strong & ~~Colonel~~ Seymour are
wounded. What do the people north think
of the attack on Charleston & did they expect
it? I have not heard direct from
the 100th but if I hear any thing about
Geo. Clark I will write to you.

I am in great haste. I never worked
so hard in my life as I am doing now
and have done for the last month or
more. I do not write to any body
but you. News is very scarce.
a dollar was offered to day for a single
coppies of the N.Y. Herald of the 19th with
and even then those that had them would
not sell. They sell in N.Y. for 2 cents
and here 2 dollars would hardly buy one.
I am well. Wish to see _____ & send all the
news. his Stoddard is well liked by his quartermaster
The Captain told me yesterday that he was going to
kick George and pay him 25 or 40 cents each pay

Your aff— son Edward

Maps

1. Charleston and its Defenses, Philadelphia Inquirer, April 11, 1863

2. Map of the Seat of War, Waters & Son, The London American, 1861

3. Assault on Battery Wagner Plan, September 1863

CHARLESTON AND ITS DEFENCES.

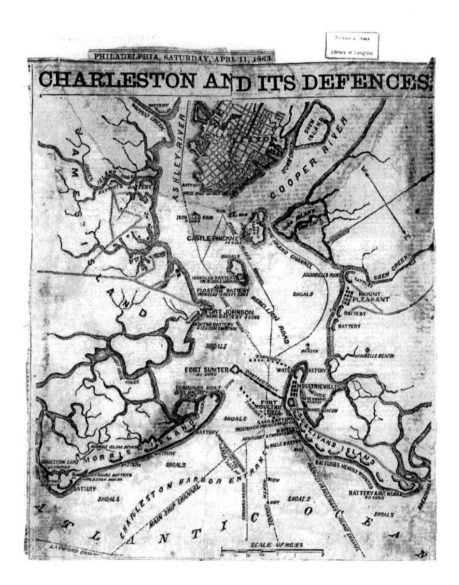

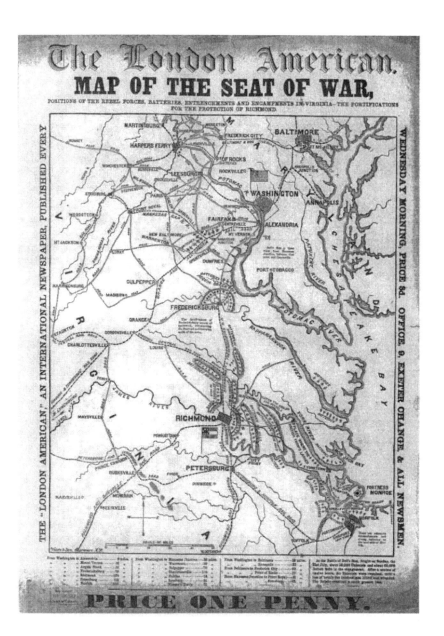

The London American.
MAP OF THE SEAT OF WAR,
POSITIONS OF THE REBEL FORCES, BATTERIES, ENTRENCHMENTS AND ENCAMPMENTS IN VIRGINIA—THE FORTIFICATIONS FOR THE PROTECTION OF RICHMOND.

THE "LONDON AMERICAN," AN INTERNATIONAL NEWSPAPER, PUBLISHED EVERY

WEDNESDAY MORNING, PRICE 3d. OFFICE 9, EXETER CHANGE & ALL NEWSMEN.

PRICE ONE PENNY.

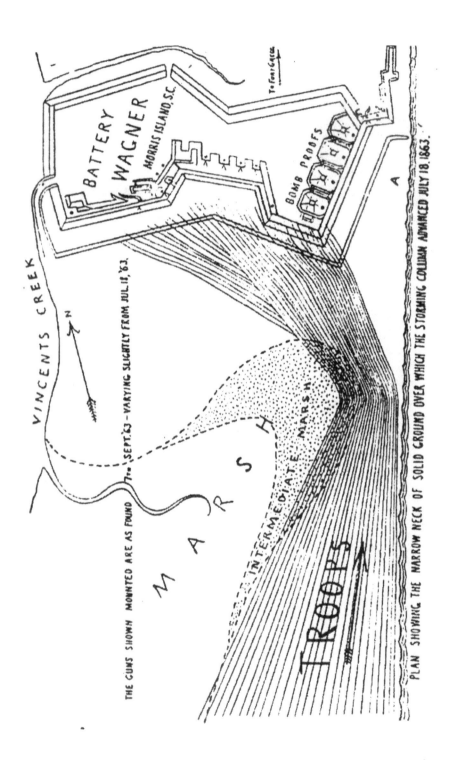

BATTERY WAGNER

MORRIS ISLAND, S.C.

VINCENTS CREEK

N

BOMB PROOFS

To Fort Gregg

A

THE GUNS SHOWN MOUNTED ARE AS FOUND 7TH SEPT.'63 — VARYING SLIGHTLY FROM JUL.18,'63.

M A R S H

INTERMEDIATE MARSH

TROOPS

PLAN SHOWING THE NARROW NECK OF SOLID GROUND OVER WHICH THE STORMING COLUMN ADVANCED JULY 18. 1863.

PREFACE

When I was about ten or eleven, I remember my grandfather taking me to the sun porch of his house and showing me a cabinet that contained souvenirs that my great-grandfather, Thomas Maharg, had brought home from the Civil War. The cabinet was arranged as if it was a memorial and was wrapped with his maroon sash. My grandfather talked about the assault on Fort Wagner and showed me a piece of shrapnel that had been embedded in my great-grandfather's lip. He also showed me my great-grandfather's discharge papers, his canteen, and a piece of a quilt. My grandfather spoke with pride that Thomas Maharg was one of the few in his Veterans Association to have been granted perpetual memberships to all of his lineal descendents; therefore, I was actually a member of the Veterans Association for the 100th Regiment.

I must admit that at that time I didn't have a full appreciation of what all these artifacts and the membership meant. Nonetheless, it must have made a significant impression on me, for from that time on, I wanted to learn as much as I could about the war experiences of my great-grandfather and his fellow soldiers. Still, as I eventually read about the 100th regiment's history and part in the Civil War, something was always missing. The books talked about strategies and officers, and yet, I was not getting any closer to my great-grandfather's personal experience. Hence, this book has been written as a means to get to know my great-grandfather and his comrades not only through their Civil War participation but also to know how they lived out the rest of their lives and preserved those recollections of their shared wartime service.

This book focuses on the lives of a few soldiers in Company H of the 100th Regiment, New York State Volunteers. It traces these men from enlistment to death and relates their experiences as soldiers in camp, battle, and prison. It is a story about young men who evolve from idealistic, adventure-seeking individuals into seasoned soldiers. Eventually they become heroes who reflect upon the past and the camaraderie established through shared times serving the Union during the Civil War.

The primary "echoes" are from the letters of Edward Cook and Alfred Lyth. Edward Cook was born in Buffalo, New York, in 1839 and was decorated for bravery and promoted to captain and first lieutenant before he was mustered out. Alfred Lyth was born in York, England, in 1844. He enlisted in August 1862 and remained on duty until December 1865. He contracted typhoid fever in July 1863 and, when well, returned to his company only to be captured and imprisoned in Andersonville from May until December of 1864. He remained in Camp Parole in Maryland until he later rejoined his company in Richmond, Virginia.

Other "echoes" are from the letters, diaries, or journals of Thomas Maharg, George Barnum, and George Stoddard. Thomas Maharg was born in Buffalo, New York, in 1842 and enlisted into service as a private at nineteen. He was promoted to sergeant in 1864. A letter is included from his brother John advising him of the death of his father; however, George Barnum had already told him of this sad loss. George Barnum was born in Buffalo, New York, in 1843. He enlisted as a private and was rapidly promoted to sergeant in 1863, second lieutenant in February 1864, and first lieutenant in May 1864. George Stoddard was born in Cleveland, Ohio, in 1838 and moved to Buffalo, New York. He enlisted in 1862.

Charles Walbridge was born in Buffalo, New York, in 1841. He was commissioned as second lieutenant in September 1861, promoted to first lieutenant, and then to captain. In 1864, he was selected to be the Depot Quartermaster for the Army of the James. Thomas Wharton was born in 1842, enlisted as a private in December 1861, and mustered out on January 20, 1865. George Stowits was born in Fort Plain, New York, in 1823 and later moved to Buffalo and became the principal of Schools 2, 10, and 11. He was promoted to major by the end of the war. He taught Edward Cook, Alfred Lyth, Thomas Maharg, George Barnum, Charles Walbridge, George Stoddard, and Thomas Wharton in the Buffalo Public School System. Not much is known about the early life of George Clark or of Edwin Nichols who was promoted to first lieutenant before being mustered out.

The book is based on unpublished letters, diaries, and notes written by these young soldiers. Through these sources, they are able to tell their own stories. They comment on everything from camp life and games, food, medical and dental care, women, religion, and politics to marches, dress drills, and fighting. Their initial exciting "expedition" and camp life turn into the horrors of adapting to battles, executions, and lost comrades. Alfred Lyth's interest in his family business is discussed no more as he must focus on his survival in battle and imprisonment at Andersonville. For a sizeable part of the remainder of the war, Edward Cook periodically notes that his friend George Clark is still missing. The soldiers eventually seem to be more and more unmoved by disease, hunger, death, and tragedy and relate these events almost with the objectivity of a reporter. Though written by different authors, the letters illustrate little disparity in relating common experiences. They reflect upon the observations of a limited number of comrades of essentially the same events. These events are reported differently only in the sense of the writer's personal interest and assessment of their importance to the reader. The letters offer a unique window into each author's mind and character. In a way, they silently express the isolation and loneliness that each man feels.

The letters and diaries are only minimally edited, so their content and character remain intact. Some words that are offensive by today's standards remain in the transcribed letters. Writing styles are varied with Alfred Lyth's long run-on sentences, punctuated only by commas, being the most difficult to read.

The letters and diaries were probably written with quill pens, which increasingly smudge as the nib of the quill wears down. Every quarter, the soldiers were able to acquire twelve quills and ink from the army as part of their stationery ration. This would not be a huge supply for a prolific letter writer. Thus, some words in the original letters are totally illegible for transcription.

Little information is provided as to strategies of battle; however, some observations from others in different companies or regiments about the assault on Fort Wagner are included. They reflect upon errors in strategy, errors by the soldiers in the 100th Regiment, and the general mass confusion that may have affected the outcome of that particular assault.

The last section encompasses the postwar years after the "boys" settle back in to "civil life" and ultimately reestablish contact with their comrades through their Veterans Association. Friendships are rekindled within this organization. The reminiscing that abounds seems to be done with surprising accuracy. Perhaps that is due to the fact that this book focuses only on average, young, unskilled men who were thrown into an adventure in which their only expectation was "to do your duty." They did not seek personal aggrandizement but rather were simply motivated by patriotism.

As we get to know these letter writers, their views, and their experiences, we are permitted to also learn about the remainder of their lives. What happened to them after the war? Were they successful in their transition to "civil life"? Were they honored upon their return? Did the camaraderie of the war remain? This book is unique in that these questions are answered. We learn of the rest of their lives and are privileged to read accounts of their reunions and gatherings. We follow the "boys" to their very graves.

I am extremely grateful to the following for their assistance and support so readily given, access to their collections, and permission to use materials where appropriate: The Library of Congress, Geography and Map Division and the Manuscript Division; John Adler, Publisher, Harpweek, Greenwich, Connecticut; Susan A. Riggs, Manuscripts and Rare Books Librarian, Special Collections, Earl Gregg Swem Library, The College of William and Mary, Williamsburg, Virginia; Patricia Virgil, former Director of Library and Archives, William Seiner, Past Executive Director, Cynthia Conides, Acting Executive Director, and Cynthia Van Ness, Director of Archives and Library, all of the Buffalo and Erie County Historical Society, Buffalo, New York; the Buffalo and Erie County Public Library; and the University of South Carolina Press. Most especially, gratitude is expressed to Edward C. Fields, Supervisor, Information Services, Department of Special Collections, Davidson Library, University of California, Santa Barbara, California, for permitting access to Edward Cook's wonderful letters, which can now be shared with the world.

Words cannot express my appreciation to my mentors: Carol Sheriff, Associate Professor of the Department of History, The College of William and Mary; Jeff Toalson; and Edward Longacre—all of whom are noted authors of Civil War books. They responded with interest to my many questions about this project and gave me words of encouragement. David Barnum provided the personal notes of George Barnum and shares a strong bond with me as a great-grandson of one of the "boys" of Company H. He, too, is a fellow perpetual member of the 100th Regiment Veterans Association.

Special recognition and appreciation is also given to my daughter, Lindsey P. Wixson, who labored tirelessly for over two years transcribing copies of the original letters of Edward Cook and Alfred Lyth and to my wife, Donna R. Wixson, who read those transcribed copies in minute detail and gave me many suggestions for improvements to the book.

I thank the families who had the foresight to preserve the letters, diaries, and records of these soldiers by donating them to the historical societies and libraries where they remain. My final word of appreciation rests with the "boys" who developed these marvelous written accounts of their war experiences and likewise authored the proceedings of their Veterans Association. Their eloquent words have truly brought me a new depth of understanding of my great-grandfather that had been missing in earlier years as well as a powerful sense of gratitude for the sacrifices made by all who fought during the Civil War.

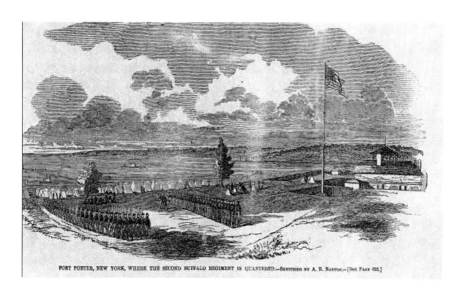

FORT PORTER, NEW YORK, WHERE THE SECOND BUFFALO REGIMENT IS QUARTERED.—Sketched by A. R. Barton.—[See Page 825.]

MILITARY LIFE

INTRODUCTION

Organization and Service of the Initial Recruits of the 100th Regiment

"We remained at Fort Porter during the winter of 1861 and '62 and I well remember the frequent discussions we had over the probabilities of our ever getting away from Buffalo, the prevailing fear being that the war would be over before we had a chance to get even as far Washington!. . . At last the long looked for orders came, and on the 7th of March, 1862 reveille sounded at an unusually early hour, the last preparations were completed, the long lines were formed, at eight o'clock we took up our march to the depot. We numbered over one thousand, and were the first *full* regiment that had left our city up to that time.

"We arrived at Washington ... and were conducted to our camp ground. Tents were issued, and we were speedily instructed in the modus operandi of pitching them. Here our first tribulation with the commissary department began, for instead of bread, rations were issued of flour, which in an uncooked state was of no earthly use to us and of coffee unburned, and ungrounded.

"One evening in the latter part of March, we broke camp with the rest of our division, marched down through the city, crossed the Potomac over the 'long bridge' and arrived in the outskirts of Alexandria about ten o'clock on a clear, cold night. We were halted by the roadside, stacked arms, and dismissed, with intimation that we could make ourselves comfortable by lying around loose, anywhere in the vicinity. This is memorable because it was our first bivouac, and that, too, at a very inclement time of the year, and under peculiarly trying circumstances, many of us having neither overcoats or blankets, having indiscreetly left them to come with the baggage. Well, we got through that night and the next, somehow, and the third day marched to the wharf and embarked with the rest of your brigade on the monster steamship *Constitution* … Many of you remember this first experience of life on a crowded transport, a state of existence with which the 100th became very familiar before its term of service was closed

"Arrived at Newport News, we were quickly established in camp at the peach orchard, or Camp Scott, as it was officially designated, and our campaign on the peninsula was begun.

"After a few days' sojourn, we advanced to Warwick Court House, and on this march realized the burden of knapsack, overcoat, blanket, arms haversack and forty rounds of ammunition, when marching under a Southern sun, and we then, for this first time, witnessed the sight of poor fellows stopping by the roadside overcome by the heat. Opening their knapsacks and throwing their trinkets and even clothing right and left, they were willing to do anything to lighten their unaccustomed load.

"We were without tents; those we had formerly used having been left with all the extra baggage. It was some days before shelter tents were received and in the meantime we made little booths, in which we weathered several severe rainstorms. Provisions were in very scant supply, owing to the great difficulty of transporting them through the deep mud and wretched roads.

" . . . after Magrauder had delayed us for a whole month, when at last our big siege guns were mounted and all preparations were made to assault his line, he took 'French leave' one night, and in the morning the fortifications in front of us were evacuated. We were quickly in pursuit but by some blunder which I never heard explained, our regiment, and I believe our whole division, marched without overcoats, blankets or knapsacks, and with only one day's rations. We supposed we were sent out for a reconnaissance, and that we would return to camp at night just as we had from similar expeditions before. This careless blunder on the part of some cost an immense and needless amount of suffering.

"The next day was the battle of Williamsburg, where the enemy under Longstreet and Magruder made a determined effort to still further delay the advance of our army. The 100th lay in the woods until late in the afternoon, although we were within distinct sound of the firing all day. There were thousands of troops like us close at hand.

"It was now dusk and we were formed in line of battle and remained there till morning. The suffering of that night will ever be remembered by all who were there. We were without overcoats or blankets, had eaten no proper food all day and now as the cold night set in became chilled through and through. Not a spark of fire was allowed along the whole line; many of the men were seized with severe pains, and as they were brought by the stretcher corps and laid in a row along the edge of the woods, where the surgeons could do but little to relieve them, their groans and agony added to their discomfort and suffering of the rest of us. It was such experiences as these that soon filled the hospitals with sick and disabled soldiers, and death was already busy gathering in his harvest.

"Well, the longest night has an ending, and the morning came at last. We found as we had turned the enemy's flank, he had evacuated his whole line of works, not to make another stand until the defenses of Richmond were reached. We therefore had nothing to do but to build great fires, lie down and rest in the warm sunshine, and wait for welcome rations which soon arrived. I shall always remember gratefully that lovely morning and the comfort it brought us...

"All the morning they have been getting their troops into position and now their solid columns and long lines speedily emerged from the dense woods which skirted the battle field, and with screeching shells and rattle of musketry, the ball opened; This was the first general battle between the Army of the Potomac and the brave foes, the Army of Northern Virginia; neither side appreciated as yet the value of rifle pits, and we stood there squarely facing the coming storm.

"Our fellows were dropping rapidly, but no attempt was made to reinforce our line, all the effort of our Commanders being to establish a second line while we held our ground in front. As they pressed us hard, with the hope of staying them yet a little longer, the order was given us to charge. This charge has always seemed to us a most desperate expedient. There was then, however, no thought of holding back, or of questioning the propriety of the order, but away we went, clambering over logs and stumps of the slashing in our front, until the fire of the enemy was so intense that no troops could breast such a storm of lead. It was in this advance and the subsequent withdrawal that we met with our heaviest losses. Soon the order came to fall back, and I can now in memory see Naglee as he rode along the rear of the line, swinging his hat, and shouting "Retreat!" "Retreat!" As we passed to the rear there was no hurry, and no panic... Thus the 100th regiment received its baptism of fire. After that eventful afternoon, we felt that we were no longer green troops, but veterans.

"In August the final abandonment of the peninsula was decided upon, and the 100th took up its line of March with the rest of the army for Fortress Monroe. The heat was intense, and we were almost choked with dust but we at least reached our goal, when, instead of embarking with the bulk of the army to go to the aid of General Pope, we were sent to Gloucester Point on the York river, directly opposite historic village of Yorktown

"Here we learned that the Board of Trade of Buffalo had adopted us as their regiment and we soon experience substantial benefits from this adoption, as scores and hundreds of new men, recruited under their influence began to arrive. The 100th now entered upon a new era of its history." Lt Col Charles E. Walbridge address at the first Annual Reunion 7/19/1887

Chapter One

Enlistment to Gloucester Point. VA.
August, 1862 to September, 1862

George Barnum, Personal Notes

"Early in 1862, a bunch of us boys in the neighborhood met at our neighbor's house one night and we began talking about the war. My recollection now is that there were about 10 of us and before we left to go home we had each promised to go down the street the next morning to a recruiting office and enlist. It was my habit every morning to drive my father down to his office, near the foot of Main Street. This morning when we passed within a block of the Post Office, I said that I would go over and get the mail and he could drive down the rest of the way. I went into the Post Office and got the mail and on the corner near by, I went to the recruiting station and signed up. When it came to my age, the recruiting officer said I would have to get my father's consent as I was not of age. I put the enlistment papers with the mail and handed them all to my father. When he came to the enlistment papers, I remember him saying "What's this?" I said I had enlisted and was going to the war. He said that I could not go since I was not of age but I said that all he had to do with give me permission which he declined to do saying I was not only not of age but I was physically incompetent to act as a soldier. I well remember that evening when father spoke to my mother about it. She did not approve but I still insisted that I was determined to go. If I did not enlist in Buffalo, I would go down to Rochester or Albany and enlist there. The next morning when I came down to breakfast, my father said that he and mother talked it over and had concluded to let me go."[1]

"The next evening when we boys assembled again, I found that

1

only one other had really enlisted. We enlisted in Company H, 100th New York Volunteers. This regiment had left Buffalo early in the spring 1,000 strong. Very soon after leaving they served under McClelland in the Peninsula campaign near Richmond. The regiment lost nearly 500 men in this campaign. Then the Buffalo Board of Trade adopted the regiment and recruited it up to full strength again. I was one of those recruits. This chum [Tom Maharg] was very close friends all during the war.

The other recruits and I left Buffalo for Albany where we were mustered in passing a thorough examination as to fitness and health. We were given a suit of soldier's clothes and a tin cup and tin plate."[2]

Letter from A. Lyth to his Parents, Sister and Brother

Barracks Albany Sep 6/62 9 am

Dear Father Mother, Sister and Brother
We arrived in Albany yesterday morning about 2 oclock and we went right away to the barracks wich is about 2 miles from the rail road depot the barracks is a very large brick building about 200 or 250 feet long an three stories high it was built for an industrial school we sleep in bunks which are placed one over another three high I sleept very comfortable in one last night but I cannot tell weather I shall sleep in one tonight or not as we expect we shall leave for New York to night but we cannot tell for certain I think by what I have heard that when we go to New York we shall go on the river by steamboat
We got all our clothes regimentals yesterday excepting our coats which some say we shall not get until we get to new york but I cannot tell I got my hat an pants two good woolen shirts simalar to what I bought in Buffalo 2 pair of good cotton flanel drawers and a knapsack we shall get stockings when we get our coats I did not take a pair of shoes because they are so very heavy they will be credited to my account and I shall get payed for them and then I will buy myself a good pair of boots as a good many of them have done I have not been into the city yet as they will not alow any of us to leave the barracks but I think we shall get out this afternoon there are about 3 or 4 hundred in the barracks at present but there squads constantaly leaving

and other acoming the other squad of Buffalo boys arrived this morning. We have very good board here We had to breakfast yesterday morning potatoes + meat good coffee and bread + excellent butter for dinner it being friday we had fish an potatoes coffee + bread + butter for supper we had good sweet corn meal + potatoes + coffee + bread + butter We have not got our state Bounty yet but we shall get it in an hour or so our squad were all examined by the doctor yesterday in which 4 did not pass him so they will not receive any State Bounty but they got to go One says he will not go and the sergent of a cavalry company say they cannot make him go.

1 oclock P.M.
We cannot get a pass to leave the barracks because the Leautenant thinks it almost certain that we shall leave here this afternoon and he wants us to keep together. We have got our Bounty. I have kept $5 of mine and sent the rest 45 home which will be delivered to you at home by a gentelman who took charge of all our Bounties that we wanted to send home. I kept $5 dollars because we do not get our moths advance pay untill we reach the regiment. We have all concluded to take our old clothes along with us. As our Leautenant says our regiment will be garrisoned for some months and they will be of service to us. I will write again when we reach New York so no more at present from
      Your Truly Affectionate Son
      Alfred Lyth
   To John Lyth Buffalo

Letter from E. Cook to his Parents

Albany around Sept. 17/62
Dear Parents
We are now stopping at our "hotel". Our sleeping room is up 3 pair of Stairs. Here is a kind of a sketch of the arrangement of the bunks. All we have to sleep on is a straw mattress without sheet or blanket. You can imagine me sitting on my bunk writing to you. We rode all night and I did not sleep a wink.
   I left off writing to go to breakfast and I have eat so much that I can

hardly breathe; we had cold corn and potatoes; first rate bread + good butter with tolerable coffee – no milk and sour sugar. We arrived at this city at 5 ½ oclock and before you were out of bed we were on the march to the tune of Yankee doodle which was whistled by Ed Cook as we had no music. We marched about 3 miles and every step of the way was up a hill. It was a good deal further than it is to our fort in Buffalo. On our way from the cars to the barracks we stole several morning papers so we have got the latest news. I will send you the one I got and you can lay it away in my trunk as a memento of the plunder we obtained on our first march.

Geo. Stoddard + I captivated the hearts of 2 young Ladies whom we saw in the arcade at Buffalo. I have heard that one of them was a Miss Lydia Day. I saw Lottie McLane + her mother at the Depot at Syracuse about 12 oclock last night to which place they had come for the purpose of seeing Lottie's future husband I suppose. Lottie looked first rate but she did not seem very sorry to have us go away. I did not get out of the cars to see her so I could not kiss her good by. She wants Lillie to write to her and I hope she would, but don't say any thing to her about it.

We feel first rate and have just been blowing the sergeant because he wants us to sweep out in our room. We may have to stay here a day or two but I hope not as I do not like the looks of the dirty bunks. We are up on a hill + have a very pleasant view of the surrounding country. The boys are just reading the paper that I am going to send to you. Our bed is on the top of the bunk and we have to climb up quite a ways like the births on a steamboat. There are 3 rows of bunks in each room and 3 stories to each bunk + 18 or so can sleep on each story; that makes 54 in a bunk + over 150 in a room.

I had another bottle of rum given to me but I gave it away when I left the cars. You need not write until as I do not know where I shall be and the letter. Tell Laura I have got along so far first rate + feel bully.
Give my love to Grandma + tell her that the boys want her to remember them. Good by.

Love to all – Private Edward L. Cook

4

Letter from E. Cook to his Parents

Albany Barracks Sept 18/62

Dear Parents

We have just rec'd orders to leave the barracks for New York to night. We are all glad to start as this barracks life is any thing but pleasant the quarters are more dirty than our old cow stable. For supper last night we had raw onions + bread without butter; for dinner yesterday we had boiled beans + fat of ham and last night every man in the company except me had an awful belly ache. There is a phrenologist up on the top bunk telling a man his character it is quite laughable; you can see by my writing that I am giving more attention to what he says than I am to the letter. He is just telling a man that he would make a good mechanic particularly a tailor I was up on top of the Capitol today and wrote my name on the dome. I saw the way lock where they weigh canal boats + had a good time generally. All the boys are in good spirits. We are going down the hudson river in the boat the moon rises about 10 o'clock and we will have a pleasant ride. I have not had my clothes off since I left the city of B. until about an hour ago and then I took a bath. The bath room had the door broken down + as another bath room is out doors and we were making a good deal of noise, every old woman would come and peak in, but we did not care for soldiers are not very particular. They have got a military hospital a little way from the barrack and the beds look so clean and the patients so comfortable that it seems just as though I should like to be sick just to go to the hospital to let them take care of me. Tell H that my pistol has been much admired by all of the boys in our room. Good by – dont fret – our forces are clearing the rebels out as fast as possible. I will try and write to you from New York. Tell Grandmother that the boys want to be remembered to her. I have lost my supper of onions + vinegar by writing to you. Good night.

Edward

Letter from A. Lyth to his Parents, Sister and Brother

Jersey City Sept 8 1862 10 am

Dear Father + Mother Sister + Brother

We left Albany last night and embarked on a steamboat and went down the Hudson river for New York where we arrived about 6 oclock this morning there we crossed the ferry to Jersey City where we are waiting at preasent for cars to take us to Baltimore. I cannot tell you weather we shall stop any length of time in any city before we reach Baltimore or not we have not got our military coats yet and do not expect too untill we reach Fortress Monroe I should like very much to hear from you but there is no use you writing until I tell you give my to sisters + brothers and Sarah Anna + William and tell Sarah I was very sorry I did not bid her good bye before I left her house I cannot write any more at present because they are all waiting for me to finis my letter for we are just going to get into the cars.

Yours Very
Respectfully, A Lyth

Letter from E. Cook to his Parents

Washington Barracks Sept 20/62

Well dear Parents here we are at last in Washington ready almost to fight and will be entirely ready as soon as we get our uniforms + rifles.

I have written to you twice before and sent you two papers. And when you write to me I want you should tell me what you have received. Geo. Stoddard wrote to his folks on the 17th and I sent my first letter. In my second letter I sent directions for you to get $50.00 for me of the Board of Trade but I put the letter in the soldiers box at the Albany Barracks just before I left for New York and forgot to put a stamp on it and did not discover my mistake until we were some ways on our march to the boat. I will repeat the directions for fear the letter did not go. I sent $50.00 State bounty to Buffalo payable to Father and if he will go to the recruiting office over the Morning Express office and inquire for Mr. Allen stating the circumstances he will get the money which you will please deposit to my credit with what I gave you in Buffalo which will be in all $110.00 I believe. Is that right?

Tell me in the first letter if the matter is all straight + satisfactorily settled. My last letter closed by saying that we were about starting for N.Y. I deposited my letter just in time to get in the ranks + answer to my name and off we went. Our march through the streets of Albany was a lively *affair. There was a large squad ahead of us but our boys were the one that attracted all the attention. Indeed where ever we go we seem to be the favorites among the other soldiers. We marched down one of the principal street of Albany and all of the girls (I was going to say good looking girls but there are no good looking girls in Albany) came out + bid us good by and threw us a kiss. I waved my kerchief so much that I almost made it. I said goodby so many times that I was almost hoarse; threw so many kisses that my lip is sore and turned round so many times that it almost made my back ache. When we got down to the boat one of our men skedaddled and the Lieutenant detailed me to go off + hunt him up. I wandered around time for a while when I returned to the boat the man was there. Our ride down the Hudson was not as pleasant as I expected for the sky was cloudy + I could not distinguish the shore very plainly. I remained on deck until 4 oclock in the morning (we started at 9 in the morning) expecting to see something grand but "I diddent see it". One of most remarkable and in fact the most astonishing thing that I witnessed on the Hudson was the very deceptive appearance of the banks of the river which, as I saw them in the evening when we were near the shore, appeared to be from 10 to 40 feet in height, but in the morning when I could compare them with large buildings on the banks they were 6 – 10 times as high as the tallest buildings, which were sometimes 4 stories high. This is the reason most likely why the scenry did not appear interresting to me in the evening. I got out of my berth the next morning at 5 ½ oclock + I cannot tell for the life of me whether I slept any that night or not. (We must start for Alexandria cant finish)*

5 ¼ oclock

After a march of about 2 miles we now find ourselves aboard of an old rotten tub, crossing the Potomac for Alexandria where our Regt will meet us in a few days) – To continue my narative of Hudson River. The scenery as it appeared during the morning was truly lovely; I cannot call it grand for I do not consider it such, the proper terms are lovely, beautiful and picturesque. We arrived at New York about 10 o'clock A.M. I bought my breakfast of the cook aboard boat for 25 cts. It consisted of beefsteak, potatoes, bread + butter + a cup of poor coffee. I could get a better meal in Buffalo for 15 cts. When we arrived in N.Y. we were marched up Broadway for about a mile + quartered in an old building fitted up for

Barracks and the smell was so bad that it almost made us sick. Not one of us eat a meal at the barracks while we staid there. We got a pass after we had been there a few minutes and we had a very pleasant time around the city. Geo. Clark + I went together and G. Stoddard + some other young man went in another direction. I first went to the shot tower, one of the highest buildings in the city. We obtained permission to go on its top and after ascending about 160 steps + 3 ladders we found ourselves many feet above the highest buildings in the city and met as grand a birds eye view of New York as it is possible to obtain. After descending the tower and performing our ablutions, we took a walk down Broadway to White Hall Street and I called on Mr. Sprague but he was not in and I did not see him but I left a card so he will know that I called. In the afternoon we took the cars + rode the full length of 5th Avenue it is a fine street of buildings but for beauty does not begin to compare with our own lovely Delaware. It contains <u>solid</u> blocks of great high brick + stone dwellings. There are spaces between the buildings but each house is masoned up close to the other all the vacancies that occur are the street. The avenues are some distance apart but the street occur at very short intervals. When we rode as far as we could go on the fifth avenue cars we crossed over to Sixth Avenue and took the cars for Central Park. (The boat is now about to land us at Alexandria so I must stop until we disembark and are marched to our quarters. If I have a good opportunity I will send this as it is and finish my recital in another letter as soon as possible.

Your Loving Son
Edward L. Cook
100th Regt. N.Y.S.V

Letter from A. Lyth to his Folks

10am Barracks Washington Sept 10 1862
Dear Folks
My last letter that I wrote you was from Jersey city I cannot tell weather you received it or not as I did not post it myself we took the cars from Jersey city through to philadelphia where we arraved about 5 oclock P.M. I shall never forget the reception the citizens of that city gave us from the depot where we landed to the Soldiers Rest which is over a mile and a half the streets where lined on both sides with young ladys welcoming us

to philadelphia the little boys would run along with us and carry our knapsacks while the ladies would grasp our hands and shake them saying welcome to philadelphia hope we shall see you again we got our suppers at the Soldiers Rest then we fell into ranks and marched through the city to another depot the biding us good by and shaking hands with us as before We embarked on the cars for Baltimore but we had not got more than 5 miles from Philadelphia when a sad accident befel us our engine broke lose from the train and another train coming behind us at full speed ran into our train as it was stoping and killed 4 four and wounded 16 of which 1 as since died and another is not expected to live the car that I was in was very badly smashed up on one end one in an being killed that sat 2 rows behind me and three badly wounded 1 slightly and one my partner had his leg hurt a piece of the car striken it but he had come along with with us and is a good deal better and march with us after the accident we encamped in an open field and carried the wounded in to a house close by the engine that run into us was totaly destroyed running half way under our hind car and bursting her boiler about 7 oclock next morning a train come along and took us to baltimore where we get dinner and then we got aboard the cars for washington. the railroad has to to be guarded between Baltimore + Washington. We keep the rebels from tearing up the track there is camps of soldiers about one mile apart the entire length of the road and a guard stationed about every ¼ of a mile but as we came near washington we saw a great many Regiments encamped but when we reached washington we saw the soldiers there is a bout 20 acres of ground covered with buildings used as Barracks an a great many camps outside I cannot tell you when we shall leave washington I have been a good deal around the city this morning and seen the Capitol which is a very large building. As I am writing there are quite a number of Regiment leaving for to chase the Rebels back out of this state which they are invading they are all in good spirits and say they will chace the Rebels Back do not write to me at present as I cannot tell you how long we shall stay here if we get our military coats here I shall send my other clothes home if not I will take them along with me to the regiment
          Your Affectionate Son
          A Lyth
P.S. excuse the writing as I have to use my hat for my writing desk on my knee

Letter from A. Lyth to his Parents

Gloucester Point opposite Yorktown Virginia
8 P.M. Sept 12 1862

Dear Father + Mother

   We left Washington on the 10ᵗʰ back again for Baltimore and then we took the steamboat For Fortress Monroe where we arrived about 6 oclock next morning we got supper on board the boat which cost each 50 cents the officers not puting rations on board then we had dinner at fortress Monroe Uncle Sam paying for it I never before had any idea of the strength of that fortress it commands the bay on one side the river on the other and all the country on the other two sides I dare say there are nearly two hundred cannon inside and some ones mounted on the beach carrying a 600 pound ball and then there is the rip raps in the middle of river where there are some more large cannon mounted and a very large fleet of ships after going all around the fortress we got our rations and embarcked on board of a steamboat for Yorktown where we arrived about dusk then we got on a ferry boat + crossed the river to Gloucester Point as we were landing it commenced to rain and was very dark we could not see the camp from where we landed is being on a hill about a ½ a mile from the shore however when we got on top of the hill we could see it in the distance and we groped our way to it and was heartly received by the boys then we searched out our respective Companys where we was treated hansomly two men turing out of their beds and giving them to myself + companion and sleeping on the floor of the tent theirselves I slept pretty Sound and rested well although it raind in torrents however it cleared up towards morning and has been a tremendous hot day we have no officers in our company except an orderly sergent which is one of the nicest men I ever came across setting men to cook breakfast for us himself getting our tents ready for us to put up we got a good breakfast and then we took a strole across the country nearly to the picket lines and went in to a house and some oyster stew which was very good then we came back and got our rig out of military clothes myself drawing a dress an overcoat + one pair of stockings then we went to our tents the men assisting us and which are very comfortable then we got supper + then had a good wash in the river which is salt. then we came back to our tent and lit our candle and I sat down and wrote this letter. this is a very strong point there being a very large fort an if with mounted guns and quite a number of on the other side of river at Yorktown besides quite a larege fleet in the river I must come to a close Give my love to sisters + brothers + tell Sarah Ann that I will write to her soon

Write to me as soon as you possibly can as I should very much like to hear from home and direct to Alfred Lyth Co. H. 100 Reg't, N.Y.S.V. Gen Peck Division, Yorktown, Virginia.

Chapter Two

Gloucester, VA
September, 1862 – December, 1862

"Well, here we are in camp in Secession soil"
E. Cook letter dated 9/21/1862

"In the beautiful autumn weather, we soon regained health and strength; our ranks were filled with new comrades, many of whom were old schoolmates and friends from home, and therefore, doublely welcome. Under our accomplished commander, we made rapid progress in drill, and we doubtless all recall with pleasure those beautiful October days and nights on picket, on the front or along the banks of Sarah's creek. Verily those tours were more like *picnic* than picket duty. In December we made that raid to Gloucester Court House, driving out the squadron of Confederate cavalry which made that village its headquarters, and how the rebel chickens and turkeys did suffer. It was one of the very few occasions on which the 100th distinguished itself in that species of warfare." Lt. Col. Charles E. Walbridge address at the first Annual Reunion, 7/18/1887

Letter from E. Cook to his Parents

Camp Elsworth Sunday Sept 21/62
Well here we are in camp on secession soil. We landed last night and were marched about 3 miles from Alexandria and were immediately marched out.

I speak of the beauty of Central Park but it far exceeds any description I had ever seen. It is about 4 or 6 miles from the foot of Broadway and across one hundred acres. The best way to reach it is to take the Broadway and 6th Avenue cars and they take the visitor direct to the park

Carriages are always standing at the terminus of the streetcars; and for 1 Dollar they will carry a person all over the ground. It takes about 1 hour

to ride through all of the park. I cannot describe the scene as it deserves.
It is nature beautified. The park is laid in a part of the city that would
be almost use less for any thing else; the ground is very uneven and stony
and in many places the huge rocks extend several feet above the surface of
the ground and the ground around the vacinity of the dirty gray rocks is
so neat and arranged as to make the very rock its self appear picturesque +
beautiful. The park as yet has no fence around it but it soon will have; the
streets of the city run through it but they in no manner interfere with it as
they are all lowered below the average level of the park. The park its self is
on high ground and the street of the park run over those of the city.

You can see by this that the park does not in any way interrupt the trafic
on the streets although the streets of the city run directly through the park
and are crossed by the park streets. They have a beautiful artificial lake in
the park which is used for rowing in summer + skating in the winter. I
saw in the park a tree planted by the Prince of Wales and another planted
by one of the Dukes who accompanied him; that which was planted by the
prince did not flourish very well and the top was cut off so that it is now a
little low English oak. The pond is alive with beautiful white swans and
in the park is a very large cage full of beautiful deer. You can well imagine
that the park must be large to allow of a place being partitioned off large
enough to allow a quantity of deer to run in. The cage that contains them
is a high wire fence painted Green and you can scarcely notice it until you
get almost to it so that a little way off the deer appear to be running at
large. The park also contains several other animals and a number of birds
in large cages. It is one of the loveliest places I ever visited and I would
any person that comes to New York not to leave the city until they have
visited Central Park. The park contains 100 acres; there is about 6 miles of
carriage way in it, and it takes about an hour to drive through it and after
a person has rode through the park and found out all the places of interest,
he wants to leave the carriage and start through it again on foot and spend
an hour at each of the places of interest in the park. After we had been
through the park we took the 6th Avenue cars and rode down to Broadway,
got out of the cars and walked up broadway as far as

[   ] Museum where I saw so many things that it is impossible to tell
you all or even to recollect them. There were wax figures + figures not of
wax; live fishes + dead fishes; animals stuffed + animals for stuffing – every
thing in fact that it is possible to imagine but the most pleasing thing that

I saw was his happy family of animals. In one cage were contained cats + rats woodchucks, raccoons, monkeys and baboons, chickens, owls and I dont know what their was not. I have got a chance to send this to the post office so I will close this + commence another immediately closed at 5 oclock P.M. on Sunday Sept 21/62

Your Loving Son
E.L. Cook
Acting Sargent
100th Regt N.Y.S.V.

P.S. When you receive my next you must read over the last part of this.

George Barnum, Personal Notes

"The Colonel of the regiment had been killed up at Fair Oaks and the regiment was in a rather disorganized condition being composed mainly of clerks and farmer boys and having officers that were not very strict. They seemed to do pretty much as they liked through the influence of the Buffalo Board of Trade they secured the services of Colonel Dandy who was at that time the Chief quarter master on General McClellan's staff and a West Point man. Our tents were put up most anywhere and I remember the first thing the Colonel did when he arrived at the regiment was to have every tent taken down. He then laid out a regular city of ten streets and every tent in line on every street. He had the ground thoroughly policed and cleaned up.

I remember the first night we went out on dress parade. The Colonel started in at one end of the regiment. My company was in the center, the color company. Soon I noticed that a lot of men were leaving the ranks and going back to their tents and could not imagine what was the trouble. When the Colonel came along some of the men had a dress coat on, some a sack coat, some had caps and some soft hats, some had shoes and some not, some had their brasses and their equipment brightened and others not. When the appearance of a man did not satisfy him, he gave him 10 minutes to go back to his tent and come back again dressed properly."[3]

14

Letter from E. Cook to his Parents, Sister and Brother

2 oclock
Gloucester Point Sept 22 1862

Dear Father Mother Sister + Brother

I had just returned from a stroll in the woods when your letter was handed in to me and you cannot tell the Joy I felt to hear from home and that you where all well. Mother should not feel so bad as I get along very well. I was very glad to hear that you were doing well in the tile business and hope you will continue to do so I should like to what kind of a burn you had in that kiln you put out the day I came away and if you have heard how Uncle Frank is geting along with his business I wish you would let me know I cannot tell you how many men there are in our regiment as there are a great many of them in the hospitals at present but I think there are about 5 or 6 hundred able bodied men in the regiment at present besides a hundred or two new recruits which started away from Buffalo before and some after our squad did the reason that those that started from Buffalo before we did have not got here I cannot learn but it is thought they got on the wrong road and went someways down towards Alexandria but we expect them along very soon there are ten companies in the regiment some of them only lacking a very few men whilst some have very few there are only 89 able bodied men in our company at present but I learn a great many of the new recruits are going to join our company I stated in my last letter which was to Sarah Ann that Capt. Hinson was under arrest and was going to be Court Martial his trial comes off to day and I do not think he will get off so easy as I first thought as is offend is serious he having got some company an some wiskey in his tent they were making a little more noise than was necessary when the Lt. Connell sent the guard to tell them to put out their light and go to bed when Capt Hinson sent back his best respects by the guard telling him to mind his own business the Goddamed dirty black Abolitionist for which language he was arrested we have not received our months pay yet but we shall get it soon as the paymaster will be along soon I should very much like to have you send me Harpers Weekly as newspapers are scarce on this side of the river and very dear as I had to pay 15 cent for one Harpers but it is not the one after the last one I had and I cannot read the story in it if you can send it after you have all read it,

I should be very much obliged send the one dated Sept 20. I have the one after that so you need not send it we have happened to get a daily paper in the company all last week but we have to go down to the boat and beseige the boy that fetches them across the river to get one then some one of the company gets upon a platform and read the war news I have done it tow or three times. I should like you to send me a Commercial Advertiser of every Saturday night as I should like to have the comfort to read a Buffalo paper once in a while no matter how old it is and what ever letters or papers you send direct as you did before as it is the right way. We have to drill 4 times a day but we have no other duty to do and we have pretty good times There are a good few darkies about here most all of them having been slaves A few nights ago we made a pretty good haul of cattle from the rebels they being fetched in by our pickets as they were on their way to the rebel army. the way we first heard of there being cattle in the vicinity a nigger came to the picket line and said there was a right smart chanch to get some cattle as there were some men going around buying all the cattle they could get and were going to take them away in the night accordingly we sent an extra company out with the pickets to capture them which they did about midnight and brought them in to camp and killed some of them the next day and eat some the next day give my love to Sarah Ann + William + all my friends.

Your Affectionate Son Alfred Lyth

Letter from A. Lyth to his Brother

Sat Sept 27 1862
Gloucester Point

Dear Brother

I am expecting a letter from you every day as father said in his letter that you was going to write to me next so having nothing to occupy my time at present I thought I write you a few lines and hope they will find you well a it leaves me at present I have pretty good times here we do not have to drill so much now as we had at first when we came here we go down to the river and catch fish + oysters and cook them I have met a few boys that I knew in Buffalo, and they tell me a good many stories of the battles they have been into The river is a first rate place to bathe in I have been in swiming twice since I have been here I was out on picket with our company on Wednesday and I had a pretty good time we have to go on at 8 oclock in the morning and stop until 9 oclock next morning there are 3 of us stationed on a post and some times 4 or 5 and we take turns watching for any signs of the Rebels and if we should happen to hear or see anything unusal we wake up our companions and alarm the other posts and if it should happen to be rebels a coming we should fire our guns and run back in to the woods on to the reserve which is stationed a piece back into the woods which are all cut down and make it very difficult for any body to pass through there only being a small foot path which one can pass through at a time then when the alarm is given the regiments turn out in line of battle and then if we should be attacked we should all march in to the fort which is a very large and strongly fortified 11 oclock night before last there was an alarm given that we were attacked by the rebels and we were all called out in line of battle and a company of volunteers deployed on to the picket line to see what the matter was and bring in the pickets but it was a false alarm some say it was a fellow saw a couple or so of mules in the pasture and though they were rebel cavelry and a good many other storys as to how it originated but however it turned out to be nothing we are at present encamped on a large common outside of the fort but we are going to have all new tents in a day or two and move inside of the fort and are likely to remain there sometime. I was very glad to here you got along very well since I left home. I have to leave my writing at present and go with my company to fire at the target.

I have just got back from shooting at the target and only 9 of us hit it out of 40 of us.

Your Loving Brother
Alfred Lyth

To John Lyth Jr, Buffalo, N.Y.

Letter from E. Cook to his Parents

Gloucester Point Va. Sept. 28th 1862

Dear Parents this is the Sabbath and although we have no service, it seems different from a week day. We slept in a tent last night and it is the first time we have slept under a covering since last Tuesday. I mailed a letter to you from Fortress Monroe on Friday day before yesterday. I had not been returned to the boat many minutes, after going to the post office, before we received orders to proceed to Suffolk opposite Norfolk in Va and before we had time to cast of the ropes + let the boat loose an other order came out as the first order and again in a few minutes came a 3ᵈ order telling us to proceed to Yorktown. This is the way that business is done in the Army; there seems to be no certainty or decision in any thing relating to Army Matters. We sailed from the Fortress about 1 oclock P.M. of Friday + arrived at Yorktown about 8 o'clock P.M. of the same day. Our ride up the York river was very pleasant, the water is salt and I sat for an hour or two watching the different kinds of sea fish that we passed on our way up. There is a kind of thing here that they call the sea nettle, when it touches you it stings like a nettle and it is nothing more than a kind of thick transparent colorless jelly and yet it has life + breathes in the water. In the evening whenever the water is disturbed it is all alive with spots of light or phosphoresant fire. It looks splendid in the evening, I can tell you. I will send back the clothes by express except my vest which I will want to use myself. From Yorktown we crossed the river to Gloucester Point, which is exactly opposite Yorktown, and remained on board the boat until morning thus making 3 nights that we were aboard of the nasty dirty lousey boat. We marched from the boat up the hill about ½ a mile + found ourselves within the lines of our regiment. You cannot guess how pleased we are to be with our regiment after being on the road so many days. We had to tent with some of the other boys last night but I suppose our tents will be here to day so we can put it up by night.

We all went outside the first line yesterday after dinner and got some oysters to eat about 3 dozen raw and if we had time I might have eat dozen more. They are very cheap here at present I am going out on the river a little ways tomorrow and get some more. They are very plenty up the river about ½ a mile above our camp and all we have to do is to pull off our clothes + wade in after them. We have not had 1 unpleasant day since we left Buffalo. Some of the days are very hot + sultry but the majority are quite pleasant. The days pass by very quickly but it seems an age almost since we left Buffalo. I have not been homesick since we left Buffalo. I would not return now if I could. We have had some pretty hard fare since we left but are very comfortably situated now. On board the boat we had hard crackers + water the first day and the crackers had both bugs + maggots in them but we did not care for that as we were pretty hungry.

We split open the crackers knocked the worms off + eat them with a relish. We had not slept more than one night with our clothes off and that was on board the boat down the Hudson. None of us are lousey as yet but the boys here tell us that we soon will be in spite of our selves. Yesterday I took a salt water bath for the first time in my life. I enjoyed it first rate. There are lots of salt water fish here if I only had hooks + lines to catch them with. I have sent you a letter asking for some things and I wish father would put a fishline in + 1 or 2 hooks. You might send them in a letter for that matter if you like. That cotton cloth you gave me will come in first rate for cleaning my musket, but woolen cloth is better + I dont care if you send me a few scraps of old woolen cloth with the other things. Tell father to ask if they ever got that roll of sheet lead if not they can get it of Ensign by paying 1\frac{00}{}$ charges!

The boys think they will stay here all winter but I do not think so. There is very little danger here except from Guerrillas. There is a band of 1000 near here somewhere but we will get them cleared on before long. G. Clark had a cholera last night but he is better today. It has been coming on him for about a week. He will get along alright now. The Lieut. wanted him to go to the doctor's office but I would not let him go. I think that all he wants now is a little rest and careful diet. We will take good care of him.

Let Father tell the directions so they can write to me. In Barnum's Museum where the have the sea fish, the have to keep them in sea water and as they would soon die if the water was not changed very often and as there is no easy mode of getting sea water how do you think Barnum manages? He has an arrangement fixed up by which a continual stream of fresh air is forced into each one of more than 100 Glass vases thus keeping the water constantly pure + wholesome.

Coming through Washington some little Negro girl was telling about a man shooting a dog + she felt very bad about it. She said "De dog diddent say nuffin to de man + de man up + shot him."

The negroes here seem to be more intelligent than the white folks and talk with less brogue than the white folks. If you had your eyes shut you could not tell the differance by hearing them talk. Write as soon and as often as you can + send along a paper once in a while. Direct to Edward L. Cook

Co. H 100th Regt. N.Y. Volunteers

19

Genl {UNKNOWN NAME} Division
Yorktown Va.

Letter from E. Cook to his Parents
Camp at Gloucester Point
Oct. 2ᵈ 1862

My Dear Parents – I have this morning a little leisure so I will commence a letter to you. I mailed my last letter to you on Sunday Sept 28/62. After dinner Sunday we had our tents given to us with orders to put them up. G. Clark + I immediately went off for the woods about half a mile to cut poles + stakes. It took us about 2 hours and when I came back one side of my face was sunburned. I did not feel it much that day but on the next day – Monday + Tuesday it smarted as if a coal of fire was held on my face. Today the skin is pealing off but it does not pain me. The sun is very hot but the air is not sultry as it is in Buffalo. The nights are not near as cold as they were at Alexandria. I was sick Sunday night but was all right again in the morning. We are right on the bank of the York river where we have saltwater to bathe in if we desire it. There are beautiful springs of pure cool spring water all along the bank of river oozing out of the sand so we do not have to use our filters. We feel that this is a great blessing after using the nasty muddy water at Alexandria. We could get pretty good water at Alexandria but we had to go about a mile or a mile + a half to get it. All the water near the camp was very impure. It may interest you perhaps if I copy a little from my diary + enlarge so I will try it.

Monday Sept. 29/62
G. Clark is quite sick to day so that he is unable to do duty. G. Stoddard does more than any thing else. There is some little insect here that stings like a mosquito. I can count 25 places on one hand + wrist where I have been stung by these insects. The flies also are very troublesome and are as thick as bees in swarming.

Tuesday Sept. 30th 1862

Our tent has been pitched low and we have been sleeping on the ground heretofore but today we took it down and moved it over onto its west side of the skirt and built a bed in it so that now we have a nice shade in front of tent in the afternoon and can sleep on our bedstead with out catching the cramp in our legs. The tent is pitched over a frame 2 feet high so we have just so much more room to stand up, the frame also is our bedstead. Our bedcords are staves and our bedding is made of leaves. We sleep now very nicely, indeed we find it quite as comfortable as a feather bed almost.

Our company came in about 2 oclock. All the company were inspected this morning. Their arms, knapsacks, tents, streets + everything were all carefully examined by all of the field officers. Every one is wondering what it is. I think likely they are testing the range on guns down on the rip raps at Fortress Monroe. This evening I took a delightful bath in the river by moonlight. The moon was so bright tonight that I finished a letter by moonlight that I had commensed this afternoon to one of my girls, and did not have time to finish before dress parade. The evenings are lovely, bright and starlight every night; we have not had one unpleasant day since we started.

They have some of the strangest games here that I ever witnessed. One of them is for one man to step in the middle of a ring and cover his face in his cap and scoop down then the other boys step up one at a time, and sometimes more, and give him an awful kick in the stern part of his body; and when he guesses the name of any one that kicks him that one takes his place in the ring and the same kind of an operation is gone through with that one. It is laughable to see the sport.

Wednesday
Oct. 1st 1862

This A.M. G. Stoddard + I went off on the beach of the river about a mile to collect a lot of boards to wall up the sides of our tent from the ground to the bed frame + to lay a floor in front of our bed. The tent is rather a rough looking place + would make you laugh somewhat to see it. The floor puts me in mind of the old floor that we used to have in the shed at the old house before we had the kitchen built on. We learned to day that the firing yesterday was from Newport News about 9 miles above Fortress Monroe on the James River + about 20 miles from here. They were testing the guns on one of the new Gunboats. We could hear the noise distinctly as if it were only a mile from us.

Thursday Oct. 2nd 1862

Some one of our boys unintentionally leaned against the front pole of our tent this morning + misplaced it and in a few minutes our tent came tumbling down over our heads and occasioned considerable merriment among the boys. It did not take many seconds for us to put it up again. We all of us had to strip naked again this morning and be examined by the doctors since we enlisted. We have not yet received our clothing or knapsacks + Guns but expect them every day. We are going to move our camp in a day or 2 about a quarter of a mile farther up the river + extend our picket line one mile farther to the front. I inclose a rough sketch of our camp + tent. I guess George S. will make a good picture + send it home. Neither of us have yet heard from home but expect a letter in a day or two. Both the boys are well again now and are able to do duty. G. Clark has had the bloody Dysentery. He looks very thin + ematiated in the face but will soon pick up again. Some how or other sickness does not seem to reduce a man as it does up north but if you are away down sick one day you are all right the next day. I should like to stay here a long time. If you want any machine needles to sew with you can get them of C.S. Pierce at his residence on Seneca Street. I don't know the number but you can find out by looking in the Directory. It is on the north side of Seneca between Michigan + Ellicott pretty near Michigan. Father knows him; he used to keep a lumber yard. Give our love to Grandma and tell her to think of us often. Ask Eliza if she ever looks in the Almanac to see if the stars are going to shine. Tell Laura to write to me and give my love to Ellen S. – when she sees her. Send as many papers as you can + write often. Let Eliza tell all the young girls of my acquaintance that I will be home one of the days + take care of those that are not used well now. Has Aunt Eliza Gone?

Goodby
Your Loving Son
Edward

Letter from E. Cook to his Parents

Camp at Gloucester point Va.
Oct. 3ᵈ 1862

Last night about 4 oclock after we had all finished our supper and settled down to read the newspaper and have a sociable chat before commencing our usual evening games, the whole camp was startled by a gun from one of the boats lying in the river between our fort + Yorktown.

There were many conjectures as to the cause of her firing but we did not learn the truth until the next morning when we ascertained that a steamer had attempted to run up the river + when she was hailed by the gun boat she did not reply so they sent a shot across her bow which had the desired effect and in the morning we saw her lying alongside of the gunboat.

G. Stoddard and I went out in front to the picket-line this morning and bought a peck of sweet potatoes. I dug them myself while Jeff the negro slave stood by and looked on said "dat he wave glad dat I wave diggin dum kase his head ached right smart." I dug just for the romance of it. The slaves and free negroes here have no idea at all of miles or distance. If you ask them how far it is to a certain place the invariable answer is a "right smart distance". "Well but how many miles is it?" "Dunno sir but it are a right smart distance I know dat." In the rear and on the right of our camp near the bank of the river stand the ruins of an old house. It has been pulled down I suppose because it obstructed the range of the gunboats on the river. All that remains of it is a tent. He is an old bachelor and is living now in an old shanty with the tent over his roof to keep it from leaking. He is very wealthy and owns the land where our camp now is. One of our boys saw a pair of children very light colored playing before a negroes house and he asked an old negro at the door whose children they were. "Dey is my daughters children" "Where is her husband?" "She dun got no husband" "Well then they ain't her children are they?" "Dey is her children" "Well but how can that be?" "Oh I know how dat can be well enough deys Massa's children too dey is. Yah! Yah! Yah!" The soldier then went to the mother and said "Are those your children?" "Yas dose is my children" "Are you married?" "No I isent married." "How then can they be your children?" "Oh Massa know dat, he know how dey be my children. Deys Massa children." This is slavery and southern chivalry.

I cannot help speaking of the sunsets and sunrises in this country. They are perfectly lovely. The sun rises now directly out of the Chesapeak bay and as I go down to the river each morning to perform my ablutions I am compelled to stop and witness the first appearance of old Sol as he rises his face up out of the water. The sun rises grandly but it does not compare with the evening sunset. We are where we can watch it until the last moment. The sky is almost always cloudless until after sunset and then as he sinks be low the horizon the clouds begin to show themselves and gradually grow more + more distinct as the sun sinks lower and lower; then the rays shoot up and change colors almost like the northern lights the edges of light vapory clouds in all shades. I have managed to tip over my inkstand but I enclose a little slip containing the words that are blotted out so you will not be at any bother to make it out. Do I write plain enough?

10/03/62

Lieut. Walbridge while we were out in the field drilling this afternoon pointed it out to us as an old house that was built before the Revolution and was used by the brittish Col. Tarleton as a hospital. At present it is a pile of bricks and 3 great high old fashioned chimneys. We had a good supper to night of sweet potatoes baked in the ashes. Our company is going out on picket Sunday. I am going out their to trade off some of our spare rations such as bread, pork, sugar + salt. We get more bread + pork than we can use and we have now [INK SPILL] about 2 lbs. of sugar that we have not used in Buffalo I [INK SPILL] 2 cents per pound. The rebels here will pay almost any [INK SPILL]. A little handful of salt will readily bring 25 cents; and they would much sooner take either sugar or salt in exchange for their pies, apples + potatoes than to have the money. We are not allowed to sell them these articles but Uncle Sam will not let us steal of them so we have to steal or march on him to do a little smuggling once in a while. I have been eating a big handful of sugar so you may know my sweet tooth does not suffer much. I caught a louse on my clothes a day or two ago and it set me looking all over for some more but I did not find any. They are great big things and the boys out here call them — "Government Lice" you can always tell them from the common vermin because they have "U.S." in great big letters branded on their backs. I saw a Buffalo Paper last night dated Saturday Sept 27/62 which said that our regiment was going to Fortress Monroe but we have received no order to that effect; on the contrary our Lieut. Colonel told some of the boys we were going to remain here all winter. As soon as any change is ordered I will inform you.

The company that went out last evening came in this morning without having met with any particular incident. We learned that their object in going was to capture a rebel mail from Richmond but they did not obtain it. Capt. has been under arrest ever since we came here and a day or two ago he was court martialed upon a charge of riotous conduct, drunkenness, using profane language, disobedience of orders, mutinous expressions and several other charges. He was tried and plead not guilty. The verdict was not guilty and his sword was returned to him to day and he appeared on dress parade this evening for the first time since we came here. It seems that he was in a tent with some other officers and remained until after 12 oclock at night drinking and making a good deal of noise and disturbing the camp. The commanding officer sent to him 3 times to have him cease and the company of officers to disperce; he refused twice and one sent back a very abusive answer to the Colonel. The 3^d time the order was accompanied by a guard with orders to pull down the tent over his head if he did not comply; and the company broke up. All these charges were read before the whole regiment at dress parade together with the language that he used against McClellen + our Colonel. He was present and heard it all – how he must have felt, if he has any manhood about him, thus to have made known, in his presence, to the common soldiers, his loaferish actions + expressions. Our time is our own from Dress Parade to 9 oclock and in that interval we can do just what we have a mind to. The companies have done so and never heard any thing from them afterward. If I can send them by Express and have them collect charges on delivery I will send them, but if not I shall sell them here to some of the contrabands. We are soldiers now and in good earnest. Tomorrow we will be put on duty and held liable to be called on for guards and picket duty and anything else that comes along. The only part of soldier life that I dread is guard duty but I shall have to do it now. We have had first-rate times so far but now then comes the tug of war. I hear the drum beating for the afternoon Battallion Drill so I must stop for the present. All but five of the recruits in our company have been taken out of what we call the awkward squad and placed in the company to drill with them. This speaks pretty well for our ability to learn although some of us had drilled before which in part accounts for it. Our company is going out on picket again Friday and I am going to take my writing materials with me and I will write you a letter while on picket duty. The two Georges have gone fishing this evening and I am all alone. The moon *is at the full and not a cloud is to be seen. I wish you could have looked in upon our company a few minutes ago as I stood over a camp fire roasting sweet potatoes in the ashes; there were about a dozen sitting + standing around the fire and I warrant that not one of them gave a single thought to the dear ones at home. The time flew swiftly by and the laugh went merrily around as each one made some witty remark or careless expression. We seem to feel just as secure here in our cotton tent with the front entirely open and the back only partly closed as we did in our own beds at home. We have roll call at 9 o'clock + we cannot retire until that hour or if we do we have to turn out again and answer to our names. The evenings passed slowly at first but now they slip by almost before we are aware of it and tattoo sounds as soon as we are ready for it.*

10/03/62

The old members of our company are out on picket to day. I suppose that the next time that they go out we shall have to go with them. The picket line is about 1 mile from our camp. I have not yet been out to it but I expect I shall take a walk out there this afternoon just for fun to see how it looks. They say there is a band of Guerrillas about 1000 strong in the neighborhood of the camp and they are the only thing we have to fear at present and I do not think there is any danger to be apprehended even from that source. There is a very strong fort a short distance in our rear and close to the bank of the river to which we can run for shelter in case we are attacked at any time. I will try + send you a plan of our camp so you will see how we are situated. Our squad began to drill this morning and drilled 2 or 3 times during the day. We have to turn out at 5 oclock in the morning and answer to roll call; immediately after roll call we have to clean up the ground in and around the tents + sweep the streets in front of our tents. This takes only about 20 minutes, then we go down to the river and perform our ablution in the spring water and by the time we return our breakfast is ready for us. Breakfast consists of roasted pea water (called coffee) and dry bread or hard tack; the bread is very unwholesome + gives me the heart burn every time I eat. I don't know what I should do if I did not have that bottle of bitters. After breakfast we drill from 7 to 8 and again from 10 to 11. At 12 we have dinner which consists generally of bean soup and bread and most generally some kind of meat once in a while we have onions and to day we are going to have potatoes for the first time 2 weeks; they are rotten but we don't care for that so long as they are potatoes, *sometimes we get dried apple sauce but it is so wormy + they are so careless in cooking it that I do not like to eat it; from 1 to 2 again we have drill + from 4 to 5. At 5 we all have to turn to dress parade when the whole Regt is drawn up into line and the Adjutant reads to us such orders as the Colonel had for the next day. After dinner we always go down to the river and wash our tin cups + plates (we only wash dishes once a day). After dress parade comes supper which like the breakfast consists of Pea Coffee + bread. This is the government food but so far we have lived better than the government allows. We have bought cheese to eat with our bread and mackerel so that we have quite a relish. We can buy sweet potatoes for $1⁰⁰ per bushel + oysters for 20 cents per quart. We are going to buy the potatoes as soon as we can get out to the picket line and then we will live rich for a short time I can tell you. Lieut. Walbridge has appointed me to keep the company accounts and I think when there is a vacancy in the ranks that one of us boys will get it. I wrote 3 letters this day so I think with my other duties I have done pretty well. In the evening we generally go down to the river and take a bath to keep ourselves clean. There is great danger in a camp of getting lousey and we are afraid of it.*

Letter from E. Cook to his Sister

Camp at Gloucester Point Tuesday Oct. 7ᵗʰ 1862

Dear Sister Eliza – As you are the only one at home from whom I have yet rec'd a letter I will direct this to you. I want you to answer it immediately and tell me how Laura directed her letter + paper she sent to me. Write + tell me immediately, even if you do not write any thing else. If I can find out how she directed I can write for it to be forwarded to me. I have asked you in 3 or 4 different letters if you received that $50⁰⁰ I sent from Albany. Was that letter containing the account of our passage through New York the only one or the first one you rec'd from me. I wrote 2 or 3 (I think 2) at Albany. Did you receive them? I wish when you answer my letters you would have them by you and read them over + note all the questions that they contain and be sure and send an answer to each + all of them. I am now permanently stationed in Co. "H" and my address is as follows
Edward L. Cook, Co. "H" 100ᵗʰ Reg't. N.Y.S.V. Washington D.C.
Be sure to put the Co. "H" on as I receive them sooner than if not put

on. *Also be careful in the figures 100ᵗʰ so that it will not be mistaken for another number.*

I think I have been very lavish with my letters to you and have often delayed writing to my acquaintances for the purpose of writing to you. I sent a letter to you yesterday and here I am writing again to day but I do not suppose I shall send it for a day or two. I would like it if you would answer each one of my letters and not wait until you have received 2 or 3 and then answer them altogether. I think you might give me the preference over what ever other correspondents you may have and always answer my letters first.

Our company returned from picket duty yesterday A.M. and most all of them had their haversacks filled with sweet potatoes which they stole from some old rebels plantation. One of the boys gave me about half a peck of nice ones. I sent a letter to you yesterday afternoon and one to Aunt Eliza at the same time. About 2 hours after I had mailed the letters I received Eliza's letter of <u>Oct. 1ˢᵗ Wed.</u> *And also a letter from Lottie McLane. She says she has not heard from Eliza. These are the only letters I have received since I left home. The one Laura wrote + the paper she sent I have not received. What date did she send it? I have received the 3 papers you sent me. G.S. has rec'd 2 letters from Flora. I think Aunt Eliza has made you quite a visit. I wish you would tell me what was in Laura's letter in case I do not receive it. Do not be afraid of writing too long letters. Tell us what folks said of us after we were gone. What with drilling + other duties and writing + bathing I manage to keep pretty busy. I do not find a soldiers life a very lazy one. There is always something to do if a person is not too lazy to do it. No person need be idle unless they are so inclined. You want to know what we call army vegetables. It is onions, parsnips, carrots, turnips, together and dried in cakes; it is very hard + brittle in this state and requires to be boiled about three times as long as vegetables generally, but when properly prepared*

Saturday Oct. 4ᵗʰ 1862

Our squad of new recruits drilled in the company with muskets for the first time this morning. We must have made pretty good advancement in order to be put in company drill so soon when we have been in the camp only one week to day, and did not commence the squad drill until last Monday. This afternoon I went down to a little kind of a brook and washed some of my things consisting of one pair of drawers, one undershirt one overshirt, 1 pair of stockings + one handkerchief. The boys say they are going to hire their washing done at 6 cents a piece but I think I can wash my own things well enough for me as long as I have plenty of water + soap. A sixpence saved is sixpence earned. I think you would have laughed to have seen me yesterday with nothing on but my hat pants + boots stooping over that pool of water and rubbing away in good earnest at that washing. I did it pretty well considering that the water was none of the cleanest and my soap not over abundant, as well as being a greenhorn at the business myself. The things are hanging across the ridge pole of my tent this evening drying in the bright moonlight. One of the boys that came down with our squad was talking with the man that owned the house used by Col. Tarleton as his hospital. He said that when the rebels held this place they turned him out of the house.

Wednesday Oct. 8th 1862

The boys returned from their fishing last evening with 4 large sea crabs and this morning we boiled them and had quite a relish. They are much finer flavored than oysters and taste very much like lobsters. You will recollect that in one of my letters I spoke of the thing they called a sea nettle – a kind of sea fish that looks like a piece of transparent jelly about the size + shape of a silver dollar with 3 or 4 long root-like appendages. I had one of them in my hand the other day; it did not affect the palm of my hand but as soon as the back of my hand touched it, the hand commenced to smart as if it was stung or burnt. Last night the boys had one of them on the dock and as soon as it came it commenced to glow like a coal of fire, so we think we can now answer the question "what is it that makes the sea look as if it was on fire?" I think it is these sea nettles that make it appear so as they come to the surface. The boys have gone fishing again this evening and perhaps may return with new developments. I just left off writing to seize my gun and answer to the call "Fall in every man the rebels are coming" I was ten times as cool as I thought I would be on receiving such an order. The order was a mistaken one and was intended for the company next to us which is going out on a reconnaissance. Our Lieutenant says we may be ordered out before morning but I think it will be nothing serious; however if it is I think I am prepared for anything in store for me. I shall wear my pistol to night as I sleep. I never undress so it will not take me long to get ready. I do not think we shall stay here long; every thing seems to indicate a movement of some kind. I do not care how soon it comes now that we have our arms + accoutrements. I hope that I am prepared to die at any moment and feel that I shall but go to meet my friends in heaven. Such a hope is the only source of comfort which the soldier has to bear him up through every hour of danger and temptation. I hope that I shall always live so that when my sands of life have reached an end, my friends may feel that I but sleep to rise again at the last day and live an everlasting life of love and joy in heaven at the throne of God.

Thursday Oct. 9th 1862

The boys came in last evening with a couple of small fish and they made us quite a nice little relish for breakfast this morning. The whole company turned out for wood this morning and collected about 2 or 3 cords enough to last for two weeks. This looks as if we were to remain for some time longer. I expected you would have written last Sunday and I should have received it to day. It takes from 4 to 5 days for a letter to come from Buffalo to our camp. You should always try and get your letters in the P.O. by evening of the day in which you write and then they leave on the early morning train and come through promptly. If you write Sundays, try and put in the mail by 4 oclock P.M. and if you can't do that be sure and put them in that same evening if you can.

Friday morning Oct. 10th 1862

It is raining this morning but not very hard. We have had breakfast and cleaned up our tent and all of us are now engaged in writing. The soil here is rather sandy, so a slight rain does not make the ground muddy. It is wet outside but our cotton covering protects us thoroughly and we are as dry and comfortable in here as you can imagine. When it stops raining we are going to put down a new floor in front of our bed. All we have at present is a lot of small pieces of wood of many sizes and shapes put together as well as different-shaped pieces will admit of being placed. I said in one of my letters it reminded me of old floors that we used to have in the old kitchen on the alley. Yesterday we found 4 nice pieces of board that will make us a first rate floor in front of our bed and we have enough to fill out to the front of our tent. We got a cracker lot the other day and made us a nice little cupboard so as to keep our victuals clean. Our tin cups and plates are all kept bright + clean and I tell you our tent inside looks as slick

+ *comfortable as the chamber in the "City of Buffalo" – all but the looking glass over head. The rain is almost stopped and I think it is going to clear up and we will have a nice day of it yet. Tell grandma we often think of her and would like to have her put in a little letter for us when you write to us and we will answer it. I have written to[+   ] but they have not yet answered it although they have had plenty of time to do so. I am not going to write to you so often after this as you do not answer my letters promptly. Tit for tat you know is fair play. The rain has stopped so I must go to work at our floor. If I was in your place I would answer letter even if I did not write more than a page or two. Give my* <u>Love</u> *to all of the* <u>Good Looking</u> *girls in Buffalo and my regards to those that are not good looking.*

<u>*Friday Evening*</u>

Oh! dear! I am so tired. We have been working hard at fixing up our tent and laying new floor until 4 oclock this P.M. and then we had to dress up for battallion drill and were on the field for 3 hours constantly performing different movements and part of the time on the double quick and most of the time our piece at the shoulder – the most tiresome way in the world to carry a musket. The Regt. received yesterday an order to appear on an undress parade with haversack containing clean change of underclothes and after review the officers are to march their men down to the river and make them take a bath. Some men in our camp make a very palateable dish especially when a little rice is added to it + a piece of meat boiled with it. You may think I am joking about the white sugar but I am not; enclosed is a sample and this is not near so white as we get sometimes. I cannot spare you much as we can sell it for 60 or 75 cents per pound over the picket line. I wish you would collect what letters I have sent you and number them. I have put on this No. 10 but I think I have written more than that but you can number them + see and then tell me when you write what number they are.

I am very glad indeed to tell you that we received our muskets, clothing, knapsacks, haversacks + canteens this day. Our muskets are the Enfield Rifle of English manufacture and considered the best in the field. Our knapsacks are of black oilcloth and our haversacks are of the same. The haversack is for carrying rations when on a march. The inside of them, that is the lining, can be taken out + washed when dirty. Our canteens are of good black tin + hold 3 pints of water. Our clothing consists of 1 pair of shoes, 2 pair of socks woollen, 1 pair of pants, 1 pair of drawers, 2 shirts – white woollen, 1 jacket, 1 frock coat – dark blue, 1 overcoat cape – light blue + 1 cap. I did not draw the cap, socks, drawers or shirts as those I now have are preferable to the government articles. We are also entitled to a blanket but as I bought one in Alexandria I did not draw any here though the government blanket is the best that can be bought and costs the least money.

[Ed Cook]

Letter from A. Lyth to his Brother

Gloucester Point Oct 7 1862

Dear Brother

I received your letter last night and was very sorry to hear that mothers thumb is so bad but I hope it will soon be better I am very well at present and am getting along finely this morning I was detailed with about ½ of our company for Fatigue duty as we call it although I assure you we do not fatigue ourselfs much we had to go inside the fort and level the ground for to pitch our new tents we started at ½ past 7 oclock to work and worked until 8 then we rested 20 minutes then worked untill 9 then we rested 20 mi. again then we worked until 10 and rested again and then we quit work a little before 11 oclock and sat down to write this letter we don't work very hard when we do work we stand + talk the bigest part of the time there was about 300 to work this morning leveling and 50 men could have done the same work in the same time if the had a work steady I am glad to hear you have got another kiln lit and hope it will turn out a good one and hope the arch has not fallen down I cannot tell you how Capt Hinson's trial came off as his sentence has never been read off on Dress Parade. You see it is in this way every day the whole Regiment has to put on their dress coat their accutriments + take their gun and go on dress parade and then if there are any new orders the adjutant reads them to the whole Regiment or if there has been any court Martials the sentences are read off Every day there is sure to be either some orders or sentences to read off But I guess Capt Hinson's turn has not come yet I have received I think all the commercial Advertisers you have sent me but as yet I have not yet received any Harpers Weeklys I think if Uncle has not got any tiles made yet that he will not get many this year I get my clothes washed first rate we get plenty of soap then I take a tub and go down to the river and wash my shirt having nothing but shirt + stockings to wash this week I took a pair of stocking + a shirt to a secesh house and they washed them for ½ a bar of extra. Last night we got a lot more men for our regiment they being alot of exchanged prisoners which were taken at the Battle of Fair Oaks + we expect a lot of new Recruits to night I had a good Bit of fun with a little nigger boy out on the picket lines the other day. he was about the size of Bill and had lips as thick as my fist he is a slave but is quite a sharp little fellow and said he was a regular secesh and he said he wanted the south to whip the north because he said if the north whips they will take the niggers up north and freeze them all to death and kill them he sung us some nigger songs and some secesh songs that the secesh soldiers had learnt him when they were camped here

Give my love to Mother + Father and all my sisters + brothers + give my Best Regards to Tommy + Martain + tell them I get along very well From Your Affect—

Brother, Alfred Lyth

Letter from E. Cook to his Parents

Picket in front of Camp at Gloucester Point Oct. 19th 1862

My Dear parents – I have two letters from home since I started, but then I suppose you do as well as your time will permit. I never can recollect what I write so I suppose I write a great many things over twice.

Last Sunday was a most tedious day for me. It rained all day + night and I was first unfortunate enough to be appointed on guard. The rules are that guards shall be on duty two hours and off four, that is they shall stand 2 hours out every six in the 24 making 8 hours standing duty. During the rest of the time they are to remain in the guard house and can go to sleep if they choose. The guard house is nothing more than a tent and is used as a prison for those who are remiss in their duty and as such persons are generally the lazy + Louzy of the regiment, the guard house is always the filthyest place in the army and no soldier will remain in it if he can help it. So in pleasant weather the guard always sleeps out of doors and in rainy weather he stands up and takes it. I obtained permission to go to my tent from 1 until 4 in the night and as guards are not allowed to remove their clothing or accoutrements I had to lay down in my wet things.

I slept for 2 hours and only dreaded to go out the more. The next day was cold but it did not rain. I had an awful head ache and a most tedious pain through the hips. The old soldiers said I was going to have the camp fever but it did not alarm me very much as I knew it was nothing but a cold. It is customary for the guard on the second day often after he goes on to act as Camp Police. Their duty is for part of them to go across the river and draw the rations the rest remain to do any little extra work the colonel may require such as cleaning up rubbish around camp. I was one of six that went over to Yorktown and obtained 2 days rations of fresh beef direct from the slaughterhouse. It weighed between 1900 + 2000 pounds. I helped handle this 5 different times in getting it from the slaughterhouse at Yorktown to the Commissary tent in our regiment. It was too much for me as I was unwell before I started having slept but little if any the night before and only 2 hours the night I was on guard; besides my hips still pained me and my head ached right smart. But I wanted to go over so as to learn if I could send my clothes home. I find there is no express office at Yorktown but the Ex. Agent comes up on the mail boat every night with the mail, and I might send them by him but it is unsafe. I think I had better sell them here for any thing I can get for them as they are scarsely worth what it will cost to send them, being completely stained with grease and soiled with dirt. The slaughterhouse was a mile out in the country beyond Yorktown and coming back I picked up a nice mess of mushrooms which I cooked for dinner on my return.

Monday Morning Oct. 20th 1862
I left off my story last night at Yorktown, which place I visited Tuesday Oct. 19/62. There was one or 2 things that I saw there that I wished to speak to you about. One of them was the chimneys. Every Southerner seems to have a particular hatred of chimneys, and so strong is that hatred that they turn their chimneys out of doors. It looks so odd to go along and see sticking out and up at the back end of the house a long chimney. It looks as if the chimney was built first and then the house added on.

Did I ever tell you what constitutes a vilage in this country? It is 1 courthouse 1 shop + 2 dwelling houses with a black smith shop in front of one of them. Only the C.H. + shop are absolutely indispensable; the dwelling houses are not necessary.

On the afternoon of my return from Yorktown a gloom was thrown over the usually pleasant countenances of those in our company by the careless act of one man shooting another. Tom Wharton was a young boy well liked by every man in the company. DeForrest the one who shot him was just as universally disliked. If the affair had been the other way there would have been very little feeling or regret. About 3 weeks ago the same DeForrest shot off his gun loaded and the ball passed through a tent + only a few inches over a man's head. The boys were in constant fear that he would do some damage and are glad now that he is in the guard house.

The Ball did not kill young Wharton but passed through the thigh of both legs and inflicted another wound of a very serious nature. The surgeon was promptly on the spot + dressed the wounds, and Wharton was then conveyed across the river to the Yorktown Hospital. Handling the beef gave me a kind of a fresh strain through the hips and I could not sleep a wink all Tuesday night. On Wednesday I was sick again and had a stiff neck but managed to get a few hours sleep and felt quite improved in the morning. I don't think I had more than six hours sleep or about 8 at the farthest from Saturday night to Last Thursday night. Thursday night I slept well + soundly and Friday I was again very much improved.

Saturday afternoon about 5 oclock the different companies were ordered out with haversacks containing clean clothes and marched down to the river to wash themselves. I went down but as I did not feel well and had just been rubbing myself with liniment the Lieut. excused me from going in.

Sunday morning both regiments stationed at this point (100th N.Y.V. + 104 Penn. Vol.) were out on parade for inspection by Major Gen. Keyes Commander of the 4th Army Corps. He is a man of commanding mein + penetrating features. After inspection of Arms the companies were dismissed to their tents + the Old Genl went through + inspected our quarters + knapsacks. When he came to our tent he stopped + asked how many lived here + if we slept warm enough. We thought we diddent + told him so. I think they will soon move us into the fort with the 104th Penn. instead of keeping us outside. Our new tents have been here for about 2 weeks but for some reason they do not give them to us. They have not yet been unpacked. Perhaps we are going to move if so that accounts for it. After inspections we went on picket as I have already informed you.

In Laura's 5 day letter she speaks of young Pixley is in the same company with us + lives just next door above. If he does not write home it is because he has too many girls to write.

Mary Scheffer's Father has been in our camp for nearly a week. He left this morning for home I sent a letter to Mary S. by him. If Lilie or Mrs. Leyman were to call on Mary S. they could learn what Mr. S. thinks of our Camp. I hope they will do so and ask him what kind of a house we live in. If they could call around in the evening, when Mr. S. is at home, they would have a pleasant time and hear him tell his own story. If they go around they must not forget to remember me to Mrs. Scheffer. Mr. S. is a very pleasant man indeed. Enclosed is a letter I received on Saturday from Aunt Eliza. She thinks it rather strange that I find time to write to her when I write such long letters home. I have not yet received the articles you sent me but I think they will come through all right. You had better not make up another box until I send you word that I have rec'd this one all right and then I will send you a list of what I need. Never send any thing by a soldier that is large or unhandy for he will surely throw it away before he gets to the regiment. It will do very well to send letters or very small packages by soldiers but nothing else. If any Lieut. told you different he must have been a green one in the business or else he wanted to steal something from the box. You wanted to know first what letters I had received from you. The first one was from Eliza dated Oct 1/62. Commenced with a pencil + ended with pen.

The second was Laura's 5 day letter + contained 3 Pages of foolscap. She is what us niggers would call a right smart gal to write 3 Pages in 5 days. The third was the one I rec'd last evening on picket + was written by both Eliza + Laura.

I have received 4 papers in all 2 at one time + 2 at another. The one containing the note for G. Clark we did not receive. So Mary has got a sewing machine well I am glad of it but I think if I had been her place I would rather have applied the money towards the purchase of a Piano. I wish I had some more of that wahoo bitters. The bottle I brought with me has been gone more than a week. It was the best thing I ever used for the heart burn, and now that it is gone I am often obliged to go without my meals. I did not eat a mouthful for dinner today after being out on picket all night. The bread we get here is very poor + indigestible and the least slice of it will give us the heart burn for hours.

I think I could relish some of those grapes that Laura says Ma bought for me but as long as I do not see them I have no desire for them. As for French Mustard we still have nearly a half bottle left. Our post on picket last night was the reserve and we had 7 men on it while the others only had 3 or 4 so we only had to stand guard two hours each during the night while on the others posts they had to stand 4 hours each. The Lieut. of our company was on the reserve and slept with us under some boards but up slanting against a rail fence.

We slept pretty well although the night was cold but not damp. When I got up to stand my 2 hours my feet were like icicles, but today I feel first rate. This ink is miserable and I almost doubt if you can make out half of this letter. G. Clark was sick again yesterday and we would not let him stand on picket last night. He is better today and is keeping quiet. I think he will be well tomorrow.

When Eliza's Laura's letter was handed to me out on the line it was so dark I could not read it so I went into a house that stood near by the post, occupied by a Mr. Shakleford, and obtained permission to read my letter by his light. The candle was nearly burned down he ordered his slave, a thick lipped negress, bring another candle. She did so and stood holding the light for me while I read. Wasent that an incident and quite romantic. Picture a sallow thin faced man with broad hat + straight coat in the background, in the foreground a young soldier reading a letter beside a table, while a shining faced + sparkling eyed negress stands grinning behind him as she bears up the flickering candle for him to see to read; on the right and in a doorway sits the mother sits a crib to sleep her young infant, while on the left and leaning on the table are 2 or 3 young children who eye with strange curiosity the group before them. It half reminds me of some of those dear old scenes we read of in the times of "76". Another thing I saw this morning reminded me very much of the old revolutionary times. About eight oclock this morning some person from outside the lines drove up to the second post to the left of us with a 2 wheeled cart load of provisions of some kind. The animal that drew the cart was a steer + was driven with a bit + lines the same as a horse. (The bit was made of a piece of wire + the lines of roap.) The man drove up to the line + was halted, the Lieut. came up and passed the cart load of provisions but the man had to remain outside. As the animals, the owner handed the lines to someone inside and that one took charge of the cart + unloaded it and then returned it. thus we pass stuff into the lines but allow nothing to be passed out. We consider that every thing that comes inside the lines is just so much taken from the rebels, whether it is intended for our troops, or those families that live inside. I am glad you *have sent me word about the fifty dollars. It makes me feel considerable more easy. It has now been more than a month since I sent it to you and as I had heard no word from you about it I almost thought that all the letters in which I had mention any thing about it had been miscarried and that you had never called for the money. I am also glad that you mentioned so specifically what letters you have rec'd from me. Your list corresponds with my memorandum exactly. I have written to Col. Belknap to forward me what letters are at Port Hospital for me but I think he will not take that trouble. Did you know that Mr. Keller (by whom you have sent letters) is the Photograph Artist that married Rebecca? He is a drunken loafer and a very unsafe person to send letters by. I don't think he ever intends coming to the reg't and if he does he cannot get a commission. All the recruits that leave Buffalo now, have to remain at Alexandria for some time before joining the regiment so you must write again soon as it will be a long time before I receive the letters from Keller. I am very glad indeed that you are so fond of your machine. When Lottie M. answers Lilie's letter you must write me what she says. I am much obliged to Laura for her word about – she knows who. When she sees her again she may tell her that I have written to her twice but rec'd no answer. Laura you tell her I want <u>her</u> to do as <u>she</u> agreed. Tell Ma that we <u>do</u> put paper on the shelves of our cupboard + have got a towel for a door in front. Our sugar last week was full of ants but we have got rid of them again. Tell Laura I find only one big mistake in her letter; she wrote the Pos. Plural of Aunt Grace – Gracies; it should be Aunt Grace's.*

Letter from E. Cook to his Parents

Camp at Gloucester Point Va. Oct. 21ˢᵗ 1862 Tuesday

Dear Parents

I wrote home to you yesterday and sent it this morning. I have been quite unwell all day. The day is not very warm but it is pleasant. G. Stoddard was taken from the roll of recruits a day or two ago and put in the company with us and today he is having his first experience in doing guard duty. It is an unpleasant duty at all times but not near as much so in pleasant weather as in cold to rainey times. I received 3 papers from you by this evenings mail.

Wednesday Oct. 22ᵈ 1862

I answered Aunt Eliza's letter today. Last night it blowed very hard so hard that it woke me up in the night with a sudden start for I thought the tent was coming down over our heads. The little caboose shook backwards + forwards + sideways + all ways but she stood up like a house built on the rocks firm and steadfast. The sand was thrown against the tightly stretched canvass and sounded for all the world like rain pelting down upon us; so that 2 or 3 times, until I found out what it was, I started up quickly, thinking the rain was pouring down in masses upon our little "shebang". This is a very windy country at this time of year. The wind is blowing constantly from one quarter or another and make things quite unpleasant when it is from the N.E.; and a little more than unpleasant when it is from the direction the cook's fires for the smoke then blows right up the streets + fills our tents

Thursday Oct 23ᵈ 1862

I received a letter this evening from [   ] clerk (Peck). It was only 1 page long and contained no news or any thing else of much interest but you need not say anything about it for I want to hear from them again. It was written on the 9ᵗʰ of Oct. and was sent to me by a recruit who did not reach here until this evening – hence the long delay.

Friday Oct. 24ᵗʰ 1862

I wrote to [   ] today and wrote them a good long letter of 4 pages like this paper I am writing on at present. I am in hopes it will shame the clerk for the little short letter he wrote to me. There is heavy + continued firing again today in the direction of Fortress Monroe but I think it is nothing more than the testing of some new guns at the rip-raps. I received a letter from the joint pens of Laura + Eliza by this evening mail. I am much obliged to you for its good full length. It is almost as good as the one I received while out on picket last Sunday. I will try and answer it tomorrow. I also received at the same time 1 paper, a Saturday evening Commercial for which I am much obliged.

Saturday, Oct. 25ᵗʰ 1862

I was this morning ordered to act as corporal of the guard today. I am very sorry for it as it will preclude the possibility of my answering your letter today. To be corporal of a guard is not quite as bad as being a guard for he does not have to walk a beat. I believe I have never told you that a guard is divided in 3 reliefs, called the 1st, 2^{d}, + 3^{d} relief. The 1st relief goes on guard for the 1st two hours and then they are relieved by the 2^{d} relief during the next two hours, and the second relief is relieve for next 2 hours by the 3^{d} relief, which at the expiration of its 2 hours is relieved by the 1st relief again + so on during the day and night. Each relief has its corporal + his duty it is to go around with his relief and assign each man his post or beat and then return to the guard house with the relieved guard. During the two hours that his relief is on guard he has to remain in the vacinity of the guard house so as to answer readily to any call from any post in case of any disturbance or any of that character; but he is not obliged to remain standing; he can sit down or take his rubber blanket and spread it on the ground + lie down, but he cannot go to sleep during the time his relief is on guard. I do not find it any trouble to keep awake; the only difficulty I complain of is not being able to sleep. I did not sleep 2 hours in the last 24. This has been a warm and beautiful day and is going to be a very mild kind of a night although I should not wonder much if it rained before long, for it is clouding up this evening and the sky is not so clear as it usually is at night. We generally have very bright + starlit nights and when they are cloudy we look for storms.

G. Stoddard went up the river this afternoon when the tide was far out, and picked up about a peck of oysters. They are very nice indeed now but when we first came here they were not quite fit to eat. Mr. Scheffer had some when he was here + he thought they were the nicest he ever eat. It took George only about five minutes to pick up 2 haversacks full, so you may form some idea of how thick they are around here. When the tide is away out at its farthest ebb, we can pick them up with out getting our feet wet. I had some of them raw with vinegar + salt + pepper for my supper this evening + they were most excellent. These are the first we have eat of our own picking. I wish father had some of them + Mr. [   ] also wouldent they smack their lips. Tell father to say to Mr. [   ] that eating the oysters here on the half shell puts me in mind of that Saturday evening at Dodd's saloon after unpacking the Gas Fixtures. Ask Mr. [   ] if he recollects it. Uncle Stoddard ought to come out here for he could get all the beans he wanted and more too. We have bean soup for dinner about nine times a week + 10 times Sundays. There were 10 Prisoners in the Guard house today and this evening they put in several more. One of the prisoners this afternoon refused to go to work, and he was tied to a post with his hands *behind him all the afternoon. At night he was handcuffed and placed in the Commissary tent under a guard. I feel sorry for the poor fellow but he is an old soldier + ought to know better. One of the prisoners put in this evening was an Irish young man. He was drunk + almost wild. He was put in for disorderly conduct after lights were ordered out (we call it after Taps). He had been counting his money and when "Taps" were sounded he put out his light and then could not find his money (He was drunk) and thought somebody had stolen it. He immediately commenced making a great noise and disturbing the Camp. The officer sent a couple of files of guards and put him in the "[   ] hole" as some of the boys call the guard house where he was quiet for about an hour. At the end of that time he said he wanted to go out, and sent a guard with him, but they had not been gone 5 minutes before the guard was calling for "Corporal of Guard!" "Corporal of Guard!" I went over to the place from where the noise came and then I learned that the prisoner had made good his escape for the night. It was dark so I did not bother myself looking for him as I knew he could not go very far. This has been the warmest + pleasantest day we have had for more than 2 weeks. I feel tip top today and shall get along first rate after this. I went down to the edge of the water yesterday when the tide was out + saw thousands of live snails in shells. These are very common things, but it is the first time in my life that I ever saw a snail in a shell. They have a kind of clam here that they call a soft shell clam. It is about 1/5 as large as the common clam + has a long neck or tube that it runs out of its shell + draws in water to its stomach, where it retains the nutritious parts + then spits out the water deprived of its nutriment. We use them for fish bait.*

Sunday, Oct. 26/62

The prisoner that ran away last night returned at day light this morning. He said he tumbled down after he got a way from the guard and laid for a few minutes and when he got up he could not find his way out of the weeds so he had to stay out there alone all night. The night was dark, and as he was drunk and there were no lights shining in the camp I do not wonder that he got lost and could not find his way back. When he fell down he scratched his face on something and this morning it was all swollen up; so on the whole I think he would have been better off to have remained in the guard house, but I suppose he thought he was going to have some fun making the Guard chase him but he got rather too much fooled for his

41

own good. It commenced to rain this morning about half an hour before I came off guard but I did not get wet as I ran into + remained in the guard house until time to be relieved by the new guard. I have had a nasty dread of any wet ever since I was on guard 2 weeks ago today. It not do me any hurt to be out last night for I feel full as well as I did yesterday and a little better. One of the young men that left Buffalo with us has been sick with the fever about 2 weeks and this morning G. Stoddard, myself + 2 others took him across the river to the hospital. We carried him on a kind of hand cot or stretcher as they call it here. He did not like the idea of going to the hospital; but when he got there and saw such nice clean rooms + warm soft beds + got on a clean pair of hospital drawers + a clean hospital shirt he said he felt better right away. It is raining hard this afternoon and I guess it will continue to do so all night. I wish Mary would send one of the "Rural New Yorkers" once in a while. We have not got the box yet but I think it will be along in a day or two as Mr. York wrote to Benson to have the Express company hunt it up. I am going to settle with York for the Express charges. I saw an advertisement in a Buffalo Paper about that [   ] that Laura spoke about in her letter. I haven't seen any thing of that letter that Ma was going to commence so many times. Did Ma give that note to Aunt Grace that I sent 2 or 3 weeks ago in a letter? G. Stoddard will not write to his folks because Aunt Grace does not answer it. Please tell her so. I have not written to [   ] Barker as yet. The girls that G. Stoddard saw at the Depot were not the [   ] girls. I do not know who they were. It is dark and so windy that I cannot keep a light burning so I will send this letter as it is. Goodby and love to all without particularizing.

Your loving son
Edward L. Cook

Letter from A. Lyth to his Folks at Home

Gloucester Point Va Oct 29 1862

Dear Folks at Home

I expect a letter from you soon but I though I might as well write you a few lines this afternoon as I cannot find any thing else to occupy my time I am very well at present and I hope these few lines will find you the same we moved our camp yesterday we did not move in to the fort as I stated we were going to move of my former letters an there is a much better camping ground close to the side of the fort outside so we took it in preferance to going into the fort it is on a gently sloping hill sloping towards the fort and as level as the little grass plot in front of our house we have got all new sibley tents. they are very large tents and 12 of us live together in one tent and have plenty of room we have got a fine set of boys in our tent Thomas Maharg is in the same tent as I am and 2 of the other boys that came from Buffalo with us and our sergent is in the tent with us and all the rest of the men are very respectable and very particular about keeping the tent clean and theirselves also I have kept my old clothes untill day before yesterday I took and sold them I had thought to send them home but there is no express hire through to here and they tell me if i send them it is ten to one that you ever get them as I know of no one who would transfer my satchel over to the express company when it reached Fortress Monroe it is different though if you was sending any thing here for the express company would transfer it right away to the mailboat for Yorktown so I should get it I wish you would send me some postage stamps as I have only one more left I sold my coat for 4 ½ dollars my hat for ½ a dollar and I gave my pants for a new carpet bag when I first thought of sending my clothes home which is very useful for putting in trinkets I kept my vest and boots and I got my boots soled + heeled for 1 ½ dollars there being a shoe maker in the Regiment who works at his trade and mends all the shoes + boots for the Regiment. There was a man belonging to our Regiment who went outside of the picket lines unnoticed the last time his company went on picket and has never returned some thought he deserted on purpose and some say he went out in search of wiskey and was taken prisoner by the gurelleas as the niggers say there is a few roaming around the country the last time I was on picket which was day before yesterday it was very stormy day raind cats and dogs as the saying is but we had good times for all of that there being 12 men left after all the other posts had been supplied with men apice and there is an old deserted secesh house on the post so we were all right and had a good time of it when it rains we have our shelter tents to take with us on picket to keep us dry but it stoped raining in the afternoon and we had a fine night I want you to send me some postage stamps as I cannot buy any here I can buy plenty of writing paper + envelopes for a cent a[   ]. I bought 30 sheets of paper yesterday and some envelopes I will write when I receive a letter which I expect to night or tomorrow night so no more at present – give my Love to all my friends and write often

    From your affectionate

Son + Brother Alfred Lyth

If you can buy more envelopes cheap + send them cheap I wish you would so. I have none + owe for 8. They cost 1 cent each at the [   ].

Rec'd 51 cents worth of Stamps

Letter from E. Cook to his Parents

Camp at Gloucester Point Va. Nov. 1862

My Dear Parents

It seems a long time since I wrote to you but it is only 3 or 4 days since I sent off my last letter to you, but if any thing happens so that I cannot write a letter every day it seems a long time when I write again. I have received your letters № 12 + 13 and the Rural New Yorker from Mr. Lyman, for which I am very much obliged to him. I am now feeling first rate and hope I shall continue so. I think that one of the boys that came down in our squad will receive a discharge in a day or two and if he does he will call on you. His name is Wm. Hart; he is well acquainted with the adopted daughter or niece of one of the [   ].

You wished to know if the oysters here were as good as those you get in Buffalo. I can only say that they are the very largest + fattest I ever saw, and if we get them + open them + then keep them exposed to the air for about 3 days until they begin to grow stale, they will then taste like the Buffalo oysters, but when we eat them as soon as we get them they taste far better than those we get in B. What did Mr. [   ] reminded him of the time we eat oysters on the half shell at Dodd's Saloon? The drum has sounded for Roll call so I can write no more this evening. Send me word as soon as you get my things ready to send to me. Don't put in any whisky unless you put in an oyster can like the pickles + seal it up. The officers open all of the boxes and if they find any liquor in they take it out. Brandy + Bitters are exempt. I do not care

We are in our Sibley tents but are not in the fort. We are encamped just in front of the fort and can skedaddle into it in double quick time in case of an attack. 'Tis true that we are willing to fight but we are more willing to go home and get a good nights rest in a soft bed. Don't worry yourself about "Farmers Joint Stock" I did not think to leave it in B. when I came away. I heard our Lieutenant say that somebody in the company seemed to have lots of Farmers Joint Stock money. I don't know of course what he meant. You ask what we think of Lincoln's proclamation. We think more of getting through with the war than we do of all the rash proclamations of our President. We think with Europe that Lincoln had better get the nigger before he sets them free. This war is nothing more than a nigger war. The nigger down here is better than a soldier. Day before yesterday a soldier was confined in a dungeon because he whipped a nigger for driving over his foot.

It is a common saying among the soldiers that a man might as well strike an officer as to strike a nigger. We are willing to fight for our flag, our country + our Constitution but we are not willing to spill our blood for the lazy and ungrateful nigger. Excuse this short + poorly written letter. I wrote in a hurry for fear I should not finish it to night and I do not think I would have time tomorrow. I will write again as soon as possible. Your Loving Son Ed Cook

Letter from A. Lyth to his Parents

Gloucester Point Va Nov 2 1862
Dear Folks at Home
I received your letters of the 22 + 26 last night and was glad to hear that you were all well and that mothers thumb was getting better. I also received the memoranda book you sent me and I prize it a great deal but I think it was unnessary to put so many postage stamps on but I took 2 of them off this morning and bought 6 pence worth of apples with them of a secesh on the picket line I am on picket to day there has been a stoppage of the mail some way between Buffalo + here because I both of your letter last night with Williams + Marys enclosed there was about a 2 bushel bag full of letters for the Regiment in consequence of the delay of the mails

Mary I was very glad to hear from you through those few lines you wrote and I received that piece of poetry + the postage stamp you sent me which I intend to keep untill I am in need of it and want it to spend I was very sorry that the shell that I sent for fanny was broken it was not a very hansome shells I exclose another one for her which I picked upon the beach yesterday whilst digging for clams it has a hole though it they say when you find a shell with a hole through it is the sign of good luck and I belive it for it was not a great whill after that I received your letters + my memoranda book.

William I was delighted to hear from you also through the few lines that you sent me if you and John were here you could have plenty of hunting if it was not war time there are plenty of wild ducks in the river and some few wild geese and there are lots of quail + medow larks thousands of them and you can get close enough to them to hit them with a short stick they are so tame and lots of wild rabbits + other game but we are not alowed to fire our guns off so we cannot get any of them but we can go a fishing or after oysters or clams I was after oysters yesterday and clams we can get oysters when the tide is out by wading into the water about 6 inch deep and pick them out with our hands by the bushel while I am writing this my companion is fixing a dish of oysters for our dinners. And when the tide is out we take and dig down into the sand for clams but we dont think as much about the clams as the oysters

John I was very glad to hear that you had got enough of tiles to fill your last kiln before the machine gave way; I was astonished to hear that you have had such a snowstorm and such cold wether but of course you cannot have such weather as we have here and it is getting well into the autumn it might be expected we have had some cool nights here but nothing like a frost as yet and one cold windy day about a week ago but as a general thing the weather is very pleasent here yet yesterday was a very warm but is not so hot today. The last time I was on picket it was just close by a small creek that runs into the river about 2 oclock in the morning there was a man observed to be crossing the stream 2 posts below the post that I was on by the sentinal on that post he halted him and wanted to know what he wanted he stated he wanted to see the Leautenant well they took charge of him and sent for the Leautenant who was on our post and he held quite a long conversation with him which we afterwards learned was that he wanted to come under the protection of our flag as he said the guerrelas that I have spoken off before are going about the country and robbing allmost all the folks of part of their winter stock and making them join the rebel army there a great many militia in this part of the country that were in the rebel army before McClellan took Yorktown but when the rebels evacuated this place they hung back in the woods + other hideing places till the Rebels got away and then they joined their wives + families and it is these deserters that the guerelas trouble principally this man was one of them and hearing

46

of their doings I suppose he determined to quit but having a great quantity of corn + fodder and some stock he wished to sell it to the government and take the money and go north accordingly the next day there was a company sent out to see that he was not molested and to assist in getting his stock and things to the river where the ferry boat run down and put them on board they were out 2 days The guerellas have ventured pretty close to the picket lines on the other side of the river and have been shot at by our pickets yesterday there came in a report that there was a body of them on this side of the river near our picket lines and the whole Regiment was called under arms and into line of Battle on the parade ground but the report turned out to be false so we soon despersed and went to our tents I must tell you that send we moved camp Thomas Maharg is in the same tent with me and we sleep together and are very comfortable. We take our 2 peices of tent that we have to carry on a march and spread them on the bunk we have raise from the floor and I have an extra blanket which was given to me by our sergant which I spread over them and then we both spread our overcoats on that and it makes quite a comfortable bed then we have a feather pillow which Tom got sent to him from home in a box amongst many other raritys. I also had a letter from Cousin William last night wich i enclose herewith that you may read it. I also send you a peice of cotton that grew on this point it is very dirty as I have had it in my pocket over a week it grow on the stalk in a bud about the size of a wallnut and then bursts open when it is ripe something like the hickory nut shells does and then it is all cotton inside simlar to the peice I send you I shall be very happy to have you send your likeness as you have promised and if I ever get a chance I will send you mine in my uniform but there is no chance around here at present I shall put my last postage stamp on this letter so if you have not sent some already I wish you would now as they are a very scarce artical around here. My love to you all so no more at present
       Your Affect Son + Brother
       Alfred Lyth

Letter from E. Cook to his Parents and Relatives

       Camp at Gloucester Point, Va Sunday Nov. 2/62
My Dear Parents + Relatives
    Last Evening our regiment received the mail for the first time in 6 days.

For some reason or other the mails are getting very tardy + irregular. I was well waiting for my mail for it brought me the writing paper, 2 letters + 7 Papers from home, 1 Letter from Mr. Lyman + 2 letters + 1 Paper from other parties. G. Clark received a letter from Eliza. I know G. Stoddard received some papers but I don't know whether he got any letters or not. I am very sorry that I cannot tent with the boys for it is not near as pleasant to be away from them. The box has not got along yet. I am almost out of postage stamps I wish you would send me a dollars worth when you write again. We cannot buy them here. What did you pay for this letter paper? It cost 24 cents. I wish you would keep an accurate account of every thing you pay out for me. If you had your cow out here I do not think you would be very fast to kill her. Milk costs 25 cents per quart and it cannot be bought for less. One of the boys in our tent has had the dysentery and he has bought 2 canteens full of milk for which he has paid 75 cents. A canteen holds a quart + a pint. Apples are worth 2 ½ cents each or more than a dollar a peck. Strong butter half lard 40 cts per pound; cheese 25 cents; boots $8^{00} a pair, wormy figs 2 cents each or $1^{00} a small box. Molassas cakes 2 for 5 cents, worth 10 cents a dozen in B. Crackers 20 cents per pound and every thing else in proportion. Albert York was put in the guard house night before last for letting one of the prisoners escape from his post while on guard. I guess he is out by this time.

Our colonel is getting so unreasonably strict that all the boys are getting down on him. He is trying to introduce his regular army rules into our volunteer regiment + he will find out one of these days that it is not going to give the best kind of satisfaction. My leg still continues very stiff + painful but I think it is now getting better. I have been up only once since last evening + that was to make me a fresh bread + water poultice. I went to the doctor yesterday morning + he excused me from duty.

This morning I did not go + so he came to my tent to see me; he told me to keep on poulticing it + it would come around all right in a few days. One of the boys in our company received a box from home night before last. It contained 2 Pillows and every thing else from bologney sausages to rich fruit cake. He gave me a large piece of cake and I can tell you it did relish nice. I think I shall send for some things in a week or two. His box was only four days in coming through. I cannot see why it is that my things do not come. I am afraid that Mr. Burson made some mistake in directing it.

I went down to the river yesterday to wash some dirty clothes that have been laying around for 3 or 4 days. I had not been down there more than 10 minutes before one of our company came running down to tell us that the long roll was beating and the regiment was out under arms. I immediately snatched up my bundle left my kettles of water on the fire and commenced hobbling up to the camp. The rest of the boys far outstripped me in the race and when I got to camp the line was dismissed and the companies were returning to their quarters. Those that were down to the river supposed as much as could be that the rebels were coming. I could not march but I knew if the regiment stood still + fired that I could shoot as fast as any one. The alarm was a false one + was ordered by the Colonel in order to teach the soldiers not to stray so far away from camp as to be out of hearing of the drum. You would have laughed I think to have seen Ed with his stiff knee hobbling along with a stick in one hand and a washboard + bundle of dirty clothes in the other. The faster I tried to go the slower I went. Several of our men were very much excited. One fellow came into my tent and commenced fumbling among one of the boys traps. He did not know where he was or what he was doing until we told him 2 or 3 times that he was in the wrong tent and then he looked around with a kind of vacant stare + tumbled out again. Another fellow, a sailor who has been here only a short time, and has been spinning off his long yarns about his daring deeds + terrible adventures ever since he came, was cooking oysters when the roll sounded. The boys said he was so scared that he turned white + so excited that he stewed his oysters twice without knowing it. There are many laughable incidents every time a regiment is ordered out, if a person is only present to witness them. After the scare was over I went down to the river again + washed my clothes. Bill Goffe helped to wash + wring them. I washed them in hot water. I had a tub + washboard so I got them pretty clean. The washboard was made out of a pine board with creases cut in it. I think when I return I shall have to hire out to do washing + darning. The letters I received were N<u>os</u>* 8 + 9. No 9 contained a letter from mother I am many times obliged to her for it + hope it will not be the last time she writes.*

I will lay down again for a short time. Well I have been lying down for about 2 hours and I think I ought to be rested, but the fact is I have lain so much in one place that I have worn the soft side of my board entirely away and have got down to the hard part where a fellow can't rest. Tom Maharg roasted me a sweet potato + boiled me an egg + toasted some bread for my supper so I have fared pretty well to day. It is almost dark now and I must turn out + poultice my knee again. Our company is on picket to day + they have got a lovely day for the duty.

Monday Morning

The gathering on my knee discharged a little last night and it feels easier this morning. I heard Saturday that Mr. [   ], the man I helped to take across the river about a week, is dead. I do not know that the report is true. I hope it is not. I have not heard from T. Wharton for several days. If he was here now he would be in my tent. I received another paper (the Christian Advocate) № 4 last evening. The inhabitants around here are Union while our forces are near + when the "rebs" are around. I would not have cared much for Mary's Ice cream but I would like some of the "Magnificent Cake" + "Elegant Sandwiches". What is the brides name? Our company when on picket yesterday saw 8 Rebel cavalry in the edge of the woods. I think I told you in my last letter that our Lieut. had been detailed to common a company from the 104 Penn, on a secret expedition. The expedition was designed to aid a Union man in recovering his property from the rebel lines so that he could move north. The Lieut. succeeded in getting away every thing that was owned by the man, including a lot of poultry.

We have only had one commissioned office in our company and a few days ago the Colonel took a lieutenant from another company and put him in command over us for a short time. The boys do not like it very well for they are afraid he will be permanently attached to our company + they do not like the idea of having a lt. placed over them. Tom Maharg gave me a couple of eggs this morning and I am going to have them cooked for my supper. I will answer Laura's letter in a day or two.

I had my fortune told yesterday as I was lying in my tent by one of the old soldiers. He believed every thing he told me as fully as if it had already come to pass. It took him about an hour to project my horoscope before he could commence to read my fortune. He foretold the future by a regular mathematical calculation based upon a system logarithms and governed by the signs of the zodiac. He paid some Judge $15 to learn him the science + he places implicit confidence in the rule. He can only foretell from the 1ˢᵗ of Jany to the 31ˢᵗ of Dec. or one year at a time and then he has to form a new *scale of figures for the next year. He said I should be in or near some little battle before long, I am to be lucky in gaming until the 20ᵗʰ of this month: I am going to receive some money. I am to receive no wounds or injuries and am going have an office in the regiment of some kind or other. This is all to take place between this + the first day of January 1863. I have heard that our Captain P.E. Dye has resigned. Do you know any thing about it? I hope the report is true for every old soldier in the company dislikes him and wishes that he may never return. Our Lieut. Walbridge is liked very much indeed. He is gentlemanly + kind to his men. He never orders them in a brusque + brutal manner but kindly requests them to do as he wishes. The boys all want him for their commander and I hope he will receive the appointment for more reasons than one. I told you in one of my other letters that I believed "Carl" to be Chas. C. Coleman. I wish you would cut out + send to me his 2ᵈ letter that you speak of in your letter,*

I have been out of my tent only once to day. My knee feels a great deal easier this afternoon. The Doctor was in again this morning to see me. He seems to be more attentive to his patients than formerly. I think I shall be around all right in 2 days. I saw a large fire night before last beyond the picket line. To day I learned that it was a large pile of wood belonging to our forces across the river which had been fired by the rebels. We had only bought it 2 or 3 days before and had no idea that any one would set fire to it. I saw an old school mate of mine to day that I never dreamed of seeing here. His name is Charley Taylor. He enlisted after I did in the navy and is now on board of the Gunboat in the river opposite our camp. He was on duty at Yorktown and knowing that myself and some others were in the camp on this side he obtained a pass and came over to see us. I was right glad to see him for I did not know that he had enlisted. It seems like old times to see an old friend. I guess I will not write any more to day for although I am not sick at all yet it makes me feel awful tired to sit up. I have got miserable ink to write with + I shall be very glad indeed when my box comes some Arnolds ink. I will send you a list of some things I want in a few days. Remember us all to all our friends. Don't forget to send the postage stamps in the first letter for I have only 5 or 6 left and they will not last long. Use care in directing the letter containing the stamps. Be sure + put on the Co "26" 100ᵗʰ Regt. N.Y.S.V. Is grandmother getting better? Laura wrote she was unwell.

Your affectionate son

E.L. Cook

Letter from E. Cook to his Parents, Relatives and Sister

Camp at Gloucester Point Va Nov. 4ᵗʰ 1862
Tuesday

My Dear Parents and Relatives – Laura in Particular
As I was sprawled out on the floor last evening I was surprised by one
of our company coming in my tent and handing me a letter done up in
a square white envelope and postmarked Buffalo. I could not imagine
who in the world it was from. I opened it + was glad to find that it
was a letter from Eliza № 10. I received all the newspapers you sent me
including Nos. 2 + 3 were not numbered. I was mistaken about the letter
signed "Carl". It was not written by Lieut. Coleman but by Capt. Morse.
I told Coleman this morning that I believed it was written by him and
he denied it and told me that Capt. Morse was the author, as did also one
other officer.
I wish when you see any letters from the 100ᵗʰ in any of the papers that
you would cut them out + send them to me. I hear to day that Tom
Wharton is improving. Mr. Stowell is dead of a certainty. G. Clark paid
25 cents for a little bottle of Oil + did not have it more than half an
hour before some one had stolen it and he saw it no more. I have got a
pretty good set of boys in my tent. I do not think any of them are thieves.
I leave my traps many of them exposed but I have had nothing stolen
from me as yet. Do you think it is worth while to continue my Eclectic
Magazine another year.
Laura how did you know that there was any argument between Nellie S.
+ myself? What did Nellie say about our argument? I guess she has been
telling tales out of school + I must give her a lecture in my next letter. Ask
her why she don't write to me.
The weather here at the time had the tornado in Buffalo was mild +
lovely and has been so for more than a week but to day it is raining +
somewhat windy. I am very much obliged to Mary for kind letter but as
I wrote to Stephen only a day or two ago I thing I shall not answer it just
at present but will try to do so shortly as soon as I have an opportunity.
I sometimes wish that you would be here to look into our tent as I am

eating my meals or as we are all stretched out on the floor of an evening ready to go to sleep and sleep till morn. Last night we had 14 persons sleeping in our tent and besides that 3 cupboards + a gun rack which of themselves occupy at least ¼ of the room in the "shebang". As an illustration of the "right smart" expression the following will answer the point as well as most any thing I know of. A woman was asked how her sick husband was getting along, she said – "He was getting right smart well but now he was getting right smart sick again. "Right Smart" + "I reckon" are the principal words of dialogue. There are a number of things that I have sent for to Mr. Comstock along with G. Clark and as their are some things that I want that Mr. Comstock cannot get I think I will leave this letter until tomorrow and finish it at that time. Geo. Stoddard is going to have some things sent in G. Clark's box + you can both take them down to Comstock's at the same time of if you prefer it you can send my stuff in a separate box + let Mr. Lyman see that they are shipped all right and take a receipt for the box and a duplicate receipt to send to me by mail. It will be the Least trouble for you send in G. Clark's box and the freight will be less than it would be the other way. If you send by Comstock he will pay the freight + I will settle with Geo. Clark.

[Ed Cook]

Letter from E. Cook
Camp at Gloucester Point Va. Nov. 4/62

Dear Sir

Your very welcome notes of the 28th came duly to hand. In the completest sense do we now realize that as cool water is to a thirsty man so is good news from a far country? A letter from a friend at home is more welcome than the richest meal that wealth could offer. It would do the heart of any one good to witness the avidity with which the poor soldier grasps his letter as his name is called. Picture a group of 7 in a common A tent. Four of the group are playing a game of euchre to quicken the slow moving steps of the coming hour of nine; two are looking on, learning to profit by the misplays of those engaged in the game; the 7th and last is writing (by the unsteady light produced by a piece of cotton cloth burning in a dish of salt pork grease) to his parents perhaps or some dear friend at home. Another group *is gathered around the dying embers of the cooks fire watching the pictures that are playing among the coals. One is telling a long + highly interesting yarn about his adventures at sea, to a listening crowd of non-believers; three others are fighting over again the great 7 Day battle at Fair Oaks and again are in full retreat down the peninsula and involuntarily look over their shoulder as if they expected to see a body of rebel cavalry in full persuit; one other is saying I wish I was in Brockways place and on my way home (Brockway has just received a discharge.) Another says yes I would give him one hundred dollars and my back pay for his papers. Another has just dropped some sweet potatoes in the ashes and stands watching them with an eager look wishing they were done for his mouth is watering for the sweet morsel, others are thinking of home and talking of fond ones not here while the last is trying to read the latest letter from the 100ᵗʰ in the daily Express of Buffalo: But Hark! The voice of "Pete came squeaking down the street. "This way boys if you want to get your mail" In an instant the "cards" are dashed aside, the "pen" is dropped, the "yarn" is broken, and the "fighting" stopped, "Brockway's discharge" forgotten, "sweet potatoes" left to burn while the "thoughts of home + fond ones" for a moment take a turn, and "letters <u>from</u> the hundredth", half read, are put away, while letters <u>for</u> the regiment hold undisputed sway. At the word letter the men in their tents come crawling out like sand crabs out of the muck. I have often laughed to see some soldier cooped up in a little shelter tent come crawling out in the morning at reveille on his hands + knees and when fairly out rise up + still up gradually until he is expanded into a good long 6 ft. man, and you wonder how in the world such a little place can contain so much flesh + bone. What do you think of 3 of us living in a little wedge shape tent 10 ft. long 6 ft. wide + not quite 5 feet high. Think of it to live + move + have our beings in such a place as this. Never go for a "sojer" boy. I suppose the people of New York State are all excitement to day and full of expectation.*

I wish I could be present to cast in my vote. I am almost inclined to believe that it would be in favor of Wordsworth although I know that the whole Southern Confederacy is not worth the precious Union blood that has already been spilled in the vain endeavor to retain it. And when we think of the vast amount that yet must flow we are ready to say let them go to the ruin they so wildly seek, but give us <u>peace</u>.

The curse of God shall yet rest upon the souls of those who have been the prime movers in this shameful rebellion and unholy war. I believe we are but little nearer the End than we were a year ago. I have not now the slightest hope of seeing my friends at home until my regiment is discharged after having served out the full term of years for which they were mustered into the service. Things of a certainty do not look near as promising as they did 2 months ago. How must it discourage the poor soldier when he learns that a place which is impregnable when garisoned by 10,000 men, has been surrendered, without a struggle, although at the time of the surrender it was defended by upwards of 11,000.

Again he is informed that an officer, when questioned as to the reason why he did not "bag" a rebel army when he had an opportunity, replied that "That is not the game the game is to maneuvre around until both armies are tired out and both sides desirous of peace to then receive the Confederate States into the Union with slavery" This is the "Game" our high Officers + Officials are playing upon the people.

Which is best? Shall we elect "Peace" parties to fill our high offices, those who openly declare themselves in favor of peace on any honorable grounds, or shall we submit to the miserable farce which is now being played off upon us, and finally find one compelled to make peace upon such terms as the "Rebs" see fit to force upon us! We have force enough to come down on the Enemy like an avalanche and crush him in an instant but we do not do it and why? Simply because that is not the "game". We have thousand of soldiers who are anxious to return to their homes and would fight like hell hounds if the could be brought into any action that they knew would be decisive, but this cannot be, and why? because such is not the "game". No! the poor soldier must remain in his camp, suffering from all camp diseases, too hot in summer + too cold in winter, with abundance of nauseating food to eat and sickening beverages to drink, no friend to comfort him if he feels despondent + unwell and no care taken of him if disease lays her pityless hand upon him; while his officers are playing at their unholy "game". Never will I advise a friend of mine to enlist until I see some signs of a disposition on the part of our "Starred" + "double Starred" strap wearers to put an end to the ruinous "game". Wait! Be drafted! Be anything but don't enlist!

The soldiers are willing and anxious to fight but we have no Generals or if we have those who are both able, and true to the Union they are kept in the background with small commands and not allowed to do any thing towards bringing this war to a speedy close. But things will not go on so always, and even now I see that the public journals are taking the matter in hand and bringing the offenders before the public and inquiring into the wherefore of certain acts of come of our high officers. I hope the time is not far away when some kind of a change will be made in our army affairs enabling us to go ahead in the work overpowering + defeating our merciless foe.

I wish you would write to me as soon as the results of to days election are made known and tell me which party is victorious. For my own part it is but little I care which party is defeated.

[Ed Cook]

Letter from E. Cook to his Mother

11/04/62

Dearest Mother.

I am a thousand times obliged to you for your kind + loving letter.

I received the letter paper you sent me and you can scarsely picture the joy I felt on receiving it. It was not from the value or scarsity of the article here but for the thought + kindness of those that sent. When I first saw it I felt almost as if I was in the presence of the dear ones at home. I never asked for it; I simply intimated that that my supply was nearly exhausted and a fresh supply was immediately sent forward. Those two pieces in Advocate that you speak of I read aloud to G. Clark one evening as he was lying on the bed not feeling very well. I was particularly well pleased with "The light in the window". The Advocate gets well read in our tent. It is handled so much that it gets completely used up before it gets round to me again. Every man in the tent reads it more or less. I am glad to know that there are prayers offered up for me. I should dread above all things to be a soldier and be without a hope based upon the Lord. It gives me confidence when fever + disease are daily visable around me; and when any danger is to be faced or any difficulty to be overcome it gives me courage and nurses my spirit to the ready performance of my duty. Not for a world would I be without my hope of future life in the world to come. Christ made the dying bed of poor Stowell a couch of peace + happiness. When I asked him, a day or two before he went to Yorktown, how he got along, he said, "Oh! Cook the knowledge of Christ does me more good that the medicine and all Else besides." "I went" said he "out in the field to day and had a sweet + happy *time in prayer to God and I feel better." He said more + I know that he had a firm hope established in the Lord.*

The weather here is lovely and has been for some time; to day the clouds look as soft + warm as in a northern summer's day. The sun is warm + pleasant. The nights are cold, very cold but in our new Sibly tents we sleep very comfortably. I am going to send home in a day or two for some things and I wish you would see to having them packed in a suitable box – light but strong. Prepay the charges clear through and be sure + take a straight receipt from the express company so that in case they are lost I can recover pay of the Ex. Company. I am well and so are both the boys. We are not homesick and have never regretted that we enlisted. If a discharge were offered us we would not now accept it. You did not tell me how to direct your letter so I send this one in care of my Father. I expect a long letter from you in reply to this + that very soon. Tell Eliza that "Carl" in the Express is Capt. Morse + [   ] is Geo. N. Stoddard. Give my respects to all my friends and if you Alice or Fannie or any of my other girls you must give my love to them. I have just rec'd Eliza's letter No 10. I will write then.

Thursday Nov. 6th 1862 - I wrote to Mr. Lyman yesterday + sent the letter in Father's care as he did not tell me how to direct his letter. I should have written to you before but I wrote a longer letter to him than I expected and there was so much noise in the tent last night that I could neither read or write or do any thing else. I got a pass to go over to Yorktown today and bought 5 cans of butter at $1⁰⁰ per can; the cans hold nearly 4 lbs. It is the best butter I have tasted since I left Albany. One can was for myself; one for G. Stoddard + the other 3 for some boys in the company. I had an excellent supper of bread + butter thickly spread with sugar. It has been raining again nearly all day but it is not very cold. Our stove makes our tent feel quite comfortable this kind of weather but as the stove pipe runs only half way up the tent you may believe our shanty is not always entirely free from smoke. Enclosed is my pass to Yorktown, please preserve it for me. I was again surprised to receive a letter from Laura N⁰ 11 this evening. The letters have been so slow in coming here-to-fore that now they come through regularly it surprises us. You ask me what I think about Jeff Davis arming the slaves. I do not think he dare do it and if he had the belief that it would aid his cause to arm the slaves, he has not got the arms to do it with unless he takes them from his white soldiers. From all that I have seen *of the negro slaves I judge them to be a very cowardly people and I would be far less afraid to meet a regiment of armed slave than I would to meet the same number of slave women armed + in line, for of the two I think the negress is more courageous + manly than the negro. I do not dream, neither does any man in the regiment dream that any trouble is to be anticipated from the Southern Confederacy arming the slave population.*

Thursday Morning I have not yet opened my little bottle of brandy and I do not intend to until there is good course to do so for the whiskey only it is good when a person comes off guard or picket to make a little hot stuff. It may sometimes prevent him from taking cold.

Laura! What in the deuce do you mean by that "Admire" *I cannot speak for the boys but* I *have used* my *housewife a number of times and find it a great convenience. I have to darn my stockings every week + a few days ago I darned the heals of one pair to keep them from wearing out. Darning is slow work for me but I manage to do it up in pretty good style + in quite a durable manner. I use the one that my girl gave me more than the one that Aunt Eliza gave me for the sake of "Auld Lang Syne". You ask why the corners are all cut off your letters? I will tell you. Do you recollect receiving one letter that had the corners [ ] up on account of being burned after being written? Well, at the same time I burned that letter the whole balance of the [ ] got burned too as both the letter and letter paper were lying together and the corner got into the flame of the candle or "slut".*

I have not written to [ ]. I called to see [ ] in New York but he was not in. I have lost his address. If I had it I think I would write to him some time when I have leisure. They say those things I called snails are *Jurywinkles but are not the kind that are good to eat. They say they are too small; they are about an inch long or less. So I have not seen a live snail after all.*

Thursday Evening Well I have finished answering Laura's part of Letter N° 12 so I will now try and answer Eliza's part. I was acting Sergeant of the Guard day before yesterday. Yesterday I did my washing + today I have been acting Sergeant of the Police and tomorrow they are going to make a special detail for me to do some carpenter work (make a door) at the Colonel's new tent so you see I have not had much time to do any writing this week, and as we are going to raise + stockade our tents

tomorrow + the day after tomorrow, and then go on picket Sunday, I d̄
know when I shall be able to write the next letter and even this I shall h̄
to cut pretty short. One of our Sergeants + a private tried to make love to ā
nigger girl a short time ago when they were on picket and the Sergeant was
put under arrest + the private was confined in a dark, damp underground
dungeon for 2 or 3 days so you see it is not very safe business. I guess Eliza,
you will have to ask Laura how to spell <u>Aunt</u> *"<u>Gracies</u>" Did Mary Scheffer*
say she would answer my letter? I guess Mr. Scheffer lived too high while
he was here – eat too many oysters, they are apt to make <u>new</u> <u>recruits</u> *sick.*
Mr. Scheffer not only had 3 blankets to sleep under but he had a good tight
tent to sleep in while we had only a shelter tent raised from the ground
about 2 feet on stakes and the wind blowing under, over + around us –
Hay!!! What!!! Right smart to sleep under those circumstances weren't we?
Hay! What! White frost on the ground too? Hay!! What!!!

[Ed Cook]

Letter from A. Lyth to his Brother

Gloucester Point Va. Thursday Nov 13 1862

Dear Brother

I take the opportunity to write you these few lines as I have nothing
else to occupie my time at present and I hope these few lines will find you
all well as it leaves me at present we are having very find weather here
at present every vistage of the snow has disappeared a day or two ago and
the sun has shone every day since and it is very warm and pleasent. There
are a great many rumors afloating around the camp at present one is that
General McClellan has left of his own accord and that Gen Burnside has
taken Command of the army but we cannot tell weather it is true or not.
we are about all fixed up around camp and it is a very fine looking Camp
and it is very admiriably situated there has been almost for the last month
rumors that the Regiment leaving this point but they all turned out to be
get-ups and at present there is a rumor that we are going to Texas but we all
know it is all a get up although we are all anxious + wishing that it may
be so as we all should like to go further south this winter although we are
so comfortable here there has been rumors of us going to Buffalo, of going to
Baltimore + to Washington to Suffolk to Albany and of even going to New

' rumors are thought little off by the more intelligent of
'beleive all the rumors It appears for a certainty that
'ough we have not had all the returns. the very fact of
· the day is that all the Republicans are in the army
... very fact that there are 76 able men in our company
. about 65 of them are voters and there are all Republicans excepting
some 6 or 7 and it is the same throughout the camp and the camps of
the other Regiments that I have been in you will the men useing various
expresions against the democrats There are 12 men in our tent and they are
all democrats but one but he is not a voter not being 18 year old. I received
the newspapers when I received Sarah Anns letter but forgot to mention the
receit of them in the letter that I wrote to her I suppose by the time that
this letter reaches you the drafting will be all over and that those that are
drafted you will have learned their names if the draft has come off as it was
to do if it has and there is any body drafted that I know I wish you would
inform me Tom + I bought a can of Butter the other day there being
     [   ] pounds in the can we paid 2 dollars for the can so we can enjoy our
good peice of bread + butter as we used to do at home it is very good butter
and besides we have some little extras that tom as got in his box he receive
from home so that we quite enjoy ourselves we sleep very comfortable in our
bunk at night*****I have just been shaved by the fifer of our company and
he has cut my hair. This fifer he his a little French boy between 18 + 19
years of age he is quite a 2^d Tom Thumb he is a bout a foot high and has
small arms + legs he has been with the Regiment ever since it left Buff he is
the smartest fifer in the Regiment and the pet of the Regiment.

[Alfred Lyth]

Letter from A. Lyth to his Folks at Home

Gloucester Point Virginia Sunday Nov 16
Dear Folks at Home
     I take this opportunity to write you these few lines having nothing else
to occupy my time at present I am expecting a letter from you by every
nights mail hence my not writing sooner + I hope these few lines will find
you all well as it leaves me at present. Last Thursday night at Roll Call
which we have every night at nine oclock we received orders to not take

of all our clothes when we retired for the night and to have everything in readyness such as our guns + equipment Canteens + [   ] there was some reports come in to the picket lines that there were some 3 or 4 hundred Rebel Cavalry about 3 miles beyond our pickets and that they might take a notion to pay us a visit through the night so we sent out an additional Company from our Regiment and one from the Regiment in the fort to act as reserves and support the pickets. however nothing occured to disturb our slumbers that night. But next day we turned a secessionist out of his house and are going to occupy it as a hospital and we set him adrift on the other side of the picket lines The reason of turning him out of his house is that he + his wife in particular were continually throwing out hints threats talking secesh and abusive language to the guard that was put over there property to keep the soldiers from molesting anything cursing the Yankees to the officers which would often call and see them so being in need of a hospital on this side of the river and this house being the very thing Uncle Sam politely helped secesh to move as Uncle Frank once politely helped us to move as was quite natural old secesh was a little vexed particularly the old woman as she said she was sorry she had not poisend a few of the yankees before this The old feller threatened to destroy the house but he was too closely watched for to get an opportunity and imagine his chagrin when the boys were helping him move of their retaining a keg of powder which they found snugly stowed away in a corner of his celler. however he is now with his friends on the other side of the picket lines to day. The next night the orders were the same as the night before. To be in readyness But still we were let sleep undisturbed that night the same as usual The next morning I was detailed for guard duty. In the afternoon there was quite a lot of Cavalry come from the other side of the river and 7 [   ] of Artillary and went outside of the picket lines. The Cavelry went out about 18 miles near Gloucester Courthouse were they got into the track of some Rebel Cavelry. The Rebels finding that our Cavelry were upon their track they turned upon a by road and skeddadled one young boy having got strayed off from the rest and somehow or other he got on the road ahead of our men and see them in the distance he thought it was some of his own men therefore he came towards them and the men say that he did open his eyes + mouth when one of our men rode from the rank and presented a pistol and demanded his surrender he was very poorly dressed having on an old tom coat raged pants old white hat shabby boots +c he was 18 years old he told me One of the other prisoners was a Rebel Cavelry Captain he was seen standing on the stoop of a house nearby and his horse hitched to a post outside He caught sight of our men at the same time and not having time to reach his horse he run into the house our men rode up at full speed and into the house after him not seeing him they began to search after him and found him stuffed between two matterases they hauled him out and disarmed him and fetched him and his horse prisoners into camp when they got into camp some of the men wanted to take his spurs from him but he pulled them off and put them in his pocket saying that was his own private property. I tell you he is a wicked looking creature and they took another prisoner and captured the Rebel mail besied some other documents and Robbed a Rebel store of a good many things such as tobaco and there was not a cavelry man in the whole squadron that hadent his haversack stuffed with chicken Geese Ducks some having 4 or 5 geese apeice and one had a live pig laid across his horseback some one thing and some another but the worst of the preformance was that a company of Infantry from the Regiment that is in the fort were attacked last night while out scouting by a few Rebel Cavalry who fired into them and killed one wounded three one of which is not expected to live and three more of them are missing But I guess we have scarte the rebels from this vicinty Our company are on picket to day but I am not with them on account of being on camp guard last night

Give my Love to All my sisters and brothers. This is Fanny's Birthday so no more at present From your

Affectionate Son, Alfred Lyth

please write soon and
Do Write to me oftener please

Letter from E. Cook to his Parents

Saturday, Nov. 23, 1862 - The night was quite cold but it was rather pleasant during the day. Since those men in the 104th Penn. Vols. were shot, a new order has been issued to the picket guards which is to allow no person to approach the lines during the day and to shoot any object that is seen approaching the picket from the Enemys country during the night. Heretofore they have allowed persons to come to the line and converse + sell provisions during the day, and in the night our orders were to challenge all persons before firing. It seems that when the 104th boys challenged the rebel *cavelry the other night they replied that they were the 107ᵗʰ Penn. Cavelry and when they were ordered to dismount one and let him advance they immediately gave the command "Right [   ] – fire!" + wheeled their horses + rode off at full speed, thus giving another example of their dastardly treachery + cowardice.*

Sunday Nov. 23ᵈ 1862 - This morning at daylight we saw the two prisoners that were taken when on that forageing party returning with their horses so I suppose the found no cause to hold them thought I firmly believe that one of them was either a Guerilla or else a rebel cavalry man and what convinces me more fully of this is the fact that a little negro boy told our Lieut. that one of them used to be his master and was now in some Virginia regiment and he told the man's name and also the name + number of the Regt. + company in which he served. When we returned from picket we went down to the target + fired off our guns. Seven shots struck the target and mine was one of them + G. Clark's another. G. Stoddard generally make a better shot than either of us.

I was in hopes that I should be able to write a letter to you to day but we had no sooner returned from our target practice than we were ordered to get ready for Brigade drill at 1 oclock. Brigade Drill on Sunday – who ever heard of such a thing? No wonder our [   ] do not conquer when such work as this is going on. It seems to me like sacriledge thus to profane the sabbath when there is no occasion for it. They might give the soldier one day in the week to devote to his own uses + purposes for I am sure he does enough for the government during week days to be entitled to the use of the sabbath. But we are soldiers + are sworn to obey our superiors so we must not murmer or complain. When we got to our tents we immediately went to work, cleaned our guns, blacked our shoes + brushed our clothes and got ready just in time to turn out as the call was beat on the drum. We had 5 Regts on the field in the 100ᵗʰ N.Y.V., the 104 Penn Vols., + 3 regts from Yorktown. Our Brigade General Naglee commanded the regiments and was accompanied by his staff + escort. We drilled about 3 hours, part of the time on the double quick and were very glad when the things over. As soon as we came off drill we had to go on dress parade and when we came off dress parade it was dark. After supper I felt tired and could not muster up courage enough to get out my writing materials and I think taking all things into consideration I am in a great measure excusable for not writing before.

Monday, Nov. 24th 1862 I received 3 papers from home this evening + 1 Letter N<u>o</u> 18. We have been busy to day putting bunks in our tent. When we have things all fixed up right in our tent I will send you a plan of it and you can compare it with the plan that Uncle David sent you. We commended altering our tent about a week ago but what with rainey weather and going on forageing expeditions + Picket we had been delayed in our work until today but now we are fairly at it again I think we will soon have it finished up. We amused our selves this evening with playing a game we call proverbs and find it very entertaining and perhaps a little instructional as it is a kind of mental disapline. It is played like this: one of the company steps outside the tent and while he is away the rest of the company chose a proverb, either religious or otherwise, and assign the words of the proverb in their proper order to the different members of the company as they sit in a circle around the stove. For instance we take the proverb "Wisdom is better than Riches" a proverb of 5 words: - the 1st word is given to the 1st man of the circle: the 2d word to the 2d man + so on. The person outside is then called in and steps up to the 1st man of the circle + asks him a question, and the answer to the question must contain the 1st word of the proverb. He then goes to the second man + asks him some question and the answer to the question must contain the 2d word of the proverb + the answer to the 3d question must contain the 3d word of the proverb + so on; and from all the answers the man must guess the proverb which is often very difficult + requires much memory to recollect all the answers. As we have voted that neither the questions or the answers shall contain any thing that is not immoral we enjoy the game very much.

Wednesday Nov. 26th 1862 – We finished the bunks in our tent yesterday. They are 2 stories high + hold 4 men 2 above + 2 below. Their are 3 of them in my tent – holding 12 men. Today I have been building a narrow movable bunk or longe for my self which I will describe when I send you a plan of my tent. It has been very rainey all the morning but cleared up at or before noon. I slept on my quilt for the first time this night. I did not like to use it before until I had a place where I could keep it out of the dirt.

The cannons on our fort have been firing shell at a target in the field front of our camp this afternoon.

Wednesday Nov 26th, 1862 evening -   It has been raining more or less all day long. I presume you are anxious by this time to hear from me again. I have been busy ever since I came from picket last Sunday so I could find no convenient time to write a letter. I had a bottle of ink come in one of G. Clarks boxes and I am using it for the first time this evening it is so much better and flows so much more readily than what I have been using that it deceives me entirely and I had these 3 large blots on the paper before I had filled my pen 3 times. I returned from Picket all safe + sound as you will learn when I get to it on my journal which I now begin where I left off in my last letter,

Thursday Nov. 27/62 I washed 2 shirts, 1 Pair stockings, 1 Pair Drawers, 3 hankerchiefs, + 1 towel this morning. We had another 3 hours battallion drill this afternoon. Our Lieut. handed me a Corporals [   ] this afternoon dating Nov. 1/62. G. Clark rec'd one also. I am still acting as Sergeant however and have some little reason to believe that I will some day receive a Sergeants [   ] but dont mention it to such a hope[   ]. We have to go on Picket again tomorrow + I will try + answer your letters there if it is warm enough to do so.

> *Good night from your Loving Son*
> *E.L. Cook*

P.S. I have not had time to read the last 3 papers you sent.

Nov. 28th 1862 Friday This was to have been our day to go on picket but as Maj or Genl Dix is expected here to review our regiment tomorrow we were ordered to remain in Camp and finish up our bunks + clean around our tents and arrange things generally so as make our camp appear as respectable as possible when the General passes through the streets. It has been a pleasant day and all the boys have been in first rate spirits. I worked pretty hard and was quite tired at night fall.

Nov. 29th 1862 Saturday We were on picket today. When we started from our tents about half past seven in the morning the weather looked rather dubious and we all thought we were going to have a wet and miserable day of it; but in a short time the clouds cleared up, the sun came out and we had a most lovely day. I had a very pleasant time reading my testament aloud to those that were on post with me and copying a letter that I had written to [ ] the day before but which was blotted so that I was ashamed to send it + so copied it over on picket. We passed the night quietly + comfortably. I stood guard only 2 ½ hours during the night but I did not sleep an hour. We were on the centre, the same line we occupied last time. When we returned from picket and went out to discharge our pieces we found our boys that were left in camp had put up a nice new target. I was the first one that shot and I plumbed the target quite nicely. After fireing our pieces we were allowed about half an hour to get ourselves ready for inspection + review. We had not time to pack our knapsacks properly and when the Colonel came to our company and saw how the knapsacks were packed he said "Oh hell! I dont want to inspect that company" and passed us by without more than a passing glance. Inspection over we were given about a quarter of an hour to rest ourselves, eat our dinner and then turn out for Brigade drill. Brigadier General Naglee drilled us for about 3 hours. We had 5 Regts. on the ground our regt., the 104th Penn. and the 11 Maine + 98th + 56th N.Y. from Yorktown across the river. We went through a great number of movements and did them up just as well as they are generally performed. But this is great Sunday work is it not? I must not stop to moralise however for if I do I shall never finish this letter.

Monday Dec. 1st 1862 I received your letter No 19 + 3 papers yesterday morning when we returned from picket, but you can form some idea of how much we have to do when I tell you that I did not get a chance to finish it until dark although I attempted to read it some half a doz. times during the afternoon drill whenever we had a chance to rest. I sent a letter to Mr. Lyman this evening.

We were ordered out for another inspection and review this afternoon at half past twelve but it commenced to rain when the line was formed so we were ordered to stack our arms and repair to our tents until the rain ceased but not to remove our accoutrements so we were kept waiting in our tents expecting every other moment to be called out and thus another afternoon passed away uselessly but I made some account of it for I finished my letter to Mr. Lyman that I commenced on picket last Saturday.

Tuesday Dec. 2ᵈ 1862   I went down to the river this morning at 8 o'clock and took a bath in salt water after having first taken a good wash in spring water. It made me feel first rate. The water however was pretty cold as also the sand I stood on to wash + dress after bathing I boiled some water and washed 2 shirts, 1 pair of stockings, one towel + a handkerchief and returned to camp just in time to fall in with the boys for company drill about 10 oclock A.M. At 1 oclock the ~~boys~~ company fell in again for target shooting. I guess they intend to make a regt. of sharpshooters of us. We fired 5 rounds of cartridge. It was rather cold in the afternoon and a wind was blowing. Forty nine shots hit the target My shooting was not of the first class but I hit the target 2 or 3 times out of 5 and could have done better if my hands had been warm enough to hold the gun steady. The 2 Georges + myself generally as good any of them and better than the majority. The shooting occupied us about 2 hours and when we came in the Lieut. told us to fall out without arms except want belt + bayonet to attend the [   ] of some soldier that was to be buried from the hospital. The order was to have the regiment in line at 3 ½ oclock but for some reason or other it did not form until 5 oclock so that we buried the soldier by moonlight. It was a solemn sight that long funeral procession and produced a feeling vastly deeper than that occasioned by the sight of a funeral at home. None of the regt had guns except the escort detailed to fire the salute over the grave of the buried soldier. We first marched to the hospital and the regiment was there drawn up in line and the escort received the body which was borne to the grave on 2 muskets and carried by 4 soldiers. The coffin was of plain neat pine and the funeral services were of course episcopalian for the Rev. Mr. [ ] officiated. The deep sad tone of the muffled drum, the sight of the escort with their arms reversed and the coffin draped in the stars + stripes as it was borne along by us as we filed off towards the grave, the slow, short step of the regiment and the silent ranks where not a word was spoken or a whisper breathed from the time the body was received until it was lowered into the silent grave; all served to produce a deep and lasting impression upon my mind. Arrived at the grave the regt was drawn up in line again and facing the grave looking towards the west. The sun had set and the moon was looking coldly down upon the solemn scene. The services were read in a [   ] and impressive tone, and as is the case with all episcopalian services was most beautiful and especially striking at such an hour as this. Behind the grave and in the west was a narrow strip of crimson light extending along the horizon for about 20 degrees while all around this little opening was a mass of dense, dark + dismal looking clouds, and when the salute was fired over the grave it seemed as though it was to waft the spirit of the dead from this drear world, through the bright window in the west to the heaven of love beyond. It is the first funeral that we have been called upon to attend since we came here although several have died out of our regt at the Yorktown Hospital. I have not learned the name of the young man that was burried or the circumstances of his decease but I will go now to our Lieut + inquire. The Lieut is not in his tent so I cannot learn the particulars that I wished but I will send them some other time.

Wednesday Dec. 3ᵈ 1862 It is raining again to day but not very hard. I am glad once in a while to have a rainey day for it gives the poor soldier in camp an opportunity to rest. As a general thing there is no drilling or fatigue duty during rainey days but this morning we had to fall out for company drill with arms but it was only for a short time.

The first sergeant drilled us and the boys behaved so badly that he could not stand the presure + had to bring them in again. He is not much liked by the men in the company. He is a little fellow and the boys rather take the advantage of him. But I do not blame them for he cannot speak to them without an oath and is not a fit person for his position. It has not been very rainey since dinner time.

When we were on Brigade drill last Sunday we had a brass band that came across the river. It played part of the time when we were marching and the music sounded perfectly delicious. It seemed as though we could march for ever if the music would only continue playing. We were tired before we commenced the drill having slept none the night before on picket but the moment the brass band struck up all thoughts of tediousness, weariness + fatigue were gone in a moment. It reminded us of Old Buffalo to hear that music and made us think of many home scenes that once gave us much pleasure. I wish I could hear lilie playing on the Piano for a few moments. Music will sound extremely sweet to us when first we hear it after our return if a return awaits us. I have now caught up with my journal so I will proceed to answer your last 3 or 4 letters. First Comes Nº 16. Tell Grandma that I run across the package of candy she sent me almost the first thing I opened. I guess I must have known it by instinct as Falstaff did the Prince. I gave some of it to the Lieut. and some to Mr.

Stowits who is stopping at the Lieuts tent acting as company clerk and I have got about half of the package still left. It is too precious to eat and so I keep it too smell of. Tell Grandma I am very, very much obliged to her for her kind present. Tell her I wish if she had time she would knit me a nice pair of ribbed mittens. She need not put in the finger if it is much trouble but I should like it better if it had both a finger + thumb but am not very particular about it. Tell Laura to tell "Adam Cook" that I found his name on one of the cans, and over his name I saw Laura's name. So! ho! Laura I guess there is some copartnership in that matter. I am very glad you sent me that oil. I can clean my gun with it in almost no time whereas it used to take me half an hour and sometimes an hour to clean it and get it in a condition to bear inspection; and another thing it tends to keep my Gun from rusting in damp days + nights. In the letter you sent by Mr. Keller, Eliza wished to know if I correspond with Mary Lane. I do not I never was acquainted with her as I know of until the evening I left Buffalo. I did not think she would call for the Picture but it is all right for I told her to do so. She wanted it for her Photograph Album. This is all that requires answering in Letter № 16 so I will go on to No 17. You want to know what kind of a looking man our Chaplain is. He is a middle aged man in appearance but I think he is not older than 35 or thereabouts. He is a well built man something under 6 feet high, I should think about 5 ft 9 inches. He is of a blond complexion and wears a heavy brown beard + [   ]. I do not think he is german and I know he has no german accent in his pronunciation but has a very clear + distinct voice. He has been here some time now and has not yet preached a sermon or had a meeting of any kind. He is Episcopalian and formerly filled the pulpit at St Pauls Church Buffalo.

You say Uncle David has about as hard a time as the soldier. I doubt it very much. Nobody knows the hardships of the soldiers life except the soldier himself for no soldier writes home all the hardships that he has to endure. I have seen the time that I would be glad to sleep in a barn at [ ] but we are over those times I hope. We are comfortably situated now and I hope we will continue so.

I would like to know if Mary [   ] had ever written to me if she has I have never received the letter. When you see her tell her that I never saw Charlie looking better than he does now. He is wearing his new coat + shoulder straps and is growing fat and better looking every day. I have got my farmers point Stock money and some of it is now circulating around among the negroes. The [   ] of the 104th [   ] never pays out anything but counterfeit money and it passes just as well as currant bank bills; in fact counterfeit money is the only kind of currant money we have at this place. I am very much pleased with the map you sent me and prefer it even to the one that George has. It is a map on which I can trace the route taken by either army as the information is acquired by the various telegraphs that reach us. Our Lieut wished me to let the map remain in his tent and I have done so. He says it is the best map he has ever seen. Those Cigars are just old comfort. Where did you buy them? The three cent ones are about as good as those that cost 5 cents. At least there is not 2 cent difference in them + in case you ever send me any more I would about as lief have the 3 cent ones. I do not smoke much only when I feel kinder lonesome. Every body in camp smokes and next time I have any thing sent to me I am going to have some smoking tobacco put in the box and have you buy me a nice little [   ] pipe. I do not want a large pipe for I do not like to smoke much tobacco at a time. I wish you would inquire the price of a nice little pipe + pipe stem of sweet briar or witch hazel wood. I really believe that smoking in camp is beneficial. It seems to destroy all bad odors that sometimes are floating around. You sent me quite a number of things that I did not expect. That Pillow is delicious and the comforter is most acceptable but if we go on a march I must throw it away. The can of jelly is a luxury and those peaches are just outstanding. That Liniment has cured one man in my tent of the Rheumatism so it has paid for itself already. The catsup is the best I ever tasted. I guess you made it different from what you used to for I did not like catsup in Buffalo. Tell [   ] I am very, very much obliged to him for the bitters he sent me. I had the heartburn day before yesterday so that I could not eat and I took a little of the bitters and it cured me right off. I think this is excellent and if the other was better than this it must have been good indeed. The raspberry vinegar I have not yet touched but I know what it is. I am going to keep it for sickness. The sleeping cap is just "old comfort" *That Molassas candy is quite a novelty but it is an excellent pastime to get it out of the can. It grows less very slowly. The bread, unfermented, had to go the rounds of the tent the first night. I finished the second loaf the last time I was on picket. Next time I want you to send me a little [   ] box. The Envelopes are first class and I am much pleased with them. I hate to use them until I have disposed of the others that you sent me. Two of the* boys in my tent received boxes the other night and both of them contained fruit cake but it did not begin to come up to the one that Mary sent me. One of the boys eat so much that he made himself sick. High living does not agree with us in camp.

As for an answer to Letter No. 18 I did not know that Andrew had tried to get Lottie McLane to correspond with him. Did he write to her and request her to answer? If so what did she say to him + how came you to hear of it. Write me the particulars for I have heard nothing about it from Lottie. I know when I was in Buffalo I tried to convince him that Lottie was vastly fond of him and endeavored to persuade him to open a correspondence with her + told him that I was very sure she would be pleased to have him write to her and would speedily answer his letter if he wrote to her but he would not do. Now that I am away I suppose he thinks it would be a first rate opportunity for him to make an advance. Never mind I am perfectly willing. I wish he would take her off my hands but don't mention a word about this to anyone whatever. About that wash, I would not mind having a washboard but we have plenty of tubs made out barrels cut down. Our washboards are made by cutting grooves in a piece of inch board. It make a very good

[   ] for army uses. Those Hey! + What! Expressions are merely slang phrases that we sometimes use here when we can't think of anything else to say. Mr. Hart got his discharge because his eyesight was imperfect + his height was under the standard. We think here that the removal of [   ] + placing B—in command is a good move. I am glad that Mr. Toye misses me so much. I wish pa would ask them to write to me even if they do not write but a word I would like to know how they are getting along. I have received only 1 letter from them since I left B. and that was the one that G. Peck wrote. Give my respect to Mrs. Toye. How does her sewing machine get along? Next time you send me a box you might fill a can or jar with some of that nice syrup. What book auction is it that that you speak of No 19? I wish I was there for I was counting on having a good winter buying some more books.

That woman that we turned out of doors we set over the picket lines so she can not do us any kind of harm. Tom Wharton is getting along finely but he will not be able to do duty for about six months. One of the boys in my tent named Hunt has had the symptoms of fever and was taken to the hospital yesterday. Good Bye I will write again soon. Give my love to Grandma + all the rest. I wish I could see little Gracie + all the rest of you.

Please send some postage stamps. I sold some of those you sent me to some of the soldiers who had none.

Your Affectionate Son Edward L. Cook

Thursday Dec. 4th 1862 Hello! here is a page I skipped + did not know it at the time until I had finished my letter but it will not do to let the letter go without filling up this page. It has been a warm + pleasant day. The regiment was called out again this afternoon to attend another funeral. It was that of a man who died in camp. He had been sick for some time but was getting well. He had received a discharge + was waiting for his papers to come so that he could go home. The night before he died he was out to the color line talking to the guard and appeared all right when he went to bed but when the boys in his tent awoke in the morning they found him dead. It was too bad and seems worse because he was on the point of going home + was probably expected by his friends. I think I have written you a good long letter I wonder if I can get it all in one envelope. Has Nellie S. called on Laura yet? When Lottie writes to Eliza, tell me what she says. Write me a good long letter next time and write soon. I have not heard from you for 4 or 5 days and it seems a long time. Time passes very quickly to me now. It is just 3 months ago today since I enlisted. It does not seem so long does it? Dont forget the Postage stamps. I have got a few yet but they are somewhat creased and soiled + I am afraid to use them for fear the letter will not go. Tell Mr. Lyman to write to me Dave White sends his regards to Eliza. Ask her what she will do with them and tell me next time Good bye No 2.

Edward

Letter from A. Lyth to his Father

Gloucester Point Va Dec 1st 1862

Dear Father

I received your letter of the 23rd and was glad to hear that you were all doing well I received the 3 dollars enclosed in it an also the note you ask me to sign I think you might just as well a drawn 100 dollars as 50 and paid it on the land for it would have lowered the interest so much more I should have answered this letter yesterday but I was not very well having had a slight touch of the ague I got 2 tablespoons full of brandy from Tom

*Maharg and ½ a tea spoonfull of red pepper and took it then I laid down
and covered myself up well and had a good sweat and it cured me and I am
as well as every today. I received Sarah Ann's letter the same time I received
yours and I will write to her soon If you send me a box you can send it as
soon as you like the sooner the better. Tom Maharg got a box a little before
Thanksgiving and I tell you we had a good time of it on thanksgiving day
we had 3 large mince pies to beef toungs and Jellies + preserves + cake to
any amount an Tomato catsup and various other things to numerous to
mention. you need not be afraid of me not receiving the box you send me
if we should move for the box will always follow the Regiment no matter
where it goes to but I guess we are going to stay here awhile longer if not
till the war is over of course this place has to be held as long as the army
goes to Richmond the road they are going now but if they should send an
army by the way of Yorktown and up the peninsula then we should stand
a chance of seeing Richmond then they would not need any troops to be left
at Yorktown or this Point*

*I am making mother a ring and will send it in the next letter I write
I wish you would send me a few postage stamps as for money that 3 dollars
will last me quite a long time but when you get an odd dollar that you have
no use for and are going to throw it away you can send it to me instead
Give my love to William + Sarah Ann I send my love to you all*

Your Son
Alfred Lyth

Letter from A. Lyth to his Brother

Gloucester Point Va Dec 9 1862

Dear Brother

*I received your letter of Nov 30th + Dec 2d last night and was very glad
to hear that you are all well as it leavese me at present as I am enjoying
very good health the weather here has been very cold for the last 2 or 3 days
but very pleasent it was very cold Saturday night we were on picket that
night but we did not feel the cold much as we had a first rate hut on our
post in fact they are built on all the posts the hut is built of the fir of the
pine trees and built up about 2 or 3 feet with ground on the outside the one
half of the hut is left uncovered so that we could have a fire in side of the
hut we kept a rousing fire all night of course we had to go outside to stand
our turn but then we would put on our overcoats and bundel ourselfs up*

well and we get along first rate Yesterday afternoon a new regiment came on this point and encamped they are a Pennsylvania Regiment of drafted men. They call theirselves drafted volunteers they appear to be about 7 or 8 hundred strong they say when they started from home they were about 9 hundred strong but they have had a great many desertions. One man told me that one of the men that was drafted got a substitute but he deserted so they have sent home after the man that was drafted They are all fine looking men there being no boys at all in the whole Regiment. We are just going on a General inspection To be inspected by Major General Dix so I must quit writing this letter at present so I will finish after I come off from inspection. I have just finished my dinner I tell you that we were hungry after coming in of Inspection Review and Brigade drill for we had all 3 of them we were Reviewed by Gen Dix and drilled by Gen Naglee then I come in and eat pretty near a pint of Bean soup ½ pound of pork pretty near a loaf of Bread and three large apples pretty soon I am going to make some mush for our suppers I bought a peck of Indian meal and Tom bought of extra molasses so we will have quite a time over our plate of mush to night we had some last night Tom is making us some lemonade as I am writing these lines so that when I finis I shall have a good glass of Lemonade There were 2 Regiment from the other side of the River over here on drill and the 2 Regiments that Belong here and the Battry. The Regiment of drafted men were not on Review we had quite a time of it on drill but there is nothing the boys like so well as when the order charge bayonets doublequick march then you should hear the Hollering and shouting and cheering

From Your Affectionate Brother
Alfred Lyth

Letter from E. Cook to his Parents

Camp at Gloucester Point Va. Dec 16/62 Tuesday
My Dear Parents
I suppose you are anxious by this time to receive a letter from me. I have just got over being sleepy since I returned from Gloucester C.H. and now I feel in first rate order to write letters. I am all dressed up in my best clothes with my face washed, my teeth cleaned+ my boots blacked preparatory to another inspection + review by Genl Keyes. It is not quite time for the review so I will improve the moments as they fly and start a letter on its

way. I suppose I must stick to the old rule and go back to the day I closed my last journal so here is at it to commence where I left off.

Wednesday Dec 10/62   I was fixing up my tent this morning about 11 oclock when one of Genl Naglee's aids came riding up to the Colonels tent and told him to have his men in readiness to march the next morning at sunrise with 5 days rations in our haversacks.   No information was given us as to where we were going but the general impression in the camp among the officers was that we were going to cross over to Yorktown and from there cross over to the James River and join the army enroute for Richmond. Therefore I sent a little note to you to that effect but happily we did not mach that way.   It took us all the afternoon to get ourselves in readiness. The inspection of arms and accoutrements was very thorough   Then the shoes had to be looked at and the haversacks + canteens examined.   It was late in the evening before the inspections were over and our rations all prepared for us.   Many of the boys felt very sad for we all thought that we should never see old camp Gloucester again.   The day has been very lovely.

Thursday Dec. 11/62   We were up bright + early this morning.   Every thing promises a fine day for marching.   It was cold last night and the ground is frozen which is quite an item in marching on this sandy soil.   We were in line about 6 oclock but did not begin our march until 7 ½ oclock. We started with 4 Regts of Infantry 4 comprised of cavalry + 4 pieces of artillery.   3 of the Infantry Regts + the cavalry companies were from the other side of the river.   We marched today to Gloucester C.H. a distance of 15 miles and arrived there about 3 o'clock.

We had just got our tents pitched and our fires made and were on the point of cooking our supper when Genl Naglee Arrived at the camp and ordered us to pass through the town + camp on the other side, so we struck tents again and marched about a ¼ of a mile.   It was dark when we broke up camp, and darker still when we pitched tents the second time. We camped in a cornfield where the corn had been cut + put in stacks preparatory to husking but I can tell you that there were very few stacks of corn left in 10 minutes after we stacked arms.   I had a nice warm bed that night although the night was cold and the ground was covered with hoar frost in the morning.   We had nothing but shelter tents but I slept very warm.   My feet were not cold once during the night.   There is something grand and enticing in this campaigning – entering and plundering are enemy's country – camping + sleeping soundly + sweetly in the very midst of danger – placing our lives in the hands of our Guards and Pickets and feeling safe + secure in their watchfulness and care. It is dangerous, it is tedious, it causes aching bones and tired limbs but somehow I love it and wished for a battle.

Friday Dec. 12 1862 The day was very lovely but not very warm. It was my turn to go on Cap. of the Guard so I was put on Picket Guard and had charge of the 3 posts on the left of the centre line and guarded one fork of a road.

There was a large house set back from the road a little ways called "Elmwood" and in the rear of the house was another large two story building used for a slave house or nigger residence. They had Geese, ducks, turkeys + chickens in the yard. I had a good dinner of chicken soup made of chicken boiled with unsifted corn meal. I tell you it was "bully! The nigger made me some hoe cakes + gave me a lot of nice turnips. I thought I fared pretty well for that day. The nigger houses are very poor affairs generally having no floor and only one room. The windows are made of old clothes. The slaves are very poorly clothed and their clothes are ragged + torn. They tell me that they have not received any clothes this year. The night was cold and I could not sleep a wink all night. They told me to put out my fires at night but I did not do it. I kept a few embers burning all night which made things a little more comfortable, and I managed to get through the night although it seemed terribly long before daylight appeared and I was right glad when the first red streakings of the morning light came shooting up the Eastern sky. The old nigger that lived in the slave house was "Uncle Pete" and a queer old "Pete" was he. He put me in mind of "Uncle Tom". A colored gal came up to the line this afternoon and gave me two big sweet potatoes. I had quite a talk with her.

Saturday Dec 13/62 I came off picket this morning. After resting a short time and reading a chapter I got up and stretched myself and then started off about 11 o'clock with G. Clark, G. Stoddard + Charlie Hunt on a foraging expedition of our own. We managed to evade the guards + pickets and got out side the lines. We soon ran a foul of a "flock" of pigs and after chasing them for about an hour we managed to separate the "flock" + lost *track of them without managing to capture any of them. Afterwards we found a barn filled with turnips + captured several of them which conveyed rich pleasure to our hungry -------*

When tired of eating turnips we roamed out into the woods again and soon caught sight of another "flock" of pigs and before many minutes had elapsed we had one of them with a bullet in his head and a knife in his heart. We hung him up on the limb of a tree and skinned him and each of us went marching into camp with a quarter of pork on our shoulder. But what was our surprise in crossing the field to find that out regiment had struck tents and gone on. We were almost dumbfounded but a guard had been left behind in charge of our knapsacks + Guns and so we fell in with the rear guard + marched on to join our regt. We marched 3 miles + found our Company who had been left behind as a reserve while the Regt moved on about 4 miles farther. We were put on picket again to night for straggling behind the regiment. But we diddent care for we thought the pig repaid us for the little matter of going on picket duty. We dont get fresh pork every day. I was glad when we had caught up to the company for I had a pretty good load to carry. Only think I had to carry my gun, my haversack, canteen, knapsack + a quarter of pork. Was that load enough? I had a good sleep tonight on picket. We had boards to lie on + boards slanted over us to keep the dew off. I slept warm + soundly until 2 o'clock + then I got up + stood the rest of the night. I felt "bully" in the morning. We had fresh pork for supper + for breakfast the next morning. I gave Dave White, Bill Gaffe + several others a good large piece of my quarter. They said it was the best meat they ever tasted. I will close this letter now + write again in a day or two.

Good bye, E l Cook

Letter from E. Cook to his Parents

Sunday Dec. 14ᵗʰ 1862

My Dear Parents

I told you in my last that I slept last night well and soundly + felt very fresh in the morning. I have a little cold but I will be careful and I think I shall soon be over it. In the field where we encamped the first time on Thursday last there were 2 tombstones. I meant to have coppied the inscriptions on them but we had to leave so soon that I had no time to do so. I recollect that one of them said "Mr" (Somebody) "Gentleman" died 1725

+ the other dated to 1723 long before the Revolution. This afternoon about 3 ½ o'clock one of the Generals Aides came out to us with orders for our officers to call in their Pickets and march back to Gloucester C.H. We obeyed very cheerfully although we did not suppose that we were going to return to our old camp. We marched the 3 miles without a rest and soon found ourselves at the Court House. As soon as we came in sight of the old camp ground and found all the tents of the other regiments struck and the men formed in line behind the musket stacks, we were very much surprised for we knew that it indicated a move of some kind and our hearts were inspired with hope. And when we moved through the town and halted on the other side and learned gradually that we were going to march back to the Old Point I tell you there was a feeling of joy ran through our hearts like wild fire and every man of us was anxious to start on the journey of 15 miles that very night and sleep not till we laid us down within our Sibley tents upon our soft and welcome beds of boards. None of us ever expected to sleep in our old bunks again; and when the word came to us the we were going back home I cannot describe the feeling of relief, from the uncertainty that up to this time had held us tightly bound. We were not kept waiting long for soon the order came to "Forward March" and the boys did forward with a will. We were tired, but we were marching home and everything was forgotten but thoughts of the camp at Gloucester Point which urged us on to new exertions + renewed efforts. When we had marched about 7 miles we were halted to wait for the balance of the regiment to come up + in the meantime some of the boys cooked their coffee for supper. When the rest of the regiment came up we started on again and at 11 oclock we were in camp once more. It was most dark when we left the C.H. We made the march in about 5 hours which is first rate time to make with knapsacks, haversacks, canteens + musket. Besides the road was very bad on the return march. The soil is sandy and the foot sinks into the road of dry sand about 3 inches every step.

When we started on the march last Wednesday the road was froze hard and the marching was very easy but it was very hard on the return.

Monday Dec. 15th 1862 I slept pretty much the whole of the morning and was much refreshed when I awoke this afternoon. I had a very tedious job of drawing and issueing rations to the company.

Tuesday Dec 16/62 We were told that there was going to be an inspection this morning at 10 oclock and so we went to work after breakfast and put in with the whole force in our tent to put our things in order, cleaned our streets, black our boots +c and were ready in time for the inspection but as fate would have it, it commenced to rain and the inspection did not come off. I rec'd this evening your letter No 22, a paper from home.

Wednesday Dec 17/62   I have been assigned the task of drilling the new recruits who have lately come into the company so I do not have to turn out to any drills but Battalion + Brigade. This afternoon we had a battalion drill of about 2 hours long. We have nothing else nowadays but battalion drills + inspections

Thursday Dec 18/62   We were on Picket to day. It was quite pleasant and warm but last night was a regular old stinger.

Friday Dec. 19ᵗʰ 1862 We came off Picket this morning. I received a letter from Eliza early this morning before I was relieved from Picket. It was numbered 24. The last one I received from Laura was No 22 and as I have rec'd No 23 I think Eliza must have made a mistake in numbering her letter. I think it should be No. 25. Dave White + myself stood our trick together on picket last night until 12 oclock and the other two on my going to bed from 12 until morning. I slept well and warmly from 12 'til daylight. We had a pit dug down in the earth about 18 inches and we slept in there. When we returned from our Expedition last Sunday night we found "Capt Dye" in Camp. He came a day or two after we left. I do not know now what was the object of our Expedition. But I think it was designed to attract the attention and perhaps draw off a little of the enemy's forces while Burnside made his attack upon Fredericksburg. How it succeeded I cannot say but I know that we drove in several hundred head of sheep + cattle and a lot of splendid horses + mules. Our Cavalry had a little brush with some Rebel Cavalry. They wounded some + put them to flight. They ran into the swamp + so escaped. None of our men were hurt. Tell Laura I have not written to E.S. for more than 2 months nor she to me. Dave White is one of the boys in my tent. I will describe him some time or other. He is a Surveyor and a subject of Great Britain but of Irish descent. He is very intelligent + witty. I like him very much. I did say to

Capt Hinson something about not knowing he was in this reg't but I never wanted to go in his company. When we left Camp I carried only my rubber blanket, my woollen blanket + lining + a pair of stocking. If we had remained away our underclothes would have been sent to us but my pillow, comfator, butter +c would have been destroyed. If you get a war map you can find Gloucester Point exactly opposite Yorktown and Gloucester C.H. is exactly north of Gloucester Point so you can trace our march of Wednesday Last week. I have 2 or 3 other letter to answer so I must close this letter. Give my love to GrandMa, Gracie, and all the children. Enclosed is a little plan of our camp at the Court House. My tent is full of smoke to night + I can hardly see to write plainly. I am going to leave off writing + don my smoking cap + puff away at a cigar. I will write again soon. Good Bye

> *Your Aff. Son*
> *Edward*

Letter from A. Lyth to his Folks at Home

Gloucester Point Va Dec 19th 1862

Dear Folks at Home

I just returned from picket this morning and to my Joy I found that my box had arrived every thing arrived save and sound except the brown jar of currence The Jar was broke but the currence were all right I cut into one of the pork pies for dinner and it went first rate Oh I am quite in love with that jar of pickels you sent me if I had to have bought that of the settlor here it would have cost me 2 dollars The pies look splendid and I am going to have some to supper to night They look like some of Sarah Anns make for They are so short and nice looking I should have had a peice to dinner but the pork pie was enough Give those kind neighbors who have sent me some of these things my best respects and tell them I am very much obliged to them for their kindness in thinking of me Then there was John's thing for a suger and the licorice too Then there is mothers cakes I know them are mothers make they are so good Who sent the apples Mother please excuse for not haveing sent you your ring I promised you but I have been so busy these last 2 weeks that I have hardly thought of it but I shall finish it soon then I will send it to you There is mothers citron + Mrs Newmans Strawberries they will be glourious on bread and the butter is splendid candy who sent that I guess it was Fanny at least I think so and that is just as good The gloves you

sent me are first rate We are having some very fine weather here at present
the day after we got in camp after the Recounoitreing expedition it was so
warm and pleasent that Tom and I and three or so more of the boys went
into the river and had a bathe of course the water was a little cool but we
had a good wash and felt all the better after it Yesterday it was pretty cold
as the wind blew from the North but toward evening the wind ceased and
it was a very pleasent night on picket and it is quite warm today I hope
this letter will find you all well and kicking as it leaves me at present The
other day I was on fatigue duty in the woods chopping down trees and the
whole day I chopped three trees down that was about 8 or 10 inches throug
the rest of the time I was either cooking something to eat over a large fire
or running round the woods after rabbits. There is an old secesh that lives
close by the woods where we were chopping and it was said that he had
threatened to shoot any one who laid a hand on any thing that he had or
if we burnt his fence rails. So to fix his lordship wherever we could see a
tree that would fall across the fence we felled it so it would fall across the
fence he came out and was in a duce of a sweat and he was told to hold his
tounge if he did not it would be the worse for him I should not like to be
a drafted soldier The drafted Regiment here are every one drafted from the
drummers to the Lt Col in fact all the Officer are drafted and they know
no more about drill than I did when I first enlisted and our officers have to
drill them with the musket so that as the officers learn they learn the men
and the drummers dont know how to play a single tune or beat a call last
night they beat the long roll for to put out the lights When the right way is
to give just three taps on the drum And the long roll is to call the Regiment
out when they are attacked by the enemey and is not to be beat on any
account except on such an occation and they will get their muskets and go
out shooting after game and get arrested some came out to the picket lines
and they asked us if we had to take our guns out on picket and they are the
laughing stock of the volunteers My Boots are giving way in the uppers and
I am going to have new fronts put on which will cost me 50 cents which I
wish you would send me as I have not got quite that amount There is some
talk of us getting paid soon but I cannot tell how soon that may be as the
pay master has been and paid the Regiments on the other side of the river
If we do not get paid befor New Years we shall have to wait 2 months more
and it is the opinion of some that we shall have to wait however if we get
paid I shall some money home and have you get me a new pair of boots but

if I get my old ones fronted they will last 2 or three months yet we can get all the shoes we want of the government but no boots Give my love to all my friends and I wish You all a merry christmas and hope you will enjoy yourselves for I think I shall for It only want 6 more day!

Your Affect Son + Brother
Alfred Lyth

Letter from A. Lyth to his Brother

Gloucester Point Va Dec 21ˢᵗ 1862

Dear Brother
    I received your letter and was very glad to hear that you were all well and enjoying good health as it leaves me at present I have just finished my dinner + we had some of the mutton that we captured on our last expedition and some of them pickels that you sent me and a peice of mince pie for desert I am glad you forgot to send me mustard as Tom got a pound of exelent mustard in his box and also a pound of black ground peper as for the sand paper it dont amount to much for I only wanted it for dressing off rings but ring making time is over so when I get mothers finished I shall have got done ring making I shall have matters done when I write my next letter We are having very pleasent weather here at present it was pretty cold last night but then it is warmer to day I am glad to hear that you are having pretty good weather for drawing and hope you will have good success I wish you would let me know if you have a large stock of tiles on hand or abut how many you have I have not seen or heard of [ ] that worked at the glass works nor did not that he had enlisted in this Regiment if he is in it I can surly find out however I will have a look around I send my love to you all Sarah Ann + William and the Neighbors So No More at present from

Your Affect Brother
Alfred Lyth

P.S. I also had a letter from Cousin William Eyeington last night and have answered it to day. Cousin wants to enlist the worst way.

Letter from E. Cook to his Parents

Camp at Gloucester Point Va Saturday Dec. 20ᵗʰ 1862

My Dear Parents
    The weather was very cold this day. We had a drill this morning but it

was so cold they did not keep us out very long. The water froze in our wash dish – we <u>have</u> a wash dish. – Some of the old soldiers never use a wash dish; they take a mouth full of water from their canteen and then spit it into their hands and wash their face but <u>we</u> don't do so <u>we</u> paid 50 cents for a wash dish and we now enjoy the rich pleasure of a comfortable morning ablution without going away down to the spring. I received your letter No. 25 this evening. I have never rec'd No 23 and I am inclined to think that you skipped from 22 to 24.

*Sunday Dec. 21*st *1862*We had a very rigorous inspection this morning by a Col. of the 98th Nyv. He was formerly Colonel of the 7th New York Militia Regiment. This afternoon I was busy for 2 or 3 hours engaged in drawing the rations for our company and afterwards issueing them to the members. It is a tedious job and not a very desirable one for Sunday but soldiers are slaves or worse than slaves and must do as they are ordered. I might almost say there is no Sabbath in the Army so little respect is paid to the day. If during the week we are ordered to clean up during the whole forenoon in expectation of a Brigade drill 3 hours long in the afternoon you will hear the boys remarking to each other "It seems to me just like Sunday; don't it to you?

Monday Dec 22^d *1862* We still retain some of the <u>forms</u> of civilization although so far away from any place where the rules of politeness are the passports to society. And what think you are these forms? One of them is to employ Monday as our washing day but although it was pleasant and would have been a good time to dip into the washtub yet we had so much to do that very few of us made the attempt. I got started and then did not through to the spring after all but never mind I guess we will have our opportunity tomorrow.

Tuesday Dec 23^d *1862* Today has been very pleasant indeed. It was so warm that it was uncomfortable drilling both this a.m. and afternoon. I have been round in my shirt sleeves all day except when we were drilling. I did my washing today under difficulties. We cannot get at our washing so early in the morning as you can at home. We are call up at sunrise but I generally am up an hour or more before that time and have a good fire going in our stove before roll call. At roll call every man (except the sick) *has to fall out and answer to his name. After roll call we sweep the street in front of our tent, fold our blankets and clean out the tent. Then comes our breakfast of greasy coffee + bread (Greasy because boiled in the same kettles that are used boiling fat pork + salt horse). By the time we have finished our breakfast it is nearly 8 o'clock. Then if we wish to do our washing we must go out and cut our wood (for we are not allowed to chop wood or make any noise before roll call) and travel down to the spring start our fire boil our water and go ahead. It is sometimes 9 o'clock before we get started: but this time there were three of us washed together. We hurried up things so that we had our breakfast finished, our wood chopped and our fire started before 8 o'clock. Drill generally takes place at 10½ o'clock but for some unaccountable reason the companies were called out this morning at 9½ o'clock and we did not have our washing quite finished but we had to leave off immediately and go up and fall in with the company or else go to the guard house. So we spilled out 2 kettles of boiling water that we just going to pour into our tub and snatched up our clothes (clean + dirty) took our kettles + washtub and started for camp on the double quick. We got there just before the roll was called and thus saved our bacon that time. After drill we went down to the spring again and started another fire and finished up our washing before we eat our dinner. After we did our washing we all stripped our selves and went into the tub and had a gay old swim. What do you think of that taking a bath with open air on the 20th of December? Oh! this is the country for me and if they ever exterminate slavery in Virginia + I am alive + well after it is done I am coming down here to live. This afternoon was our day for Target Practice but instead of that we had to have one of those long and hated battalion drills. Somehow or other every time that it is our turn to go target shooting we have to have a battalion drill and get cheated out of our fun. I am afraid this lovely weather is but the forerunner of a heavy storm. Tomorrow is our picket day and I am hoping that it will not rain until after we return. It is just like spring weather so lovely that I cannot describe it. We have heard heavy cannonading this afternoon + this evening there was a report that there had been a battle at Williamsburg – 12 miles from here. I received 3 papers from you this evening. I wish you could send one at a time + send them oftener for when you send so many they sometimes get torn + worn by sending before I have an opportunity to read them – but I am much obliged* to you for them in any form and you of course must accommodate your own convenience in sending them rather than heeding my likes + dislikes.

Wednesday Dec 24ᵗʰ 1862 Well here I am on Picket. The day is not as pleasant as it was yesterday and feels a little like rain but I am in hopes that it will be postponed until tomorrow for I would rather have someone else on picket when it rains. It is no pleasant job in wet weather but on fine days I would rather be on picket than in camp for there is more variety. Twenty 4ᵗʰ of Dec. Day before Christmas. Happy times there will be in Buffalo tonight + happier still tomorrow morning but there is no Christmas Eve for the poor soldier. My Christmas Eve will be spent in the open air, the stars twinkling laughingly and the new moon smiling down upon me. With my long gray coat closely buttoned up around me and my musket over my shoulder, Christmas Eve will find me walking my narrow "beat" looking towards the enemy + thinking of my home. It was indeed a happy hour and one that I shall ne'er regret for having spent it as I did. I was straining my gaze into the darkness before me and yet my thoughts were wandering off in a few different directions and dwelling upon a holier and a happier theme.

Thursday Evening I am quite certain that we shall leave this camp in a very short time. I dread it for I shall have to leave so many comfortable things and valuable articles. I almost wish that you had not sent some of them but if I should have to leave them now I think I have received the value of them already in the comfort I have received from them already.

I destroyed all of my letters this evening. There was 30 or more of them and it was like pulling a tooth for each letter that I burned. I should have left them if I had thought there was any hope of our staying here. I had expected as much as could be that I should receive a letter from you to night but it did not come and I felt disappointed. I have not received a letter from you since last Saturday and it seems a very long time now that we are thinking of moving and do not know as we shall stay to see another mail come into our quarters. But if we move, the letters will follow the regiment so that if we do not receive them here we shall get them after we leave. This has not been a Merry Christmas to us for the knowledge that we are going to leave our nice comfortable winter quarters to go we know not where, has cast a kind of silent gloom over the minds + feelings of the soldiers that even the thought of the enjoyment that roams the hearts of the dear ones at the north on this anniversary of our Savior's Birth could not produce a happier state of feeling. Some few in our tent had calculated on having something a little extra for dinner to day but this rumor has knocked it all in the head and about drove the thought of eating from our minds. If we have to move I will drop you a line just before we start I hope we are not going to join the Army under the immediate command of Burnside. I would rather go to Carolina or even Texas than to form part of the Army opposite Fredericksburg. Is it not shameful the way our poor soldiers were slaughtered before the entrenchments on those heights near the city? I have almost lost confidence in Burnside. You do not hear all the news for I do not think the papers dare publish everything. You should read the letters that some of our boys receive from boys in Burnside's army. It is from them + from them only that you can get the facts of the engagement. But it is almost time for Roll call so I must close my letter and make my bed. Remember me in your prayers and bear in mind that where 2 or 3 shall ask any thing in the name of the Lord that he will give it unto them. Give my love to Grandma and all the children. Tell Sammy that I do not forget him because I do not always speak of him. GoodBye.

From Your Affectionate Son
Edward

Letter from A. Lyth to his Brother

Gloucester Point Va Dec 23ᵈ 1862

Dear Brother

I take my pen to write these few lines hoping they will find you all well and enjoying good health as it leaves me at present. We are having a spell of splended warm weather here at present 2 more days and it will be Christmas though when this reches you I guess will be near New Year I sent mothers ring in this letter since I have finished it I begin to fear that it is a little to small but if it is John can take sand paper and work it out a little larger but he must not take a pocket knife to it. The star is made out of a 3 cent peice We got the news last night that the governer of Pennsylvania has ordered all the Pennsylvania troops home Some think he has not the power to do so and some say he can time will tell You hear all the war news befor we do so of course I cannot tell you what you do not know. We have *heard that they mean to consentrate a large army before Fredricksburgh and march through in spite of all obstacles I wish he may When you direct my letters direct Alfred Lyth Co H 100 Regt N.Y. Div. Gloucester Point Washington D.C. In them Harpers Weekly you sent in the box there is some very splendid illustrations of the army There is one of where the cavelry are deployed a scrimeshers it reminds me of our tramp that we had out to Gloucester Court House The most amusing feature of that march was to see the niggers They would flock to the roadside by hundreds some bowing and saying how is you masser. Youre grining Some shaking with fear and some of the knowing ones kicking up all sorts of cappers It is quite a show to see such a lot of the colored race together some great big thick lip and as black as midnight some little bit of monkeys that can hardly crawl. We met a nigger on the road out there who had a pair of what he called new shoes. I never saw such shoes I think the {unknown word} was about ½ {unknown word} it was green in places and quite rotten one shoe was about half an inch longer than the other one was {unknown word} the ties and the other peaked and such workmanship never was seen it looked as if they had been cut out of a dead pig with a skull hatchet it is no used me trying to describe them shoes I was astounded he said he had to pay 5 dollars for them and they could not be bought for less and a pair of {unknown word} such as we should get in Buffalo for 5 ½ or 6 dollars he said cost from 35 to 40 dollars*

Dec 25 Christmas I wonder how {unknown word} folks at home spend Christmas eve are spending Christmas Well I have an idea how we spent last Christmas and I think you will enjoy yourself quite as well this Christmas eve and are spending Christmas well I think you would The weather is very pleasent and warm just like spring in the month of May Well yesterday it was our turn to go on picket and stay until this morning the picket that we releaved stated that they had seen Indications of the enemy lurking around so we were told to keep good look out Through the day some niggers came to the lines and reported that there were lots of Rebels outside ready to attack us through the night The picket line about 1 mile and a half from camp now so they have to establish a reserve half way between the camp and the picket lines so 2/3 of the company had to go on picket and the rest stay at the reserve I was on the reserve. Then for the night we had to establish a telegraph between the Reserve and picket line so they post three men from the reserve at equal distances so that if they was any disturbance on the picket lines they should fire their peices + then fall back on the reserve They relieved the men on telagraph every hour so we had to stand an hour and sleep if we wanted to for 4 hours but we did not sleep much Capt Dye was with us Everything went all straight untill about 11 oclock when we heard some firing but it was not in our company it was to our left from Co Gs pickets the firing aroused the camps and the Regiments were drawn up in line of battle and {unknown word} fires were kindled all along the banks of the river so as the gun boats would see to get range over our soldires heads I went on telagraph at 10 to 11 oclock and we heard quite a number of shots fired on the outside of the line and once {unknown word} of 10 or 12 muskets was fired at once but not near enough to the line to create any alarm Then we would hear an occational shot and the wizzing of a bullet through the air. We kept hearing shots fired all along the line untill about three oclock in the morning when the firing by our men became very rapid first the pickets would fire then the camp guards then back again to the picket lines and we could hear the bullets whiseling above our heads in all directions Then Capt Dye ordered us to fall in the ranks {unknown word} and fix bayonets and be ready for any insurergensey. The Capt was a little figity but he took things pretty cool Boys say he keep cool but get excited I guess he was more excited than any of us Wait boys says he till we find out where the line is attacked then we will fall back in good order. however after all we were not attacked by any {unknown word} although there was some firing outside of the lines and one of Co G men shot a large sow that was approaching the lines in the he thought it was a man however he got some fresh pork by the bargain. So that is the way I past my Christmas eve I found an old secesh pouder horn hang on a bush last night so I have sent it to Buffalo by little Ragapelt belonging to our company who has got his discharge for disability he is only enlisted some 3 months I have directed him to leave it at {unknown name} store but I have sent the ring I made for Mother in this letter. When we got into camp this morning we received marching orders Where we are going we do not know nor do we care Wheather we are going to leave Gloucester Point for good or weather we are going to come back again I can not tell but if you write direct Washington D.C. Give my love to all my friends and Relations so No more at present. Your Affect Brother

Alfred Lyth

Letter from E. Cook to Parents

Thursday Dec. 25th 1862

My Dear Parents
    As I came in from Picket this morning I was handed a letter from Mr. Lyman containing stamps. Tell him I am very much obliged to him both for the letter + stamps. We did not spend a very quiet time on picket last night. About 10 oclock the Balance of the regiment, left in camp, was called out in line of battle and after remaining some time were sent back to their tents and ordered to sleep on their arms. About 11 or 12 oclock our Lieut came round to the different posts and ordered out what little fire we had and told us to keep a sharp look out to the front. About 3 o'clock they commenced to fire on the line and it ran along from post to post like wild fire. In a few minutes we heard the long roll beat in our camp and in the fort. We were more than a mile and a half from camp but we heard the drum distinctly. The men on all the reserves were drawn up in line and some of post fell back to the reserve. We did not see any enemy and I thought it would be time enough to fall back when we could see the danger in our front so our post stood fast not knowing what danger might come but determined to do our best + fight manfully if necessity demanded. The firing began on the extreme left of the Picket Line. What originated it I do not know but they say that our boys were fired on first. After the first rapid round the firing ceased except a few straggling shots now + then. I stood guard from 8 to 12 and then from the time the firing began (3 o'clock) until morning so I did not get much sleep last night. I was sound asleep when the firing began and had to be awaked by the sentinel on guard. I could scarcely have believed that anyone should sleep so sound in the open air, surrounded and in the midst of danger, that the firing of a gun would not awake him; but we become so accustomed to these feelings that we sleep just as sweetly as in our beds at home. And another strange thing – At the first call of the sentinel, as he said "Cook! Wake up! there is firing on the picket, I was wide awake in a moment. The low voice of the sentinel accomplished what a whole volley of musketry on the reserve could not do. There was very heavy cannonading away off the South East of us all day yesterday and continued during the early part of the evening. I think they are fighting down there somewhere. Our company Cooks were up the whole of last

night cooking rations for a 2-days march. They are ordered to keep 2 days rations cooked ahead all the time so as the regiment can be ready to leave at a moments notice. I think we are not going to stay here very long. Every thing seems to indicate a breaking up of camp. I am very sorry for I think that we will never see again as pleasant a camp as this we now have. As soon as I finish this letter I am going to pack my knapsack with such things as I want to take with me so as to be ready for a start at any time the order comes. I had a happy time last night from 8 to 12 while I was sentinel. The time passed by very swiftly and did not seem more than 2 hours. I was thinking of my house and holding sweet yet silent intercourse with My Lord + Savior while others were buried in their Slumbers.

So we went back to our quarters feeling sad and sorrowful and in an hour we were on our way. If I had time I could fill a letter moralizing on thoughts + Ideas presented on that evening but I cannot afford the time; suffice it to say that our camp at Gloucester Point we called "Home" and when we left it, it was like leaving a dear friend and tearing us away from dear enjoyment to send us into misery. We formed in line and marched down to the dock and went on board of a Transport. I was on deck with my company. It was a pretty cold place but I preferred it to the dirt + stink that I would have to endure if I had slept in the hold or between decks.

After we had all got snugly esconced in our blankets and just dropping off to sleep about 9 o'clock we were ordered too get up and fall out in line under arms for the pickets of the 169th regt of Penn. Draffted men who take our place had got scared and been driven in. So we turned out and marched up the bank into the fort. Every man praying for a fight so that we would not have to leave the "Point". But the fight would not come. After waiting there for more than an hour we learned that the report was false and marched back to the boat again. I slept on the boat pretty well but rather cold for the wind blew considerable strong.

Saturday Dec. 27th 1862 We were busy all the morning getting army wagons and provisions aboard the boat. Nobody knows where we are going or when we are going to start. It rained this afternoon and was misty all the morning. The boat started from the dock about 2 oclock this P.M. and arrived at Fortress Monroe at 5½ oclock. It rained very hard at night + I could not stand the pressure so I picked up my dudds + went away down *into the hole of the vessel and made my bed down there among the dirt + rubbish. The boat anchored off Fortress Monroe so that even if there was any bilge water in the vessel it did not trouble us any. We saw the 2 monitors as we came to anchor in the bay this afternoon. They are queer looking things and it does not seem as though they could do much damage. They were sunk down to the waters edge and only the towers were visible.*

Sunday Dec. 28th 1862 This morning the boat drew up to the dock and the men were ordered to stay aboard and a guard was placed on the dock to keep them aboard but the men couldent see the point and in 5 minutes myself + any quantity of others were past the guard and standing around the counter of a negro pedlers shop waiting our turn to be waited upon. I bought some fresh bread + molassas cakes and stole a good drink of cider out of the hole in a cider barrel and went on board again. Quite a spree for Sunday was it not? But I suppose that not half of the men knew that it was Sunday. All the stores but one were shut up and I could not think for some time what the cause could be until finally it came to mind that it was Sunday. The mail came aboard at Fortress Monroe + I recd a letter on small note paper No 25. I was very glad to hear from you. We weighed anchor and left the Port about 6 oclock this evening. A pack of sealed orders came aboard just before we left containing information as to our destination but they cannot be opened until we are at sea. I slept on deck but not very well for it was cold + windy.

Letter from A. Lyth to Folks at Home

Fortress Monroe Va Dec 28th 1862

Dear Folks at home

We embarked on board of a transport day before yesterday about 7 oclock at night all of our Regiment going on board of one transport. It not being a very large boat we were pretty crowded. Four companys of which ours was one took the upper deck and the other six companys the lower deck. We left only the one Regiment of drafted men and the Battery at the point. We had all got laid down and most of us asleep when we were roused up it being reported that the pickets were attacked so we had to rouse up and go ashore we marched into the fort and got behind the breast works and loaded our guns and laid in waiting for the Rebs to come and we lay there in the cold night air untill about 1 oclock and we heard nothing of any Rebels a coming so we marched back to the boat and got a board and had a good sleep the rest of the night – The next morning they sent 2 companys back to camp the Capt of the boat refuseing to take the whole Regt. We learnt that it was a false alarm calling us out the night before one of the pickets thought he saw some body crossing the line and he fired and the men being green at picketing a lot of them fired their peices hence the alarm. Pretty near all the next day was taken up in getting the stores on board we had 14 days rations on board We got under way about 3 oclock for the fortress were we arrived at 6 oclock we anchored out in the bay opposite the fort There was quite a lot of gun boats anchored all around us 2 of which were of the Monitor build It commenced to rain so us fellows on the upper deck had to put below and stow in any little corner we could find some even slept on deck in all the rain I did not sleep any at all myself I was tramping all over the craft seeing the fun Where ever there was any The men were stowed so thick on the lower deck that there was not room to get from one hatch to the other and if a man should try to walk through the men he would shure to get triped over then he would fall across 3 or 4 of the men then when he had just got up another push he was sure to get and over he would go again and so on till he got through In the morning it cleared up and we got our quarters on the upper deck again and it is very warm and pleasent to day Our boat is at present up by the dock getting water + coals they put guards on the dock to keep the men on board but it was of no use for they all made a rush for the shore the boys were bound to get ashore Tom + I went ashore and bought 4 loaves of fresh bread and we drew 2 loaves that night so we were well off for bread We got under way about sundown and we learnt that we were bound for Beaufort North Carolina

> Morehead City – North Carolina Dec 30 – 1862
We arrived on the coast of this State opposite Beaufort last night before sun down we run up the signal for a pilot but he did not come untill the next morning and he piloted us into morehead city which is just across the river from Beaufort and marched about 3 miles to a place called Carolina City we are at present encamped to wait for the rest of the Brigade to come up and then I think we are going to Willmington. Give my love to all
> I should have wrote more but the Capt is waiting for to post them
>> Your Affect Son
>> Alfred Lyth

Letter from E. Cook to his Parents

Monday Dec. 29<u>th</u> *1862 The weather is cold but clear + pleasant. The orders were opened last night as we rounded the cape into the sea and this morning I learn that we are going to Beaufort to cooperate with Gel Foster. I am glad we are not going with Burnside. We came to an anchor off Beaufort City in N.C. about 6 o'clock P.M. I saw the sun rise in the sea this morning it was a most beautiful sight but mother can describe it to you much better than I can so I will not attempt it.*

Tuesday Dec 30/62 We landed at Moorhead City opposite Beaufort this A.M. The regiment marched up the railroad track about 3 miles to Carolina City and encamped. I was left behind to help unload the boat and put the stuff aboard of the cars + when we had done that we put our Knapsacks +c on the cars and rode up to the reg't. We overtook them just as they halted and had the pleasure of assisting in pitching the camp. We have to sleep now in the little shelter tents open at both ends. G. Clark G. Stoddard T. Maharg + myself tent together. G. Clark + I went out + got some boards + made a floor to sleep on. I slept warm + well but about the middle of the night I awoke with a very queer sensation about my head. I couldent think what it was but I soon learned that it was raining into my tent + running under my head so I got up + put my rubber blanket at the end + stopped the opening + went back to bed again + slept well till morning, when I felt much rested.

Wednesday Dec. 31/62 This morning I got up + built a fire, boiled the coffee + fried or warmed up some sweet potatoes and had a first rate meal for a Soldier. Then I went out with a party + got wood for the cooks, drew the company rations and assisted at making out the muster roll for pay. We were mustered in for pay this morning but nobody knows when we will get it. I was up all night helping our Orderly Sergeant finish up his pay roll. It is an almost endless job to make out the muster rolls for pay. I was tired out when morning came but the rolls were finished. This noon in opening one of those cans of pickles that you sent me I cut a horrid little hole in my first finger with the sharp tin and the rag around it is in the way.

Christmas Eve. I was on picket as I told you in my last letter and this New Year Eve I was up + working all night.

Jan 2/63 We are considerable farther south than we were in Virginia but we are right on the sea shore and it is much colder I think than it is in Virginia where we left. All the male inhabitants from little boys 10 years old + upwards chew tobacco and all the females from little girls to old women smoke pipes + chew snuff on the end of a stick. It makes me sick as I write about it. It is the most disgusting habit I ever knew. The corners of the girls mouths are constantly dirtied up with the nasty snuff. Instead of having carpets they sprinkle their floors with fine sand and use the whole room for a large spit box. The girls squirt the snuff juice out of their mouths and between their teeth as far and as forcibly as any man who has chewed tobacco for years. The soil of this point is sandy dry + unproductive. Scrub or live oak flourishes abundantly and of swamps there are no end. The pine tree also grows extensively and they make tar here in great abundance. There are not near as many slaves here as in Virginia and the rank South feeling is not found here. All that the people here want is to be let alone. I am writing now in a secesh house just behind our company and it was here that Mr. Stowits + I made out the pay rolls the other night. I expect that we shall be in the next batch that takes place in North Carolina so watch the papers closely. We came down here to fight + any day we may be cut down by the bullet or the sword. This may be my last letter but I hope not. If I am killed in battle I have the happy knowledge that you will not mourn for me for you will feel that I am not dead but only sleeping. not dead but only gone before. Mourn not for me if I am killed; weep not a tear, then smile and feel that to a home I've gone where lives not sin or guile. My peace with my dear Savior now is made and I am free to part in peace with friends + life whene'er the time shall be. Then mourn not for a single hour but spend an hour in prayer beseeching that through Christ dear Lord we'll meet together there.

    Farewell if this should be my last. Adieu if I should write again.
Your Loving Son, Edward
    Write often and direct as before.
    We have no regular mail here. We have just heard that the Monitor which was to have cooperated with us is wrecked it may alter our destiny.

Chapter Three

Operations near Port Royal, Beaufort and Hilton Head, SC
January, 1863 to March, 1863

"Our camp at Gloucester Point we called "home" and when we left it, it was like leaving a dear friend and tearing us away from dear enjoyment to send us into misery" E. Cook letter dated 12/25/62

"A soldier's life is full of surprises, and just as we were nicely fixed for the winter at Gloucester Point, with our fire places built and our Sibley tents stockaded and floored, marching orders came, this time to go by water, and embarking on the old tub Belvidere, away we speed southward.

After a rough passage we arrived at Morehead City, N.C., which we found was to be the rendezvous for a great expedition. After 1 week of delay we put to sea again, on the fine steamer New England, and the morning of January 31, 1863, a lovely morning, entered with the rest of the fleet the noble harbor of Port Royal. The sight, as the mist lifted and disclosed the beautiful surroundings and the great fleet, with colors flying and bands playing, steaming up the bay, was one never to be forgotten." Lt. Col. Charles E. Walbridge address at the first Annual Reunion 7/18/1888

Letter from E. Cook to his Parents, Relations and Friends

Camp of the 100th Regt. N.Y.S.V. at Carolina City, N.C.
Jany. 2d, 1863

My Dear Parents Relations + Friends
*   I cannot write much of a letter to you this time for the first finger of my right-hand is done up in a rag and I have to handle my pen with the wrong fingers which makes it very difficult to write. but I will do as well as I can so here goes. I must continue on in my old style and write in journal form. First – let me light my cigar + then I will start.*
*   My cigar is going + I have tightened up the rag on my finger so that it*

is a little more out of the way and now I will reherse what is written in my diary since I wrote to you last.

Letter from E. Cook to his Folks at Home

Carolina City Jan 3ᵈ 1863

Dear Folks at home

We are still laid at Carolina City but are expecting to be on the move every hour or we may stay here a week or so yet Yesterday 2 more Regts Joined us and we expect that the rest of our Brigade will be up to day some are landing now They have expected some very bad new with them They say that the old Monitor was lost off Cape Hatteras which if it is true it is a great loss to us at present as she was one of the boats that was going to Willmington with us I am enjoying very good health and I hope you are doing the same. It is very good weather here yesterday it was a little cold as the wind blew from the all day but to day it is very warm not only warm but the sun shines down very hot upon us The people in this vicinity are not such rank secesh as those in Virgina some profess to be union and others dont seem to care how the thing goes only the war was settled.

Letter from A. Lyth to his Father and Mother

Carolina City N.C. Jan 6ᵗʰ 1863

Dear Father + Mother

I have just received your kind letter of the 25ᵗʰ containing 25 cts each from all of you which comes in handy at present I cannot tell you how soon we will get paid but it is all the talk now how ever when we get paid we shall get 4 months pay as we were mustered in for 2 months more the last of Dec. We are mustered in every 2 months for the 2 months pay due us so when the pay master comes pays you all you are mustered in for no matter if you have 10 months pay coming in to you as some in our company have as they were in the hospital when the pay master was paying off the Regt I was very glad to hear that you were all enjoying good health as it leaves me at present I am sitting in house writing this letter as we do not have very good accomodations in our little shelter tents for writing when it rains and blows as it does at present but there is signs of it clearing up The house is situated in the rear of our camp Just at the foot of our company street. If you have not sent me any boots yet you need not as I cannot tell when I shall get them although I shall get them sometime if you have sent them Just as I was going to take my boots to get fixed we got marching orders so I drew a pair of army shoes and threw my boots away but if I get my boots they will come in handy for the wet weather next spring but the army shoes are much better to march in than boots so if I get boots I shall keep a pair of shoes to march in as a great many of the rest do. You say Mr. Robson has proposed to sell you the whole concern for 3 thousand dollars and you say I must give you my opinion about it Of course it would be a great deal more pleasent I know to have every thing to yourself if you think you could clear it. But you know best. John say that Mr. Pierce came and took the old mare to winter again. I hope he realey will bring her back in better condition than he did last spring We are still at Carolina City and we are begining to think we may stay here a week or two yet as we are encamp here while every day there is other Regts arriving and they are put on board of the car and sent right forward to Newbern to Reenforce Foster. Our whole Brigade is encamped here we had a Cavelry man from Newbern yesterday visiting his brother who is in this Regt he says they think up at Newbern we are encamped here to bring up the rear of the army when all the reinforcements have arrived he say the talk up at Newbern is that we are to go and take Willmington and cutting of the Rebel supplies from that place and then to proceed to either to Charleston or to go on the back track to Richmond but it is only suppositions but suppositions are sometimes right he says that there are at Newbern at present there are between 50 and 60 thousand troops. It is a courious fact that in this part of the country that both men + women and even children to as small as sister Fanny either smoke or chew tobacco in the house I am writing there is an old woman + 3 daughters one about 19 the other 16 or 17 and they both smoke and the old woman smokes the other is about as old as fanny and she smokes when she gets a hold of a pipe then she has 2 sons one about the size of Billy the other smaller and they both chew and smoke tobacco. You must keep on writing a usal as we shall get the mail here twice a week if not oftener and I shall always continue to write as usal myself Give my best Respects to all the neighbors I send my love to you all so no more at present from

Your Affect Son Alfred Lyth

P.S. It has stoped raining Capt Dye and our Doctor have just been shipwreck in a small boat they went over to Beaufort this morning in a small boat and they under took to return when they saw the storm coming up but were overtaken in it and capsized but were saved by a boat that put out from the dock after them the Capt has just come into this house for some clean clothes that he got washed and ironed here and says he had a narrow escape.

Letter from E. Cook to his Parents

Camp of the 100th Regt. N.Y.S.V.
Thursday Evening Jany 8/63
Carolina City N.C.

My dear Parents

I am still in the land of the living. I sent you a letter a few days ago containing some very pretty little shells. As soon as you receive them I wish you would write + let me know. There is one among them that I prize very highly. It is a little white shell something like a snail shell but has a rough kind of surface being furnished with thin shell or blade like projections. Please take care of it for me as I think very much of it. You will know it as soon as you see it for it is different from all the rest.

Thursday Jany 1st 1863 The weather was rather cool in the morning but in the afternoon it was quite warm. You wanted to know how I spent my Christmas. I wrote home + told you that my Christmas Eve was spent very pleasantly on picket and my Christmas day rather sadly in camp. And now I suppose you would like to know how I spent my New Year Day – calling day – open house day – the day of all the year most loved by us young sparks. I will tell you how I spent it. New Years Eve, or the night before New Years, Mr. Stowits (an orderly Sergeant) and my self were up all night making the pay rolls for our Co. I had a sore finger + could not write so he did the writing and I did the calling off.

New Years Morning I was on camp guard. I did not have to stand sentinel or walk a beat (Corporals are exempt from such duty) but I had to be up and around during the day and had to go round with my relief twice during the night. The guard had a house to stay in but it was just as bad as out doors for there was no door and the windows were broken out. Many of the boys remained out side by the fire when they were off duty but I went inside + laid down + had 2 good naps. I can assure you I thought of home many times during the day + wished I was safely returned again. I read my Testament in the afternoon as I laid out on the bank of the sound basking in the delicious rays of a January Sun. I fear if I had been in Buffalo my little testament would have been unnoticed in the usual hurry and excitement of the day. I hope and trust that before another year is ended this unnatural war will have closed and we all be returned to our homes in safety and security under the old stars + stripes.

Friday Jany 2ᵈ 1863 the weather was pleasant.

Saturday Jany 3ᵈ 1863 the weather was decidedly hot. We had battalion drill in the afternoon, and with the fine dust which we kicked up as we marched, + the heat of the sun we had no very enviable time I can assure you.

Sunday Jany 4ᵗʰ 1863 The day was cool. We had a regimental inspection this morning at 9 AM. The Colonel when he came to me and inspected my knapsack remarked, "There, there, that's the way to pack your knapsacks" It was quite a compliment for <u>him</u> *who never compliments anybody. As soon as inspection was over Geo. Clark and myself went down to the beach and heated some water in a tin pail and took a general wash.*

Monday Jany 5ᵗʰ 1863 We had quite a lively time this evening playing a game they call prison. Myself and another Corporal chose an equal number of men and then we take two points on opposite sides of the field and a few feet to the right or left of the points we select other points which we call the prisons; then each side tries to catch the men of the other side when they are off their point or home. And when they are caught they have to remain on the prison until some of their own side can come up and touch them and get them off. The side that catches the most men + keeps them from the other side is the victor. Just as the drum beat for roll call, my side had every man from the other side on our prison so my victory was complete.

Tuesday Jany 6th 1863 - *The weather was rainy and in these little shelter tents it is most miserable living in damp days. The dreariness of today however was greatly relieved and my heart was gladdened by unexpectedly receiving a letter from you. It was one written by Laura about Christmas time and contained 7 dollars in joint stock money for which I am much obliged. But what if the box should not be sent on to the regiment. It was directed to Gloucester Point and perhaps it may lay there for months and George not receive it, but no that can't be for Dick Allen who got drunk at Fortress Monroe and was left behind has just come to the regiment and says there is a box for G.S. at Newbern so if we go on to Newbern pretty soon George will get it. They say some of the boxes have been broken and perhaps George's is among the number.*

This afternoon a train of came down from Newbern with commissary stores and express freight for our Brigade. But I must stop writing for a little while and take another delightful smoke from my cunning little genuine pipe.

Well I have enjoyed my smoke and now here goes again again. George's box came through all right. Tell Aunt Grace I have helped to demolish her mince pies and am ready to pronounce them the best I ever ate. We made a grand charge upon them but they stood it like veterans. They were almost too many for us but our superior skill and unquenchable fiery determination finally conquered them. We have utterly destroyed many of them and now we are somewhat pacified and shall attack the rest as it suits our best convenience. The Head cheese was rich but I guess it had been frozen and thawed out again on its journey here.. Tell Grandma that her candy was most acceptable but among us three it did not last long. Did Grandma knit my mittens? They are much better than I expected: warm + thick and a perfect fit. I shall throw away my fur gloves before I part with my mittens. I am a thousand times obliged to the doner and hope the gloves and my pipe may remain my companions until the war is closed and finally return with the present owner when all danger is passed having served their country together.

Saturday Jany 10ᵗʰ 1863. Our Company went on today. The day was pleasant and warm but a little cloudy. I was lucky enough to be on the reserve post for the first time since I first went on picket. The reserve was quartered in a little country meeting house so they had a better place to stay than if they had been in camp. I improved the time and the convenience of the seats + house by writing a good part of this letter and reading my testament. About Six o'clock in the evening it began to rain and it did rain right smart until about 1 o'clock at night. It was the hardest rain I have seen since I left home. The lightning flashed and it thundered terrible for a short time. It was fortunate for the boys that were out doors that the rain was warm so that they did not chill when they were wet through. The picket were all posted in the woods and had such large fires that all the rain could not put them out. There was a very apparent diminution of the rail fences in the neighborhood of the different post when daylight did appear. I considered myself very fortunate in being allowed to have a dry bench to lie on and a tight roof to remain under. I did not sleep any, for about nine o'clock in the evening I was taken with violent pains in the bowels and a nausea at the stomach. I throwed up about 3 days rations but did not feel any better. In the morning I made me a strong sling of the brandy you sent me and after a while I felt much better so that when we were relieved I started with the rest of the boys and marched into camp.

Sunday Jany 11/63 The day was warm and pleasant after the terrible rain of last night. The soil is so sandy that at 9 o'clock not a trace of the rain was discernable in our camp or on our parade ground. I felt much better when I reached camp than I did when I started from the reserve. Either the brandy that I took this morning or the walk did me good. I felt rather weak after the severe nausea of last night and as soon as possible I laid down and did not get up again until dress parade just before sunset. I ate a slice of bread and drank a little coffee for supper. This constituted my breakfast, dinner + supper. The Captains excused me from appearing at roll call to night and I went to bed early in the evening. I must have caught cold in the early part of last evening for I have sharp rheumatic pains darting from one joint to another in the lower part of my body but I think I shall sleep well + feel better in the morning. Monday Jany 12/63 Geo. Stoddard played the mother part last evening and made up my bed and tucked me in so that I slept warm + well and this morning I feel first rate. I took another warm bath this morning and this evening with the exception of a slight pain in my bowels I feel perfectly well. I am writing on a table in a house with a warm fire blazing in the fireplace. Geo Stoddard is writing to Flora and has just finished his letter. The candle has almost burned out and so I must stop. I think we shall leave here in a few days. Keep on writing as heretofore. Tell Mary + Laura out the inclosed notes in envelopes and send them to the proper persons. Tell Mary tell Fannie that I have written to her but have received no answer.

Your Loving Soldier Son
Edward

Letter from E. Cook to his Parents

Head Quarters 2ᵈ Brig. Naglee's Div.
Carolina City Jany. 1863

My dear Parents

It is Sunday and as I have a little time to spare I will commence a letter to you and finish my journal to this date if possible. I am now no longer with the 100ᵗʰ Reg't. I have delivered up my musket and accoutrements and hope I shall never have to carry them again. My journal will explain matters so I will hasten to it.

January 13ᵗʰ 1863. Our Lieut. Walbridge has lately been appointed Brigade Quartermaster and this morning he saw me in our company street and told me to come over to his office about 8 ½ oclock am. Previous to this he had told me that he thought he should need a clerk and he said he had been thinking of me. I replied that I should like the appointment very much and he said he would remember me if he should decide upon taking anyone. Here the conversation ended and I had but small expectations of receiving the appointment, but this morning almost unexpectedly he requested me to come to his office, so I got myself up as neatly as a common soldier can – blacked my boots, washed face +c and went over. The Lieut. told me that he should want me there and as soon as he could see the commander of the Brigade he would get an order to have me detailed as Clerk in the Quartermaster Department. He spoke to Capt. Dye about the matter and the Capt. gave his consent although I do not much think that he wanted me to leave the Company as I have since been told that if I had remained with the Company I should have received a Sergeant's warrant and stood a good chance of being Ord^ly Sergeant as soon as our present Sergeant receives his commission as Lieut. which he expects very shortly. But I think the place which I now how have is preferable to a Sergeant's warrant for I have no musket to carry and as our office is always at Brigade Head Quarters I shall fare as well as the best.

Before the Lieut made his choice known to me he inquired of our Orderly Sargeant Mr. Stowits (formerly a highly respected teacher of Buffalo) concerning my mathematical abilities. Mr. Stowits gave him an answer that was satisfactory I presume for the matter has been decided and here I am. This afternoon I went down to Morehead City to draw some stationary for the Quartermaster Dept. The city contains less than 300 inhabitants and not more than 20 or 30 houses it is built on the sand of the sea shore and has a decided bleak appearance like an outcast and out of the way village. There is a large military R.R. Depot at the boat landing and this I presume is what has laid the foundation for a city at such a strange point as the sea shore sand.

January 14th 1863 My Captain told me today that the order had come from Head Quarters to detail me as Clerk in the Q.M. Dept. so the thing is now fixed and determined upon. I have to thank Mr. Stowits in part for putting in a good word for me at the right opportunity but above all I am thankful to God for I feel + have felt that it is the answer of a gracious God to the earnest applications of a loving mother + prayerful relatives. You have prayed for my safe return and I trust that the same good being who has thus far kept me from sickness and disease will still continue to afford me his divine protection and finally grant that I may return to you in good bodily health + spiritual condition. Pray on, pray ever, remembering that "whatsoever ye ask in faith, believing it shall be given unto you.

January 15/63 I was sent to Newbern today about 31 miles up the railroad on some business for the Lieut.

The orders he gave me were these "I want you to see Lt. Prouty, Ordinance Officer, and hand these papers to him. I can't tell you where you will find him but you must hunt him up" This was rather uncousling orders but I told him I would do my best and started off. I got to Newbern about 5 o'clock. It was raining + growing dark very fast but I rushed around from one place to another and finally found Lt. Prouty and did up my business with him in short measure. I then went to the Provost Marshall's office to get a pass as no soldier's allowed to go about the streets after dark. I did not care about going round the City but I knew the 67ʰ Ohio was somewhere in the vicinity of Newbern + I wanted to see him. When I got to the Provost Marshall's office he was gone and I had to wait until the Officer of the Guard came in and get a pass of him. He gave me a pass to take me out of the City to the Camp of the 67ʰ Ohio. The difficult thing was to find where the regiment lay. I went to the Post Quarter Master's office and that was shut up so I could not find out anything there but I enquired of a soldier standing near and he told me there were some Ohio Regts away off to the right of the City so I started at haphazard off in the direction pointed out. When I reached the outskirts of the town I inquired of another soldier who told me I was on the right road and said the 67ʰ Lay about a mile out of the City. I walked about a mile further on and met an officer of whom I again inquired. He told me he was a Lieut. in the 67ʰ and that I was on the right road but the regt Lay about a mile + a half further on. It was dark + raining and a strange road. I was about persuaded to turn back but decided to go on. I went forward more than a mile passed many regiments but none of them knew anything of the 67ʰ. I saw a group of soldiers standing in the road + of them I inquired. One replied that the 67ʰ was on the other side of the woods about ¾ of a mile further on. The distance began to grow shorter instead of longer as in the first instance + I was encouraged to go on. I finally reached the regt all in a perspiration from my fast walking and found Uncle David in a tent visiting someone of his comrades. He asked me in and we had a smoke together out of my tobacco + talked over matters + things in general and the folks at home in particular. He looks poor and complains much of a pain in his back occasioned by heavy lifting about 6 weeks ago. He does not much like the army and says it is worse than sailoring. I slept with him that night and Eat Breakfast next morning. He says it is 4 miles from the Camp to Newbern but he calls it five.

January 16 (63) with Uncle David - After Breakfast, I walked to Newbern again and got there just in time to take the nine o'clock train for Carolina City. It is cold + rainy today and coming down on the cars I grew quite *chilly from having perspired freely on my walk from the 67th camp to the city.   The line of road from Carolina City to Newbern is very dreary. I do not think there are six houses along the entire 30 miles. The wood is all pitch pine and nearly every tree has been barked + scraped for the pitch that flows from the tree. You have seen the Virginia pine, but the pine that grows here is as much worse than the Virginia pine as that is worse than our own Northern pine. North Carolina is a great state for tar making. The tar is made from the pitch or gum that flows from the pine.*

January 17th 1863 The weather still continues very cold I almost froze last night. I still sleep in the tent with the boys. The wind blew almost like a hurricane. We expect to move from here every day. I hope I shall hear from you before we go. I have rec'd no letter from you that was written since Christmas.

There is a report that the mail has been stopped both ways but whether it is true or not I do not know. If it is the case then you have not heard from me in nearly a month and must be very anxious but for your sakes I hope it is not so as I wish you to hear from me whether I hear from you or not.

Sunday January 18/63 This has seemed the most like Sunday to me of any Sabbath we have had since I enlisted the Army. I am writing tonight, as you will see by the heading of my letter, at headquarters of our Brigade. The quarters are in a depot and if it were not for the stove which is red hot beside me I should almost freeze as I am writing for the floor is made of rough planks with a crack of about an inch in width between every plank and there is an <u>open work</u> window sash over every door in the building. I am writing in a hurry for the regiments are going to begin to embark tomorrow and I do not expect to have a moment of spare time. I will write again as soon as possible. I am anxious to hear from you for I am reduced down to the last stamp. I suppose you know better than I do myself where we are going to but the rumor prevails here now that we are going farther south to Wilmington in this state or else to Charleston in South Carolina. Remember me to all the folks and write as often as usual and direct as heretofore for I shall get all the letters some time or other.

Good night – Pray for me
Your loving Son
Edward.

Please preserve the inclosed papers.

Letter from A. Lyth to his Father

Beaufort Harbor Jan 21ˢᵗ 1863

Dear Father

Our Regt is at present on the steam ship New England anchored out in the harbor between the citys of Beaufort + Morehead City there are 9 Regts altogether embarked on board of different transports awaiting orders we do not know where we are bound for. The Monitors and other gun boats left here some days ago We have not received any mail these last 2 or 3 weeks so I have not heard from you in that time but I hope these few lines will find you all well as it leavese me at present We are a little crouded on board of this boat but ours is the largest Regt in the whole lot which makes us more crouded than the other Regts. but we have got the best transport in the whole lot we have pretty good weather on the whole but it was a very heavy rain storm last night but it is cleared up this morning. We have not got our pay as we expected before we left and it make the boys feel quite bad and there is a great deal of talk of stacking arms if they do not pay us soon untill they do pay us. I send my love to you all so no more at present.

from your affect Son
Alf. Lyth

Letter from E. Cook to his Parents

Qrters 2ᵈ Brigade Naglee's Division
U.S. Steamer New England
Jany 22ᵈ 1863

My dear Parents

All of our regiments are now embarked on their respective transports and I think we shall stand for our place of destination either today or tomorrow. The 100ᵗʰ regiment is on board of the Steamer "New England". We do not yet know where we are going but then opinion generally prevailing is that we are bound for either Charleston or Wilmington. Our Division General

"Naglee" is on board of our boat + also Col. Davis the Commander of our Brigade so that this Vessel is General Head with a vengence. I am quartered in the Cabin but have to sleep on the floor as all the state rooms are occupied by the Officers and then there is not room enough for them all. There are two regiments of Soldiers on board and there is not room enough for them in the hold and between decks so many of them have to sleep on deck. It is shameful how little care is taken of the poor soldier on board of transports. They are stowed away like so many cattle + left to take care of themselves as best they can. The officers are assigned to good snug quarters and little do they care how the privates get along. The welfare of the soldier seems to be the last thought of the officers on board of vessels.

It rained hard last night and I felt sorry indeed for the poor men who had to lay out on deck during the storm. How true it is that exposure kills as many as the bullet.

Monday Jany 19/63 The 100th left camp this morning at 8 o'clock to embark on the Steamer "New England" I do not know when I shall see the boys again but I hope before long. I went to Morehead City again this afternoon on business for the Quartermaster. I have plenty of riding to do and that is just what I like. Cornelius [ ] is Brigade Ordnance Sergeant and has his office in the same room as myself. If any of you should see any of his folks tell them he is well and looking first rate. He and I had a splendid ride on horseback the other evening. We rode all along the beach both ways as far as we could go. I had a delightful time and enjoyed myself tiptop. I wish I could send home some of the strange fish we find around here such as the starfish which looks like a 5 pointed star, the Porcupine fish which is covered with sharp pointed quills about 1 ½ inches in length, the toad fish which is said to be poisonous when it bites and is so strong in the jaws that when it bites at a stick it can hold itself out straight and be carried all around the camp in that manner.

Tuesday Jany 20th 1863 I rode to Morehead City again this afternoon to turn in some Quartermaster stores that we do not wish to take with us. It rained and blowed very hard at night.

Wednesday Jany 21/63 We left our quarters this morning about nine oclock to embark on board the transport; our baggage was boarded on some *platform car but there was no engine at hand to pull us down to Morehead City where the boat was anchored so all hands – Officers, Clerks, and privates turned to and undertook to push her down – 3 ½ miles.*

We run the cars about ½ a mile when we saw the engine coming up to meet us and so we all jumped on the cars and rode down the rest of the way much obliged to the engine for her assistance. It was rainy by spells all day and as I have said before, at night it rained very hard.

Thursday Jany 22/63 I slept first rate last night on the floor of the Cabin and after a good wash I feel in excellent condition this morning. We are lying at anchor this morning off fort Macon and near Morehead City. A schooner swung round with the tide this morning and striking her stern against our vessel, smashed her small boat to pieces. Afterwards our steamer by some means or other run into the steamer and tore away part of the other steamer's stern.

I shall be glad when we get out of this harbor and in the open sea where we shall have plenty of room. I do dread to be on board of these miserable transports. Many of them are not sea worthy but I think though that all those that are going with us are good sound sea going vessels and I have no doubt that we shall reach our journeys end in safety if no violent storm occurs on the passage. I learned yesterday why we have received no mail from the north. It is detained at Fortress Monroe along with almost numberless Express boxes for the Brigade. It was expected that our stoppage at Morehead + Carolina City would only be of one or two days duration and that we should immediately start on and complete our journey. And as they expected us to move everyday they would not forward the mail until they received another notice that we had landed at some place where we were going to remain for some time. I suppose when the mail does come at last that there will be any quantity of letters for me and newspapers in abundance. One of our Clerks went up to Newbern the other day to draw some forage for the horses and the Lieut. at our request gave him an order to get a negro cook for our regiment, but he was so busy while there drawing the forage that he did not have time to attend to it. He brought back the order and I will send it in this letter to you for preservation. I will also send a copy of Genl Naglee's order Nº 3 which I wish you would preserve for me. I will now stop for a few minutes and take a smoke from my pipe.

*Friday Jany. 23/63 My few minutes smoking turned out to be a few hours. We seem to have any quantity of accidents as we lay moored in this harbor. The water is very shallow and in places where the water seems deep enough at high tide it is not deep enough to float a boat when she swings round as the tide goes out. Yesterday evening or just at dusk I was sitting in the cabin when I heard a terrible crash and thought the whole side of the vessel was breaking in. I went on deck to see what was the matter and there alongside of us lay a large boat with her prow jammed into our wheelhouse. She tore us up badly but did not injure the wheel. This morning one of the Gunboats laying in sight of us got in shoal water and one of the other boats broke two large ropes in trying to pull her off the bar. No one was hurt when the ropes broke but it was high fun to see the officers on the decks of the boats scatter as the rope come coiling swiftly up towards them.
The day is cloudy and quite chilly. We have not seen the sun for several days. I presume he will give us a good shine when he does come out and scorch things considerable. There are some little signs that the weather is going to clear and give us the balance of the day pleasant + sunshiny.*

We have the brigade brass band on board with us and during the hours of mealtime they occupy the quarter deck and discourse sweet strains of soul stirring music to our greedy ears and enliven the dull + slow passing hours with their lively and cheering notes. Music I presume sounds doubly sweet to us because it recalls the happy hours that we have spent while listening to its sounds at home, us with the light fantastic toe we tripped the joyous measure and felt that each new note that came brought with it pleasure.

Letter from A. Lyth to his Father

Beaufort Harbor N.C. Jan 24th 1863

*Dear Father
    Since I wrote my last letter we have learnt that we shall not receive any mail untill we reach our destination for we are on the move now and may leave this place any moment so if the mail was forwarded to this place we might not be here to receive it. I hope these few lines will find you all well and in good health as it leaves me at present. Night before last there was*

one of the transports in this harbor caught fire below deck she was anchored about 100 feet from where we are anchored so of course we had a fair view of her the fire broke out about 3 oclock in the morning it did not get much head way before it was discovered She was not loaded with soldiers the men aboard of her we could see we exerting theirselves to extinguish the flames but it kept gaining on them untill they got their engine to work pumping water into the flames then they got the better of it and pretty soon extinguished them altogether she was not much burnt above deck as most of the fire was below deck although the flames rushed very fierce. When Gen Heckman took up his quarters on board of this boat he had with the rest of his duds 8 barrels of wiskey fetched aboard he fetched 5 or 6 men to guard his wiskey and other property but it was of no use some of the men have made to or three ralleys upon the wiskey barrells but the ralley they made last night was the most destructive one as a whole crowd went on the ralley some seized hold of the guards and overpowered them while some others stove in the heads of the barrell and was dipping the wiskey out and pasing it around and helping theirselves and it took some 20 guards + officers to make them quit 2 of the officers got a good pounding in the dark severl of the men were put under arrest and some were arrested and hand cuffed and tied up. one boy about 18 or 19 years old that they were trying to put the handcuffs on made desperate resistance he would not let the guards tie him at all and when the officers undertook to tie him he kicked one hit another with his fist and then run and 2 of the guards was put under arrest for not doing their duty and stoping him with the point of the bayonet when he run. they soon overhauled him again and the officer again undertook to handcuff him with the assistance of 2 of the guards but they had pretty tough work he cursed and he swore and call the officres every thing he could think of and he snatched one of the guards bayonet and made a rush at an officer and would have run it into him if he had not been caught hold of behind and held back they put the handcuffs on to him and tied his feet then tied him to a post but some how or other he got the hand cuffs off untied himself and threw the handcuffs overboard but they soon tied him up again After all this had happened those that had just got enough of the wiskey to put them up to more devilment made a break on the Sutter shop after tobacco and other things where they had another battle with the guards and officers all the ringleaders they arrested and took them over to the flag ship where they tied them to the mast all night and they are going

to court marshall them and I guess it will go pretty rough with some of them
there is only one in our company in the mess at all. Day before yesterday
I went up the masts of a brig that lay along side of our boat furnishing us
with coal and counted the number of vessels steamers + gunboats anchored
in this harbor there being 57 in all of which 10 or 11 are large steam
transports loaded each with Regt of soldiers all day yesterday and to there
is quite a fleet of steamers coming in to be load with soldiers to go with us
and we have learned that there is a large fleet fitting up in New York either
to go with us or follow us up I cannot tell for sure where we are going we
still thing that we are going to Willmington then to Charleston but that is
an supposition this morning there was one of the boys fell over board but he
was soon got out of water after getting a ducking the weather is very fine I
cannot tell when we shall sail as we learn we shall have to wait untill the
troops come down from Newbern and embark on board of the transports
that came in yesterday. I send you all my love and give my best respects to
the Neighbors.

From Your Affect Son
Alfred Lyth

P.S.   please keep on writing to me as usal and oftener if any thing as
you cannot tell how all us soldiers feel when we hear from home. It is
the hardest thing we have to put up with at present is the stoppage of our
mail.

Letter from E. Cook to his Parents

Saturday Jany 24/63 The day was rather pleasant and for a short time
during the afternoon the sun showed us his face and looked down upon us
quite pleasantly and made every thing look smilingly. For a wonder we did
run into any other vessel last night or have any other vessel run into us as
we swung around with the tide. I have been very busy today writing for
the quartermaster. We are going to try and complete our monthly return
for Jan'y while we are lying at anchor in this harbor. It is a good long job
but I do not think the boat will leave for 6 or 10 days and that will give
us time enough to complete our papers + then we will have nothing to do

*while we are sailing on the expedition. Another large fleet of vessels and steamers came into the harbor this morning to receive the balance of our division. Gen. Naglee left our boat this morning and went on board the "Secor". I am glad he has left for it was a kind of constraint to have him on Board. C. [ ] was on the "New England" yesterday and he says the 100*th *have got first rate quarters and are in good spirits. Some of them broke into a whiskey barrel and got drunk yesterday, and this evening they brought 14 of them on to our vessel and tied them to the yard arm. Some of the 104*th *Pa. Vols. have formed a kind of Minstrel Band and this evening they gave us an exhibition in the cabin it was very interesting and laughable. I enjoyed it highly. Give my love to all the folks. I will write again in a few days before we leave the vessel.*

Good Bye
Your Aff. Son
Edward.

Letter from E. Cook to his Parents

*Head Quarters 2*d *Brigade Naglee's Division*
On board Steamship "New England}" Jany 27/63

Sunday Jany 25/63
     Dear Parents – I will commence another letter to you but I do not think I shall send it until I receive a letter from you for I have only one post stamp left and I must keep that in case of an emergency and I do not like to run the risk of sending letters without stamping them. I hope I shall hear from home very soon. A month seems a long while to wait for a letter when I have been accustomed to receive letters every week. I am anxious to hear from home but more still am I anxious that you should hear from me for I can imagine just how you will feel if my letters are detained here instead of being sent to their destination.
     Lt. Walbridge told me today that he saw one of our old schoolmates yesterday and who do you think it was? You recollect the Mr. Dennis that used to live in the Clarendon and was acquainted with Mr. Lee's family?

112

Well it was his son. His is a Lieutenant in some company of Artillery or Cavalry and is going on this expedition with us – perhaps I will have an opportunity of seeing and speaking with him. Did I ever tell you that Lt. Walbridge was one of my schoolmates? He used to attend the Central at the same time that Dennis and I did. There are a great many of the old Central schoolboys in the army scattered around in different parts of the Country. Joyous indeed will be the time when the war is ended and we all can meet again in our own loved city and grasp each others hand in cordial friendship and upon the same or equal footings. There we shall not know each other by the rank we hold in military life, but again, as before the war broke out, "The Mind shall be the measure of the man" and by this only can we justly claim a rank above the level of mankind.

Monday Jany 26ᵗʰ 1863 Yesterday was the finest day we have had in some length of time. Lt. Walbridge went to Newbern yesterday to draw some clothing and I assisted in rowing him to shore. On returning to our vessel after landing him on the dock at Morehead we passed the New England and I got off and went on board of her and had a good long visit with the boys. They are much more comfortably situated and not near as crowded as the soldiers on our own vessel. They are all in good spirits and all are anxious to be on the way to Wilmington or where ever we else we are going to. We are no wiser now as to our destination than we were when we first left Gloucester Point just a month ago today.

Tuesday Jan'y 27ᵗʰ 1863 Rainy + dismal. We had a court marshal on board of our vessel to try some of the soldiers engaged in the rumpus on the New England Last Saturday. It seems that it was quite a serious matter instead of being a small affair as I first supposed. The boys told me over there Sunday that it was a regular mutiny and that the officers did not dare to leave their cabin and go down on the first deck among the drunken and furious men. Some of the privates told the officers to their face that they would shoot them the first opportunity that was offered them in battle. They only managed to secure the Leaders by having the orderly sergeants read to them a fictitious order to detail them on detached service where they would draw 25 cents per day extra pay. This mislead them and when they were ordered to sling their knapsacks and shoulder their muskets + embark in the small boat they hesitated not a moment but willingly obeyed the order and suffered themselves to be brought to our ship but how their countenances fell when on arriving here they had their arms taken from them and were strapped to a beam on the wheelhouse.

Fifteen of the worst cases in the regiment were thus secured and I have no doubt that the court marshal will inflict on them all very severe penalties for their offences.

Wednesday January 28ᵗʰ 1863 Another cold and windy day. I think we should have sailed to day but for the storm and dead head wind. The pilots will not venture out in such weather

Thursday Jany 29/63 The wind still blows very hard but it has changed around quarter. The mouth of harbor is guarded by one long continuous line of breakers. There is apparently no opening to admit of the passage of vessels and an inexperienced hand would stand an equal chance of running a vessel out to sea and of running her into the ground. Our pilot has been on board since yesterday morning and so I think we shall leave as soon as circumstances will permit.

The schooners are sailing out thick and fast this afternoon and the sea seems almost covered with them. It is splendid sight to see them hoist sail and move proudly past us one after another as thick as they can move. It seems as though they would run into us or else run into each other so close do they come to us, so narrow is the harbor and so quickly do they follow one another in their passage out into the sea. Hello some of the steamers are going out. The [   ] is started on her way and there look is the New England weighing anchor to follow after her. I wonder if we are going this afternoon. Genl Naglee has just come aboard of our vessel again and is going to have his Hd Qrs. here. I am sorry for that because I do not like to have him around. "Man the windlass" shouts the captain and soon the anchor is upon our deck and we are speeding on our way.

The channel through the breakers is very narrow and in going out we tried to pass between a vessel + a propeller + in doing so the vessel swung round and struck her jib boom in our wheel house. It cracked her boom and stove in our wheel house but did no serious damage to either of us. We are out to sea, sailing south west along the coast of North Carolina. It is rumored now that we are going to Port Royal. We left our harbor at 4 o'clock this afternoon.

Friday Jany 30/63 Pleasant but very windy and the sea quite rough. You might go to any part of the ship + you would be sure to see somebody "casting up their accounts" Sea sickness is prevelent. I caught a bad cold in my head night before last and I feel very chilly to day. I have not yet been sea sick and I do not think I shall during this trip although the sea runs very high. We passed a gunboat to day scuddling before the wind with only her top sails set. It was a rich sight for me. The hands gave us 3 cheers as they passed by. Towards evening we ran into a school of porpoises or some other kind of fish. They followed us for a long ways and came up close along side the vessel   It was fun to see them jump out of the water + skip over the waves. Finally when they got tired of following us they turned around and went back and we saw them no more.

Saturday Jany 31ˢᵗ 1863 This is a lovely morning the air feels like, and reminds us of one of those lovely spring morning at the North. How I would like to be there now and on just such a morning as this that meets us out to sea. We took a pilot aboard early this morning after lying at anchor for about an hour before daylight so I know that we are about to enter some port although when we received the pilot, no land was in sight on either side. I wonder where we are and what harbor we are going to enter. My wonderment is soon dispelled for about eight oclock we heave in sight of land and at 9 am we drop anchor in the harbor of "Port Royal" off "Hilton Head". We are now in the pestilential state of South Carolina — the viper from which has eminated the rank poison of secession that now has been distilled into the veins of every state in the once lovely South. In the state of the "Palmetto Flag" that has led many brave and true hearts to a base and ignominious death in the unholy cause of rebelion. In the state of the "Palmetto Tree" that now warms over the grave of noble souls now hushed in the silent sleep of death.

We passed one of the "monitors" this morning on her way up the coast. She was in tow of another Steam Gunboat and was probably going to blockade some harbor on the coast. We heard firing early this morning away to the South of us and have since learned that it was a naval engagement near Savannah about 20 miles below this harbor. I have not heard the results of the engagement but probably will hear by tomorrow and will let you know.

The New England came in the 2ᵈ boat after us and is all right. During the day a number of other steamers entered the harbor but as yet no sail vessels have made their appearance. I do not know as yet whether we are going to disembark at this point or whether they intend to land us further up the river or take us further down the coast and disembark us in the vicinity of Savannah. All is doubt and uncertainty, and perhaps it is well that it is so for the soldiers' sake. He knows not whether he is going to a place of safety or to meet his dreadful death but only hopes that the next night may bring him as safe and soft a bed as that on which he slept the night before. The soldier is, in the judgement of the world, the lowest of all low classes that earn their bread by the sweat of their brow. His friends at home forget and forsake him, but absence chills their recollection and his occupation cools their love, + they soon entirely cease to think of that which is so distasteful to their mind and unpleasant to their feelings (I speak not of <u>Relatives</u> *but of those who once have called us* <u>friend</u>*) but the soldier has two friends –* <u>God</u> *+* <u>uncertainty</u> *– that will never desert him though all else may forget him.   This has been a truly lovely day.   The trees are plainly visible on the shores both sides of us and are as bright and green as though it were the better part of time when every thing up north that bears the name of vegetation has reached its fullest and completest growth and beauty. The air feels {UNKNOWN WORD} and bracing giving health to all on board. If I were rich I think that I should always spend this season of the year at some seaport town in Southern latitudes. Our boat lies at anchor as quiet and immoveable apparently as if it were some proud and haughty thing that had been here for ages, so still and motionless is the bosom of water on which we float.*

Letter from A. Lyth to his Father

Sat Jan 31ˢᵗ 1863
Port Royal Entrance
on Board the steamship
New England

Dear Father

I received your letter of Jan 16 Just about 2 hours before this fleet set sail from Beaufort Harbor. This makes the six[th] letter I have wrote since the one dated Morehead city Dec 30 so you see I have not neglected writing the reason that you have not received them is that the mail has been stoped but I guess you will have received some of them letters before this. The reason I suppose that Mr. Maharg + Mr. Barnum did not hear from their sons is that they did not write untill we got to Carolina City and their letter did not go up untill my second. It is useless for you ever to feel uneasy about me as when we are on the move as we are now our mail is always most stoped for a few days We started Thursday afternoon about 3 oclock and arrived here Just before daylight this morning When we started the wind blew pretty strong and the sea rolled pretty heavy most all the Regt was sea sick yesterday myself among the rest Tom Maharg was not but George Barnum was as bad as myself and this morning we felt allright and are in very good health and I hope you will be in as good health as myself There was some 20 scooners started out of Beaufort belonging to our expedition just before the Steamers loaded with troops started and I tell you it looked splendid to see as many scooners all about the same size and with all their sails spread they were all loaded with the horses, provisions, ammunition +c then after they had all got out of the harbor the Steamers put out with the troops the vessels have not arrived here as yet. This morning Just outside of the harbor we met a large gunboat going out having the Passaic one of the Monitor Build of gun boats we passed close past her we had a fair view of her. It was a splendid sight to see her cutting through the water as the sea had calmed through the night it was quite smothe she stood about a foot out of the water her deck was clear of everything and as smothe as a peice of glass only the turret and the crew were to be seen on deck as she past by us the whole Regt gave her three hearty cheers which were as heartly responded to by her crew. We are still on board of the boat and I cannot tell weather we are going to land here or not it is the opion of a great many that we are not going to land here. It is very pleasent and warm here to day. We can see Fort Walker + Fort Beauregard from the boat as we lay in the harbor. I wish that mother would get some of that checked stuff and make me two shirts as the shirts they have here are very miserable things being both to short in the sleeves and body they are not near as good as the government shirts we drew at Albany. The men will not wear them when they can get others from home or buy some of the suttlers for which he charges like he *does for every thing else then I should like a pair of suspenders you can send these when you send my boots but don't send them untill I send for them. I received the letter you speak of all of the children having sent me some small change and as I said in the answer to that letter it came in very handy I spent the last of it to day. I will close this letter with my love to you all and hope to have another from you soon they say we shall receive all our back mail when we reach our destination were that is I cannot tell you probaly Savanna. No more at present*

From Your Affect Son
Alfred Lyth

write soon
send me some postage stamps

P.S. if we land here you can expect another letter in a day or two or if we stay in this harbor. And if we leave here on this boat I will write as soon as we arrive at another port.

Letter from A. Lyth to his Sister

Steamship New England Feb 1ˢᵗ 1863
Port Royal Entrance S.C.

Dear Sister

I hope these few lines will find you all well and in good health as it leaves me at present It would be useless for me to describe our passage down here as I wrote the whole account of it yesterday in a letter that I wrote to father which of course you will have read I simply am writing these few lines to you to pass away time as we are puzzeled to find anything to do on board of this boat having nothing to do but eat and drink and sleep It is very pleasent to sit were I am at present and cast your eyes on this harbor. to the right we see Fort Beauregard and some 4 or 5 large gun boats one of which is the renouned Ironsides and there are 2 large full rigged men of war and quite a number of small government transports Then in the center of the harbor our fleet of some 22 or 23 large steamers are anchored some of them containing 2 Regiments while more of them have less than one Regt. then to the left of these are quite a number of vessels of all sorts anchored and we can also see Fort Walker very plain and the town of Hilton Head which is a very neat looking place as far as we can Judege from here

The weather is very pleasent and it is very warm. I cannot tell weather we are going to land here or not or weather they are going to take us somewere else before they land us it is the opinion amongst us that we shall leave here soon on board of this boat although we cannot tell as yet. As I cannot think of anything else to write about I must close with my love to you all
Your Truly Affect Brother
Alfred Lyth

Write soon.

Letter from Ed Cook to his Parents

Sunday Feby 1ˢᵗ 1863 Another bright and holy Sabbath; but no sweet chimes to greet our ears or deep toned bells to send their joyous notes across the wave to where over vessel lies. 'Twill be a novelty to us when first again we have the church bells pealing forth their solemn call to morning worship. It is now more than 4 month since I have been in a church or heard the sound of a church bell.

The gunboat "Ironsides", which has been lying at anchor near us, went out to sea this morning. There are several more gunboats lying in this harbor and among them the large sail frigates with 2 + 3 tiers of guns named respectively the "Wabash" and "Vermont". They are the largest vessels I have yet seen afloat. The day has been very pleasant and comfortable. I have learned that the firing we heard yesterday was near Savannah. During a fog the Rebels sent out one of their "Rams" which attacked some of our vessels loaded with troops and captured one or two of them, upon hearing of which the monitor went down and drove her in and our forces now hold possession of the mouth of Savannah harbor.

Some of our Gunboats lately captured a Brittish vessel that was trying to run the blockade. She had on board 600 barrels of powder intended for the "Rebs". She was brought into this harbor sometime during the day but I was below and did not see her as I would have wished to. I fear I am forming bad habits down here for although I have read 8 or 10 chapters in my testament this morning yet the greater part of the day was devoted to novel reading. *The time hands heavy on our hands aboard this transport, but as soon as we land I shall have no time to spare for such light, idle and unbeneficial reading.*

Monday Feby 2ᵈ 1863 Another pleasant day. Our Boat made another short trip this afternoon and now we are lying at the landing of Beaufort S.C. Thursday afternoon we left the harbor of Beaufort N.C. and now lying at Beaufort S.C. I hope you have a map at home so that you can trace out these different points through which we may pass in this Compaigne. Beaufort is up the river about eight miles above Hilton Head. The river is very narrow but so deep that the largest ships can run up to Beaufort. But just above here the river divides into two forks and is not wide enough to allow of the passage of vessels. The harbor at Hilton Head, which is nothing more than the mouth of, Beaufort is called the finest harbor south of New York. Hundreds of vessels of the largest build could anchor in it with perfect security to themselves and to each other. At Hilton Hd, there are 2 rebels forts – "Forts Walker" + "Beauregard" – on either side of the harbor which were captured by our forces last spring I think it was. I believe it was here that Capt. Budd U.S.N. of Buffalo lost his life while rowing up the river to make a reconnaisance. This whole vacinity is called "Port Royal". If we land here at Beaufort as they say we are going to do tomorrow morning I shall be able to give you some kind of a description of the place. As I see it from the vessel it appears very neat + clean with many very pretty Southern style residencies. The regiment that guards the place is a negro one. Their uniform is a dark blue jacket + red pants. They appear similar to show monkeys at a little distance but they feel as proud as a pet Peacock. Give my love to Grandma, and Sammy and Annie, Lillie and all the rest of the children and kiss little Gracie for the Soldier boy. I have rec'd. no letter yet.

> *Good Bye*
> *Your Aff. Son*
> *Edward*

Chapter Four

Operations on St Helena Island, SC
February, 1863 – April, 1863

"Yesterday morning we took our wash tub our clean clothes a couple of camp kettles and material for making a fire and went to a spring which is near our camp. I fill our wash tub with cold water and striped naked and had a good wash so did Tom. Then we changed our clothes and washed the ones we took off and had a regular washing day of it." A. Lyth letter dated 2/12/1863

". . . we landed on the lovely island of St Helena, and soon were occupied with the ordinary routine of camp life. When at last all things were ready, and the advance on Charleston was commenced, the 100th, as usual, was selected to lead off, and once more we embarked on the briny deep." Lt. Col. Charles E. Walbridge address at the first Annual Reunion 7/18/1887.

Letter from A. Lyth to his Father

Steamship New England
Port Royal Entrance Feb 3 1863

Dear Father

I hope these few lines will find you all well and in good health as it leaves me at present. we are as yet laying on board of ship in this harbor and are likely to lay here some time yet untill this expedition is fairly fited out which as we learn will take some time yet. Yesterday our boat ran alongside the dock and let us go ashore for a few hours. The whole Regt went ashore taking with us our guns and accutrements. We marched a short distance along the beach and stacked arms then we broke ranks and put off in vairous directions as suited ourselves. I took a tramp up in the town of Hilton Head which is a very busy place although it don't appear to have

121

been much of a place before the war broke out. There are a great many government store houses the whole place being built over with them. Then there is a large yard covered all over with large heaps of solid shot of all sizes and some two or three acres covered over with large seige guns and small cannon then there is some large mortars which measure some five feet high as they lay on the ground in fact they are thicker across the muzzel than it is in length Then there is a splendid Battery of six brass cannons mounted with the ammunition wagons ready for the feild. Then I took a stroll round Fort Walker which is a very strong fort on account of their being a large amount of heavy seige guns that are mounted all round it. The time I was there they were fireing at a target out in the water. They made some pretty good shots. Then I took a walk up the main thouroughfare where I could have bought a good many thing that took my fancy if I had only had a little money and I could have got my likeness taken if I could have got the money. I don't think we shall have to be without much longer as they say we shall be paid off before we start on this expedition they say the paymasters is on the way here now. It is certain that we are either bound for Charleston or Savanna so very likely the next you hear from me it will be from either of those places. But of course I shall write every few days weather the mail leaves or not. I close these few with my love to you all so no more at present

From Your Affect Son
Alfred Lyth

Letter from A. Lyth to his Brother

Steamship New England
Port Royal Entrance off Hilton Head
Sat Feb 7th 1863 S.C.

Dear Brother
I take this opportunity having nothing else to do hoping they will find you well and in good health as it leaves me at present. We are still laying in this harbor either waiting for orders or more forces. They are talking of going ashore when the weather as it has been raining for these last 2 or 3 days but the sun rose splendid this morning The Capt said day before

yesterday that we should go ashore and camp as soon as the weather was a little better so we expect that we shall go either to day or tomorrow. We have very easey times on board of this boat but I like the land a great deal better. I said in my last letter that I wrote home that we were either bound for Charleston or Savanna but to tell the truth we don't know were we are going as it is only known by the commander of this expedition We do not receive any letters now at all nor we will not untill we reach some place were we know we shall stop some 8 or 10 days so that we shall have time to send for it to fortress Monroe and time for it to return I have got a good ring made for you. It is not quite finished yet but I will send it in my next letter. Just as I am writing this they are raising the anchor so I will stop here and tell you weather we land or not

Sunday Feb 8th 1863
We run about 2 miles further up the harbor yesterday and cast anchor again. This morning some of the Regts are landing and going ashore to dig wells and to prepare us a camping ground so I guess we shall go ashore tomorrow. This is a very warm day. Tom and I took our tents and pitched them on the Hurricane deck of this boat and it is very pleasent to sit under it and write. We lay pretty close to the shore and have a very fine view of it. It appears to be high and dry. We can see the soldiers that have gone ashore building their camps and cooking their dinners over their camp fires I have nothing more to write at present so I will conclude with my love for you and all the folks.

From Your Brother
Alfred Lyth

Write soon
*   Tell Father to tell me were to express my money if we get paid which is very likely. If I get paid before I get the answer to this I will direct John Lyth Buffalo Puffer Street – Cold Spring*

Letter from E. Cook to his Parents

Q.M. Department H'd. Qrs. 2d Brig. Naglee's Div.
On board Steam Transport "[   ]" anchor'd of Beaufort S.C.

My Dear Parents

Tuesday Feby 3ᵈ 1863 The two regiments on board this vessel disembarked this morning for a day or two while the boat hands clean the ship. It was a great joy to the boys to see their feet on land once more. It will give them an opportunity to clean themselves and wash their clothes if nothing more. Close by the landing is a cotton mill that runs 9 gins. All the hands employed are negroes – men + women – except the overseer who is white.

When reading of Whitney, the inventor of the cotton gin, I have many times desired to see the operation of one of these wonderful inventions and here unexpectedly the wish is gratified. The machines used in the factory here are of very simple construction. They are run by steam power and the work is performed by a roller around which is glued a leather strap running diagonally like a screw. As this revolves it pulls the cotton from the seed with great perfection. After witnessing the operations of the machines I went out on the beach and had a hunt. I found one big one about 20 little young ones and 50 nits. I gave my clothes to the wash woman and told her if there was one on them when she returned them I wouldent pay her a red. These are the first I have found on my clothes since I enlisted, but this is the result of living on board of transports. In the afternoon I took a stroll around town. Those who have been here for some length of time say that when they first came here it was one of the loveliest places they ever saw; Every yard was filled with flowers and every street shaded with beautiful trees. Orange trees are common and Lemon trees abundant. The walks were all nicely kept and every thing was loveliness, but now the fences are broken or destroyed entirely, the houses are torn and dilapidated, the flowers plants + fine shrubery are trodden down and they say it does not look like the same place. Still there are some beautiful residences here yet but there are no occupants for them except officers + niggers. You have seen orange + Lemon trees but they bear no comparison to those down here. I saw an orange tree to day that was as high as a 2 ½ or 3 story house and a large and beautiful tree it was I tell you. They are about as common here as peach trees in Cleveland. Some flowers are in blossom here now. This afternoon I picked a full blown Dandelion. It was a beauty in my eyes for it made me think of home. This is the place which when taken contained only 1 white man. Dont you recollect the papers spoke of him. Well I saw him this afternoon and bought some peanuts in his store. His name is

Allen. He is an elderly looking man of medium height, Greyish hair and wears spectacles. I have had quite a spree of it to day. It was quite a novelty for us to be in a town of any size. Beaufort formerly contained about 2000 inhabitants. Very many of the houses that were formerly occupied by the residents as dwellings are now turned into stores + shops.

I bought my dinner to day in a small eating house. It consisted of Pork Steak, Pancakes + coffee. It is the first <u>meal</u> *that I have had since I left home. There is a negro regiment here that was raised in this state. They went down the coast a few days ago in transports and had a fight. They say they fought well. As we came up the river yesterday we saw a small steamer that was captured from the rebels by a negro some time last summer. She was fitted out at Charleston and was built with especial referance to speed. The negro that captured her was employed with several others as one of the boat hands. One night when the officers were ashore the negro got up steam and run her out. The rebels fired on her from the forts and sent boats out after her but she was too quick for them and the negro run her safely into this harbor. She is lying at this place now. The negro who captured her has just been pointed out to me in a little sail boat which he owns himself and takes great pride in sailing round the harbor. He is only half black and is quite intelligent looking.*

There is a printing office at this place and they get off quite a respectable looking paper. One of the clerks gave me one of them and I will send it to you tomorrow to preserve until I return. Did you ever get that package of small sea shells that I sent home to you?

I think that I never told you that in the box that George Clark sent to Comstock when we left. There was a blanket, a pair of pant, a coat, a quilt, and one or two shirts that belonged to me. If you have not already received them you had better call on Mr. C. and inquire about them for they worth having.

Wednesday February 4th 1863 The boat was thoroughly cleaned and scrubbed yesterday in the absence of the troops and this afternoon they came aboard again feeling refreshed after their stay ashore. When I came to look for my newspaper this morning to send home I found it gone. Someone stole it out of my portfolio where I put it when I had finished writing last evening. I bought another one this afternoon and sent it to you along with another old secession sheet which I found on board of the boat. I wish you would keep them both and be careful with them. The day has been quite chilly. This is the coldest and most disagreeable season of the year in this latitude.

Thursday February 5/63 Cold + Rainey We moved down the river this morning towards Hilton Head and about 3 miles from it to what is called Helena Island. It is expected that we will land here and remain about 15 days. It is rumored that the Gunboats are out of ammunition and as we can do nothing without them, we have got to wait here until they can obtain it from the northern depots.

Friday Feby. 6/63 Very Cold.   We are still laying where we anchored yesterday and still no signs of landing. Some body stole my Haversack from the cabin last night. It contained my Pocket Knife, fork + spoon combined, about a pound of butter, a bag of coffee, my brandy + a little bitters. I was very sorry but it cannot avail to find the thief.

Saturday Feby 7th 1863 The weather is still cold. George S. Marlin a member of the 104th Pa. Vols. died in the Cabin last night. He had what is called the ship fever. This afternoon they took his body and carried it to Hilton Head (3 miles from where the [   ] lies) and buried it on shore. I went down to Stilton on the boat that carried the body and went all over fort Walker. It is a small fort and was originally built by the Rebs, but it mounts a great many guns and commands both the harbor and the country in the rear. It is an Earthwork with wooden stockades outside the breastwork pointed at the top. Some of the old rebel guns are still mounted on the fort. They are known by their having either the English coat of arms or the Palmetto Tree cast in the butt of the gun. There is another fort of about the same size on the other side of the harbor which was formerly called "Fort Beauregard". While I was at the Head the gunners were firing at a target out in the mouth of the harbor. They aimed with great accuracy and if the target had been a vessel she would have been completely riddled with shot by the time the practice was finished.

Sunday Feb'y 8th 1863 This morning I read 8 or 10 chapters in my dear little testament and in the evening I employed my time in thinking of my parents + relatives at the fireside at home.

Monday Feby. 9ᵗʰ 1863   I went to Hilton head this morning in a small row boat to draw rations for the Brigade + the Ambulance Corps. After I had got the rations and had them loaded on a cart and hauled on the dock I found the small boat just starting off and the four rowers in it. It seems they got a chance to be tugged up by a steamer + so they thought they would not wait for me and the rations. Well when I found the boat was gone and no chances of its coming back again I turned the cart around on the dock and took the rations back to where I got them. In turning around the dock was narrow and I spilt two boxes of Hard bread in the river, then I had to go to work and get a boat and skull it out into the river against the tide all alone and pick up the boxes of bread which by the time I got to them were perfectly water soaked and heavy as lead but I managed to get them into the boat + hoisted them up onto the dock and put them on the cart and by the time I did that I was so fagged out that I could scarcely lift 10 pounds. I thought I should have to stay at the head all night without a blanket or overcoat or a single red cent in my pocket. But as luck seemed to turn, about dark the "Secor" came alongside the wharf and they told me she was going to the [   ]. So I got on board of her and at 10 o'clock I was landed.

Tuesday Feby 10/63 Went to Hilton Head again today and had the rations that I dun yesterday brought up on a schooner. The weather for the past two days has been warm and pleasant. The birds sing so sweetly in the warm mornings that it almost makes me love the sunny South to hear the joyful songs they warble from their little swelling throats.

Wednesday Feby 11/63 The troops were landed this day from the different boats and are encamped on this Island where I am now writing namely St. Helena Island S.C. I have been working pretty hard all the day getting thing ashore from there and looking to other matters for the Quartermaster.

Thursday Feby 12/63 This afternoon we were busy issueing out clothing to the different regiments in our Brigade. There are no springs on this Island and therefore each company has had to dig its own well. We have three at headquarters. The soil is dry and sandy and very easy digging. We reach water at the depth of 6 or 10 feet from the surface. We cannot dig them any deeper than that for at that depth we reach a quicksand which caves in as fast as we can dig it. As soon as we reach water we sink a cracker box or a barrel and that completes our well. The water of course is nothing but surface water but it is good enough for a soldier I suppose.

Friday Feby 13/63 The weather is still warm and at times even sultry. The nights are cool and are always accompanied by heavy dews which has given many of us a severe cold in the head. I had a sore throte the other morning but it worked off during the day. The first night the troop landed on this Island they burned up a negro settlement. It seems one of the negroes shot a soldier of the 9th New Jerseys which so exasperated some of the members of the regiment that they burned up every negro house they could find, furniture and all. The negroes put on a good many airs since they have raised a regiment in the part of the country and they had made their brags that they had cooled down and scared our regiment of white soldiers who landed on this Island and they thought they could do the same to these troops, but how vain are all the calculations + expectations of ambitious man as the smoking ruins of their once loved homes will now bear witness.

Saturday Feby 14/63 The day has been dismal and rainey since 12 or 1 oclock. I started with a squad of men to go to Hilton Head to draw some more clothing for the regiments but it came on so stormy and foggy that the boat did not land us we had to come back without it.

Sunday Feby 15th 1863 Another Lovely Sabbath greets the soldier at his camp on <u>Land</u> and right glad are we to be allowed to spend it in our camp instead of being on the water put up in a foul unhealthy ship. This Sabbath is a doubly dear one for we have heard from – <u>Home</u> for the first time since Christmas. The Adams Express Steamer arrived yesterday and brought with her our old mail that has been on the way so long. It was sent from the boat up to Camp as soon as she landed and when I got back from H. Head I went over to the regiment and got all my letters and papers from G. Stoddard who had drawn them for me. I rec'd 5 letters from home, 1 from Aunt Eliza + 1 from Lottie L. McLain. The last letter from home was mailed on the 19th of January so I have not rec'd any late news. The Letters were numbered as follows 1-No. 26 1-No. 27 2 – No. 28 1 – No. 29.   I am surprised to hear that [   ] have got Father charged with 5 or 6 dollars. I think if they look on their books again they will find a number *of credits in father's favor that will equal or more than equal the debits. He had better speak to them about it again and ask them to let him see the account. I know they will do just what is right in the matter if he will only convince them in a quiet manner of their mistake and show them where they are wrong. If I was only there I could settle it in no time. That wash dish belongs to Geo. Clark but he says you can have it to remember him by only try and keep it until he returns. I left mine at the point when we came away; there was no room in the box to send it home. We are no longer in Genl Peck's Division so you need not put that on my letters. Direct to E.L. Cook Co "H" 100th Regt. N.Y.S.V. Washington – D.C. 2^d Brigade Naglee's Division or the last may be abbreviated as follows – 2^d Brig. Naglee's Div.*

I was reading letters from 4 until 8 oclock last evening and I have not yet had time to read any of my papers. I must try and answer Aunt Eliza's letter to day if possible. She say she has written to me and sent several papers but I have not rec'd any of them.

I am going to send you, in an Envelope a small paper that is printed at Hilton Head and some cotton that I took from the "Gin" at Beaufort S.C. and a sprig of palmetto with the edges cut off, and a map of Morehead City and one or two other things that I wish you to keep for me. Tell Mary that I am very much obliged to her for the present of that pipe and tobacco. The "bacca" is all gone but we expect the paymaster here in a few days and then I will get a fresh supply and try and send you some money to boot. We can buy butter here for 35 cents per pound and apples for 2 ½ cents each – 2 for 5 cents.

That young man that was shot is getting along finely and is now with the company I believe doing light duty. I read aloud the sentence in your last letter where you say that you do not see how we manage to keep warm. Why as I am now writing I am almost sweltering and every one is complaining of the heat. Both ends of the tent are thrown open to afford a draft and still I am perspiring with the heat. Only think what it will be in July and August. I am sorry that Father + Gracie have been sick. How are times at home? I will send you some money as soon as I get paid. I am entirely out of money and have borrowed some besides to buy a little butter with. I have spent less money than either of the Georges since I left home. I can not give you much of a description of this Island as I have not been around any as yet. Hilton Head is quite a business place. It was formerly a kind of a watering place with 2 or 3 large hotels and a few small dwellings. It is now all military. Some of the government store houses for Commissary stores are 500 or 600 feet long. There are any quantity of cannon there ready for shipment where ever they are needed. They have got a horse railroad running on the dock and into all the store houses by means of which they discharge the cargos of the different vessels that arrive at the dock, loaded with government stores. I noticed many of the stores or Sutter shops are built in such a manner that they can be taken apart + moved or transported to any other part of the country. They are patented and are called "Patent adjustable houses". They are made in Baltimore I think and brought down here + sold. They can be taken all to pieces like a play thing in 15 or 20 minutes and set up again in a very short time. They have doors, glass windows, steps, rafters, floor + every thing complete.

As regards this expedition I think it is so far a failure. I do not think that it was the intention of our General to have us land here but go right on to our place of destination + do quickly whatever we were designed to do.

But there was some difficulty arose between Genl Foster + Genl Hunter as to who should command and now Foster has gone back to Newbern or to Washington and we are going to stay here about a month until things are settled one way or another.

By that time the Rebs will know where we are going and be prepared for us and beat us as usual. I know we are not going to stay here long for the vessels that brought us down here are still at anchor in the harbor and another reason is that Genl Naglee will not let the officers draw any large tents for he says they have no means to transport them. I am in first rate quarters. We have a large hospital tent for an office and an "A" tent for 2 of us two sleep in. The other 2 clerks sleep in the office. I have a nice soft + warm bed of Hay.

> Good Bye   Write soon
> Your Aff. Son
> Edward L. Cook

Letter from A. Lyth to his Father and Mother

St Helena Island S.C.
Feb 12 1863

Dear Father + Mother
    We landed day before yesterday at this place which is about three or four miles from Hilton Head it is bounded on two sides by the harbor and on the other two by the river. It is a very pleasent place there are some large plantations on it. When we landed here it was so hot that the sweat poured down off from us in fact it is the month of July here. When we reached our camping ground we all had to strip and go in our shirt sleeves to pitch our tents and then we had enough to do. but towards night it was very pleasent. We are encamped on a small plantation I should say it is about as large as the lot where the race course is. Upon at the north end of the plantation is the negro huts or houses worked the plantation before the war broke out. Just as we had got our tent pitched some boys from another Regt. told us that one of their boys had been shot at by the niggers and that they were very sasy to the soldiers the story got in circulation amongst all the soldiers in this vicinity and it was not very long before there was a lot assembled around the negro shantys then they commenced and went in and took every thing that took their fancy. They took all the chickens + pigs they could lay hold on and opened the sweet potatoes pies which were very numerous and took all the sweet potatoes they wanted. I got a good mess of them. Then the negro fled as the soldier commenced to tear down the out houses for lumber for to lay floors to our tents Some of the negros were well suplied with both household furniture as well as clothing in some of their houses I saw some of as fine linen as ever I saw. In one of the out houses there was a sail boat and two or three pots of paint. one of the boys took the pot of white paint and painted the boat all over with it another took and painted the name 'Gen Hunter' on the stern with red. Then they painted it 2 or three colors then a croud got hold of the boat and took it down to the water and lanched her. At night not being satisfied with what was already done the shantys was set fire to which illuminated the whole plantation Just as some of the men were about setting fire to one of the buildings I steped in to it and saw a loft were the boys had not noticed before I jumped into it and they handed me a candle there was a good many articles stowed away. different

things that must have blonged to the Rebels when they had possesion of this place. Then there was a bag in which there was 3 nice shoulders an 3 nice hams I pitched down the shoulders to the boys and 2 of the hams retaining a good ham for myself we have had some of it cooked and it is as splendid ham as ever I tasted. I got a good wash tub which I found very usefull the next day for washing in Yesterday morning we took our wash tub our clean clothes a couple of camp kettles and material for making a fire and went to a spring which is near our camp. I fill our wash tub with cold water and striped naked and had a good wash so did Tom Then we changed our clothes and washed the ones we took off and had a regular washing day of it. Our Regt. is very healthey as for myself I never enjoyed better health in my life and I hope you are all doing the same at home. As for the war you will know better than myself how it is progressing but it seams to be going in favor of our cause. I guess you have heard of the prize that our gun boats captured off Charleston I saw it coming in as they fetched it into this harbor. I can not tell how long we shall stay here but it is supposed we shall stay long enough to receive our mail I hope so as I should like to hear from you again. I think we will get paid this week but weather we get 4 months pay or 2 months I cannot tell some think we shall only get 2 month as the pay master has not got our pay rolls for the last mustering he having left Washington befor our pay rolls were sent in. If you write a letter and direct it to hilton head S.C. so that I may have a chance of getting a letter before the regular mail would come from Washington

I have sent John this ring and I expect he will send me one for a keepsake I should like a good pocket hankercheif when you send my box Give my love to Sarah Ann and William and all the neighbors.

From Your Affect Son
Alfred

P.S. I forgot to mention before that we can hear the bull frogs every night Just the same as we do to home in the summer evenings The niggers here say that there is alligatoes about here in the summer time

Letter from A. Lyth to his Father and Mother

Feb 17. 1863
St Helena Island South Carolina

Dear Father + Mother
I received your kind letter of the 30th of Jan containing a few pins and some thread and was very glad to hear that you were all well and in good spirits. You say that [   ] about our provisions. the reason is that we have no reason to do so. Of course something we have to put up with little inconvenient which of course cannot be helped. For instance the second night that we were on this Island we had to do without our cup of coffee as the commisary had run out there being a certain number of days rations put aboard of the and some of the men having taken it without premission. They forgot their patriotism and called Uncle Sam and all the officers all the hard names they could think off. So to the quality of our provisions of course we cannot expect such daintys as we get to home but we get good solid food. We have excellent hard tack which is the most common name our crackers go under. They are not like some that I have seen full of little black bugs and maggots but they are fresh ones and very good ones. Then we draw salt pork raw so that we may fry it whenever we take a fancy Then we have salt horse or beef boiled every other day Then every day to dinner we have boiled beans in the shape of soup or rice and some potatoes we had boiled potatoes and beef to dinner to day. Then we had some oyster soup which Tom Maharg made he having bought a pint of oysters. Of course when we are on the march we do not have all these as the cook do not have any more time than to cook our coffee for us. Then it is that we need a little cash to buy things. We are about giving up hopes of being paid they are so long of coming around. You need not send me a box as yet for we cannot tell how soon we shall leave here. Tell mother I gave the box and old Jars to some of the soldiers that were left to garrison the point only keeping one of the fruit Jars to carry some butter in which we had left and that I traded at Carolina City for sweet potatoes. I had forgot to ask you in my other letters weather that boy had left that powder horn that I sent John for a Christmas present. Tom Maharg's father said in one of his letters that he had been to their house And that he had told them that Tom had been home sick. Now neither Tom nor I have had one days sickness since we came to the Regt

except that one day I had a touch of the ague and we are both always in good spirits Our Regt has always been in good health take as a whole The old members say it never was a healthy as it has been these last six months there has only been about 4 deaths in the whole Regt since I Joined it. Now if you ever see that young lieing theiving monkey I wish you would ask him for that horn I sent. It belonged to some sesesher of Gloucester I must close with my love to you all give my love to Sarah Ann + William.

From your affect Son Alfred

P.S. write soon

Letter from A. Lyth to his Father and Mother

St Helena Island S.C. Feb 19. 1863

Dear Father + Mother

   Having nothing else to do at present I take the oppertunity to write you a few lines hoping they will find you all well as it leaves me at present. To day it is very warm. we were on a General Review this morning The Review not coming off yesterday morning as I stated in my letter of day before yesterday on account of a little rain storm that passed over here at that time. We fell into line at nine oclock and marched about a mile and a half from our camp to a large cleering it being the nearest place large enough for the occasion. I tell you it is a fine sight to see a lot of soldiers on a Review The field that we were Reviewed in is bordered by little clumps of bushes all round which look at from a distance they looked as if niggier heads grew on them and when you get a little nearer they looked like a target painted black with a white spot in the center as they were all grining their teeth at us All the time we were on Review and at present we can hear very heavy cannonadeing it is supposed that our gunboats are giving the rebels old harry in some place. likely you will know by the time this reaches you what it all means. I guess you will have heard before this about the taking fort Mcallister on the Savanna river and the capture of the Rebel gun boat in that vicinity and if you can scare up the paper with the account of the capture I wish you would send it I should like you to send me a daily every now + then Fort Mcallister is not a very great distance from here we heard the cannonadeing very distinct when it was taken and when the news of the capture came here the first Brigade station on this Island and encamped next to our Brigade were put under marching orders and they left the same night about 12 oclock and were gone away 24 hours when they returned and encamped as usul. We cannot get a chance to talk with any of them as we are not allowed to leave our own camp on account of the Robberies being purtrated by some scamps belonging to the different Regts encamped here To day Tom Maharg bought 3 oranges of some nigger pedlers which grew some 2 miles from camp they say there is a great many oranges grows on this Island, those that Tom bought were very good but sour.

I wonder if you know how it is that Captain Hinson came to get his discharge if you have not it is worth while telling you. Having left his seat in the cars on his route to Washington a short time when the train had stoped at a station on his returning he found his seat occupied by gentleman in citizens dress whom he commenced to abuse shamefully and curse and swear at him in a most beastly manner. When whom should this gentleman turn out to be but Major Gen Couch who on arriving at Washington kindly procured the brave Capt his discharge Billy said in his letter that it was freezing very hard. We never have any frost down here Well the other night after roll call which is at 8 oclock I went to the spring and got a wash tub half full of water and set it in our company street in front of our tent and striped naked and Tom and I and Mr Murry who is tenting with us jumped in the tub and had a good wash and then went to bed so you may know what kind of weather we have here. I must conclude with my love to you dear Father + Mother and give my best respects to Mr. Barnum and tell him if he like hooking fence rails he had better enlist for a soldier for he can have all he wants to hook No more at present.

From Your Affect Son
Alfred

Write soon

Letter from A. Lyth to his Brother

Camp of the 100th Regt N.Y.S. Vol.
St Helena Island March 3 1863

Dear Brother

On Sunday we received quite a large amount of mail from Washington there was nothing for me from home but there was two very neat valentines. I cannot tell who sent them as I do not know the handwriting. I wish you would please tell me who sent them for I am sure you know and there is no use keeping me in the dark about them. Last Saturday a couple of the boys and myself were out in the woods on an exploring expeidition on our own account we me some of the crew of the New England They told us that they} were making preparations for sailing and it was supposed they would be ready in 8 or 10 days from that time. There was a detail to assist in putting rations aboard of some of the steamers. They said as far as they could learn that our destination would be Charleston. The gunboats and the 7 monitors are getting ready for the attack of the forts in Charleston harbor and Savanna also. On our ramble through the woods we came across a great many wild flowers in full bloom and there are any amount of wild orange + plumb trees the plumb trees are covered with blooms and the peach trees on a plantation that we were on were in full blom There are any quantity of birds of every description and plenty of bull frogs + snakes oft when we are out drilling we get come across snakes on our drill ground. Those men that charged upon the wiskey on board of the boat have been court Martialed and all but five have received their sentance. They received their sentance according to the charges proved against them some of the charges prefered against some of them was unsoldierly conduct preditual to good order and for forming in mutiny on board of the Steamship New England and also for trying to strike their superior officer and one had the additional charge of having tried to shoot Lt. Col. C.N. Otis at Carolina City and trying to run a bayonet into him. I forget weather I ever mentioned the accurance to you before however it did happen the mans name is John Riley. he having got some wiskey into him he was making a disturbance in camp when the Lean Col came and had him arrested and taken to the guard house when he got to the guard house he grabed a loaded musket run apeice from the guards and aimed at the Lt. Col and pulled the trigger but of course the gun did not go off it not being loaded} Then he made a rush at him with the bayonet but of coures he was secured before he could do any harm his sentance is that he shall searve out the term of his enlistment on any government fort or Work as they see fit to put him at and to wear a ball and chain attached to his right leg. the ball to weigh 2{unknown number} pounds and the chain to be six feet long one week in each and every month commenceing the first day of every month and to be dishonorable discharged when the time expires one of the others sentance was nearly the same some have got a year and the ball + chain 1 week in every month some have got six months and the ball + chain 2 weeks in every month and they all forfeit all pay due to them from the Government The one that belongs to our company that was in the mess they cannot do anything with as he is not sworn into the service having left Buffalo some time after we left of his own accord to join the Regt Not having taken a cent of Bounty money or received a cent of pay from the government Capt Dye has resigned they say and is a going to come home on account of his health When you write direct as usal to hilton head if you do not hear of our Regt leaving through the newspapers. I should like you to send me a newspaper once in a while John I wish you would tell the folks to any one of their likeness taken and send it to me as I should like to have some of your likenesses My Love to you all and Sarah Ann + William also.

Your Affect Brother
Alfred
write soon

Letter from E. Cook to his Parents

Quartermaster Department
Headquarters 2ᵈ Brig. Naglee's Div.
St. Helena Island Feby 22/63

My dear Parents
    Monday Feby 16ᵗʰ 1863 Went to Hilton Head to draw some clothing from there to the troops on this Island. Could not get the papers certified to and had to return minus the clothing. Brought back with me a large mail for the 100ᵗʰ Regt. among which was 2 letters and several papers for

myself. One of the letters was from Mary and one from you. I answered Mary's 2 or 3 days ago.

Tuesday Feby 17-63 The Lieut. went to Hilton Head again today to draw the clothing which he + I were after yesterday. He did not return tonight and I guess he has not been able to get it. I wrote to Aunt Eliza today.

Wednesday Feby 18/63 Rainey in Morning. The Lieut ret'd to camp this afternoon he has got the clothing and sent me down to the Head to get it shipped to this Island. I wrote to Mary this morning. In the afternoon I went down to Hilton Head agreeable to the Lieut's order to get the clothing sent up. I could not get a boat to carry it up this afternoon so I had to remain all night. There is so much animosity between the commander of our expedition and Genl Hunter who comds. the troops in this dept. that it is hard work to get him/Hunter to give the soldiers their necessary clothing + rations.

Thursday Feby 19-63 I slept last evening in a cot at the "Port Royal House". I had a good soft bed and a pillow to lie my head on but I could not sleep much. I have got so used to lying out doors and in a tent that it does not seem like home to sleep in a house. When I was on the transport I caught cold the first or second night that I slept in the cabin and I did not get rid of it entirely until I got on shore but I had not been here more than 4 or 5 days before all traces of it had left me.

I almost think that if I ever get safely to "B" again that I will be surprising you by ordering my bed made in the wood pile or on the housetop where I can get the air and keep from catching cold. I paid 25 cents for my bed last night before I laid my head on it and in the A.M. I wished I had it back again to buy my breakfast with for I felt a little hungry having had nothing to eat since yesterday noon. About nine oclock, as I was waiting on the wharf for the boat to come up and take my good on board, I saw a couple of hardtacks lying on the dirty ground which I eagerly snatched up and commenced to devour when a negro exclaimed "[   ]!" I knew what he meant but I walked hurridly on and had the tacks used up before the poor nigger could recover from the surprise which my refusal to obey his order had occasioned. After a while when the boat got ready (and she waited until she did get a <u>*good*</u> *ready) she came alongside the pier nose end*

138

foremost and after they had put fifty horses on board of her I managed to get the boxes of clothing +c put onto her and off we started for the Island of St. Helena where we arrived just about dinner time and the first thing I did was to take a horse and ride up to camp and eat my supper for last night which consisted of "Baked Beans"; and my breakfast for this morning which consisted of Baked Beans + the two hard tacks I stole from the nigger; and my dinner for this noon which I think consisted of Baked Beans. These 3 meals being finished I again jumped onto my horse and started for the pier and arrived there just as the boat had managed to get into a good place where she could land the horses conveniently and with safety. I helped get the boxes on shore and load them in the wagon. There were 3 army wagon loads of them (13 large boxes) Well we got them to camp and before night we had them all distributed except a very few articles to the 100th Regt. That was considerable of a number of incidents for one day. Perhaps you dont believe all the minor technicalities but I gave you the "facts" and leave you to draw your own conclusions as Dave White tells me when he think I am inclined to join myself to the doubting persuasion.

Friday Feby 20th 1863 They are holding a court martial in our officer tent for the trial of those prisoners engaged in the mutiny of board the Steamer New England while at Beaufort Harbor N.C. It will go pretty hard with some of them. I know that one is to receive 6 months hard labor on the rip raps with hard tack and water for his victuals + drink and his pays to be kept back. Some of the poor fellows I think will have to serve out the balance of their time at the same place and on the same fare. We finished issueing the balance of our clothing this morning. The Lieut. says that this Department is the hardest place to get clothing that he ever knew. It will be just a week tomorrow that he first made a requisition for the articles which reached only yesterday.

The delay of course is caused by the personal animosity that is felt between the leading officers Genl Hunter does not relish the idea of giving clothing and food to Genl [   ] men although we have no other means of feeding and clothing the soldiers. Hunter has just issued an order forbidding any of his quartermasters or officers issueing any more clothing or ration to our men or food for our horses and mules. This is a very bad aspect of affairs but I am in hopes that it will not last long.

Saturday Feby 21st *1863 I will say for the especial benefit of Eliza that Dave White has been appointed Corporal and a day or two ago he was detailed from his company and regiment to do provost guard duty. If he knew I was writing home he would certainly send his love to Eliza but as he does not know it and I have no way of informing him she must of necessity overlook his absence and take the will for the deed. I will say for the benefit of Mother that the tin wash dish does not belong to me but to Geo Clark and he says mother may have it on conditions that she keeps it until he returns, to remember him by while he is absent.*

Sunday Feby 22^{d} *1863 Washingtons Birth day anniversary. Raining in the morning, very pleasant in the afternoon. The Shipping have all their flags floating in the air and all their signals flying in the breeze in honor of this great day in our nations history. I hope the next anniversary of this day may find me witnessing the celebration of it in the beautiful street of my own loved home but I am very much afraid my hope will not be realized for I do not think this war will find an end in one year. I am glad to see the government changing its plans and tactics. I am in hopes that they are tired of finding their efforts their money and the precious lives of the poor soldiers in the vain attempt to take the Godforsaken city of Richmond. I hope the scene of war now is to be removed from the unlucky state of Virginia and shifted to the South + West where our arms have always been successful and where we may yet hope to meet and conquer our traitorous enemy. I believe the only true way to end this war successfully for ourselves and in the short speedy and lasting manner to attack, take + keep all the seaport towns and then move up from all points and cut off the enemies supplies and he will be obliged to yield. I think it is useless to try + take Richmond for even if we take it from the North the loss of life in the struggle will never be repay'd by the good we will gain or the advantage we will derive from the victory. If we take Richmond the enemy have command of the railroads to Petersberg and can speedily transfer all their men + stores to that place and fortify it fully as strong as Richmond or Fredericksburg now is. This is their policy in this war and the only way in which they can hold their own and if our government keeps on in the blind course which they seem to have been persevering for the last year and a half I am fearful that it will prove most ruinous to our cause and fatal to our success. I cannot send a very long letter as I hear the boat is going tomorrow and I must post this in*

the mail bag tonight so Good night give love to Grandma and all the folks
+ write soon

P.S. *Green Pea vines are up about 4 inches!*

Letter from E. Cook to his Parents

*Headquarters 2ᵈ Brig. Naglee's division
St. Helena Island Monday Feby 23/63*

My dear Parents

I am going to commence another letter to you so as to have it ready
whenever there is a mail leaves this place for the month. I took a little walk
down the road this morning and had a little visit with Uncle David. He
is getting a little better but is still excused from drill and all heavy duty.
He went over to the 100ᵗʰ Regt the other day and had a visit with the two
Georges. He had heard from his wife and knew that Sammy had gone
home. Aunt Harriet told him that Sammy was home sick and so she went
to "B" and took him home.

Tuesday Feby 24ᵗʰ 1863 Weather just warm enough to be pleasant and cool
enough to be comfortable. 'Lovely' is the word that best describes it. There
was a grand review this morning of all the troops on this Island by Genl
Hunter. The parade was formed on a plantation about a mile to the rear of
the camps. There were 5 Brigades of 18 regiments – over 10,000 men. It
took upward of 2 hours for the troops to pass the colors or stand point of the
General. I was up in a large tree and had a good view of all of the troops in
the field. I saw Genl Hunter, Genl Seymour, Genl Terry, Gen Naglee (our
present commander) + some others who I do not recollect. Seymour + Terry
are on Hunters Staff. I do not like the military appearance of Gen Hunter.
When he shuts his mouth, turns his head to one side and cocks up his eye to
squint under one corner of his old French military hat, he reminds me for
all the world of [   ]. He is bald on the top of his head and as he is quite
an elderly man and has jet black hair I am inclined to think that he is vain
enough to use hair dye.

The two Generals on his staff are both very insignificant looking men.
Our general Naglee, who commands the troop on this island and who is only
a Brigadier, is by far the most military + intelligent looking general that I

have yet seen. He is about 45 years of age. His hair is sprinkled with gray and adds to his noble appearance. He is a small man and lightly built but has an iron frame. His eye is narrow and long and never at rest; its color is jet black and being sunken a little under the eye brows it gives him a very penetrating look. I think he knows more than Hunter could ever learn. He is loved by all of the soldiers although he never speaks to one of them, and it is very seldom that he ever addresses a remark to an officer of the Line. I never saw him laugh and only once have I ever seen a <u>large</u> *smile on his countenance and then I was so surprised that I have not yet forgotten it. I should hate to be led into battle by Genl Hunter for I have no confidence in his ability but under Genl Naglee I should feel perfectly secure on that point. He is a general who will not send where* <u>he</u> *dare not go.*

Friday Feby 27<u>th</u> 1863 I was out in the woods this morning with a team and got a load of pine boughs + laid them down in our office to keep the dust from rising. They make a splendid floor and carpet, and keep our papers clean.

Saturday Feby 28<u>th</u> 1863 I have been down to Hilton Head all this day with the quartermaster drawing clothing for the different regiments of this brigade. We had 25 large boxes and 9 nine bales. It was about eight o'clock when we returned.

Sunday March 1<u>st</u> 1863 This morning early I went down to the dock with a squad of men to take our clothing off the boat and load the teams to haul it up to our office. It was 10 oclock when we got the things all up to camp and commenced issueing. And about 4 oclock when we had got all through, and I had just washed myself and put on my uniform, the mail came in and I rec'd your letter No 31 and one from Mr. Lyman and a lot of newspapers.

Tell Mary that Fannie has written to me. I am as glad as 5 dollars that you have rec'd the little sea shells I sent you. Tell Mr. Lyman I will answer his letter in a day or two. This is the first Sabbath that I have had any work to do since I have been in this department, and we would not have issued this lot if it were not for the fact that we expect to move every day and it is necessary the soldiers should have their clothes before they go. We have received the news that the rebel boat Nashville has been destroyed by one of our Monitors (the "Montauk") They say the first shot that the "Montauk" fired was a 15 inch shell and went right through the "Nashville" and exploded inside. I think we are going into battle in a few days. I believe the scene will be James Island near Charleston S.C. and the prospects are that it will be a very bloody battle. If we take the Island then the city of Charleston will soon be in our possession. I hear that the mail is going out tomorrow so I will not have time to write a long letter.

Monday March 2ᵈ 1863 I built a bunk in my sleeping tent this morning and laid a floor in front of the bunk so that I now have tip top quarters and good times.

The report that the "Nashville" is destroyed is confirmed to day I will try and write again before we leave the island. There is a report current that our gunboats are [ ] away at Savannah today. I wonder if it is true.

The mail is ready so I must close. Write to me very soon and give my love to Grandma and all the rest. The boys are both well. We have now 4 if not 5 Monitors in these waters at present. They are going with us when we go.

Good Bye Your Aff. Son Edward L. Cook

100ᵗʰ Regt Co. H.
Direct to Washington D.C.
2ᵈ Brig. Naglees Div.

Letter from E. Cook to his Parents

St. Helena Island S.C.

Monday Feby 23ᵈ 1863 I do not feel in a writing mood to day but I must not lett my letter writing behind. I saw uncle David this morning and had a little talk with him about different matters + things.

The movement of armies works about some strange occurances. Who ever thought that in this war Uncle David + I would be encamped within 10 minutes walk of each other when our homes are a whole days journey from one anothers but so it is and any time when I feel so inclined I just take a hop, skip + a jump and light right down in his tent.

I think I am bewitched today. Here I have been copying from my Diary of Feby 23ᵈ when my last letter closed my journal up to March 3ᵈ so I must begin again.

Tuesday March 3/63 Weather cold

Wednesday 4/63 Very cold I reckon the new congress meets today. We soldiers are building great air castles on the expected doings of the new democratic congress. Some are expecting congress to order home the troops, some expect the declaration of a dishonorable peace and may expect an armistice during which time we can have a furlough to go home, but I expect things to go on as they have heretofore slowly and ineffectually.

Thursday March 5/63 Read letter No 32 from Eliza. We rec'd news to day that our favorite commander Genl. Naglee had been relieved from his command by order of Genl Hunter. I have considered Genl. Naglee the moving spirit in this expedition and now that he has gone I am afraid that it will be some time before we make a move towards the completion of the design for which this expedition was fitted out. Each day of delay adds strength to the enemy and weakens our forces in more ways than one. I trust my suspicions are not true but I am fearful that our next engagement will be a Fredericksburg repeated. There is not the least news as to when we are going to move. The quartermasters commenced to put rations aboard of their respective boats last week but their operations were suspected at the close of the first days week and now we are in a quandary. Some think we are going to return to Newbern, others believe that we are to remain here during the summer and some few think that we are going to make a move upon Charleston or Savannah, and upon taking either of the places remain and do garrison duty until the opening of another Campaign. Of course none of us know certainly what is going to take place but nearly all think that the removal of Genl Naglee will very seriously affect the design of the expedition and perhaps quash it entirely.

Friday March 6/63 Pleasant I wrote to Mr. Lyman this afternoon. I presume that you will receive the letter several days before this reaches you. If you should see any letters from the 100ᵗʰ in any of the newspapers I wish you would send either me the paper or else cut the piece out and send it in a letter.

Saturday March 7/63 Pleasant I went down to Hilton Head to day to draw new blouses for the 100ᵗʰ Regt but could not get them. It seems as if the officers could not provide clothing enough onto the men. Nearly every man in the Regt now has a dress coat + fatigue jacket and when he receives the blouse he will have to throw his Jacket for he cannot carry all of them.

   I saw a man on the dock to day dressed in diving armor. He was a hideous looking object with the great Copper helmet over his head with 3 little windows in it. I was almost afraid of him. He went into the river and under a boat to find a leak that was fast filling her with water. There are 6 monitors in the river about a mile from our camp. I passed by them in the boat to day I saw the Montauk that blew up the Rebel boat Nashville One of them has a lot of cannonball holes through her smoke pipe. They are all in here to coal up. This looks a little like doing something

Sunday March 8ᵗʰ 1863 Pleasant day but for some reason or other I had the blues the very worst kind. I tried to write to you 2 or 3 times but I had to leave off often having blundered one page and made the mistake which you see on the first page of this letter. Genl. Naglee leaves for the North tomorrow. He has appointed a meeting with all the officers at 10 oclock am to bid them farewell. Very many of the soldiers + officers in his old brigade are in hopes that the war Dept will give him another command in the Western part of Virginia and if such a thing takes place they are in hope that he will reclaim his old brigade and get an order to have it moved to where he is and placed under his command.

Monday March 9ᵗʰ 1863 Rained a very little in the morning but soon cleared off and was pleasant the remainder of the day. I went over to our transport to see about getting off some ammunition While I was there the boat crew rec'd a mail so I guess we will receive our by tomorrow. However I will not delay this letter but if receive a letter from you I will soon let you know about it. It was worth 5 dollars to me to hear that you had rec'd all of my letters so far and among the others, the one containing the little shells some of which were really beautiful, and I wished you to get them principally because they would serve as a memoir of our short sojourn in North Carolina.

Next time you write please tell me what regiment Morris is in. I would not lend any more if I was in your place. As I returned to camp yesterday I met Uncle David he had recd a letter from Grandma written about the middle of February I believe. I saw the letter that Henry Stoddard wrote home It is strong secesh. I inclose some flowers and a description of transport life written by one of the 52^d Penn. boys. I gave D. White the respect that Eliza sent to him. He incloses his own description of himself – please preserve it for me. It is an Acrostic. The first letters of each when combined read as follows "To Miss Eliza G. Cook" I told him I would copy it off for him before I sent it but you can do it for him. Only preserve the original for me.

Give my love to Grandma and all the folks. Tell Aunt Grace the boys are well. The Regt. generally is quite free of sickness; I wish I could say the same of all the regiments on the Island.
Kiss little Gracie and remember me to Lillian + tell May to write when she has time. Hoping this will find you in as well as it leaves me. I remain your affectionate son.

Edward L. Cook

Letter from E. Cook to his Parents and Relatives

St. Helena Island S.C.

My dear Parents + Relatives – I have not rec'd a letter from you in a long time and I had made up my mind not to write to you again until I rec'd a letter from home but I find that I can not be so hard hearted for although it is very vexatious and provoking to have the mail brought into camp and see letters pass round to the other boys without receiving a single one my self, yet my natural feelings will not allow me to retaliate upon those who seemingly forget me. There have been some 3 or 4 mails brought to our camp within the past 2 or 3 weeks, but neither letter or paper did I receive by any of them. However I presume that I am just as much thought of as before and must attribute this apparent neglect to household duties and *other unavoidable difficulties and obstacles that present themselves which are paramount to writing to "The boy that's gone for a sojer" and so I must overlook them and as I know you love to hear from me just as much as at any time heretofore I will withdraw my unfeeling resolution and send you another letter hoping thereby to set you a good example which I trust you will see fit to follow – So here goes!*

Tuesday March 10ᵗʰ 1863 The letter I sent you yesterday was number 35 but as forgot to date it you can put the number on yourself. All of your letters so far have come through straight and correctly but you are cheating yourself for I have 2 or 3 times rec'd 2 letters with the same number on them.

Wednesday March 11ᵗʰ 1863   Pleasant

Thursday March 12ᵗʰ 1862 Went to Hilton Head to draw stationary

Friday March 13ᵗʰ 1863 Windy and dusty. I thought by the appearance of the foliage and every thing that surrounds us that they never had any snow down this way but I am mistaken for today we had a tremendeous snow storm of sand. When the wind blows as it does to day it reminds me of a good old fashioned winter storm home when the wind whistles through the crevices and the snow come drifting in from every direction. The soil here is light and sandy and the March winds take it up in boat loads and drift over the country and out to Sea. The plantations after one of these strong winds present the facsimile of a snow field at the North. The ridges are leveled down + the furrows filled up until the whole surface is smooth and level as a frozen lake. When the roads are much traveled in dry weather, the ground instead of becoming hard and packed is cut up light + loose and when walking over it, the sensation is like walking in dry snow or flour. I never walk down the road to the boat landing without thinking of tromping through the snow at home.

Sat. March 14ᵗʰ 1863   Pleasant but warm

Sunday March 15ᵗʰ 1863 Very warm. I presume that it is nearly as hot here to day as you will have it in the month of June or July. This afternoon immediately after dinner one of my fellow clerks and myself took a horseback ride out into the country about 6 miles. This morning I attended a meeting at the 104th P. Vols. Two converts were babtized by sprinkling. Our Chaplain has not preached once since he came to us. I am growing chilly so I will give you a short description of my ride tomorrow. I am waiting anxiously for a letter from home

Now for a description of my ride. The day was very warm in fact most uncomfortably so and so we could not ride very fast for fear of injuring the horses so we took it slow and leisurely and had a better opportunity of viewing the country through which we rode. The road is much cut up and in many places is just like meal but in the spots, where the bridle path is diverged a very little from the main road, the riding is beautiful. Nearly the whole length of the road, over which we passed, is lined on both sides with shady trees and shrubbery and part of it passes through a pine forrest. In many places the branches of the trees join each other over head and form a screen from the sun at all hours of the day. It is delightful to ride through these natural arbors at any time and particularly so on a warm day like this. When about 4 or 5 miles from camp we came upon a country church + grave yard. There was one large vault and many tombs. Nearly all of the stones were inscribed with the name of the church and the same of the vaults. There are six families of this name in the immediate vicinity and all of them own large plantations. The church was used only for the worship of the "Whites" and its religious denomination was Methodist Episcopal. I learned all this from an old Negro slave who passed by just as we demounted. I asked him what religion he believed in and he said Methodist. He said he did not think the Episcopal church was religious like the Methodist. He thought it was a queer kind of Church, he did not quite understand it, he thought the minister in that church preached more about how to till the land and raise the crops and tell the planters how to make money. I think the poor nigger was not far from right. The side door of the church was opened so I entered and as I did so I instinctively took off my hat for I felt as though I was in the near presence of God and a strong spell seemed to pervade the little church. On the pulpit laid a large gilt edge bible and in the choir was a small organ. I went upstairs to see it and found it was opened and ready for the fingers of some skilled one to touch its pure white keys; but when I put my hand to the bellows handle I found it had been disconnected from the pipes and would omit no sound.

148

The gilt edge bible + organ are things that I did not expect to find in an out of the way place like this. I tore 2 feathers from a fan that I found in the church and I send them home as a memento of my ride. About a mile farther on the road we came upon another much larger but less picturesque looking church – Methodist – and devoted to the use of the slaves on the plantations. After passing a glance at the large brick church and its surrounding we paid a short visit to a small negro settlement. In many instances two families are crowded into a small house and every thing would look dirty and squallid. I think the slaves fared better when they were under their masters than they do at present when they have no one to look after them. There are any quantity of "<u>South</u> <u>Carolina</u> <u>Cabbage</u>" out a mile or two from camp. They do not grow more than 20 feet high and instead of having branches at the top as other trees do they have a kind of cabbage head of long pointed leaves that all grow out from the same trunk. This is the celebrated "Palmetto tree".

The residences of the planters instead of being along the side of the road the same as in our country are away back in the fields out of sight of the road. A person could ride for miles and not see a house but let him turn off at any of the little shady bridle paths that seem to lead nowhere in particular + right into the thickest part of the woods in general and if he continues to follow it for a short distance it will invariably lead him to the door of some planters house.

When we returned it was nearly dark and our horses were still in good spirits. I had a most pleasant ride and enjoyed it hugely. I think I shall take another stroll next Sunday if I can get a horse. Yesterday we had a feast. I forgot to tell you about it. What do you think it consisted of? Well I know you cannot guess so I will tell you. It was <u>milk</u> in our coffee at dinner. It was a luxury not dreamed of until we had sat down to the table and found the cup of milk placed thereon. I drank 4 or 5 cups of the coffee just for the sake of getting the milk and then only stopped because the supply of coffee did not hold out. This morning I listened to a sermon preached by the Chaplain of the 104th Penn. Vols. It was not very eloquent but was to the point and purpose. He urged upon the soldiers the necessity of being prepared at any moment to meet their maker. Two of the men were baptized previous to the sermon by sprinkling which shows that he labors with some effect.

Monday March 16th 1863 Went to Hilton Head with the quartermaster to draw some camp equipage.

Tuesday + Wednesday March 17 + 18 Pleasant

Thursday March 19th   Very cold at night so that we could not sleep comfortably

Friday March 20th Still cold and damp. This morning the Regt. rec'd orders to keep their knapsacks packed and hold themselves in readiness to march at a moments notice + in about an hour or less the boys were ready for a start. At sunset they rec'd the following order "Soldiers of the 100th your good name and discipline has at last reached the military authorities. You are to lead the <u>Advance</u> on <u>Charleston</u>.

Saturday March 21st 1863 The regiment has not gone yet. The day is very cold and rainey. We have a stove in our office tent which keeps us somewhat comfortable. I went over to the regiment this P.M. and found both the Georges in their bunks with their blankets tucked around them trying to keep warm. I am sorry for them and almost feel that I do wrong to remain away from the regiment. I should not be surprised if I went back to it on the first of next month. It is awful lonesome for me to be away from the boys. I have the blues to day; and not receiving any words from home does not improve my feelings a bit.

Sunday March 22d 1863 The weather is very warm again to day. The reg't is to leave at 4 oclock to day. They are going to embark for "Cole" Island near Charleston. There is a Rebel battery within two miles of where they are going to land. The mail leaves tomorrow so I must send this tonight. I have just heard that the 100th does not leave until tomorrow on account of it being low tide this P.M. and the boat cannot get to the dock to take them on board. One of the boys in our company named John was pretty severely injured this P.M. by having a stick run into his eye. He will probably lose the sight. He is now in our office tent + I have made him a good soft bed and he feels comfortable but his eye pains very badly. Good Bye Love to all, write soon Ever your affectionate Son

> *Edward L. Cook*
> *Co H; 100th N.Y.V.,*
> *Hilton Head SC*

Letter from A. Lyth to his Brother

Camp of the 100ᵗʰ Regt N.Y.S. Vol.
St Helena Island S.C. March 16 1863

Dear Brother

Having nothing else to occupy my time I thought I would write you these few lines hopeing they will find you in good health as it leaves me at present It is very warm weather here at present and I tell you it was pretty warm on drill this morning We have Brigade drill every morning now and are very likely to have it every morning for a week to come every time we come off from drill we have to take a good wash for after sweating the dust settles right into our skin so that if we don't wash right away it would be pretty hard to get the dirt off. Tom Maharg and I take a good wash all over every 4 or 5 days

The other day quite a lot of us boys went out a rabbit hunting there are quite a large amount of rabbits around here we all took a short club then we all would surround any likely place where we thought there were any rabbits Then one or two of the boys would run into the ring and scare up the rabbits an when they would try to run past us they were sure to get knocked over with a club and when there was a large field of long dry grass one would go to the windy side of it and set fire to the grass while the rest of us would string our selves on the oppisite side ready for the rabbits when they made their appearance we set a small woods afire in this way where the trees grew very thick + lushey then you should have seen the rabbits skeddadling from underneath the underbrush and the havock we made of them. Golly and you should have seen the field of grass and the bush on fire the flames flew up a mile high and the noise it made was like a continual roar of artillery and big guns There are Two Indians in our Regt both belonging to our company and they make bows + arrows and go hunting rabbits with us Our Col issued an order to have this Regt supplied with blouces well of course we all have to take one which makes us all have an overcoat dress coat blouse and Jacket or roundabout so we call them now since we have got these blouses which by the way are very comfortable things this summer time being very thin and light and the only thing that we can get to drill in with comfort we have no use for our Jackets and the first march we go on we will have to throw them away now pretty near every *man in the Regt has a new jacket that he drew at Gloucester Point now some grumble very much at having to draw these but I and a good many more do not care so much but there are a good many who have familys to home to support hence they do not want to be buying clothes all the time now those Jackets cost $5.50 and have to be cast away. I dont care it takes half of pay I am bound to have desent clothes and look respectable I have draw a dollar or two of my account already and I it will take 6 or 7 dollars to clothe me the rest of my year out.*

Mail's has come

Dear Brother John I just received your letter containing a few lines from Father an a dollar and a few lines from Will + five cents from fanny I was very glad to hear that you were all well. I never received the letter that you sent me informing me that you received the powder horn and I guess I have lost 2 letters since we left Gloucester Point. We have not got paid and I cannot tell when we will but we have hopes of getting it soon no more at present

From Your Affectionate Brother

Alfred

Letter from A. Lyth to his Father and Mother

On Board of the Steamer Expounder
off Hilton Head S.C. Mar 24 1863

Dear Father + Mother

I have just received a letter from you dated March 2 stating that there were 5 or 6 letters on the way one with a ring in one with a dollar I received one some time ago with a ring in and one with stamps in then I receive one about 7 or 8 days ago with a dollar from yourself and five cents from fanny Then I received alot of harpers weeklys altogether and some harpers and an express day before yesterday. On sunday last we got orders to strike tent and pack Knapsacks and get ready to go aboard of the boat we got everything in readyness and gave away our bunks and other things that we could not carry along with us when the order came to pitch tents again as we could not go aboard untill the next morning we pitched our tents again and slept under them untill morning when we got a board of the steamship Expounder + went over to Hilton Head where we went ashore for the purpose of exchanging our guns for new ones which we did

We gave in our Enfield and got the Austrian rifel they were made in this country although they are the Austrian style we do not like them so well as we did our old ones and I guess they are not as serviceable for from their appearance they look as if they had been got up in very cheap style. however they all being new guns they look pretty well we got aboard of the boat again and put out into the stream where we droped anchor. It is said that we shall put out early tomorrow morning. As far as I can learn we are going to Coal Island near Charleston. There are some gun boats going with us. You say you cannot see how all the negros should be punished for the wrong doings of a few. I and a good many more in the army are of the same opinion but there are a lot of the boys that hates the sight of the negros and they improve every opportunity they can get to abuse them It goes against them when orders are read that they are not allowed outside of the camp guard and the negros employed by the government are allowed to go where they please I have seen 2 or 3 of the Couriors articals about this Regt which they say they obtained from Soldiers letters from this Regt which speak of its spirit of demorilzation under its present Commander Col Dandy it is readily imagined where such sentiments come from no doubt from some unruly fellow who had been Court Martialed and five or ten dollars stoped off his pay. of course the officers some of them get drunk sometimes but they are put under arrest for it and have to suffer the consequences. one of the articals runs down our Col and does not senture Lt Col Otis or Major Nash but gives them praise now if our Col does ever happen to get too much he keeps in his tent which Col Otis + Maj Nash does not though Col Otis is the best hearted old man in the business and thinks a good deal of the boys and the boys think a good deal of him but Major Nash is the only officer in the Regt at the present who the most of the boys do not like he is a regular drunken bully who has been under arrest for a while back for getting drunk and pounding a couple of officers belonging to another Regt however enough of this now about the Chaplin the last mail we received but one there were 5 daily papers for George Barnum, when the mail was assorted at Brigade headquarters Ed Cook a fellow detailed from our Company for assisting in coping of orders and doing other writing saw these five papers for George and saw them put in the mail bag and sent over to the Regt for the Chaplin to assort out for the different Companies when the mail was distribeted Geo only got one paper. It turned out that the Chaplin had retained them to read. he made the excuse that some of the officers had took them to read.

however he has not seen the end of the matter yet as some of the boys have swore to pay him for robbing the mail in that manner as a good many of the boys oft miss newspapers The Board of Trade had better have kept the Rev Mr. Linn in Buffalo. so no more at present and I hope these few lines will find you all in good health as it leaves me at present

From Your Affect

Son Alfred

write soon

Chapter Five

Operations on Folly and Morris Island, SC
Pre Assault of Fort Wagner

April, 1863 – June, 1863

"The Belvidere the transport that was loaded with stores provisions + ammunition go over the bar all safe but our boat being heavyer loaded and drawing more water she ran aground. which gave her an awful racking. Seeing the predicament one of the small gunboats came and hitched on and tired to draw us off but our boat was set fast in the sand that it was only straining both boats to get her off so they had to get some of the Regt. off in small boats . . . It was pretty tough work getting the men from one boat to the other as the sea was pretty rough and they most all got pretty good duckings as the waves would break right over the top of the small boats." A. Lyth letter dated 3/28/1863

". . . after day break we could see some of the Rebel come to shore + shoot ducks and come within easy range of our guns. I should like to have tried my hand at them but we had strick orders not to fire if we had of course we might have expected the same from the rebels. " A. Lythe letter dated 4/9/1863

"Company H has got the finest camp I ever saw. The tents are all trimmed with cedar boughs and present a splendid appearance. At the lower end of the street, where the Captain's tent is, an arch is erected in which the letter H + {unknown} 100 are hanging. Their street is thoroughly cleaned every morning and looks as neat as a new pin. The General passed through the other day and remarked he did not see why all the companies could not have as fine a camp as Co H." E. Cook letter dated 5/23/1863

"Cole's Island was soon reached, and from our camp on the wretched little sand-spit we looked of across the marshes to the deserted hamlet of Legarville, or across the Stono toward Kiowa, or over toward the island of Folly, and wondered what there was beyond." Lt Col Charles E. Walbridge address at the first Annual Reunion 7/1/8/1887

"The men of Company H will recall with pleasure the period in which we were detached as a permanent picket guard near Pawnee Landing, and would likely need to be reminded of our picturesque little camp under the great magnolia trees, with the large palmetto at the head of the street." Lt. Col Charles E. Walbridge address at the first Annual Reunion, 7/18/1887

Letter from A. Lyth to the Folks at Home
Coals Island S.C. March 28ᵗʰ 1863

Dear Folks at Home

When I last wrote we were on board of the steamer Expounder Ready to put out We started Thursday morning at 4 oclock and arrived oppisite the sand bar between us and our destination but having arrived to late for crossing the bar as the tide was too low we had to put into a harbor some 9 miles north where we should be under the protecktion of the gun boats. The next morning we put back again so as to be in time to cross the bar at high tide. The pilot that we had was Robert Small the negro that stole the boat planter from the rebels about a year ago and fetched her out of Charleston harbor you remember there was an account of it in Harpers Weekly at the time The Belvidere the transport that was loaded with stores provisions + ammunition got over the bar all safe but our being heavyer loaded and drawing more water she run aground. Which gave her an awful racking. seeing us in this predicement one of the small gun boats came and hitched on and tried to draw us off but our boat was set so fast in the sand that it was only straining both boats to get her off so they had to get some of the Regt off in small boats and take them aboard off the Belvidere. It was pretty tough work getting the men from one boat to the other as the sea was pretty rough and they most all got pretty good duckings as the waves would break right over the top of the small boats. The rebels fired a shell or two at us when we were stuck on the bar but we were quite out of their range. They were transfering the Regt from one boat to the other till dark when the sea was too rough for to venture any more but having got all off but three companys our Co being still on the Capt thought he could get over after the tide came up to its full hight which would be at 12 oclock at night. Well we got off at that time with a good deal of straining and run into a small harbor oppsite Coals Island which is about 2 miles from a small place called Le Grangeville which place we can distingush men with the naked eye and it is said the rebels have artillery planted in fact it is the very place where the rebels captured our gunboat the Isaac Smith The gun boats can run clean round this Island We can see the signal lights from fort Sumter.

By the way our Col has got 2 brass Artillery peices for this Regt and I had the good luck to get attached to one off the cannon They took two men from every Co They took volunteers The half of the Co wanted to go but I an another young fellow got the start of the rest We have got both of the peices planted in the rear of the Regt and all we have to do is to drill a little once in a while whilst the rest of the Regt have got a great deal of fatigue work to do such as dig wells sinks unload the Belvidere of her cargo build bridges where the Rebs had destroyed them across a creek that runs through this Island.

You can Address to Hilton Head as usal as our have to go there before they come here. Give my best Respects to all the neighbors. My love to you all

Your Affect Son + Brother
Alfred Lyth

Letter from A. Lyth to the Folks at Home

about 4 mils from Charleston
Follys Island S.C. April 9th 63

Dear Folks at Home

I take this opportunity to write to you again as it is the first chance I have had to write since we left Coles Island I received last night 2 letters from you both containing a skein of thread and one six postage stamps also 3 harpers and 2 other papers the new york weekly times We left Coles Island on sunday night April 5th I am with the company again as we did not fetch those peices of Artillery with us but left them to protect Coles Island with an other Regt. We embarked on leaving coles Island on a large flat scow, somewhat larger than a canal boat and in quite a large number of small boats attached to the scow then as steamers hitched on to us to tow us out the harbor + across the river to follys Iland we started out at about 12 oclock in the night I tell you it was a fine night to see the whole Regt in small boats all in tow of the steamer on that moonlight night we all loaded our guns and primed them as we expected that we should be fired into on landing we run as near the shore as we could with the boats but they being heavly loaded we had to jump out + and wade some 200 feet to the shore in wadin to the shore we got in places where the water was up to our hips but we got ashore all safe Admiral Comodore Dupont superintended the landing of the troops when we were laned the boats were sent back for more troops we deployed 2 Co as schrimmerisher across the Island and commenced the advance that night expecting every minute come upon some rebel forification which if we had I suppose we should have charged upon Our march was very slow as we had to feel our way we marched along the beach untill about 12 oclock the next day when we had ourselves in the woods untill night should come so that we could resume the march again we rested untill 12 oclock at night and then we fell in and resumed the march along the sea shore which was very fatigueing untill we came within ½ a mile to the furtherest extremity of the Island without encountering any thing but some old deserted brest works when we came to a halt and the troops hid theirselves in the woods where the underbrush was very thick all this time we had to live on crackers and salt horse and pork + water as we durst not build fires to cook coffee we had just got settled down when our Co + 2 others had to go on picket our Co had the right which was at the furtherest extremity of the Island right on the river or creek which divides this Island from Morris Island we were posted behind bushes an a cautioned not to show ourselves at the peril of our lives we had great scrambling through the bushes to get to our positions on picket at day break in the morning we could see the rebels runing around on the other side of the river very plain and could see the fort on the other side of the river with the guns mounted on it our forces lay right in under the guns of the fort and if the rebs had known our position they would certainly have shelled us which of course the result would have been very serious to us after day break in the morning we could see some of the Rebel come to the shore + shoot ducks and come within easy range of our guns I should liked to have tried my hand at them but we had strick orders not to fire if we had of course we might have expected the same from the rebels. we lay watching them all day but of course they found out of our presence but of course they could only see an odd man now + then and did not know of the close proximity of our forces occasionly in the afternoon. The men exposed theirselves but the rebels did not fire but the Gen and a couple of Cols and some other officers exposed theirselves and they got a couple of rifle bullets flying after them in double quick time but it did not hit any of them. along in the afternoon the ironsides crossed the bar + some of the monitors after her and made for Charleston harbor Fort

[   ] emieadate opened upon them we could see the shell burst very plainly + see the water spurt up in the air when the shell + shot struck the

water we could see the flag flying over fort Sumter + see every shot that was fired from where we were we should think that most all the fireing was done by the forts + land battries it is supposed by us that they just went into the harbor to find the range of the rebel guns get the range of the forts and hunt up the torpedoes. we thought once we could see one burst for there was an awful column of smoke rose in the air at once then a report above all the cannonadeing. the fireing ceased just before sunset after going it a great rate for about 3 hours. we stood picket all the next night again on account that they could not releive us as the rebels we on the watch all the while we could hear the railroad wistle in very distinct in Charleston and the drums of the various Rebels camps on James + Morrises Island + could see a Rebel Regt on drill we stayed on picket untill yesterday in the afternoon when the picket was drawn in we had to make our way to the Regt without being seen leaving one man to fire on the rebels if they attempted to cross the stream and then to retreat if they came across we had to crawl on our hand + knees through the wood + underbrush till we joined the Regt so that the rebels would not know that we had drawn our pickets in we joined the Regt and then we marched about ¾ of a mile back under the cover of the woods and then encamped in the woods we are allowed to build fires in the hollows where they are well protecked by brush + trees in the day time + cook coffee. There are quite a number of cannon planted in our front in case of an attack which is not very likely as the Rebels will wait for us to attack them in their fortifications which peice of business will be done by our gunboats on the final attack on Charleston the 2 turret monitor is sunk on the bar not a great ways from here I suppose before this reaches you will have an account of the whole affair in the newspapers so you will know more than I can tell you of the affair if our forces are succesful in this undertaking I shall very likely celebrate my birthday in the city of Charleston

Dear Brother I want you to answer this letter right away and tell me how you are all getting along and how the times are in old Buffalo, I should like to know how old Martin is getting along and if he is going to work for dad this summer Tell me all the news about Cold Springs. I send my love to Sarah Ann William + the children + also all the folks at home Tell Sister Sarah that I have been waiting very anxiously for a great while back to have a few lines from her and that I wish she would write as it always give me pleasure to read her letters

Dear Father + Mother   I think I do not miss many of the letters you write if any. There is some enemy to this Regt some wares who writes such disgraseful letters about us we have allway had the praise of being a good disciplined and cleanly looking Regt in speaking of Lice who ever wrote it it is a malicious falsehood of course in those 22 days that were aboard of the New England there were a great many lice amongst the soldiers + officers too as we lay almost stowed on top of one an other.   but as soon as we got ashore the whole Regt most went off to a little stream and striped naked and washed all over and built fires + washed + boiled all their clothes and dried them the same
so no more at present

From Your Affect
Brother Alfred

Letter from E. Cook to his Parents

Beaufort S.C. April 15ᵗʰ 1863

My dear Parents
     Having a little leisure this afternoon I will improve it by writing to you. You will see by the heading of my letter that we are now at Beaufort which place I have once before described to you but the more I see of the City or village the more I like it. I think I should be work out the balance of my time in this locality; best <u>all of this</u> in its place. Instead of running ahead of time I must go back to the old form and journalize so you will know how I came here and what I have been about in the interim.

Friday April 3ᵈ 1863   The day was pleasant and it has done much towards making me feel well again.

Saturday April 4ᵗʰ 1863 Pleasant. The Brigade rec'd orders yesterday to embark and accordingly one of the regiments left night and our headquarters broke up housekeeping this afternoon. All the rest of the troops on the island will embark this evening. Us clerks are going on a Schooner as we prefer that way of going to being with a lot of soldiers on the boat.
We have got a sleep in the hold but there are lot of oats + hay on board so

that we will have a good soft bed to lie on and will be quite comfortable if the weather is pleasant. We are going in the direction of Charleston but how near to the city I do not know.

Sunday April 5th 1863 Pleasant but not warm This morning early the Propeller came along side us and passed us a line. She is going to tow us as the wind is not in our favor. We have 22 horses on board the schooner belonging to different officers. As soon as we had crossed the bar at the mouth of Port Royal harbor, the captain of our schooner the "Maryland" opened his sealed orders and we learned that we are going to North River about 25 miles this side of Charleston.

There are several regiment now encamped on the bank of the river so there is probably no danger attending our entrance at that point

The 100th Regt. is still on Cole's Island so far as I can learn and they are still the Advance reg't

We crossed the Bar and anchored in the North River a little before dark. It is part of Stevenson's Brigade (to which the 100th belongs) that is encamped here. Before they landed here our Gunboats shelled the woods and they were not attacked and have not seen the enemy since they landed. There are 2 or 3 gunboats that lie here all the time to assist and protect the troops that are stationed here. There is a small village off towards Charleston about a mile. I would like to pay it a visit but dont suppose I shall have a chance to do so. It has one or two good sized churches. I can just see the Spires rising above the other buildings.

Monday, Tuesday, Wednesday, Thursday April 6th 7th 8th + 9th All pleasant days and heavy dews like rain at night. Still lying at our same anchorage. I have had no opportunity to go on shore and no particular desire to go even if I had an opportunity as the scene does not look very inviting. The time hangs heavy on my hands on board the "Maryland" but it has been somewhat Relieved by a book named "Like & Unlike". It is a first rate story and will do no one any hurt to read it. It will interest much while reading it and leave a good impression when you have finished it. I have heard while lying here that when our men first landed here some of the soldiers strayed off to the village in the distance that I spoke about and a number of them were taken prisoners and several are wounded + one killed. Since then all of the "rebs" have cleared out for fear of the punishment that awaited them if they remained. We can occasionally hear *the firing at Charleston. A steamer came in yesterday and told us that our monitors have been firing continuously for the past 3 or 4 days. One of them has been disabled by the steel shot which the rebs shoot at them and she has had to go back to Port Royal. There is a rumor that the double turret monitor has been destroyed. I do not know as it is true however.*

Friday April 10th 1863 Windy but pleasant on the water. A steamer came in about noon with the news that since the troops left Hilton Head and Beaufort, to come down here, the Rebs have been up the river and burned one of our Gunboats that laid somewhere above Beaufort so we have got to go back there and protect the place. About 2 oclock this P.M. the "Tillie" again took us in tow and we started back. When we had crossed the bar we hoisted our sails and told the "Tillie" cast off our line. She did so and at the same time bid us farewell expecting to leave us behind but the laugh was on the other side when we had spread all our sail and in a few minutes run by Miss "Tillie" with a cheer. The little schooner almost stood on her side but the way she came through was a caution. We run in ahead of every thing except two steamers which had the start of us and were almost out of sight when we got under way. But we kept so close to them that we could see them when they went they crossed the bar at Port Royal. She came to an anchor in the river about half way between Hilton Head and St. Helena at 7½ oclock P.M. which is about 3 or 4 hours better time than we made on the passage to Edisto. The Tillie was 4 or 5 miles astern of us when we came in and I guess she did not enter the harbor until the next morning.

Saturday April 11th 1863 Very warm This morning a tug boat took us to the dock at Hilton Head and we were transferred with our mess chest and the Horses to the Ferry boat that runs to Beaufort. She left the Pier about 3 o'clock and arrived at Beaufort about 5 o'clock. We got a team to carry up our things and about six oclock we again found ourselves in a tent at the Hd. Quarters of the 1st Brigade. We have had no dinner and so a cup of black tea + a piece of bread without butter was highly relished for supper.

Col. Davis has selected a most delightful spot for his head quarters. The tents are pitched under the branches of a small Grove of large and wide spreading live oak trees in what was formerly a public square or park (apparently). One of our boys bought a bottle of Whiskey, old rye whiskey, gimme some of your rot gut. I had 3 good drinks of it and it was just enough to make me want one more but it was lucky for me that I could not get one more for if I had I should have been rightly slight.

There are some very pretty residences in the town and the shrubbery and shade trees are truly delicious. An officer who visited Beaufort about 5 years ago says it was then one of the loveliest places in the south and was occupied by the wealthiest men in South Carolina. And even now in its present torn condition I can easily find cause to believe his assertion is true.

Sunday April 12ᵗʰ 1863 Pleasant I wrote to Mr. Lyman this afternoon and I hope he will send me a speedy answer and tell me all the news. It is reported here that there has been a rupture between Genl Hunter and Admiral Dupont who has command of the naval forces now in front of Charleston. Genl Hunter is very anxious to reap all the Glory resulting from the taking of Charleston and claimed that as Duponts fleet was in his (Hunters) Dept, Dupont was subject to his command, as soon as the vessels came inside of the bar at Charleston. Some misunderstanding arose between them in regard to this matter and they of course had to quarrel. I hear that Hunter has recalled all the land forces from the vacinity of Charleston and that the attack has been stopped or abandoned and Dupont has gone to Washington for orders. If Mr. Lyman hears any thing about this or sees any thing about it in the papers I wish he would write me the particulars. I think that as Charleston can only be taken by water, that Dupont who evidently knows his business should be allowed to use his own judgment and go on and do the best he can without any of Hunters interference. When I had finished my letter to Mr. Lyman I went to church. It is only a few rods from where we are encamped. The congregation was black and the persuasion I think is Methodist. The preacher was a white man and preached a very good sermon. There were many of the negro soldiers and some few white soldiers present but any quantity of negro wenches of all colors.

At the close of the meeting and after the Benediction was pronounced they struck up a song and then while singing went through an odd form of hand shaking – keeping time in the shakes to the cadence of the song. In the evening as I heard the bells pealing out their joyous imitation I could not resist the appeal and again I went to meeting but to another and a larger church. This time I was a little late and as all the seats downstairs were full I had to go up gallery. The congregation were all males with the exception of 4 or 5 females (officers wives I presume) It seemed like old times to be seated in this church and I could almost fancy I was back in B again (As I am writing I hear the slow and regular beating of the muffled drum. Another soldier is going to his last long home. They carry one or more past here every day) Pardon this digression but that slow and solemn music which has just struck up recalls sad thoughts and I could not help mentioning it. The music, the ambulance bearing the pine coffin covered by the American flag, the sad procession following the corpse to its grave, remind me but too fearfully that my time may not be far distant. We know not the day nor the hour. Heavenly Father! grant that in our blessed redeemer I may ever be prepared for death when thou shall call me!

Instead of preaching this evening they had a prayer meeting and well indeed did I enjoy it. The hand of Jesus is at work in this town and many conversions are being made. The meeting is lead by a regularly ordained minister, but is sustained by the soldiers. It is a soldiers meeting. They are going to hold meetings every evening during the coming week so that I shall have other opportunities of attending if we remain here. The church is as large I think as the baptists church in B and is painted and adorned inside very tastefully

Monday April 13th 1863 Very warm I have sent you two "Free Souths" one of them is an old one and contains the conclusion of the story. I sent you part of it once before. I went to prayer meeting again this evening. I tell you it is delicious to be allowed again to sit and listen to the singing and bow to the prayers that are offered up and hear the words of exhultation. It reminds me of the days when I first held a hope of everlasting life through our redeemers blood and again how fully do I realize that there is no real happiness save in Jesus Christ

Tuesday April 14th 1863 Rained last night pleasant during the day. The troops stationed here consisting of 7 Regts of Infty and about 4 companies of Artillery were reviewed by Genl [   ]. This evening it rained quite hard and as it was dreary at the tent I thought I would go to the prayer meeting again. I went and was repaid so well that I think I shall go again tomorrow. Every evening there are several persons use to request the prayers of their comrads in their behalf. We have been very busy to day drawing + issuing camp equipage to the regiments.

Wednesday April 15ᵗʰ 1863 Very windy I built a bunk in my tent to day. I have been sleeping on the ground but there are so many toads hopping round here that I dont like the idea of lying so low. I have not noticed a letter from you since March 24ᵗʰ I presume that there some at the Regt for me. I have just heard the 100ᵗʰ is coming back again and we are all going to Newberne N.C.

Good Bye
Your Aff Son
Edward L. Cook

Letter from A Lyth to his Father and Mother

Coles Island S.C. April 14 63

Dear Father + Mother

I received 3 letters from you on the 10ᵗʰ + three newspapers The Letters were dated Mar 23 + 26 + April 1 I was very glad to hear that you were all well as the last letter stated my health was never better than at the present We have left Folly Island and returned to our old camp on Coles Island and another Regt has taken our place on Follys Is On the night of the 9 + 10ᵗʰ a squad of rebels of about 100 or 150 in number came across from Morris Island and got in rear of our outposts that were set out there to watch signals and give the alarm if the Rebels came across at a certain point. They came on at about 12 oclock in the night and were approaching one of our posts when the man on guard who belong to our Co halted them 'Who comes There' 'Friends' Halt friends + give the counter sign. yes we will give you the counter sign you yankee s-n b-h upon whitch they emiately fired a volly right at him The other 2 men on post with him ran and got away but he was shot in the right shoulder then he to run when they fired again one ball hiting him in the heel passing through his heel and coming out of his ankle. The Rebels came up to him asked him what Regt he belonged to he told them the 100ᵗʰ N.Y. they asked him his name he told them it was Charles Sabin. they asked him how many forces we had on that Island he told them he did not know as we were the first Regt on and he had not been to the rear to see if there were any more Then he asked the officer what his name was

165

and he said Col Howard They then left him finding he could not walk and he lay there 2 or 3 hours before he was picked up he was a first rate fellow and his loss is very much regreted in the Company. When they left him they past close past other posts but the men were hid in the grass and they did not see them only one of our company was hollering Corporal when the rebels heard him they said something when he said don't shoot. Oh no we wont shoot you come fall in + come along so they took him prisoner right within arms length of two other fellows that were hid in the grass. his name was John McDonal he was an old sailor The next night there was a stronger picket line thrown out and the next night a whole Regt went on picket and a 12 pounder howitzer which us that maned the brass peices at this Island had to take care of and a Co from our Regt to support us Our Col was up with us all night so was our doctor by the way I never told you that our Col was a Georgia man Though I guess there is not a better union man.

From your Affect Alfred

Letter from E. Cook to his Parents

Beaufort S.C. April 16th 1863

My dear Parents

My ink is low thick and poor, so I am afraid I shall make but a sorry looking letter of this which I am now writing. I presume you have heard or rather will have heard by the time that this reaches you that the 100th has been in a fight or skirmish. I have not heard the particulars and at present can give you no deffinite information in regard to the matter. One of the soldiers was brought up here last night and placed in one of the many hospitals. His leg was off below the knee. As near as I can learn the fight took place on the picket line. One of the pickets challanged an approaching body of troops who replied by a volley of musketry and then retreated; how true this is I do not know. Another account states that our men made a reconnaissance to one of the adjacent islands and met with sharp resistance. I presume you will hear the facts of the case before I do as George Stoddard will of course write to his folks about it. I am almost ashamed to remain here while the regiment is off many miles and in dangerous sections. I feel as though I ought to be with them and doing my part of any fighting is going on. The regiment rec'd orders a day or two ago to return to St. Helena and my heart was glad at the expectation of seeing all the boys again but in a few hours after the order was sent to them to return, Genl Hunter rec'd directions from the war department to attack and take Charleston at all hazards and immediately he sent off another boat to the 100ᵗʰ to countermand the first order and consequently all my hopes were dashed to the ground. We expect orders to embark every day.

The report here is that we are to take Charleston if we sink every "Monitor" and kill half our men in the attempt. There is so much feeling in the north in regard to this expedition that it seems it is actually necessary to the sustainment of our cause Charleston should float the stars + stripes before any other movement of our armies takes place. The papers at the north and the northern people have a very inaccurate idea of our military strength in this department. It is confidently stated that we have 30,000 men to cooperate with the naval force and more expected, whereas, we have at no time been able to bring forward more than 16,000 and today as one whole brigade has left this point for Newberne N.C. we can not show for active operations above 12,000 to 15,000 men including niggers, cavalry, artillery + infantry. Nor have I heard of any reinforcements that were expected here. In fact there is no point whence we can draw more troops unless we take them from the Dept. of Virginia for Genl Foster is hemmed in by the enemy in North Carolina + Hunter was obliged to send a whole brigade from the forces here to relieve Foster of the difficulty in which he has very foolishly placed himself. I do not see for my part what becomes of all the soldiers. It has always been the cry since the war broke out "More men" more men" "reinforcements, reinforcement" And the general who really needs them can seldom or never obtain them. But they can be kept in large bodies doing nothing, accomplishing nothing where they are not needed at all or where a small force and light artillery would answer the purpose just as well. But we are going to Charleston with our little handful of 12 or 15 thousand men and we are going to trust to God and the righteousness of our cause for the complete and perfect fulfillment of the hard task which is alloted to us to perform. And I believe that God will bring us out conquerors for I trust that He is on our side. The issue now seems to be <u>freedom</u> or <u>slavery</u> and can it be that God will favor the cause *of slavery? I do not believe it. From the very first outbreak I thought that this war would result in the abolition of slavery, and I then believed that God permitted it only for that purpose and I am now more fully and firmly convinced of it than ever before and I can not come to any other conclusion than that this is <u>God's</u> war and He is on the side of freedom.*

I have been to prayer meeting every evening this week and I do not regret the time that I spend going there. Even if I were not a professed Christian I should rejoice at the work of salvation which is going here among the soldiers. It has been said that a soldier cannot be a Christian but one evening spent in this town at the soldiers prayer meeting will give the lie to every and all such assertions and prove direct that a Soldier can be a Christian. It would do the heart of many Christians good to come down here and remain about two weeks to see the good work that is going on in this department both among the soldiers and the once neglected slave.

I traded a pair of pants to day with one of the Adjt. Genl's clerks and got a dollar to boot so I am now in funds, after paying some little debts, to the amount of 50 cents. I am quite rich dont you think so? If I can learn what hospital that wounded man is in I will try and visit him and if I do I will let you know

Friday April 17th 1863 Very warm indeed I went to St. Helena this morning on the boat to bring up our mules + army wagons which we left behind us when we embarked for Edisto. Besides the mules + wagons there was a half months forage of oats + hay for 32 mules which we had to bring along. We loaded it onto the eight wagons and drove down to the landing. When the boat came up about 4 o'clock we had a gangway made of heavy timber + planks which we ran onto the boat and over this we were able to take the wagons onto the boat without unloading them and when we got to Beaufort we were able as the tide was high to run them off in the same manner. I was highly pleased with the job for transporting wagons + mules is usually considered a very unpleasant + difficult job as we generally have to take the wagons to pieces in order to load them. I never saw any thing go off so nicely + smoothly as the work of today and I could not help remarking that if every undertaking during this war had been as successful as ours of moving the wagons our country would present a far different picture from that which now presents itself to our disheartened + discouraged citizens and soldiers.

Letter from A. Lyth to his Father and Mother

Folly Island S.C.
Tuesday April 21ˢᵗ 63

Dear Father + Mother
Our Regt has at last received its pay we received it last night + I have put $50 in the chaplins hands to deliver to Buffalo by order of the Col. There is a great many of the boys are sending their money by mail in preferance of sending it by him as they are afraid to trust him but I think that he will deliver it safe for his own interests + however I have let him have mine and hope he will deliver it safe I got $78 + 40 cts which leaves me $28.48 which I think I shall need for if I should happen to have the bad luck to be taken prisoner or wounded I shall need it a great many of the boys are keeping all theirs till after the coming conflict I guess the final attack on Charleston will have commenced befor this reaches you I understand that Admiral Dupont has orders to take Charlston or sink the fleet we left Coles Island April 15ᵗʰ + landed again on this Island the same day we fetched our 2 peices of Artillery with us + have them planted near the head Quarters + have our tent pitched in the woods near our peices so that we shall be on hand if the rebels show their noses. we have very easy times of it while the Regt has to go on picket every 3ᵈ day we are bothered by the mosquitos + nats a great deal + there is whole Regts of wood ticks + snakes the boys oft get a snake in their beds I was setting in one of the boys tents one afternoon having a chat when all at once a snake about three + half feet long stuck his head from under the palmeto leaves that the bed was made of and commenced crawling out by degrees we let him get about ½ way out when we gave him a knock that settled him.

April 22 1863 I understand that the attack on Charleston will commence within the next 4 days + one day has past The monitor Passaic is going to lead the ironclads into the harbor + will be immeadeately by the ironsides + the other monitors then the others bring up the rear The Pawnee Wabash + the McDonal will be in the river between this + James + Morris Island + will shell all the woods within their reach so as to leave the road clear for the troops to cross over + walk into Charleston I suppose our 2 peices will have a chance to do some talking besides 9 other peices that are on this island A day or two ago the 3 or 4 rebel pickets + our pickets laid down their guns and each came to their own edge of the stream the rebels commences to black gaurd our fellows then they asked our fellow if they would trade coffee + sugar for tobacco or any thing they had they said they would give almost anything for a little salt and they asked if our boys would exchance newspapers They our men said they could not trade newspapers till they got premision from our officers but said they could let them have sugar + coffee when the rebels heard that they began to strip off to swim the stream for to make the exchange but our boys told them to float what they wanted to send across on little boats or board + they would do the same which they did I heard that they sent over a newpaper for a little salt

The day before we came on this Island this last time one of the 62ᵈ Ohio boys shot one of their Captain he was officer of the day + he was making his round on the picket line in the night when on coming near the sentinals post the sentinal sung out who comes there Halt three times when receiveing no answer he fired and shot him dead
I hope these few lines will find you all well + in good health as it leaves me at present My love to you all

> *From Your Affect*
> *Son Alfred*

write soon

Letter from E. Cook to Parents and Relatives

Beaufort S.C. April 22ᵈ 1863

My dear Parents + Relatives
I hope you are all enjoying as good health and feeling as well as I do at present. We have all been pretty busy to day issuing the "A" or "Common" tents to the regiments. Heretofore the soldiers have been living in the little shelter tents but now they can make themselves more comfortable and have a better protection from the heavy dews and rain.

Thursday April 23ᵈ 1863 Very pleasant There was a large mail came up to day but no letter for me. I presume my letters still go to the 100ᵗʰ Regt. You must not direct to the regiment hereafter for if you do I do not know when I shall receive them. I have sent for those that are there now and expect them in a few days. I will let you know if I receive them.

Friday April 24th 1863 Very warm this A.M. very windy this P.M. I saw a paper from the north to day and it gives a very gloomy account of the conditions of our affairs. The "Cut-off" at Vicksburg is a failure + our army of the West is acting on the defensive. Rosencranz is in danger of being surrounded + cut off. Genl Foster is surrounded and if not relieved he will have to surrender. The attack on Charleston is a failure. The Copperhead sentiment at the north is fearfully increasing. Treasonable remarks against our President + Cabinet are common in the daily journals and altogether it seems as though our cause to day look more gloomy than did that of the rebels a year ago. The 100th Regt has been paid off and I presume they are overflowing with money. The Boys in Co. "H" owe me about $5#. I wish I was there to get it. I am going to Hilton Head tomorrow to try my luck, although I have little hope of getting my pay as I was not present at the last muster.

Saturday April 25th 1863 Warm I went to Hilton Head this morning and paid a visit to the paymaster who paid the 100th. I found him very kind and obliging and upon stating my case and producing my credentials he paid me without any hesitation and told me send along as soon as possible all others who were on detached service as clerks or teamsters from the 100th. I wrote a short letter to you from Hilton Head saying that I would send you some money by the next boat but afterwards I concluded to send it the boat which leaves tomorrow and so I gave it to the Express Company and before this reaches you I trust that you will have rec'd it all right. The amount was $5 and the charges which I paid on it were 75 cents + 25 cts for insurance making $1# in all. You will not have to pay any charges on it of any kind as I have paid them all in full. You can have the money if you want it but if you do not then you can put it in the bank in my name and let it be drawing interest. You have my blank checks and any time that you want money I hope you will not be afraid to draw it and use it. Answer this letter the same day that you receive it and let me know if you have rec'd the money. How I wish I could follow the money and enter your door a few moments after you receive it. It seems a long time since I heard *from you and so it is, for I have not rec'd a letter from you since March 24th more than a month ago. I hope you will always be prompt in answering my letters for if you do not answer* <u>immediately</u> *upon receiving the letters then the answers have to lay over until the mail steamer makes another round trip. Whenever you hear by telegraph or otherwise that the steamer is in New York then you must immediately get a letter in the mail for me. Direct to Edward L. Cook Q.M. Dept. Davis' Brigade, Port Royal S.C.*

Sunday April 26th 1863 Pleasant I went to Hilton Head this morning with the intention of remaining all night and going to the 100th early Monday morning but while at the Head he saw the Chaplain of the 100th who told him that our letters had been remailed to us and were now at Beaufort Post office so there was no use in going to the regiment at present + therefore we were surprised to see him step into our tent just as we had finished our evening meal. Chaplain goes north to day with and carries with him about $2000 for the soldiers.

Monday April 27th 1863 Pleasant I went down to the post office this morning and rec'd two letters from home one written by Eliza + the other by Laura. The first contained one dollar or 2-50 cent stamps. Neither of them were numbered so I numbered them 34 + 35. I am afraid you are spoiling Gracie and indeed by the tone of your remarks about her I think she is already spoiled. I am much obliged to you dear mother for the one dollar you sent me although at present I do not need it still I will keep it for a while and perhaps send it to you with some more besides. I do not see what put the idea in your heads that we could resign and go home. There is no way of getting out of the picnic expect through sickness, inability or death. I have serious thoughts about being mustered out of the 100th and joining one of the negro regiments for 5 years that are raising here in South Carolina. I have no more of those sitting pictures than what you have got but if you mail any more of them go to on the west side of Main Street between Mohawk + Court near Seibetrut's old drug store and as the have the negatives they can soon print off some more of the pictures. Tell Eliza those 2 words on the end of the paper that Dave White sent have nothing to do with the poetry. I dont know how they came there. They are Indian names. Tell Laura I do not know how great a Friend I am in the opinion of Ella H. but I think very much of her letters and should dislike very much *to have her cease corresponding with me. Her letter are lively, ladylike and interesting and will bear inspection and re-reading, and as regards my opinion of the young lady herself I have only to say that I very likely will express that opinion to Miss Ella before I communicate it to Laura and the world at large. I am afraid I shall not get the tobacco you sent to me in G C's box as the 100th is away up almost to Charleston but I am going up there as soon as we get our April Papers made up and sent off if nothing intervenes. I guess I must have been mistaken about those shirts – very likely I lost them in moving our camp at Gloucester Point. I have not rec'd any of the papers that Laura says she sent me. As regards my going back to the regiment I am liable to be ordered back at any time as the 100th is now out of Davis' Brigade and consequently this quarter master cannot retain me if Colonel of the 100th orders me back. Lt. Walbridge returned to the regiment on the 2^d of April and Lt. [ ] 52^d Pa. Vols. is now our quarter master. I do not know where uncle David's regiment is stationed at present. I was today offered the position of Clerk in the Post Quarter Masters office at Beaufort but I did not accept as I would rather be in the camp and on the field. If Geo Stoddard had been here I could have got him the place but the parties could not wait so long as to have him detailed from the regiment.*

Thursday afternoon Very warm We feasted again this noon on Codfish balls and right tempting and delicious they were I can tell you. [ ] went to Hilton Head this morning but I expect him to return this evening. I think he will up some letters for me. He is detailed from here as Clerk for Genl. Hunter's Adjutant General and he is going to try and get me in the same office. I think if I can get there I shall stand a good chance of obtaining a commission in one of the Negro Regiments as this place. As I write two companies of Negro Soldiers are marching across the park and it is a fact that they <u>march</u> <u>better</u> than the White Soldiers. Whether they do so from pride or on account of the natural capacity which possess of keeping time + step I cannot say; but whatever may be the cause the fact is true. Everybody around here says they are going to make good soldiers + I believe it is true.

I took a short horseback ride this afternoon through the cool and shady streets of Beaufort. I enjoyed it very muchly. I hope you will answer this letter soon as you receive it. I want to go to church this evening so I can write no more and as this is the last day of the month I think I will conclude this and commence anew tomorrow on the next letter. Next Monday May 4th I shall have been in Uncle Sams employ 8 months and have never yet been in a battle while many other poor fellows have measured their length on the cold damp ground for the last time and now sleep in death. I think the rumor that we are to go to Newbern N.C. unless Hunter immediately attacks Charleston is true. I wish I had the tobacco you sent me. We cannot get any good tobacco here and we are obliged to smoke evenings to keep the little biting pestering sand flies + gnats away from us. They bite as hard as mosquitoes. Give my love to Grandma and kiss little Gracie. Tell Annie + Lillian I have not forgotten them and often think of them and all the rest. Remember me to Mr. Dinwoodie who sent his respects to me, and believe me ever your affectionate son   *Direct to*

                                              Edward L. Cook

> *Q.M. Dept.*
> *1st Brigade*
> *Heckman's Division*
> *Port Royal*
> *S.C.*

Letter from Al. Lyth to his Brother

Follys Island S.C. April 28

Dear Brother

    I received your letter of the 17th + 2 harpers + a Weekly [ ] I was very glad to hear that you were all well as it leaves me at present. Charleston has not been attacked yet as it was supposed it would be before this of course I can not tell you the reason but I should think there is some good reason or it would not be delayed so long Our cannon is at the head of the Island we can see the rebels Just across the stream from us {unknown words} + can holler over to them they have a large gun {unknown words} + exchange newspapers + coffee +c give them for tobacco I must write you a little description of this Island it is about 7 miles long + varys from a mile to a mile + a half in width there never was any more than one house on it + that is where the Genl has his head Quarters the land is worthless for cultivation except a small peice Just around the White house as it is called

There are a great many palmeto + June trees + a few red cedar plenty of snakes I guess when this summer get a little more entranced we shall have rattle snakes copperheads + other poisonous snakes but I guess we shall be off from it before that time for the last week we have had the woods on fire on this Island but the fire had gone down pretty much last night I sent $5 home last week + I guess you will have received it before this.

April 30th

Every thing as yet is quite in this quarter every day when the tide is out we go down to the beach an have a talk with the Rebels yesterday they sent over a boat to us something in the shape of the monitor to day we have been shaping it over + puting a turret on of a quart cup with a hole through for a port hole + a cannon gun stuck through the hole then we put a flag on which has + eagle + coat of arms on + say the union for ever in large colored letters then we printed + addition which made it read *The union for ever Thats what the matter Fighting for no niggers.* From where we talk across to the rebels we can see fort Sumter very plain can see the warehouses on sulivan Island + the church stepels in Charleston city. Just across the river where we talk with the rebs there are 2 large guns mounted on a fortification + yesterday some one of the boys hollered over + asked them what kind of wood those guns were made off when they told us to come over + we should find out.

May 1st 1863

Dear Brother I should have finshed + posted this letter before this but for the last week our peice has been about 3 miles away from the Regt + I had no chance to post it but last night we moved our peice

We cannot get the 'New South' here as well as I could at Hilton Head so I cannot send them to you regular

A.L.

Send a letter a couple of days before you send me a box informing me of it as the express boxes some times come quicker than the mail and send a letter the day you express the box

The mail arrived here this morning by the Steamer Fulton but as my letters would be directed to the hospital I shall not get them untill day after tomorrow then I will write again

Letter from A. Lyth to his Folks at Home

Follys Island S.C.
May 4ᵗʰ 1863

Dear Folks at home

It is some 7 or 8 days since we received a mail but are expecting one every day I thought I would write you these few lines + enclose my ambrotype which I got taken day before yesterday I do not know weather you could tell It was me or not If you did not know beforehand The man that is takeing them has no accommodations whatever he has only a little shanty about 20 feet long + the instrement is not so large as our magic lantern + he has a few panes of glass for a sky light he takes a good many ambrotypes but he has not taken one good one yet he took mine 3 times before I would take it the first time I was taken standing up with gun + accutrements but he could not take me standing nor any one over 4 feet 6 or 8 in then he took me setting down the next time + I had on an Artillery belt + swords + it showed pretty good but the features were as black as a nigger The last time I had an Artillery belt + sword but it did not show on the picture at all + one side of the face is pretty darck but it was as good a picture as he could take so I gave him a dollar which is the price he asks + took it so you must take it as it with the hopes of getting a better one when I can get it taken in deggeorian gallery in Charleston I go into the sea to have a bath every other day The water is quite warm + it is glorious to go in when the tide is coming in full force + have a good racing of from the breakers or to go out beyond the breakers + let the tide wash you ashore Every thing is at the stand still here at the present time with the exception that there was another 2 or 3 Regts come on this Island.

I hope these few lines will find you all in good health + spirits as it leaves me at present I should like to know how Sarah Ann + the youngster gets along

My love to you all
so no more at present
From Your Affect
Son + Brother
Alfred Lyth

P.S. I suppose by this you are busy at till making I want you to tell me how you are getting along

Alfred

This letter will be posted tomorrow morning which is your birthday you are 17 years old tomorrow I should very much like to see you now you must have grown some since I left home now if it is a fine day tomorrow I am going down to the landing on this Island and get my ambrotype taken + after you read this letter the first chance you get I want you to get yours taken and send it to me.

    Give my love to William + Sarah Ann + the children I sent my love to Father + Mother + all so I must close here

From Your Affect
Brother Alfred
WRITE Soon

P.S. I shall write again in a couple of days

Letter from A. Lyth to his Father and Mother

Follys Island S.C. May 9th 63

Dear Father + Mother

    The mail arrived here yesterday and fetched me a couple of papers the Tribune [ ] with the illustration of our Regt landing on Coles Island The picture is a very good resembleance + I acually think I can see myself there helping to get those peices of Artillery ashore I received no letter whatever by this mail + was very much disappointed as it is over two weeks since we received the last mail. Every thing in this quarter as yet is at a stand still in the shape of an advance on Charleston but are very busy building fortifications + diging rifle pits making roads.. They have got a fine little fort built for our cannon + we are settled in it. We fired a few shell over into the wood on James Island the other day I have been put in charge of the ammunition and when the gun is in action I have to pass out the kind of ammunition the Leaut calls for + to cut the fuse of the shell we have very easy time as {missing words} drill one hour a day then the rest of the time is our own The other day we killed a large poisonous snake he was some five feet in length and as thick as a persons wrist in the thickest part of him we tied a

177

string to him and hung him up in a palmetto tree in emblem of the Southern
Confederacy Yesterday there was quite a phenomena occur on this Island in
the afternoon a black cloud was observed rising in the west and it rose untill
it came directly over the point of this Island + about 60 or 70 rods from were
we are stationed when it began to desend rapidly in the shape of a waterspout
but when it got very near to the ground it turned into a whirlwind then the
waterspout burst into a mist + spray and began to ascend with greater rapidty
than it came down then the whirlwind followed {missing words} and took the
sand over a hundred feet high it crossed over on to the of Morris Island then
worked off on to the ocean + carried the water a considerable distance into
the air I wish you would send me a couple of watch keys in the first letter you
write + you can send that brass watch chain if you think it will come in an
envelope I have bought me a pretty good watch of one of the boys of another
Regt that was pretty hard up and I have lost the cord + key that was attached
to it while scrambling through the bushes the other day I must close now
hoping these few lines will find you all in good health + spirits as it leaves me
at present Give my love to William + Sarah Ann and let me know how they
are getting along My love to you all

Your Affect Son Alfred

N.B. write soon let me know that you are alive

For How pleasant {missing words}
Amid lifes changing scenes
Some friend from whom the rays
Of heavenly nature gleams
From whom when weary hours
To us are lingering near
The light of love can shine
To fill the Heart with cheer

How pleasent tis to feel
The kind and fostering care
Of those who seek our good
And who our sorrows share
Then let us strive to be
A friend to all in need
That we from them may reap
The blessing of the deed

P.S. I have just learned the Arago is at Hilton Head with another mail for us so I expect something by here.

Letter from E. Cook to his Parents

Beaufort S.C. May 7ᵗʰ 1863
My dear Parents
     We completed our monthly papers yesterday evening and now for a day or two I shall have some leisure time on my hands. After this week we are going to draw and issue a large amount of clothing + camp equipage which will keep us employed for a short time and when that is over I am going to try and get a pass to go to the reg't.
     [   ] is there now and we expect him back tonight but as Co "H" is detatched from the regiment and some 3 miles away from it I am afraid he will not go there for my letters. I received a letter from G. Clark a day or two ago which I inclose to you. His surmises in regard to another attack on Charleston I think are unfounded for Genl. Hunter is granting furloughs to all the soldiers (Officers + Privates) who send in a request for one, and I think he would not do so if he intended to make another attack this summer. I presume I could come home for a month if I wanted to but I do not see any use in doing so as it would cost me considerable money. If I could have obtained a furlough at the time they were raising the negro regiment in "B" I should have gone home and tried to obtain a commission in said regiment. As things stand now I think I had better remain as I am, for I do not suppose there is any chance of bettering myself and if not I had better stay and keep my money for better and useful purposes.

Saturday May 9ᵗʰ 1863 We had a very heavy thunder + lightning storm on the 5ᵗʰ of this month and since then the weather has been most deliciously cool and pleasant. An incident occurred here a few days ago which is worthy of note. A negress living in a house a few rods from our headquarters wanted something to put in her fireplace to put her pots + kettles on so what do you think she did. I have heard of foolish women before but I <u>never</u> *heard of so foolish a woman as [   ]. She went into the artillery camp adjoining her house and took up a loaded shell. She used it one day successfully but the second day the heat of the fire exploded it and the pieces of shell went flying in all directions. There were several persons in the house at the time but providentially none were injured save herself. One piece of shell struck her arm and tore a frightful gash but did not break the bones. I heard the crash when the shell burst and some one standing near me remarked that it was an explosion but neither of us imagined at the time that it was any thing of seriousness. It is very strange that more were not injured as there were several in the house.*

The "Arago" arrived at Hilton Head yesterday and I expect a letter from you acknowledging the receipt of the Fifty dollars I sent you. When I get my extra duty pay I will send you some more for your own use

Laura said some time ago that she wrote something for the newspapers and was going to send me the papers. What was it she wrote? Also one of you said you had some <u>news</u> to tell me but could <u>not tell</u> it until July.

What is the news? Dont write any thing about such uncertainties, unless you can tell me what it is at the time you write it. I dont like to be kept in such suspense and would rather that you would not write to me at all. How is Grandma? I am afraid if she dont keep up good spirits that we will not have the happiness of seeing her on our return. I think if we take Charleston the war will soon be ended. What do you think? Give my love to Grandma and tell her to keep up good spirits for our sake remember me to all the folks and tell them all to write to me as often as possible. How are all the girls? Have you any news from the 74ᵗʰ Regt.

I hear Lee has recrossed the Potomac.

> *Good Bye again*
> *Edward*

George Stoddard Diary

May 12ᵗʰ, 1863
Folly Island, SC

There days were spent with ill success in fishing & the nights succeeding in dreaming of mud, dog-sharks, "bites", catfish, shrimp, minnows and every thing connected with the "divine art"; all muddled in heterogeneous confusion

Have suffered some with tooth aches. Screwed up courage & had it extracted this morning.[4]

May 14ᵗʰ, 1863
Folly Island, SC

Heavy fighting was heard in the direction of cln. The Rebels report that they have got a new general in command of them – General Starvation. The also report the evacuation of Vicksburg.

All day today they have been firing guns every one half hour, and all their flags are at half mast. They say in token of respect for the loss of a great General, either Longstreet or Lee, I was unable to learn which. {Jackson died of wounds at about this time.}

Lieutenant Coleman was accidentally shot yesterday by a revolver in the hands of a cavalry officer. The ball entered his chin, penetrating the lower jaw & passed out near his right ear. Both officers were slightly "sprung".⁵

May 20ᵗʰ, 1863
Folly Island, SC

Yesterday nothing of importance, except Ed Cook's visiting from Beaufort, S.C. He is well. It is uncertain yet whether he will rejoin the regt. or not. He is pleasantly situated up there; camped in a cool grove. Rather lonesome & mail not to be depended on, both of which tend to create a desire to come back again.

He thinks our camp is the finest he ever witnessed. It is really a pretty place, not a tent to be seen, everything is covered up with evergreen, cedar & the palmetto leaves. Most of the leisure time is spent improving and beautifying camp. Considerable taste is exhibited in the display of fancy devices by way of arches, shields, verdure letters of cedar, etc.⁶

Letter from E. Cook to Parents

*Q. M. Dept. 1*st *Brig. {unknown} Div.*
*Beaufort S.C. May 24*th *1863*

My dear Parents
    *I returned last evening from a visit to the 100*th *Reg't. on Folly Island and the first news I heard on my return was that all the detached men were ordered to report to their regiments. So tomorrow I must again join my company. I cannot say that I am sorry for it although if the order had not been received I think I should have remained where I am. If the regiment goes into a fight I want to be with it and try and earn another step in the line of promotion.*
    *[   ] received notice on the 16*th *that he had been promoted to 2*^d *Lieutenant and on the 17*th *we both started for the regiment. He to report for duty + I to make a visit. The boat did not leave Hilton Head until the next day and so we had to remain all night at the Port Royal house. I thought I was going to have a good nights rest but the flies troubled me so that I could not sleep and I had to get up in the middle of the night and put on my pants and shove the bottoms of them in my stockings to prevent being eat up entirely. The next day I left but {unknown name} had "Wet" his Commission so many times that things were rather messed up in his head and he got life. When I sailed from Folly Island he had not yet arrived on Folly Island May 10*th *1863*
    I took a walk out to the head of the island and had a sight of Sumter.

*May 20*th *1863 Geo. Clark + I took a walk this afternoon and by the courtesy of the "Signal Officer" were permitted to ascend the "Lookout" and take a peep through the Telescope. We saw Sentinels walking in the Ramparts of Sumter + boatsmen rowing in the river. We could also look down into Charleston. There are 2 Rebel camps about 3 miles from Co "H" and I could distinctly see the "rebs" walking through the streets of their camp ground.*
    The woods on the island used to be full of snakes but the underbrush has been burned out and the dead snakes are lying thick as peas. There are any quantity of fireflies in the woods which the boys find quite useful + convenient. They (the boys) are not allowed to impose themselves or have

any fires so when they are on guard at night they catch a fire fly and put him in their hats and the fly will give light enough to show the time on the face of a watch.

There are also a great number of chammeleons in the woods. They look like a lizard but sometimes they are Green then yellow, brown and I dont know what other colors. Sharks are also quite numerous. Some of the soldiers killed one of the tiger sharks on the beach that weighed 380 pounds. It was left in a kind of basin when the tide went out. One of the boys, not knowing what it was, took hold of its tail when it immediately turned round and inflicted a serious bite on the arm or leg of this soldier.

Saturday May 23/63 I returned from Folly Island to day only to learn that I have got to rejoin my regiment on Monday. Geo. Clark is now Orderly Sergeant which would have been my position if I had remained with the Company.

Co "H" has got the finest camp I ever saw. The tents are all trimmed with cedar boughs and present a splendid appearance. At the lower end of the street, where the Captains tent is, an arch is erected in which the letter "H" + {unknown} 100 are hanging. Their street is thoroughly cleaned every morning and look as neat as a new pin. The General passed through the other day and remarked that he did not see why all the companies could not have as fine a camp as Co "H". Wood ticks are countless. Geo. Stoddard pulled 10 or 12 off his body in one day. Stinging Gnats fill the air and the only way the boys can live with them is to put a smoking brand inside their tent which drives away the gnats + mosquitoes at the expense of suffocation.

Sunday April 24th

I rec'd letter No 44 from Eliza. I am glad you received the fifty dollars I sent you. The letter contained 5 Postage Stamps. I am much obliged to Eliza for the long letter and hope she will always write at an equal length. I have not received the letters between 39 + 44 namely 40, 41, 42 + 43. I think they are at the regiment. So the 21st *has got home again at last. I hope I shall live to march into Buffalo at some future day along with the Bloody Hundredth as every body calls us. Direct your letters to Edward L. Cook Co. H. 100*[th] *Regt. N.Y.S. Vols. Port Royal S.C. Direct in a good plain hand and always pay the full postage on your letters. I have written in a hurry because I have got considerable to do before I leave for the regt. When I get there I will write you a good long letter. Two men out of our company are going home on furloughs and I have given them a little box of shells to leave at Comstocks for you please call + get them + preserve them. Some of them were picked up in sight of Fort Sumter. I think I shall send another little box home by Old Jacob Seibold's son who will call on you So be prepared. They will be packed in the Mohair Moss that grows on live oak trees and which will be more of a curiosity than the shells. Perhaps if the two Georges and myself can get a furlough together we will do so in July or August but some of us care much abougt going home. I dont know what I should do if I was out of the army. I am not much regretful at being ordered back to my regiment but I shall miss my good living. Write to me soon as you receive this and direct as above. Please preserve the inclosed passes {unknown} forget to call at Comstocks for the shells. If young Seibold calls on you use him well. Good Bye Give my love to all the folks and remember me to Grandma in particular.*

Letter from A. Lyth to his Brother

Follys Island S.C. May 25th 63

Dear Brother

Day before yesterday I received the two Harpers and the weekly you sent me The report here now is that Hooker was driven back across the Rappachanack and that he was going to be superseded by Gen Heintzelman however we cannot beleive all the reports we receive here all is quite in this quarter but yesterday there were a few heavy guns fired from fort Sumter it is thought they were fired for a salute although they were not fire as salutes are generaly fired The weather here is pretty warm now a days but we have very good times as we have nothing much to do We are living here better than ever we have done since I came into the army our Regt has got a bakery built and we get 3 loaves of soft bread every five days and all the hard bread we have a mind to eat which is very little The last time we drew rations we drew some of those decicated potatoes there is so much talk about but we dont think much of them the we drew some dried vegitables which are dried and pressed for the army use it is called vegitabel soup well it makes a good soup for a change once in a while but we think it is better suited for pig feed but we cannot grumble for we have plenty of meat and there are plenty of sutlers on the Island for to get some little extras so we have a good time of it. We go into the sea every evening and have a bathe. By the way I must tell you of a little occurance that happened in our Regt a couple of week ago There has been a promotion of Company offices in our Regt and a couple of orderly Sergt have got Commisions. There is a kind of a simple fellow in Co. F. so some of the boys told him if he should try hard he might get a Commission So he said he would try if they would help him so as he could not write he got one of them to write him out a recommend and they all were to sign it which they all did They read it to him when they got through and read it thus. Since I enlisted in this army I have done my duty as a soldier I have never been in the guard house seldom on the doctors list never been court martialed and thus they read on giving such a glowing description of himself that he was sure of getting his commission but the document read quite the contraery stating Since I enlisted in this army I have never done my duty as a soldier should do I have been in the guard house a great many times and Court martialed some 6 or 7 times I often play up sick and go to the doctors to get excused from duty and thus it ran on giving him the worst kind of a caracter so they told him to take the paper and show it to the Captain The captain some how or other having heard of the affair took the paper when he presented it to him and read it without a smile and told him to take it to the doctor and let him see it then to go to the AdJuntant then to the Col well he went to the doctor in high spirits as the Capt had said nothing against it when the doctor read it he hunted him out of his tent double quick but not caring for the doctor much he went to the adjutant after the adjutant had read it he smiled and told it was all right he then went to the Col the Col took the paper and read it and then he handed it back to him and told him to go to his camp away he went back and the Capt asked him what the Col said he told him the adjutant told him it was all right and when the Col read it he had said nothing against it well said the captain you'll get your commision he went and told all the boys he was going to get his commision and that he would remember the services they had rendered him in helping to get it and he treated them to 12 dollars worth of wine he met the orderly sergent of his company who had Just been promoted and said oh…you can put on style with your shoulder straps but maybe in a week I can play as much of that as you can now that is a very good one but John if the Joke 4 or 5 and myself *have on hand at present don't beat it I'm a dutchman when it is complete I will let you know of it*

I must come to a close now hoping these few lines will find you all in good health as it leaves me at present Give my Love to Sarah Ann and tell her to excuse me for not writing in so long but I will write in a day or two Give my best respects to William and the Neighbors

From Your Affect
Brother Alfred

P.S. write soon and let me know how the business is getting along

As I have been writing these few lines the gunboat Com. McDonough has been pitching a few shell over into the woods on James Island our Lt was saying we might have to throw over a few before the day was over.

George Stoddard Diary

May 27th, 1863
Folly Island, SC

We have had soft bread once or twice, the first leaving St. Helena. We turn out now with white gloves, polished boots and brasses, and a general fancy get up throughout. Rumor afloat to the effect that we will soon move. The weather is fine. And the General says that Co. H camps looks like a Fourth of July celebration with its arbors, arches & green trimmings.

There are high old times in the regt. now. Col Dandy is drunk all the time; most of the officers ditto. Some are under arrest & a number are about to resign. The men are court martialed and heavily fines for the most trifling offences. To be seen with a dress coat on, to wear pants in boots, to have a button off or one unbuttoned, the least deficiency in the polish of boots, a soil on white gloves; or, in fact, any of those little shortcomings that to men of the field seems inevitable, is certain to cost, by way of fines, from three to five dollars.

One captain is at present under arrest for going on picket with boots drawn over his pants, another was served the same for appearing on dress parade with the "straps" off from his shoulder. Another officer is under arrest for associating with his men; talking in familiar terms to his private. The Colonel is doing all in his power to get the officers and men under his heel. The officers are sending in their resignations daily.

Co. Dandy, in a mad drunken prank the other night, after being challenged rushed by a picket post shouting "Col. Stewart of the Confederate Cavalry". The astonished sentinel, knowing his voice perfectly well, was at a loss what to do. The Col. put the whole post in the guard house for not firing on him.[7]

Letter from A. Lyth to his Brother

Folly's Island S.C. May 31ˢᵗ 63

Dear Brother

 I received your kind letter of May the 14ᵗʰ and was very glad to hear that you were all enjoying good health as it leaves me at present. I hope you will have sent me you ambrotype before this as you promised I am glad to hear that father has got plenty of draining to do I guess though by this reaches you you will have commenced hole makeing but I guess you can not {missing word} untill the shed is rebuilt I wish you would tell me how many thousand brick can be made in a day by the new brick machine and how many hands it takes to work it Artillery men carry a sword and revolver but as yet we have not got them our Lt made out a recquisition for them but they had not any in the ordance department here. I guess we shall get them some time.

 For the last week past Captain Paine of our Regt has been takeing scouting parties on to James Island he has brought in a great deal of valuable information he found some four company of Rebel cavelry camped on James Island right opposite the Gen Headquarters they were covered from sight by the woods Last night some four or five hundred men went over under {missing word} and of our Col to attack them and drive them away or capture them and a small gun boat ran up a little inlet to render them a little assistance if nessary The gun boat has been throwing shell all the morning into the wood and we think she has made a few of them bite the dust the gun boat is a very short distance from us in fact we can holler over to them if nessary and they hear us our cannon are guarding the inlet that the gun boat has gone up in.

*June 1*st

Our men succeeded yesterday in driving the rebels and the took several prisoners *The rest run leaving their haversacks behind* *The grub in their haversacks was very poor there being nothing much but hominy and mollassas* *Our men after {missing words} made their way to a small fort with three guns mounted on it they were very cautious in getting up when they got as near as they could with out being seen they made a charge but upon captureing the fort they found that the guns were nothing but {unknown word} Logo.* *Then they pushed up a little further and came to a large house where there was a gun mounted in the window it also proved to be a wooden gun some of the boys went into the house and tumbled the gun out of the window* *They then returned the gun boat threw a few shell and returned also* *In one of his scouts Capt Payne discovered a boat loaded with food and clothing* *That two men belonging to one of our transports had smuggled over to the rebels* *They came across the boat as it lay loaded with goods by the shore of Johns Island one man was sitting in the boat while the other had gone off.* *They arested the man that was in the boat and then fixed bayonets to wait for whoever else might come but as no one made their appearance Capt Payne be a cautious man thought he would retire with what he had already got and make sure of it it is found out that these two men have been makeing it a business of smuggleing goods on dark nights over to the rebels* *I should like to see the fellow that they found in the boat strung up by the neck I wish he might fall into Gen Burnsides hands.*

Dear Brother I must close with this little birthday present to you. My love to you all

From your Affect Brother Alfred

N.B. There has been rumor around here that the gun boats are going into Charleston harbor agin this week but I guess there is no truth in the report

Letter from A. Lyth to his Sister

Folly Island June 1ˢᵗ 63

Dear Sister Mary

    I received your kind letter of May 14 with great pleasure and was glad to hear that you were enjoying good health. Tell fanny it may be not very long before I come home Our Regts time will be out in 18 months and then I'll come but it is to be hoped that the war will be over before that time

From Your Loving
Brother, Alfred

Write Soon

Letter from A. Lyth to his Folks at Home

Folly Island S.C. June 5ᵗʰ 1863

Dear Folks at Home

    I take the opportunity of writing you these few lines having nothing else at present to ocupy my time or mind hopeing they will find you all in good health and spirits as it leaves me at present. We are having some pretty warm weather here but the troops on this Island are as yet very healthy though yesterday a Lt of the 4 New Hampshire Regt died very suddenly by the black vomit The evening before he was playing with the boys of his company They will send his body home to day They say that the troops are not so healthy in other places in this department as they are here. It is rumored that all the troops on this Island except a Reg't or two are going to join the Potomac army and that a Brigade of negro troops are going to take their place here It is said that our Regt is a going to stay on account of it being the healthiest on the Island They are now issueing orders that solders shall do no duty whatever except picket duty only in the cool of the evening They will have no drill and they will only have dress parade in the cool of the evening I wish you could only see our Regt some time as they turn out for dress parade every man has his belts and shoes so that you might see yourself in them and each man has two pair of white gloves so he has to turn out with a clean pair on all such occations and they must be clean

189

and neat in all respects and they are the largest Regt on the Island I tell you it looks splendid. Our Col is getting very strick though. We are pretty well fortified on this Island and now they are busy mounting seige peices on the fortifications The principal ones are those that are bearing on the Rebel fortifications on Morris Island. But the rebels are not idle all this time. I was down to the point of this Island the other day and see the rebels are mounting peices on the point of Morris Island bearing on this Island.

The day before yesterday a black snake came into my tent and commenced eating some crackers that I had soaking in a cup some half a dozen of us got sticks to kill him but he run up a tree and down another one before we knew where he was we had just killed 2 snakes simlar to him the day before.

Dear Brother I must close now with my Love to you all. Give my Love to Sarah Ann and William and the children

From Your Affect Brother, Alfred

Letter from E. Cook to his Parents

Post Q.M. Office Folly Island S.C. June 7

My dear Parents

I have not time to write you a long letter but I will do so very soon.

I rejoined my company one week ago last Saturday and yesterday I was again detailed for duty in the Q.M. Dept. with the regt. I went on picket 3 times.

Our company has been recalled to the regiment + Co "C" has taken our place. The boys did not much like the change at first but they do not mind it much now. They will have to go on picket or guard once in 4 days, whereas when we were out to the battery the boys had to go on picket or guard twice in five days. The ocean is about a ¼ of a mile from the regiment and we take a bath in the surf every day. Write to me soon and direct to Co "H" 100th Regt. N.Y.S. Vols. Folly Island S.C.

I have had first rate health ever since I came down here. The weather is <u>Hot</u> *Furloughs are played out for the present I rec'd a letter from Mr.*

190

Lyman the last mail. Tell all the folk to write to me. The boys are both well. Write Soon.

Good bye
Your Aff Son, Edward L. Cook

Letter from A. Lyth to his Father and Mother

Folly Island South Carolina June 9th 63

Dear Father and Mother

I received your kind letter of May 25th also 2 Harpers Weekly's and 2 Weekly times I was very glad to hear that you were all well and in good health as it leaves me at present There has been orders read off that the troops of this department are all to be furnished with straw hats which will be furnished to us soon and the order also states that the men are to no fatigue work and as little other duty as possible through the day That the men should be furnished with fishing material and that they should fish in the morn and evening for the good of their health The order also states that every soldier should cover his tent with brush that is green limbs of trees and so forth and that every soldier must strike his tent twice a week and air it and all his clothing. All the tents in our detachment have our tents so fixed so we can take them down and put them up again in 3 minute We all have an abor of green bush built over them and another built in front in which we pass the warm hours of the day either reading or writing playing cards or passing the time away some how at our leasure Just as I was writing the last sentence small green snake fell out of a tree Just over my tent it fell on the tent then slid down to the ground near my feet were I soon put an end to him. Take things on the whole we should get along very well on this Island if it was not for the mosquitoes I tell you it makes a person open his eyes when a half a dozen come buzzing him when he has laid down to sleep each one carrying a brick under his wing to sharpen his bill with and I think it would astonish you to see a couple of them take hold of a large black snake and carry him off to feed their young ones

The capture of Vicksburg is great news here and if it proves true as there is no doubt it will it is a hard blow to the rebels

June 10ᵗʰ

Our company that has been supporting our Battery ever since we have been on the Island has been ordered back to the Regt and Co C has taken their place They are trying to get Captain Walbridge of our Co to take the office of headquarter master on this Island but he tells the boys if it is possible he will remain with the company although the quarter master is a higher office and more pay and of course no duty in the field only as staff officer. Capt Walbridge is loved by all the men in the Co and he is the best officer to his men in the whole Regt and the boys of other companys wish he was their Capt he once threw up the office of Brigade quartermaster to Join the company {unknown word} Negro Regt made a raid down here at Beaufort S.C. the started from Beaufort towards the interior of the state for the purpose of destroying a bridge they burnt houses took some cattle and destroyed a very great quantity of Rebel property but they did not succeed in destroying the bridge as they were attacked Just as they were about to commence the destrucktion and they made a hasty retreat not knowing how strong the force might be that was attacking them the returned with about 700 contrabands the next day they enlisted some 250 of them and had them drilling. I must close my letter with my love to you all give love to Sarah Ann and William and the children and let me know How the Youngster gets along

From Your Affect Son Alfred

P.S. answer soon

Letter from A. Lyth to his Brother

Folly Island S.C. June 11

Dear Brother

I hope these few lines will find you all in good health as it leaves me at present. There is not much news about here at present except that a British Steamer tried to run the blockade this morning into Charleston harbor but our blockadeing fleet caught them at the game and put after them and gave her two or three broadside and drover her in the beach of this Island where the crew tried to escape in the small boats on to Morris Island setting fire to the Steamer before leaving her Our men commenced to fire in to them as they were leaving the Steamer The rebels seeing this They commenced throwing shell at our men Who have to retire and let the men escape and the Steamer burn she is a fine looking steamer The rebels are awful mad and they hollered over and told our men they would pay them for that our men have to keep out of their sight now.

It is said there are very few rebel troops about here at present it is supposed they have gone to reinforce the Rebels at Vicksbourg now would be the time to attack Charleston if our fleet were ready. The last reports we have here are up to the Guns They state that Grant has Vickbourg surrounded and is in a fair way of takeing it but it is feared here that he may yet be foiled but I sincerely hope not.

I send you a paper which is published at Beaufort in this state it is not much of a paper as it oft contains many false rumors +c it is a week old now but I thought I would send it however

To day I see a black snake have a bird in its mouth carring it of I took a stick and got the bird away from the snake but the snake got away from me

June 12

That Steamer I mentioned in the fore part of this letter is run ashore between this Island and Morris Island the fire went out after burning the stearn of her off so now you see she sit upon the shore with all her merchandise in yet but the rebels cant go and get it out a we have quite a number of large guns bearing upon her nor we cant go to her as the rebels have the same They report our men killed one of the crew as they were escapeing this morning Last night our men fire a few shot at the Steamer by some long range 32 {unknown word} we have mounted on this Island They hit here once and some times threw over her but they did not destroy her it is thought that we will have to destroy her yet Dear Brother I must close with my love to you all

From Your Affect
Brother Alfred
write soon

Chapter Six

Operations on Folly Island and Morris Island, SC
June, 1863 – July, 1863

"Do not say anything to any one for I may be mistaken about it. All the work here is done at night. If a boat comes in during the day she has to lay until night before we discharge her. Everything is done very quiet. A regiment of troops landed here a night or two ago and persons sleeping within a few yards of the shove knew nothing about it. We have got some heavy siege guns planted right under the nose of the rebs that will make them squirm when we unmake them + open upon the [unknown]." E. Cook letter dated 6/20/1863

"Work was at once commenced on the batteries at the head of the Island. This was done at night, and with the enemy on Morris Island was so near to us that great precautions were necessary to conceal our operations. No loud words of command were spoken, the chains of the wagons were wrapped with cloths to prevent them rattling, and horse teams were used in the work, as mules might betray the presence of a working party by their familiar 'hee-haw'." Lt Col. Charles E. Walbridge address at the first Annual Reunion. 7/18/1888

George Stoddard's Diary

June 17th, 1863
Folly Island
Knowing that the officer of the day would never wet his skin to visit our post, I concluded to try my hand at fishing. Rigging up a pole I cast in. The first haul was something I knew could not be a fish and when landed the night proved too dark to see it; so I took my gun — which was stuck bayonet downward in the ground by my side — and smashed the animal with the butt. The next haul was a toad fish, a little fighting devil, said to be poison, who made a noise similar to the cluck of a setting hen. The next was a crab, as a severe pinch in my fingers attested. Now a crab is something I abhor. It makes me shutter to touch one by daylight and groping about their claws in

the dark was more than I could endure. The "gooseflesh" raised all over my body and I made up my mind to give up fishing for the night in disgust, or despair, or fear, I hardly know which. At any rate, I kept "crawling" until I was back to my post away from the edge of the water. In the morning I found the first haul to have been a crab.

I watched for Jonney Reb a half hour, when the reeling person got the predominance again and I concluded to try my luck in resuming fishing again.

Ten minutes and no bite. I kept on in an active lookout and presently I imagined that I saw a man cautiously approaching me. I dropped the pole and seized the gun. My pole at the same instantly settled on the oyster shells at my feet. I looked down and with a couple of jerks it started off towards the water. I tried to stop it with my feet but could not. It went scooting through the water leaving a long luminous wake behind it. I as so absorbed in this performance that I had quite forgotten the man. But after the first surprise was over I looked for him and he was gone. Supposing myself mistaken I paid no further attention to it.

Drawing a handline from my pocket, I baited & threw it in. Waiting a while, there were two sharp pulls and I commenced to draw. By the weight I knew it was a big fellow. A few yards of the line in and I heard a dry stick crack. I very reluctantly dropped the line and took the gun,. Three or four rods off, I saw a man coming. I let him get near enough & then challenged. "Friend with the countersign" answered he.

Recognizing the voice as one of the boys on post on the other end of the little island, and not caring to lose the fish that I had hooked, I waived ceremony and hollowed our "Hello, Brad, is that you?"

"Yes"

"Come on then, I have got a whole or something less in tow."

When I hauled in the fish – a huge catfish – there was something attached to him. On examination, it proved to be my lost line, pole, hook, and everything else, all in good order.

I then related the circumstances of losing it to Brad, when he said, "Guess it was me you saw. I was coming down to see what time it was, when I saw you down in near the water among the grass, and you seemed to be stooping or creeping suspiciously I thought it best to go back and get my gun & find out what you were. I did not know but what it was a rebel spy scouting around."[8]

Friday, June 19, 1863
Folly Island

. . . Lieut. Stowits' company had been detailed to work at the head of the island. He being sick was left behind in his tent all alone. He sent for me to come and see him. I found him quite sick with camp fever. Could do but little to help him. Slept tonight in his tent to be on hand in case of emergency. He was restless & lay the whole night tossing about in high fever.[9]

Letter from E. Cook to his Parents

Quartermasters office
Folly Island S.C. June 20/63

My dear Parents

I have now rec'd all of your letters except Nos 36 + 37, 40 + 46. I presume they will be along one of these day. I have been very busy so far in the office, but I am going to have some one here to help me as soon as the Quartermaster can find a good man. I rec'd 2 papers from you yesterday. I wrote to Mr. Lyman two or three days ago.

Thursday June 11th 1863 After sunset it commenced to pour. You will never know what is meant by "rain storm" until you have been down here. The night was dark as pitch. I had to get up from my bed + walk over to the boatmen's quarters + get them to take me over to one of the steamers in I had to deliver some dispatches. It was so dark that I could not see down to my feet + the only way I could make any headway was to stand still in the rain until a flash of lightning would show me the ground for a short distance and then I would start on a double quick and go it blind until I thought I had got as far as it was safe for a man to go with his eyes shut and then I would stop and wait again for another flash of lightning to guide me on my journey. One I fell into a slop hole but quickly tumbled out again without doing much damage.

Friday June 12ᵗʰ 1863 The rebs commenced to shell us to day from their batteries on Morris Island. Some of the shells passed through the place where our company was encamped when I joined it on this island.

They have not done much damage as yet. A piece of shell chopped a niggers head off but if he had remained in his proper place he would not have been killed. Some of the shell fell into one of our camps + compelled one or two regiments to move back a short distance. Our outer pickets are on the extreme point of this island and only a short distance from the rebel works. They have got holes dug in the sand and when they see a shell coming they dive down into their holes until the thing passes over and then they leap up onto the bank and shout + wave their hats to the rebs until they see the smoke from a cannon and then they dive down again and repeat the same operation. Oh! yes there is considerable fun about in as so long as the shells dont hurt any body.

Thursday June 18/63 I was threatened with fever to day but a dose of [ ] appears to have broken it up.

Friday June 19ᵗʰ 1863 We had a terrible thunder + lightning storm here to day. The claps of thunder sounded just like a large building falling, cracking, to the ground in our immediate vicinity.

Saturday June 20/63 The rebs have not shelled us any today. We will soon be ready to open upon them the most terrible fire they have ever rec'd in this department. We shall commence operations here sooner than I expected. Indeed I should not be at all surprised if before you receive another letter from me, you should hear through the newspapers of the commencement of operations on Charleston. Do not say anything about this to any one for I may be mistaken about it. All the work here is done in the night. If a boat comes in during the day she has to lay until night before we discharge her. Everything is done very quiet. A regiment of troop landed here a night or two ago and persons sleeping within a few yards of the shove knew nothing about it. We have got some heavy seige guns planted right under the nose of the rebs that will make them squirm when we unmask them + open upon the {unknown}. We have been sending mules teams up to these guns with supplies of ammunition in the night, but Genl. Gilmore ordered us to stop sending mule teams for they made too much noise in the night when they brayed. *Genl. Hunter has been relieved + Genl. Gilmore takes his place. Gilmore is a trump. He appears to never rest. He is everywhere at the same moment. He leaves Hilton Head at 4 o'clock in the morning to go down the coast + take note of what is going on among our forces in the vacinity of Savannah Every body expects he will be gone about two days and just as likely as not before night he will be walking through our unfinished works away up here near Charleston. He is a regular driver for doing business and I am in hopes of the highest kind that he will accomplish something worthy of the valor of the troops on this island. Nearly all of the boys down here are young men and old veterans. I guess every regiment down here had been in the field during one or more campaigns, except one – the 7th New Hampshire which has never been in a fight. Every thing has gone on finely so far. The rebs have only killed one or two of our men. If any thing occurs I will write and let you know immediately.*

We have a jug of whiskey sitting in our office all the time so I have plenty to drink (that is if I want to drink it). The water here is <u>miserable</u> + so we put a little whiskey into our drink to keep us from catching the fever. I would give 4 shillings for a days rations of good water.

It is a long time since I have had a drink of water that I could relish.

Write to me very soon. Give my love to Grandma + the children {unknown} + Lillian. Tell Mr. Lyman to write me all the news.

Good Bye from your Aff Son

Edward L. Cook

Direct to }   *Co "H" 100 N.Y.V.*

Folly Island SC

Letter from A. Lyth to his Brother

Folly Island S.C. June 21st 63

Dear Brother

I take this oppertunity of writing these few lines having nothing else at present to occupy my time In this section they are makeing preperations for an attack the engineer corps on this Island with some two or three infantry companys are working every night building fortifications on the point of this Island right under the rebel batteries They work nights and sleep day time for if they work day time they will be seen by the enemy Their work is hid from the sight of the rebels partly by being under cover of the woods and partly by small trees and bushes placed so as to conseal our opperations Last night they mounted 2 heavy guns and they will mount some every night now untill they get them all in position. It is the beleif of all on this Island that the attack on Charleston will commence the next full tide which will be when the moon is full and we shall have full moon in about 2 weeks from now As far as we can learn is that when the iron clads go into Charleston harbor and open on the forts our batteries on the front of this Island will open on the Morris Island batteries with the assistance of the gun boat Com McDonough. While our batteries on Seabrook Island will open also and some gun boats go up the rivers and come up in the rear of Charleston so you see when the ball does open there will be some lively times our peices will remain in the position they are at present untill the surrender of Morris Ile when we may have to take a more advance position. all this is founded on appearances and general beleif as we have heard no official orders as to when the attack is to begin. though it is know that when the attack does commence it will open as I have stated above. we are getting reinforcements of infantry on this Island. Our Regt which has been an independent Battalion ever since we left St Helena Island is at last been put in a Brigade Capt Paine went on a recconoisence on James Island yesterday and he has just returned with four rebel deserters who joined him while he was on James Island and they say that there are quite a number more would desert but the can't get away as they are afraid to approach our lines in the night for fear of being shot and they don't have a chance in the day time. They confirm the belief that there are very few rebel troops in this vicinity they say that there is no more than about five thousand in and about Charleston they say at one time they had barely enough men to work the guns on the fortifications and do picket and guard duty

June 22^d

To day we have 8 more deserters from the rebels 4 of them came on board of the ironsides 2 of them we carrying despatches from fort Sumter to fort Moultere and the other two were carring dspatches from fort Moultere to Morris Island they all got into a boat together with their despatches and instead of fetching them around the shore to Morris Island they put out to sea and carried their despatches on board of the iron sides The commander of the iron sides sent the despatches on to this Island to be opened by Gen Gillmore as they related to land operations The men are to be kept aboard of the iron sides untill the attack on Charleston is over as they know just where the torpedoes are placed The other 4 who came by land are of the same company that those were that Capt Paine fetched in yesterday They belong to the 1ˢᵗ S.C. Heavy Artillery they say that pretty much all of their Co would desert if they could swim and was sure they could reach our lines in safty but they say they are afraid as they are held under such strict orders if they should be caught deserting the would be shot without trial and if they are away and miss one roll call they are put in ball and chain One of the men that came across to day his brother came with Capt Paine yesterday, and he told us boys that last night as he was set in his tent another fellow came to him and began to taunt him to let his brother go off like that and not go with him then he said there was another day to come yet and they went right to work then to plan out a way to get off as they were coming through the rebel lines they were fired upon by the rebel pickets and they had to run through a big marsh where the mud was up to their waist where two of them gave out while the other two made good their escape to the edge of the river opposite the Gen Head Quarters where they signaled with a white handkercheif and our men went over in a boat and fetched them over a few hours after the other 2 made their appearance. one of the deserters was a Buffalo man and one a Ohio man the other were cast Tennessee They all agree as to the number of troops about Charleston. And they all say that when our monitors were in Charleston harbor on the 7 of April if they had kept up the bombardment an hour or two longer that we should have been in possession of Charleston that day they say that Gen Ripley actualy signaled from his quaters to fort Sumter for to surrender and the Col in Comand of fort Sumter signaled back for him to dry up he knew his own business best They say they are kept in ignorance of it if their army lose a victory they say they did not know of the capture of that rebel ram by our Monitor only the 4 that fetched the despches had heard any thing about it and they say the people in Charleston feel verry bad about it. The artillery men say they had it read off at dress parade to them that the Confederates had drove us Yankee's of off this Island They get very good clothese over there one of them that fetched his knapsack along he had two pair of pants one pair bran new and the other pair he had only had them on once and he had a pretty good pair on he had two shirts in 2 pair of

200

stockings and vairious other Knicnacs they are the worst of for shoes than anything. They say they get very poor grub over there for breakfast they get cornmeal bread and sugar for dinner they either get boiled rice or hominy sometimes with a little molasses and they have the same for supper as for breakfast they very seldom get meat and when they do get it it is only a few ounces they get When they came over here one of our boys asked them if they would take a cup of coffee which he did not say no we got some coffee some fresh bread and butter and some meat for them It would have done your heart good to see them fellows how they relished that breakfast one fellow grabed a big slab of bacon in his fist and held it up and hollered out 3 cheers for the old stars and stripes yet boys They say that when the war first broke out the enlisted of their own accord but had served their time out and were pressed in again one says they kept him in jail 8 weeks before he would take arms again one of them is known first rate by some of the 67 Ohio as he came from the same town that they did.

June 23ʳᵈ

    $26 To day we have been paid 2 months pay I think I shall may be kneed all that I drew as I had spend all I kept out of last pay having bought a watch out of it. Dear Brother Tell father if he can make any use or nead that money at all that is in the bank all he has to do is to draw it out The 4 of July will soon be here and I suppose you will have a great celebration of it in Buffalo but I guess we will be having a grander celebration here as it is stated that the attack is to begin on that day and one day will settle the affair The orders of Gen Gillmore are to have every thing ready for the attack by to morrow night on this Island. I must tell you a little story of Gen Gillmore since he has took command of this Island. I guess I have mentioned befor that Gen Gillmore was building some very good fortifications on this Island but that most of them were around his Head Quarters and at the landing where our ships came in from sea and right in our rear some even pointing out to sea where our own gun boats lay Now when he was riding around with Gen Gillmore he asked him how he liked his fortifications Gen Gillmore said he liked them first rate if he had got the Island on a pivot (so he could swing it round) since that time the troops on the Island have been busy plant guns in our front where there are needed Dear Brother I must conclude now with my love to you all We expect a *mail in day after tomorrow and I expect 2 or 3 letters as it is a good while since we had mail write soon*

   From Your Affectionate Brother Alfred

George Stoddard's Diary

Folly Island, SC

Bill of Fare for the month of June 1863

   Motives of curiosity prompt me to keep a memorandum of our grub. I choose June, and will continue it through the month.

   Observe! That, being in camp now, with every facility for obtaining rations, that this month will be a sample of the best. Instead of hard tack we occasionally get soft bread, which is a luxury beyond the common order of things. This since May.

   Breakfast is always hard tack and coffee; always the same for supper.

   For Diner

June 1 Salt Horse & Hard tack
2	*Boiled Rice and molasses*
3	*5 Boiled Potatoes*
4	*Pea Soup (Detestable)*
5	*Boiled Peas*
6	*Rice Soup & fresh beef*
7	*5 Boiled Potatoes*
8	*Split Peas boiled*
9	*Split Peas boiled*
10	*Boiled Rice & fresh meat*
11	*Boiled Rice & molasses*
12	*Bean Soup*
13	*Pea Soup*
14	*Peas & salt Horse*
15	*Desiccated Vegetables*
16	*Split Peas again*
17	*Peas split and Boiled Rice*
18	*Rice & molasses*

19	*Coffee & Bacon*
20	*Desiccated Vegetables*
21	*Desiccated Vegetables*
22	*Bean Soup*

Salt pork can be had any time by going too the Bbl. and cutting it off.[10]

Letter from A. Lyth to his Father and Mother

Folly Island S.C. June 25

Dear Father + Mother

I received your kind letter of June the 7th and was very glad to hear that you were enjoying good health as it leaves me at present

As regards that leave of absance you speak off there is no athority for any of the new recruits to expect any this year. There was order issued for to give all the men in this department fourlough and arrange it so 4 or 5 should leave every Co every 10 days but the order was countermanded Just after the first squd left here for Hilton Head which was some 3 or 4 weeks ago and the last we heard from them they had not left there which was 5 days ago but they expected to leave for home the next day There will be no more fourlough granted untill after the attack on Charleston for which every thing has to be in readyness by next Wednesday and it is thouht the attack will commence on the 4 of July. Yesterday the rebels commenced to shell our picket lines and reserves killing 2 or 3 men of the 62 Ohio I suppose the account that you read in the newspaper of our being attacked by the rebels has some reference to their shelling of our pickets of whitch I spoke in one of my former letters but none of our Regt have been hurt or taken prisoners as none of it were in the vicinity except myself and a couple of other boys belonging to our detachment. I am very sorry that you did not send me the box as it would have come in very handy Just at present as I have only got one good shirt and I dont want to wear any more government shirts so last night I went to the sutlers and bought a good one which cost me three dollars I wish you would send the box of immeadately for if we are not on this Island by the time it gets here we shall be in Charleston Address it A.L. Co H 110 R NYSV Hilton Head S.C. camp on Folly Island

I should like John very much to send me his ambrotype and not let any foolish newspaper reports stop him any more. I should like to have all your likenesses but when John gets his let fanny have hers taken the same time and send them both

I must close now with my love to you all we expect another mail in tomorrow as the Argo is due then and she is our regular mail steamer I will write in a day or two again. Give my love to Sarah Ann and William and the Children and let me know how they all get along.

From Your Affec Son Alfred Lyth

P.S. I also received 2 weekly times and three Harpers

Letter from A. Lyth to his Sister

Folly Island S.C. June 27th 63

Dear Sister

I received your kind letter of June 11th and was very glad to hear that you were all well and in good health as it leaves me at present Just as I received your letter last night the orders were going round to every Regt and battery on this Island for to get prepared for the attack and be ready on a moments notice to open on the rebels No soldier is allowed to roam around the Island as we used to do as there are guards posted all over the Island to arrest all they find without a pass. I have a pass that will pass me any where on the island so you see I have a good chance to see what is going on The attack will not begin untill the morning of the 4 of July so you see when all the peacefull citizens of Buffalo are woke from their nights rest by the noise of your cannons in the park. The soldiers in the vicinity of Charlston will be tumbleing out of their bunks and grasping their arm tightening their belts eager for the fight and victory

Yesterday every man in our Regt all drew a new india rubber blanket and new hats. The kind of hats we drew are those tall drab plug broad rim hats and when the Regt got them on we looked like a Regt of farmers though *they are an excellent thing in this hot country Then we drew mosquitoes bars. these bars are 7 ½ feet long a little over 2 feet broad and 3 feet high they are wove like braze about as close as a sand sive now we fix these over our bunks and get in let down the front curin then we are in a cage out of the musquitoes reach but still if you get under your bars in the evening you can see them come and light on your bars and stick their bills out at you. The Regt has draw all new A tents so the soldiers wont have to carry our shelter tents any more the teams will carry the tents here after all that our musquitoes bars weigh when rolled up to put in the knapsack is 3 ounces Dear Sister there is no danger of me ever doing any thing so that I shall be court martialed Yesterday I was at a court martial of one of our corporals for striking a man. Our Leautenant acted as President Our Sergent acted as Judge advocate and myself and the other Corporal and a private formed the court The prisoner was fetched up before the court he pleaded guilty he was found guilty. Then the court retired to pass his sentence Now we could have had the prisoner reduced to the ranks or fined him a months pay but we did not like to do that as he was always a very good fellow so we sentenced him to ask the pardon of the party offended*

Dear Sister I must close this letter with my love to you all so no more at present.

> *From Your*
> *Affect Brother*
> *Alfred*

write soon

Letter from A. Lyth to his Father and Mother

> *Folly Island S.C. July 2ᵈ 63*

Dear Father + Mother
*   I received your kind letter of June 19ᵗʰ containing three postage stamps I was sorry to hear that John was sick but I hope he is all right by this. I hope you will have a good kiln and good success to the whole season but the way Mr. Robson goes into brick making don't look very brilliant I cannot*

tell you for sure weather the attack on Charleston will commence as soon as expected on account of Admiral Footes illness but they are still making extencive preparations in this section and for the last 4 or 5 days the troops have had to drill 6 hours a day scrimish and Batallion drill. We are having some hot weather here at present but we oft have a thunder shower here but they never last long but when it thunders its what you may call thunder there's as much difference between this thunder and the thunder we have at home as there is between the report of a small pistol and a cannon

I never received that book on Phonorgraphy I wrote for to Ci and I guess I never shall as it is nearly 2 months since I wrote for it Dear Folks you must excuse my short letter as I intend to write again in a day or two Give my love to Wm + Sarah I send my love to you all

From Your Affect Son
Alfred

P.S. dont neglect to write soon

Letter from E. Cook to his Parents

Q.M. office July 2ᵈ 1863
Folly Island S.C.

My dear Parents

I have been working hard at my papers all day and all the evening also until now. I have a very small piece of candle left just an inch long so I must write hastily if I finish my letter to night.

I think I have rec'd very nearly all of your letters but I do not keep any account of them any more because half of them are not numbered and the other half are numbered wrong. I am in good health and feeling first rate. There is going to be some fighting down here one of these days if we can judge by appearances. I hope our side will be successful. We are all anxious to hear from Vicksburg + Pennsylvania. A monitor came in our harbor last night which looks like work. I think as soon as all the iron clads are ready for action we will open the attack on Charleston again. The men who started from here about a month ago to go home on furloughs returned last week without getting any further on their journeys than Hilton Head.

The poor fellows felt very much disappointed and I am very sorry for them. I rec'd two months pay about a week ago. Geo. Stoddard is detailed in the Q.M. Dept. at this point. He likes the place very much. He is military store keeper for the command on this island.

It is quite a responsible position but the employment suits George to a dot. And he is well qualified for it. He keeps every thing as neat + straight as a pin and his mode of keeping the accounts of the stores is excellent.

Laura can do just as she and you like about going to the Seminary but if there is any chance of her graduating in any reasonable length of time at the Central I would much rather that she would remain there at least until I return for two reasons first I think the discipline, system and tuition is far more perfect at the Central than it is at the Seminary. And Secondly if she should ever desire to become teacher in any of the public schools she will be shown a preferance on account of graduating at the Central. However if she should desire and you should wish her to attend the Seminary I will do any thin to the extent of $100# towards paying her tuition and clothing bill. And you can draw that much from my bank account at any time you like for that purpose.

I have not heard from Lottie {unknown name} for nearly 2 months. I suppose she has got struck with some fellow that diddent go to the war. Heigh ho!

I am glad the 7th has gone I would have give a years pay to have been {unknown} and gone with them. I am having an easy time in comparison with the rest of the boys in the regt., although I have to work all day long from the time I get up until it is too dark to see and then if I have candles I have to go it at night. I have not had a chance to visit the company since I left although I see some of the boys down here every day. We have a Barrel of Whiskey in my office all the time on tap for fatigue {unknown}. I am allowed whisky rations a gill a day but I very seldom take that all and when I do it is in small quantities. The regiments on the island are working day and night. Sometimes I have to get up 2 or 3 times in the night to give whiskey to working parties. You would be surprised to see the minimum amount of work that has been accomplished here in the last 10 or 12 days in sight + range of the enemies guns. But they do not know it for all the work is done at night. We will be all ready to open on them in less than a week and I think it will make them open their eyes. My inch of candle is most burned down and I will bid you good bye now so that if it goes out at any moment my letter will be finished. Give my love to Grandma. I hope she will be well soon. I wish I could see her. Tell her to try and keep up her spirits until we return and all of us see her again. I wish I could do something for her. I think she will be pleased to know that G.S. is in the Q.M. Dept. and does not have to carry a musket a lil out in the heavy night dews on picket duty. I saw G. Clark today. He is looking well. He was down here. I hope you will continue to write to me as heretofore and even oftener. Although I have not much time to answer. I think after the fight I shall have more time to myself. What made Geo. Peck leave Hardiker + Toye: Tell Mr. "H" that I have far more complicated work in the Q.M. office than I had in his office. I could have told them what Charlie was before they employed him. What is H. Phillips doing now? I suppose you think when I speak of my office that I am in a building but it is not so. I do all my writing in a tent where the wind has free play with my papers, and sometimes plays them out of doors. We drawed Mosquito bars + felt hats last month for all the troops on the island. Tell Mr. Lyman not to go to the war even for 3 months if he can avoid it. I still have plenty of paper and envelopes. Give my love to all hands. Next time I write to will take more time than 15 minutes and write plainer. I hope with a very little patience + perseverance you will be able to make this all out. Good Bye from your Aff Son. in the army of the U.S. of America. – Edward

I send you Twenty dollars which you can use as you see fit. If you have no use for it you had better put it in the bank as soon as possible in order that it may draw interest on my account. Ed.

Chapter Seven

Operations on Folly Island and Morris Island
Assault on Fort Wagner
July, 1863 – September, 1863

"Our part of Regt was in the fight. Our pieces remain in their old position. I believe there was quite a number wounded some very badly. They established a hospital near were our pieces are. I am about well now but a little week as yet I hope that these few lines find you all in good health." A. Lythe letter dated 7/10/1863

"All I believe we would have taken the fort if it had been daylight as it was so dark that our men shot one another our Regt fired a volly in the 48th and 67th fired 3 vollys into us killing & wounding a great many." T. Maharg letter dated 7/26/1863

"Unfortunately for us, the assault on Wagner was deferred until daybreak the next morning, by which the enemy as well as ourselves, were prepared for the struggle. Though our brave fellows reached the work, crossed the ditch, and even scaled the parapet, they could not maintain their footing and were driven back with severe loss, having their killed and wounded in the hands of the enemy. Then there was a week's delay, during which the iron-clads daily poured their shot into the fort, and we could see the great showers of beach and dust displaced as the shell struck the work, while the garrison remained practically unharmed within the massive bomb-proofs. During this week of waiting, more troops had been landed, more guns put in position, and all preparations were made for another and desperate attempt to take the fort."
Lt. Col. Charles E. Walbridge address at the first Annual Reunion 7/18/1887

"My comrades, let us in fancy transport ourselves this afternoon from these pleasant groves to that sandy island on the coast of South Carolina. Not a solitary tree shades us from the scorching heat, while the white sand reflects the sunlight with dazzling brightness. As we cast our gaze around the horizon and recall the scene that once was so familiar to us, in our rear lie the woods of Folly Island, across the marshes we see Secessionville in the distance, then the dark woods over on Black Island, then more marshes like a giant prairie, with Fort Sumter silent and sullen rising beyond them. On our right is the blue ocean with the blockading squadron in the offing, and the ironclads closer in shore. Since early morning the land batteries and the fleet have been hammering away at Wagner until at last the guns of the fort are silenced. All day you have been lying with other troops along the beach below the Beacon House, waiting for the decision of the Commanding General, and at last the order comes shall be stormed after dark.

How can we describe the horrors of a night attack, when friends as well as foes are concealed from view, or only revealed by the flashes of the guns; when it is almost impossible to convey orders, or to bring up re-inforcements, and when those who succeed in reaching the parapet, find themselves unsupported and alone. Just as the assault was made, a tremendous thunderstorm commenced, and the flashes of lightning and the roar of heaven's artillery added to the terrors of the scene. General Strong's brigade formed the first line, and went in gallantly, but Strong himself was soon mortally wounded, the gallant young Colonel Shaw of the 54th Massachusetts was killed, many others had fallen, and soon the whole line was driven back. Putnam's brigade, to which the 100th belongs, pressed forward through the storm of fire and through the flying fugitives of the first line, with a stern determination to carry the fort in spite of all obstacles.

You reach the other ditch, cross it beneath the plunging fire from the crest and commence the struggle for the parapet; a foothold is gained on one corner and messengers are dispatched from re-inforcements, but Colonel Putnam, like scores of others, is killed within the fort and the enemy pour out of the bomb-proofs, and have the advantage in their familiarity with the place, while you have, as it were, to feel your way in the dark, that all your sacrifice proves in vain, and the word is passed to fall back. Retreating under such circumstances is almost as fatal as advancing, and many a poor fellow fell during the retreat. The 100th lost heavily in this fearful night attack." Lt Col Charles E. Walbridge address at the first Annual Reunion 7/18/1887

Letter from A. Lyth to his Father and Mother

Folly Island S.C. July 10th 63

Dear Father + Mother

    I take this oppertunity of writing you these few lines not knowing when they will leave here as the operations against Charleston commenced this morning The batteries on this Island opened as 5 oclock this morning against the rebel batteries on the point of Morris I. after between 2 + 3 hours Bombarding The rebels guns were nearly silenced Gen Strong crossed folly river with his brigade and some negro troops and worked himself into the rear of the rebel batteries and captured all the rebs before the reingforcements that were coming up could reach them Our part of Regt was in the fight Our peices remain in their old position I belive there was quite a number wounded some very badly They established the hospital near were our peices are I am about well now though I am a little weak as yet I hope these few lines will find you all in good health

I should have wrote more particulars but you will see them in the papers. I send my love to you all

From Your Affect

Son Alfred

PS Write soon

Clara Barton's Letter to Elvira Stone, July 11, 1863

"While all were tired and hot and faint with the terrible days work in such a scalding sun, and such a climate, what should happen as if Heaven sent, but that the little steamer which came for our wounded should bring us the glorious, glorious news" that Vicksburg had fallen to Grant and that Lee's army had been *"defeated and largely captured"* at Gettysburg in Pennsylvania. The news, she added, *"had an electric effect on Gillmore's troops. They were no longer tired or hungry or faint, neither could they talk, they just shouted and wept. Oh, these are glorious days, and the sunlight is breaking through. I began to see some prospect of rest for these tired armies, some husbands and fathers left to waiting wives and little ones art home"*[11]

Clara Barton's Letter to Dear Friends, December. 8, 1863

"It seemed as if day light would never come" When it did come, it revealed a hideous sight: Dead men, black and white, littered the beach for almost a mile. At Wagner, dozens of corpses, many dismembered, were stacked up in the moat and along the parapets."[12]

Edwin Nichols Diary

Saturday – July 18 - We had been lying down about half an hour and nearly all fast asleep when we were called up and ordered to go support the pickets. Between 10 and 11 o'clock we were visited by just another thunder storm as we had the night before. It does not often fall to the lot exposed to such storms two nights in succession. The storm lasted until seven o'clock this morning. We are now lying behind the sand hills to keep clear of the enemy's shot and shell which has and is now dropping too near to be pleasant. Our gun boats are now coming up and I guess they will have something else to attend to besides shell us.

Sunday – July 19 - We joined the regiment about noon and formed line of battle on the beach. About the same time the monitors and ironsides moved up and opened on Wagner, and continued blazing away until after sundown. Then commenced the horrid strife as to who should be master of Fort Wagner. The first brigade, commanded by General Strong, and headed by the 54th Massachusetts colored regiment led the attack and was repulsed with great slaughter. The second brigade followed and was also repulsed. The 7th N. H. was a little in advance of our regiment and succeeded in getting very near the fort, and a few men got inside, but could not stand the fearful fire they were exposed to, and those that were not cut down, retreated.

Our regiment marched in line of battle and kept a good line until they got near the fort, in spite of the gaps that were constantly made in its ranks; but the men closed up, and on they went without wavering or taking any notice of their comrades falling around them. It was now dark and the rebels were pouring murderous fire of grape and canister shot and shell from every gun they could bring to bear on us, besides musketry and hand-grenades. No tongue can tell or pen describe that terrible scene

Some of our men got inside the fort and held part of it for some time, in spite of musketry, hand-grenades and everything else the rebels could bring against us. Had reinforcements come up at this time the fort would have been ours, but none came, and those that were not killed or wounded made their way out again as best they could. As I crossed the moat on my way out again, it appeared to be full of dead and wounded soldiers, with no help for them; as it was certain death to any man who attempted to rescue them.

At this time the groans of the wounded and dying were fearful to hear and were enough to appall the bravest amongst us.

A second time the regiment formed, or rather the remains of it, and marched back again; but before we got near the fort the orders were countermanded – all was lost.

We had seven companies in the fight and all the officers that are present now are the colonel, two captains and one lieutenant. Company C lost 32, killed, wounded or missing, but there is scarcely a man in the company but what was shot, through some part of his clothes, Yesterday there was not a better, or finer, or larger regiment in the department; today it would make a man's heart ache to look upon it. Today our men are burying the dead and caring for the wounded.

Tuesday, 21ˢᵗ – We had a dress parade last evening and all the officers we could muster were Col. Dandy, Capt. Evert, now acting adjutant, Capt. Bailey, and Lieut. Howell. It was a hard site to look upon and caused quite a sensation amongst the spectators, as well it might.[13]

Letter from E. Cook to Parents

Folly Island S.C.
July 19ᵗʰ 1863

My dear Parents

We had another terrible battle last night. Yesterday as soon as the rain ceased in the morning about 10 o'clock the firing began and continued until 8 or 9 oclock at night without ceasing. Sumter fired about 3 times a minute and all day long it was one continual boom, boom, and boom without any ceasing. Last night our boys made a charge, the 100ᵗʰ was in it. We lost very heavily, the rebs bayoneted out wounded. We were repulsed again in the charge. I think now that Genl. Gilmore will try some other way to take it. I think this fort is the only one that will give us any trouble. If we take this we will have Charleston.

Rebel Officers, taken prisoners, say that we can take "Sumter" but all H-l cant take "Wagner". It is steel cased + casemated with railroad iron {unknown} from the casemates so that it is perfectly Bombproof.

I think we will take within a fortnight our loss is terrible. Our *regiment lost all their field officers all the hire offices but five. Our Major was wounded. Genls. Strong + Seymour were wounded. What do the people north think of the attack on Charleston? Did the expect it? I have not heard direct from the 100th but if I hear any thing about Geo. Clark I will write to you.*

I am in great haste. I never worked so hard in my life as I am doing now and have done for the last month or more. I do not write to any body but you. News is very scarce. A Dollar was offered to day for a single coppies of the N.Y. Herald of the 15th and even then those that had them would not sell. They sell in N.Y. for 2 cents and here 2 dollars would hardly buy one. I am well. Write to me soon + send all the news. Geo. Stoddard is well liked by his Quartermaster. The Captain told me yesterday that he was going to keep George and pay him 25 or 40 cents extra pay.

> *Your Aff Son*
> *Edward*

Clara Barton's Letter to Brown and Duer, March 13, 1864

"I can never for get the patient bravery with which they endured their wounds received in the cruel assault upon Wagner, as hour after hour they lay in the wt sand, just back of the growling guns waiting their turn for the knife or the splint and bandage . . . and when ever I met one who was giving his life out with his blood, I could not forbear hastening to tell him . . . that he was the soldier of freedom. . ."[14]

Clara Barton's Letter to Mr. Parker, December 9, 1863

"We have captured one fort – Gregg – and one charred house – Wagner- and we have built one cemetery, Morris Island. The thousand little sand hills that glitter in the pale moon light are a thousand headstones, and the restless ocean waves that roll and break upon the whitened beach sing an eternal requiem to the toil-worn, gallant dead who sleep inside."[15]

Report of Major Lewis Butler, 67ᵗʰ Ohio Infantry, of the Assault of
Battery Wagner, July 18, 1863

HDQRS. 67ᵗʰ Regiment, OHIO VOL. INFANTRY, Hilton Head, S. C.,
February 2, 1864
Brigadier-General SEYMOUR,
Commanding U. S. Forces, Hilton Head

GENERAL: Agreeable to your request I have the honor to report that
on the evening of July 18, 1863, in the charge on Wagner, my regiment,
the 67ᵗʰ Ohio Volunteer Infantry, went into the charge third in line of
Putnam's brigade in the following order, in deployed column, First, 7ᵗʰ
New Hampshire, second, 100th New York, third, 67ᵗʰ Ohio; fourth 62ⁿᵈ
Ohio, Lieutenant Colonel Steele; our brigade preceded by Strong's brigade.
For some reason unknown to me, our brigade was halted near the beacon-
house, and Strong's brigade allowed to proceed on toward the fort. After
remaining some twenty minutes we were ordered forward under a most
galling fire. When about the fifth parallel our columns were very much
disturbed by stragglers from Strong's brigade and the breaking of the 100ᵗʰ
New York. It was here that we met the 3ʳᵈ New Hampshire and 9ᵗʰ Maine
moving back by the flank. Upon arriving near the glacis the balance of
Strong's brigade were lying down. Upon our brigade coming up, they arose
and the final assault was made. Of the number that gained the fort from
each regiment, I am not able to say but this I was state, that the only
regiments that showed anything approaching organization at this time
were the 48ᵗʰ New York, 6ᵗʰ Connecticut, 7ᵗʰ New Hampshire, 67ᵗʰ and
62ⁿᵈ Ohio. A few men of the 54ᵗʰ Massachusetts (colored) and a few of
the 100th New York were in the fort, but upon calling for the officers
none reported to me from either of those regiments. I believe that in all
there were not more than between 400 to 500 men in the fort from both
brigades.... I then called a council of the officers in the fort, not wishing to
hazard anything further with out their co-operation. All agreed to hold out
until we could hear from the rear. After waiting twice the length of time
which I knew would require to move Stevenson's brigade to our support, at
about 10:30 o'clock, observing that the rebels were being re-enforced and
we were making preparations for a sally upon both flanks, I gave the order
to retire. ...... John B. Chapman, of our regiment, who was wounded and

going to the rear, saw Colonel Dandy, just above the battery inquiring for his regiment. And was informed that he would find it in the rear.. . . In conclusion let me say that the repulse we suffered was entirely owing to our not being promptly sustained, and the consequence the numerous loss of life and expenditure of money which had to be incurred to regain the position we had gained at so fearful a loss of life, and might have been held at a light expense to what it eventually cost. In this report I have not attempted to give anything coloring which did not belong to it, but as nearly as possible give you a plain statement of facts which came under my notice. Of the scenes of carnage, of the determined valor of the troops, I need not speak, but the fact that they gained the fort amid the darkness of the night and under as withering a fire as any troops were ever exposed, and held it near three hours against fearful odds, speaks a volume for the personal courage of the men which cannot be written.

Very respectfully, your obedient servant,
Lewis Butler
Major 67th Ohio Volunteer Infantry[16]

Other Perspectives

"The battle is over; it is midnight; the ocean beach is crowded with the dead, the dying, and the wounded. It is with difficulty you can urge your horse through to Light-house Inlet. Faint lights are glimmering in the sand-holes and rifle pits to the right as you pass down the beach. In these holes many a poor wounded and bleeding soldier has laid down to his last sleep. Friends are bending over them to stanch their wounds, or bind up their shattered limbs; but the deathly glare from sunken eyes tells that their kind services are all in vain."[17]

"Before leaving for the assault, Col. Putman ordered his men not to cap their muskets, for he anticipated that the assault would be accomplished by the use of bayonets if it came to a fight. The 100ths New York, which was positioned behind the 7th New Hampshire, disobeyed that order. Their Colonel, George B. Dandy, said that his men never fired without orders. Within only an hour, Dandy's statement would be sadly disapproved."[18]

"The next regiment in our rear (the One Hundredth New York) came promptly up to the ditch and in the darkness, which was only lighted by the flashes of the guns, saw the parapet covered with men, and supposing them to be Confederates, fired into them, undoubtedly killing and wounding many of our men. As it now became very dark, we could only see our way when the flashes of the rebel guns which swept the moat, lit up the ghastly scene for a moment only but at short intervals."[19]

"His (Putnam's) 100th N. Y. advanced near to the works, but in the confusion, and darkness poured a volley into our own (54th Mass. Regiment) in the salient and then retired."[20]

Letter from A. Lyth to his Folks at Home

Hilton Head Hospital
July 21st 63

Dear Folks at Home
I was taken pretty bad with the diorea when I was on Folly Island and they put me a board of the Hospital boat were I was 4 or 5 days then they fetched us to the Hospitale here I have about got over the diorea and am gaining strength pretty fast Our Regt has been in a fight and is nearly cut to peices you will have seen the account in the papers before this reaches you A good many of the wounded came down on the boat that I came on I must close now excuse my short letter From Your Loving Son, Alfred

Letter from E. Cook to his Parents

Office [   ] Folly Island S.C.

My dear parents
I suppose you feel rather lonesome. I rec'd 2 letters from Laura this morning. One of them told me you had rec'd the 20 dollars I sent you and the other one said Laura, Mary + Gracie were going to start in a day or

two for Bridgeport. I think I will send you 20 dollars more in this letter although it is somewhat scaley + riskey to be sending uncle Sam Lincoln's money over the world with no thing to protect it but an envelope. I am not in good health, nor have I been for several days. The heat is oppressive and causes a headache each day. We have considerable wind but as this island is white sand the wind becomes so heated in passing over it that when it reaches us it is oppressive instead of luxurious. We have lightning every night but little rain + thunder. When it does thunder it sounds as if every thing was going to pieces. The lightning is grand and very different from the lightning we have up north. I am stationed now with Capt. Walbridge at the north end of Folly Island S.C. and right opposite Morris Island. I can have a plain + close view of every shot + shell that is fired by either side. There has been but little firing within the last 3 or 4 days. I should not wonder if the rebs were preparing for some kind of a move to cut us off. In the meantime our men are working hard every night with a few hundred yards of "Wagner" and within short rifle range of the sharp shooters. I guess some of our men are killed every day but the work goes on steadily + surely + all the rebs can do won't stop or impede our progress. If we can't batter down the hellish Iron hung institution we will dig under it and blow it into dust. Laura thinks we cannot take "Wagner". I think that before the 1ˢᵗ of Jany 1864 we will have Wagner, Sumter, Charleston + all.

I fear that there is but little or no hope that we shall ever see George Clark again. Nothing has yet been heard from him. I have written to his brother for instructions in regard to the disposal of his effects. Dr. Howell wants me to come back to the company and be orderly sergeant. What would you advise me to do about it. I do not think I shall get my extra duty pay in the Q.M. Dept. for that has been stopped by an act of Congress and I am now working again for $10 # per month and patriotism.

I do not have to work as hard as I used to last month and in June, nor am I able to do it even if I had to. My head troubles me so that even in writing this letter page + a half I have had to knock off 2 or 3 times. Except the heat I am doing first rate. I am so fat that I think you would hardly know me. The sand is very fine and seems to sift right through a persons clothes and makes him feel nasty + dirty all the time. Oh won't I be glad when I can get back into old Buff and get off this dirty soldiers toggery and put on a nice clean shirt of pure white cotton and sleep between cotton sheets and have a chance to bathe in fresh water. I am sick of this *salt water bathing. It is well enough in cool weather, but in these hot days it acts on the perspiration of the body just as water does on oil – It don't mix; and when we come out of the water in stead of feeling nice + clean we feel just as if we had been in an oil can. Our Batteries will be ready to open on Sumter in about a week. I will write you all the news just as fast as possible. I think it is very likely that when our batteries are ready to open they will fire right over "Wagner" and try breach "Sumter".*

I am glad Grandma is getting better. I hope she will keep up good spirits and live to see whoever is left of us return to our loved homes again. I wish I could say that I believed George Clark was wounded + a prisoner but I fear that he was killed in the ditch of "Wagner" and buried by the rebels.

Charlie Shaffer has got his discharge and has gone home. He took a small package of shells for you and if he does not send them over then Eliza had better call and get them at his house. Capt. Walbridge had Geo Clark's opera glasses and a few days ago he lent them to Capt. Payne our "Yankee Scout" who had lost his own in one of his expeditions to Charleston. The first night that he went out with Geo. C's glasses he was captured and is now a prisoner in Charleston. Capt. Walbridge says he will pay for the glasses if Capt. Payne does not return with them. If I send any money in this letter I wish you would answer it immediately and let me know that you receive it all right.

Our iron clads have just began again for the first time in 3 or 4 days to pop away at Wagner. I can plainly see the sand fly up in clouds where the huge balls strike. There is a great smoke rising on Morris Island about halfway up and near Wagner. It looks as if something was burning.

Fort Sumter has just fired her warning gun. It does not appear to be more than a mile from here yet it is about 3 or 4 miles. The evenings are cool but the nights are warm with very little air stirring. Fort Sumter's flag is still flying although her evening gun has fired. I am strongly inclined to believe that within 10 days from this time there will be no rebels on Sumter. Our Batteries + floating batteries are almost finished and there will be but little delay in getting them to work after they are finished. Write to me as often as you can and tell me what the buffalo people say of the 100th Regt. in the last fight. Some of Co "H" boys were inside fort "Wagner" for nearly an hour but they were not supported and finally had to back out again.

I have just returned from supper and as it is too dark to see I must stop. I will write again soon.

I enclose 20 Dollars

Edward L. Cook
Co H 100 N.Y. Voles

Letter from T. Maher to A. Lyth

Morris Isl. July 26

Friend Al

Jim {unknown name} received your letter yesterday + I had the pleasure of reading it. We have had a pretty hard fight here lately it was on the evading of the 18ᵗʰ that we charged on fort Wagner & was drove back after holding it about two hours. All I believe we would have taken the fort if it had been daylight as it was it was so dark that our men shot one another our Regt fired a volly into the 48ᵗʰ and the 67ᵗʰ fired 3 vollys into us killing & wounding a great many.

All our Col. is a [ ] the last time I seen him in the fight he was in the line of file closers back of the flag he told us to keep as near the flag as we could. The 9ᵗʰ M was the Regt. a head of us and when they got about ¼ mile from the fort they broke and run through our lines which was enough to make any Regt. brake but ours did not flinch but went on loosing men at every step the first that fell was {unknown word} & John Allen and then Tom Wharton To was on my left + Townsend was on my right – they are both gone. Geo Clark I guess is killed for we have not heard any thing from him Lient Runkill is killed + a great many more. There was 22 killed wounded & missing in our Camp. Major Nash was wounded and our Adjutant is missing Roby Henderson is wounded in the foot I seen him when he was shot. All they talk of opening again to morrow the rebles keep up a brisk canonading on our pickets and there is more or less hurt every day we have been on picket twice the first time Camp I had 7 men wounded and the last time there was five our Camp done the scrimmishing last time + we went with in 10 yards of the Rebles picket it was so dark we could not see them but one of our boys coughed + bang went a musket right at his nose but did not hurt him Give my respects to all the boys there and tell them to wright soon.

Yours For Ever Tom Maharg

Letter from A. Lyth to his Father and Mother

Ward F
General Hospital
Hilton Head S.C. July 29ᵗʰ 63

Dear Father + Mother
I am getting my strength slowly but surely I have had a slight touch of the typhoid fever but have got entirely clear of that. I have not received my mail from the Regt yet but expect too in a day or two so I have not learned which of the boys in our Co came out of the fight safe. They are going to seige those forts and not make any more charges with the infantry on them I must close as I have nothing else to write about Give my love to Sarah Ann + William an the children. I send my love to you all
From Your Loving Son
Alfred

Letter from E. Cook to his Parents

Folly Island S.C. July 29ᵗʰ 1863

My dear Parents
The weather is decidedly warm, but we do not feel the heat very much because we are on the beach of the ocean and generally have a cool sea breeze blowing all day.
I am afraid Geo. Clark is either a prisoner or else something worse. No trace can be found of him: he was wounded + left on the field. I have inquired of every body that knew him but no one saw any thing of him after he fell. <u>One</u> *of the trio has gone; who shall the next be. The Lieut. of our company wants me to come back to the company and be orderly sergeant, but I have refused to go unless the boys of the company express the wish to have me that position. I told him I would come back as a corporal if he thought it was for the good of the company but I would not overstep any of the other noncommissioned officers. He replied that he did not want me back unless I came as orderly sergt. I do not know what steps he will take in the matter but I think I shall have to return to my company before*

many days. I shall try my best to have Geo. Stoddard remain where he is. He is getting almost as fat as I am on high living.

We expect an attack from the rebs on this end of the Island every night. It is the only hope of the rebs attack us here and move up. They could do it to for we have no troops down here and our men are working now to get things in readiness but it will take us some little time get prepared for an attack. The officer commanding our river battery, and the only battery that commands the river both ways and the only battery that could be used against an attacking party, says that if the rebs should come down on us now, we could do nothing to oppose them but would have to desert this end of the island and 10 large guns, and retreat to Morris Island.

I have just this minute rec'd a letter from you but I have not had time to read it. The mail is just going to close and I must finish this letter or I shall be too late. Write to me very often and tell me in your next letter if you recd the 20 dollars I sent home about a month ago. I am afraid you never got it. I have 50 dollars now but I do not like to send it until I hear from the last I sent. I have managed to skim over your letter. I am glad Grandma's better give her my love. I am afraid she will never see poor Geo. Clark again. I rec'd a lot of his papers this mail. I wish he was here to read them.

I am acquainted with Halsey. I think he is a good fellow for his kind. The furlough men who took my shells were recalled before they got to Buffalo. In fact they were stopped at Hilton Head and not allowed to proceed. I have written to Henry C Clark about Geo. but I could give him no hope.

Give my love to all and tell them to write.

> *Good Bye in Haste*
> *Your Aff. Son*
> *Edward L. Cook*
> *Co H. 100 N.Y.V.*
> *Morris Island*

S.C.

P.S. Fort Wagner is not yet taken. It is a hard nut to crack.

Letter from A. Lyth to his Brother

Ward F.
General Hospital
Hilton Head Aug 6th 63

Dear Brother
I have not received my mail from the Regt yet but expect to get it in a few days. I am gain strength slowly. It is very warm here the themometer stands generaly at from 80 to 85° in the shade where there is a slight breeze too. I never lay in any in the day time now I sometimes go over to the reading room and get a hold of a book and sit where the wind of the ocean can blow at me then I pass away a good many hours reading then when I get tired of reading I go and a walk upon the shady side of the hospital there is a stoop built all round the hospital and it is quite pleasent to walk up and down from one end to the other till you are tired of walking then there are benches you can sit down and rest upon. I make my own bed every morning I get along first rate at it and make a bed look as nice and tidy as any of the nurses. Water + Musk melons have been ripe around here these three weeks the docter allows me to eat a peice of melon once in a while and an orange whenever I can get one but he wont let me eat nuts of any kind and he say I must not eat sweet cakes or pie as they would spoil my stomach at present so I dont touch any thing of that sort. There are Just 27 men in our company as it is now on Morris Island with the Regt but there are 8 or 10 sick in the hospital and I guess 4 or 5 of the wound will get well enough to do duty again. Our Co had some 60 odd men before the fight. I enclose letter Tom Maharg wrote me giving one a descripion of the fight. I recived another from Tom Russell telling me the names of those left in the Co. I wish you would address my letters to
Alfred Lyth
General Hospital
Ward F
Hilton Head S.C.
as I am likely to stay here this month out any way as the doctor here wont let any body go back to their Regts untill he is perfectly sure they are able to do duty again particularly this hot weather I have seen fellows that run

around all day long who look to have got their strength ask the doctor if they could go back to their Regts and he would say no you had better stay here a little longer than go back to your Regt and be taken sick again right off. I tell you when a soldier is stricken down with sickness and he is laid upon his sick bed then he wishes himself at that home he has left. Oh! how he wishes he could be amongst the kind friends he has left he thinks of his and what care she would take of him if he were but at home I know those were my thoughts as I lay sick in bed in the hospital and I have heard a good many say the same. Give my love to Sarah Ann + William + the Children My love to you all

From Your Loving Brother Alfred Lyth

Our Regt has been paid off again but I missed being paid on account of being in the hospital I Should have sent 25 dollars home out of the 26 if I had got paid

Alfred

Letter from E. Cook to his Parents

Q.M. Office Folly Island S.C.
Aug. 6th 1863 Sunday

Dear Parents

I rec'd a letter from Eliza, one from Mary + Laura and 2 papers from you. I cannot write you a long letter but I will send you a short line for I know that you will like to hear from me. I am well and in good spirits. We have not yet taken Charleston, Wagner or Gregg. Sumter is completely used up. The firing to day has been terrific from our batteries; the rebs reply from Charleston and the James Island batteries at long intervals.

Monday Morning Aug. 7th 1863 Hurrah! Forts Wagner + Gregg are ours. The rebs skeddaddled last night leaving their dead unburied in the fort. They say the stench of dead bodies was so great that our boys could not stay in the fort. Our firing was so rapid + hot that they could not bury their dead. We were going to charge on the works this morning but before we could see to move the rebs had evacuated + we found an empty fort. We lost no man Except those killed by torpedoes buried in the earth and only a few in that manner.

Sumter is a pile of ruins without shape or form. We will soon have her however. Beauregard refuses to surrender her, but Gillmore says "Then blow her to pieces." The papers are wondering why we do not have Charleston, but it is not because we have not got it in our power. We have the guns in position and the shells filled and any time that Gillmore gives the word, Charleston is doomed.

Evening of Monday
The Ironclads have moved up in front of Sumter and are shelling "{unknown}" and the other batteries on Sulivans Island oposite Wagner.

Tuesday Morning
One of the Magazines was blown up this morning. The Iron clads are pouring in their big 15 inch shells without any signs of ceasing. Our men are in the best kind of spirits and hopeful of success I suppose you will have heard all this news long before this reaches you but this will serve to confirm it. Goodbye. write soon. I am very busy and cannot write a long letter. I will write a letter every day and send off whenever I have a chance.

Your Aff Son
Lyman Cook   Edward L. Cook
Buffalo N.Y. }   Co H 100th N.Y.V.

Letter from A. Lyth to his Father and Mother

Ward F. General Hospital Hilton Head S.C.
Aug 9th 1863

Dear Father + Mother
I received your kind letters of July the 5th + 12th. Also Johns of the 12th containing his photograph which I think is taken very well and is a very good likeness of John. I also received 2 harpers + a commercial advertizer. Father there is not much use you sending me any more weekly times as we always have the news here before I get the papers as they always send the

New York papers down here as soon as published and I always get a chance to see some of them. Then we have the news printed in the New + the Free South every week. Though the harpers you can send and a Buffalo paper once in awhile. I am gaining every day and getting along first rate and I was very glad to hear you were all enjoying good health. it is very warm to day the thermometer stands at 86°. The troops on Morris Island are having pretty tough times Our Regt. have been up 5 nights out of 7 this last week working in the trenches + mounting heavy seige guns and doing picket duty I have had another letter from Tom Maharg and it was him that sent me my mail from the Regt he says they are making great preparations there he says there are as many as 75 heavy seige guns + mortars planted on the island bearing on fort Wagner and they are still mounting more he say they have got one three. four two. + five one. hundred pounders to mount yet and they are expected to have every thing ready by the 10th which is tomorrow when it is thought they will open on the rebels with their land batteries and the monitors and gun boats in the harbor will open on them too. he says their picket duty is pretty hard they have to go within 600 yards of fort Wagner and lay in rifle pits 24 hours and dare not show their heads for rebel sharpshooters and shells. They are receiving reinforcements so the duty will not be so heavy on them Give me best respects Robert Townsend and tell him his brother is amongst the missing of this last fight of the officers that went into the fight only 4 came out safe one was Col Dandy + Capt Everts of C° Leaut Howell who was in command of our C° and Leaut Sheffer. Capt Paine was on a scout the time of the fight and his C° was not in the fight as they were on picket on another part of the island. Give my best respects to martin. Now I must close with my love to you all, Wm Sarah and the family also

From Your Loving Son
Alfred Lyth

write soon

Letter from A. Lyth to his Father and Mother

Ward F. General Hospital Hilton Head S.C.
Aug 14th 1863

Dear Father + Mother
    I have received three Harpers Weekly a Buffalo paper and a Weekly times since I last wrote last and the mail Steamer Fulton has arrived from New York so I expect my mail to come up from the Regt in a day or two. I am gaining fast and am in very good spirits I hope you are all enjoying good health and in good spirits. This last week we have had pretty hot weather here the themometer in the shade for the last five days has been from 90 to 93° and in the sun it was 110 degrees now you must know that is what you may call warm weather I have not heard from the Regt since I last wrote but we heard the rebels made an attack on our batteries but were repulsed with heavy loss to the rebels. To day it is quite cool we have a nice breeze off the ocean and the themometer is only 83 degrees in the shade Melons in this part of the country are all about gone there are a few tomatoes that the negroes peddel around and you can buy them very cheap of them when I buy five cents worth I have enough for three meals and I can get plenty of vinegar + plenty sugar to fix them up as they are both used on the table in the dining room where I go to get my meals When this place was taken by our forces all the rebels and planters cleared out double quick and you should have see them run as the negroes say they left household property and Negros behind in their haste to get away so the Negros what staid settled down on their massas plantation and raise produce for to keep themselves on in the winter time and raise a great quantity of stuff which they sell to the soldiers they are begining to dig sweet potatoes for Imeaditate use but they generally leave them in the ground untill the latter part of September or the month of October. Peaches are begining to get ripe. Now I think I must come to a close as I shall write again in a few days. Give my best respects to Bill Clifton. Give my love to W^m + Sarah Ann and the family I send my best respects to all the neighbors + let me know how they are all getting along My love to you all
        From Your Loving Son,
        Alfred Lyth

Letter from A. Lyth to his Father and Mother

Ward F. General Hospital
Hilton Head S.C. Aug 20ᵗʰ 1863

Dear Father + Mother
        I received your kind letters of July 21ˢᵗ and August the 2ᵈ and was very glad to hear that you were all well and in good health. I think that mother if she would not trouble herself so much when you hear of my taken with a little sickness it would be a great deal better for herself and I am sure it would not greive me so much as when I hear tell of her being so much affected. Always rest assured that I shall always let you know the worst in such cases I must say with regret though that for the last week I have been very bad again in the diorea but are getting along pretty well now as I have again got over it. We have had some nice cool weather here for the last four or five days though it has been rainey most all the time and sometimes it would blow a regular gale of wind from the north. In directing my letters to the hospital here you should leave out the Co. H 100 Regt N.Y.S.V. or they will sure go to the Regt and then have to be sent back from the Regt here which takes a week or more

August 21ˢᵗ 1863
        Dear Folks when you hear of an arrival from Port Royal unless it is the mail Steamer, the Arago, or the Fulton, you need not expect any mail from me as those are our mail steamers for this department and other boats are seldom trusted with the mail but I shall always contrive to have a letter on either of these steamers when they leave this port. These envelops that I have got printed with your name I got from Ohio with a lot of writing paper that has got the N. York State arms at the head, some printing that wants filling out to make the date of your letters +c I will write my next letter on one of them. I sent a dollar for it when I was with the Regt and got it since I came to the hospital there were 25 envelops + more paper than I know what to do with here in the hospital. I received that book on Phonography when I was on Folly Ile but since I have had it I have never had time or been well enough to study it so I think when I rejoin the Regt I shall send it home. There is a rumor that our Regt is either to come here or go to Beaufort which is only eleven miles from here to receive the conscripts and

they come from New York as our Regt is to be filled up by conscripts They had the chance to come here once before about 3 weeks since but they would not come then now I suppose they have got to come if the rumor is true, but there is not much faith in the rumor. I see by a Buffalo paper received by one of our Co in the same ward that I am that they have commenced drafting in Buffalo and that it goes on very quitely. I received Harpers Weekly and a times with the letters. I think it is about time to close now. Give my love to Sarah Ann and W^m* and I wonder you don't mention them in your letters. I have not had one from Sarah Ann this long time. Give my best respects to Cris and the rest of the men Tell Robert Townsend that his brother may be a prisoner in Charleston as he is amongts the missing as it is not known that he was killed Now I must close with my Love to you all*

From Your Loving
Son Alfred

Letter from A. Lyth to his Brother

(Printed Stationary)
HEAD QUARTERS
Co H, 100 Reg't NYS Vol. Infantry,
Camp, _____ 1863

Ward F. General Hospital Hilton Head S.C.
*Aug 29*th *1863*

Dear Brother
   I hope these few lines will find you all in good health. I am getting along first rate at present and I am very hearty and in good spirits. and my health is getting better every day. but the doctor won't let me go back to the Regt as he say I would not be able to stand the heavy duty that the Regt has to preform now. I am very sorry to say that Tom Maharg has been wounded the last time the Co was on picket the wound is not a very serious one but it is in a very bad place as he was hit in the upper lip and the letter I received from Sergt Warham say it is swollen very badly. I have not received any mail from the last mail steamer which came in but I guess it is

229

on account of Tom Maharg being wounded as he was the one who always sent me my letters after they had gone to the Regt but there is the Fulton coming into the harbor at the present moment and I expect a letter on her There is not much use me saying any thing about how things are progressing in this department for you will see all in the newspapers that I could tell you. it is the opinion here that Charleston will be in our possession shortly.

Dear Brother day after tomorrow I shall have been just one year in the service but if all goes on well I expect I shall see you all again before another year passed away There is some prospects at present of the war coming to a speedy close well the sooner the better. I think I must close now as there is no particular news here at present but I shall write again in a few days. Give my best respects to Cris, Robert Townsend and all my acquaintances. Give my love to Wᵐ and Sarah Ann. My love to you all so no more at present from your

Loving Brother
Alfred Lyth

P.S. Write soon and let me know how you are getting along

Chapter Eight

Operations on Folly and Morris Islands
Post-Assault Field Operations
September, 1863 – April, 1864

"Forts Wagner + Gregg were evacuated a few nights ago. If I don't forget it I will send you a piece of Rebel Hard Tack taken out of Fort Gregg. Our men were all in line ready to make another charge where a deserter came and informed us that the fort was being deserted. The feeling among our men was like an arising from the dead to life. At first the word was whispered down the line "Wagner's Evacuated". The men would not believe it but as the truth became apparent a long drawn sigh of relief came welling up from the bosom of more than one poor soldier who has supposed that the next morning sun would shine upon his corpse. Wagner, the hated, hellish Wagner is ours with out a loss of another man. The stench in the fort was sickening. Thirty dead bodies were in one pile without the appearance of a wound or scratch, probably suffocated. In one of the splinter proofs were found two bodies hanging probably for attempting to desert."
E. Cook letter dated 9/10/1863

"During the siege the losses of the regiment were 104 in killed or wounded – not counting the losses from the night attack of the 18th of July. When at last the fifth parallel was completed, and all preparations were made for the final assault, to our great relief the enemy evacuated the fort under cover of night, and Morris Island was ours without further bloodshed." Lt Col Charles E. Walbridge address at the first Annual Reunion 7/18/1887

Letter from T. Maharg to A. Lyth

Hundredth Regt Camp
on Morris Isl Sep 2/63

Friend Al

    I read your letter directed to John Warham + I was sory to hear that you ware taken sick again but I hope it will not last long + I hope to see you back soon Al John Warham was killed on the night of the 31 while on picket in the trenches he was on post + a shell came from Wagner + bursted right over him tareing him dreadfuly he never knew what struck him Al the Regt is having some hard times now we have the advance + have to go on picket every third night besides camp guard All there is not a time our Regt went up in the trenches but we have lost from 10 to 12 killed + wounded Stives was wonded in the foot the same night Warham was killed + has gone off some where. Dave White was slighlty wounded in the sholdier but he is with the company not fit for duty. I got a Slight touch of a shell on the lip but it is all right now but it was enough to let me taste how a little more would feal. Al we are now not more than 95 yards from fort Wagner when we go on picket. Al we got a small mail this afternoon + there was nuthing but two papers for you I send them this afternoon. Al how does Wm King, Wm Goff + all the rest of the boys that is at Hilton head get along. Fort Sumter looks hard it looks as though a brick team had run away + spilt the Bricks where it is no shape no form to it I guess It will never do Johny reb much good any more. Al I see by the papers I got to day that the 49 was coming down here to help us I hope they are for I know some of the boys. Well I must close now for it is after four oclock + pretty near coffee time + then dress parade so you see I havent much time. The Company all send there love to you + all the rest of the boys

From Your Friend
+ Tentmate
Tom

P.S. Jim Dick is home I dont know weather he has got his discharge or not

Letter from E. Cook to Parents

To Lyman Cook
Buffalo N.Y.
Folly Island S.C. Sept. 10/63

My dear parents
    I have about an inch of candle left after having finished my work this evening and its light shall be devoted to your use. More than a year has now passed since I joined the volunteers. It does not seem so long does it? But when I think of the many things that have transpired in that short space of time then it seems as though I had been a long time away from my dear old home a very long while. One think, within that time 2 or 3 of my girls have got married and I dont know how many more are contemplating the same act so that by the time I return there will be none of them left for me. But never mind "Ed" + I have got a plan of our own. And I will it to you if you wont tell any body. I have got a country girl picked out that none of you know any thing about and when I return Ed + I are going to marry her – perhaps – and take father's land warrant and go out and locate it and turn cozy old farmers in short order. Will you come out and visit us once in a while? I would tell you the girls name but I do not know it myself although I know that there is such a girl.
    Forts Wagner + Gregg were evacuated a few nights ago. If I dont forget it I will send you a piece of Rebel Hard Tack taken out of Fort Gregg. Our men were all in line ready to make another charge when a deserter came and informed us that the fort was being deserted. The feeling among our men was like an arising from the dead to life. At first as the word was whispered down the line "Wagner's Evacuated", the men would not believe it but as the truth became apparent a long drawn sigh of relief came welling up from the bosom of more than one poor soldier who has supposed that the next morning sun would shine upon his corpse. Wagner, the hated, hellish Wagner is ours without the loss of another man. The Stench in the fort was sickening. Thirty dead bodies were in one pile without the appearance of a wound or scratch, probably suffocated. In one of the splinter proofs were found two bodies hanging probably for attempting to desert. Our men have dug up 30 or more torpedoes buried in and around the fort. The large magazine in Wagner has not yet been opened as it is feared that on opening

the door the magazine will explode. The rebs are now shelling Wagner + Gregg to keep our men out of them but they dont hurt us much. The navy made an assault in small boats upon Sumter night before last and lost 100 men without accomplishing any thing. The gunboats exploded a magazine near fort {unknown} on Sulivan's Island day before yesterday and burned several buildings in {unknown}. As soon as the obstructions are removed from the river the gunboats will move up past the batteries and attack them in the rear. The navy has not helped us much as yet and every body seems dissatisfied with their apparent unconcern in the siege. They would not have gone in day before yesterday if one the Monitors had not got aground and {unknown} fired on her and the others had to go in + help her until it was high tide + she floated.

My sheet is full so I must stop writing. Good Bye Write often to your Affectionate Son.

Edward L. Cook
Co "H" 100ᵗʰ N.Y.V.

Sept 11/63 <u>Evening</u>

I think our land forces are now going to have a short resting spell. I dont think though that Genl. Gilmore will keep them idle very long. This is the most unhealthy month in the South and he may perhaps keep them inactive until next month but no longer. It is my opinion also that only a small force of men and artillery will be kept on Morris Island. If the Iron clads do not soon succeed in reducing the long line of batteries on Sullivans Island, I think our general will take the job into his own hands, and by some move, get possession of the Island with his land forces. We have just heard the news that {unknown} has obtained possession of Chattanooga but the news is so good that we do not believe it. We do believe however that "Wagner" + "Gregg" are ours and Sumter soon will be. Several deserters came into our lines today from James Island S.C. They say that there is very much dissatisfaction among the rebel troops and that they are quarreling and fighting + murdering among themselves. The Georgia + North Carolina troops are calling to go home and protect themselves from {unknown}'s army who is threatening to invade their state with a large army. But Beauregard has them fixed for he has got the Georgia boys on James Island and the North Carolina troops on Sulivans Island and the South Carolina troops garrisoning Charleston + {unknown}. So there is no chance for them to escape. Still every few days some of the most venturesome will swim the rivers + wade + crawl through the intervening swamps and come into our lines. Those that came last report that the conviction among the Officers and men of the rebel troops is that the City of Charleston must fall before long.

Their conviction is most certainly right, and no one among our troops has ever entertained the first doubt since we took Morris Island, that the fate of Charleston was as surely declared as though it had been written in letters of fire upon the vault of heaven. One of the greatest pieces of strategy + engineering that has proved successful, during this war (or in any war) was the taking of the lower end Morris Island. When we were strongest the Enemy thought we were weekest. While we were daily receiving reinforcements of troops, ordnance + ammunition, they thought we were evacuating. While we were building our sand batteries opposite and within pistol shot of their high sand hill batteries and while we had a large force to sustain the working party, they thought we had but a small picket posted along the beach and bank; and so confident were they that this supposition of theirs was correct and that we were evacuating that it was their intention to have attacked us the night that we opened on them but something prevented them. Right under the mouths of their guns we planted our mortars + erected our cannon, and to use their own language "Stole from them Morris Island.". The only drawback, the only mismove that has been made by Gilmore on this campaigne was the false + fatal one of attacking by Storm the hell-hole "Wagner" on the night of July 18/63. Every thing else has worked beautifully except our little 200 pounder "Swamp Angel" which is a too much inclined to hide herself in the mud when our folks make her speak.

Letter from A. Lyth to his Folks at Home

General Hospital Hilton Head S.C.
Sept 11ᵗʰ/63

Dear Folks at Home
I take this opertunity of writing these few lines having nothing esle particular to occupy time at present and I hope they will find you all in

235

good health and spirits and doing well as it leaves me at present. It is just one year yesterday since I joined my Regt at Gloucester Point Va. Now last night I sat up untill one oclock to attend to the wounded for you see it greatly releives the nurses when they can get some one that is kind enough to sit up half a night for them once in a while as I was saying I sat up untill one oclock well long before that time I got tired of reading so I shut up my book and got to thinking of all I had past through this last year of the jolly times we had while peacefully encamped at Gloucester Point of the trials and hardships we have past through since we left that beautifull camp up to the present time. Now in all the letters that I have wrote to you this past year I believed I have never complained of any hardships because when on the march or on board of transports I always could find enough other subjects to write about without troubeling you at the time with complaints as I had learnt to put up with them in fact thought very little of them myself for what with change of scenes and other matters of interest which always present themselves to soldiers while traveling from one place to another they have very little time to worry theirselves with the hardships they may have to put up with at the time. Now I think when I come home again I think you will not find me grumbling at trifles as I oft remember I used to do when there was no occation to grumble at all and willing to eat my bread without butter without saying a word when I can't get butter I can remember of making many a meal this past year of to or three 'hard tack' and water or a cup of coffee without milk or sugar and propby the hard tack would be full of bugs or crawling with maggots. other times we have made a meal out of two hard tack a peice of salt junk about the size of an egg and a drink of water but I must say Uncle Sam never lets his children go hungry when they are where he can get provisions up to them. When we first went on to Folly Island we put three days rations in our haversacks. well we took three days rations of hard tack and meat we got our coffee and sugar but we could not take our beans rice and potatoes which were left on Coles island in charge of the cooks. now you see if we had stayed on Coles island we should have had our full rations but as it was we got our three days rations of hard tack and meat so you see we had to pinch ourselves and some would have their grub all finised on the breakfast of the third day and as we did not get any more untill the afternoon of the next 4th day they had to pretty short the fourth day. we were not allowed to build fires the first two days so we had to live on hard tack and junk and water and the water we got was from wells that we dug in the sand with our hands and peices of sticks but after we got settled there and our cooks came up with the back rations and what with them and the fresh ones we drew we had a fat time of it and all the time the Reg't was on the island we lived quite happy although there was an awful amount of duty to preform but of course I had not much to do on account of being detached in the artillery. Now you may think having never been in a government hospital where it is full of wounded men just from the battle field that a green horn like myself would be let sit up half a night to act as nurse. now in our ward at present there are only twenty six men and half of these only are wounded men the rest are convalsences like myself. all the wounded men but two have their wounds healed up or nearly so but the other two have to have their wounds kept constantly wet with cold water. so you see that all a nurse has to do in the night is to keep their wounds wet one of them is wounded in the leg he was hit with one of these infernal rifle balls which are filled same as shell and burst after strikeing a fellow this bursted after it got into his leg and the doctors could never get out all the peices. The other one was wounded in four places one was a rifle ball going in to his left eye and coming out of this mouth fetching a few of his front teeth with it the other three are flesh wounds one on the hip the other two are one on each side of his rump so you see he must have suffered some at first when he received his wounds but now he is doing very well. I received a letter from cousin William to day and I wrote answer they are all in good health. I was down on the beach this evening and as usal saw the rebel prisoners going in bathing there is some five or six hundred at the provo guard house and every evening some three or four hundred of them are let out under a guard for the purpose of bathing and it is quite a sight to see them runing around the beach every evening they are mostly North Carolina troops and will most all take the oath of allegience and go north I must quit writing any more to night as it is about my bedtime I will finis in a day or two.

Sept 16th Yesterday it commenced to cloud up and to day it is raining I am doing well as usal and I may have to go back to my Regt soon how as they are sending some away every day now, and they are going to send a lot of the wounded north in a few days. I begin to think it is time that I was back again to the Regt and that I had been here long enough. The duty is not so heavy in the Reg't now as it was before the fall of fort Wagner and I think Gen Gillmore is giving the boys a bit of a resting spell untill the navy fetches fort Moultre and other batteries to time so that by and our troops may take peacefull possesion of the city and the sooner that comes to pass I think the better as it is fully expected that the fall of Charleston will be a death blow to the rebelion and I sincerly hope it may all the rebel prisoners that have been brought here that belong to North Carolina Tennesee Regts are strong against the rebels and will take the oath of alleigence and even some of the South Carolina Georgia Alabama and Mississippi Regts will take the oath sooner than go back to the confederacy, I have heard that Robert Townsend's brother is a prisoner so if Robert don't know it already I wish you would let him know of it and Give him my respects I oft wonder that Mary and William dont write a letter to me once in a while now. It is a good long time since either of wrote me a letter now I should like them both to write to me every once in a while for I should like to see if they are improving any in their writing and I should like to know how they are getting along and how Fanny is prospering and to know if she has forgot her big brother App or Appe as she used to call me. Give me love to Sarah Ann and William and the family and let me know how they are getting along. I have not had a letter from Sarah Ann this long while and I oft wonder what is the reason she does not write to me Give my respects to all the neighbors. My love to you all

From Your Ever Affectionate Son

Alfred

P.S. write soon and let me know how you are getting along and how the business is prospering so no more at present

Letter from J. Marharg to T. Maharg

September, 1863
Buffalo

Dear Broth {Tom Maharg}:
    Yours of the 9ᵗʰ came to hand and I was glad to hear from you to know that you were well. The time you wrote the letter you had not heard of Fathers death but since it was received it we got me from you stating Geo.

Burnham had got the news and had told you the next morning after his death. Aunt Hatti wrote you a short letter but you did not say anything about receiving it. I will now give you the details concerning his death. Thursday, September 10ᵗʰ, 1863, Father went down town with his horse in the morning feeling pretty well but he did not stay long before he returned home sick. Mother put mustard plasters on his stomach he vomited and seemed to feel better but that pain in his stomach seemed to stick with him he lay around on the lounge and acted the same as usual when sick Saturday and Sunday he fed the chickens and lay on the lounge and read Monday morning he wake Nan and myself up. When I came home at noon I went upstairs and had a talk with him and came to the conclusion that he would sell his horse and told me where he thought he could sell him Monday Uncle Hugh came up to see him and father sat up on the side of the bed and talked with him. When he was getting up Uncle attempted to help him and Father told him he need not mind for he could get up himself and only wanted to set up for awhile and rest himself. Uncle went home about nine o'clock and thinking not death was so near at hand. When I came home that night and had my supper I sent for the Doctor because he had taken some physic and it had not operated. The dr. told me to have Mother give him an injection so I coming home and bought a seringe and Mother gave him the injection. After I got home and had to go up to Aleo Vickerefts store with a fenlbs of candies which were broken in a box sold to him and collect the bill that he had oued Uncle. His store is on the corner and ninth and Carolina Streets. Coming home I stopped in Slocums and add was very glad to see me as there were no one home but Mary and Sidney. I had not been that very long before Aunt Kate and Mary come over there and said Father was worse and I did not feel very alarmed but came home immediately and actually think I have very often see Father as bad as he was then but he had kept growing worse. 15 or 20 minutes before he died he asked me if it was not late. I told him not very. He said he would like a lemon but he thought it was to late the stores would be all closed. I went immediately over to Morrisons and woke him up and got his lemons. Before this he had sent many and Hugh after the doctor and as I was coming home I met him after we had a good meeting. I asked him if there was anything we could do for him He said he though he was breathing his last. I did not believe him and thought that it was impossible for Father to die. He finally rolled over with his face to the front of the bed and gulped twice and his ….

Moved gently to the world beyond the skies to the God who gave it there to be met by an unimaginable company of angels and escorted to the throne of God to sing praise and be as one of them waiting for you and me and the rest of us who he has worked so hard and thought so much to join him in heaven. Oh Thos let us strive not to let his teachings be lost and let us follow in his footsteps. Lead as pure a life as he has it is the only way that we can ever hope to meet him. Thos we are only deprived of a Father a short time and we must consider that supreani home has been very linent and merciful towards us by not calling him away from us before but sparing his life till we are all able to do for ourselves. Won mary and father are called away leaving mother and a large family of small children........Dear brother do not let this blow overcome you for it is Providence and he must certainly work out his ends The Dr. said that the night he died it is nothing more than we have all to come it in the road we have all go to go Father had only got there ahead of us Only think of it we have all got to go the same road and O Thos I only .. me may be as well as prepared for ... as he was. I feel very lonely in that fact as had not a friend on earth but undoubtedly time will blot out a feeling as cares come. First we need to remember that we have a mother which will crave all our feeling and love as we left to on well with no earthly adviser let us use discretion in all our works and learn to contend with the world and honest upright man and be a respect to the names of our worthy and deceased Father and an honor to our Mother and mail it be the will of God to return you safe home to your waiting ..... All the folks send their love.

 From your closest affectionate Brother John Maharg.

If you want to keep this letter you can send it back and I will take care of it for you.

Letter from E. Cook to his Parents and Relatives

Office H.H. Q.M. Folly Island S.C.
Sept. 16/63 Evening

My dear Parents and relatives
 I rec'd, 2 or 3 day ago, a good long letter from Eliza, a letter from Mr. Lyman written Last July and 2 papers from you namely the Weekly Express

+ *Moores Rural New Yorker for all of which I am very much obliged. I think I receive all the papers you send me. You wonder that I write such short letters. You would not wonder much if you was here and saw the other writing that I do. Much as I love to read, and highly as I prize "Moore's Rural New Yorker" and the Weekly Express I have not yet had time look at either of them. It has been write, write, write from breakfast to supper time for the last 3 months except 1 or two little short resting spells. I have just this minute finished my August papers and now I grasp the first leisure time offered me to answer your letter. Our business in July was so mixed and extensive that it took me all the month of August and the first week of September to straighten out things and make the returns. Up to the first of Sept, Capt. Walbridge did more business than all the rest of the Quarter Masters on the island put together; but hereafter it is going to be much lighter and I am going to have comparatively easy times and considerable leisure which I shall try and improve by catching up with my back correspondance, and atoning for past delinquencies. Speaking of those dirty soldiers — you must recollect that a soldier cannot dig ditches and do soldiers fatigue work and keep their clothes clean. And besides if those soldiers had new shoes + pants they were in their knapsacks waiting to be put on when they drew near their cherished homes.*

I am dirty now, dirty pants, dirty blouse and old cap. I almost believe not know me if you should see me. I never carry any extra clothes in my knapsack except shirts + stockings. I draw a pair of pants + wear them right straight along weekdays + Sundays until they are worn out + unfit for service, or unpassable on an inspection. Dirt is the soldiers badge of honor, for parlor soldiers who live in nice clean barracks and do Garrison duty on forts &c that can keep themselves looking clean It is as impossible for a soldier in the field, who has to skirmish & picket, to keep himself clean as it is for a pig in an irishman's shanty to appear like a lady in a drawing room. The Rebs think that dirt is their best friend for it protects them, as at Wagner, from assaults. Gillmore too is a friend to dirt. He gave the following toast immediately after the fall of Wagner in the presence of a number of officers of rank & his personal staff. "Spades are Trumps" Wagner + Gregg are ours and Sumter to a mass {unknown} bricks and mortar. I am in hopes that the navy will soon make an assault upon and finish the work which Gillmore has so ably commenced. I suppose that many of the people of the North are wondering why the Iron Clads do not run the Gauntlet of {unknown word}, Battery {unknown word}, Johnson, {unknown word}, {unknown word}, and the host of others, but they seem to forget that this harbor is filled with obstruction in the shape of immense chains, torpedoes &c. These have got to be removed before our vessels can pass up the channel. The torpedoes are connected by wires to an electric battery in Sumter so that they can be fired at any time when a vessel is passing over them. When we get possession of Sumter we can explode these torpedoes or render them harmless at any time but so long as rebels enough remain in Sumter to discharge the torpedoes our Iron Clads are useless.

This is why the rebs hold on to Sumter with such tenacity – although Gregg + Wagner have been lost to them and Charleston is within range of our guns. Again many at the North are wondering why Gillmore dont burn the city treason when it is said to be in his power to do so. You may depend upon it that there is good reason for this delay but neither the general or any one else has yet seen fit to give the reason to the public. I flatter myself that I can solve the mystery but I cannot reveal it. Suffice it to say that we have got more than one gun mounted in <u>easy</u> range of Charleston in position that the rebs know not of + will not know until they are unmasked and opened by the order of the general, when every body shall learn why he does not shell Charleston.

Furloughs are now being granted to the troops in this department but I shall not apply for one. We are having a kind of resting spell, and nothing further will be done at present by the land forces, until about the 1st of November when I think our guns will again pour out their masses of shell & shot. I have received two letters from Lottie {unknown name}. One of them dated last July. Some how or other her letters do not come very straight. She said her mother was going to visit Buffalo. Did she call on you?

Eliza wants to know why Fannie Porter married that fellow. I guess love was not the main mover in the match. I reckon as how she got tired of waiting for me and thought that 3 years was a long time & was very precarious and uncertain. She had an offer and thought she had better take a whole man than wait for two years and then perhaps get only a part of a man besides losing so much valuable time without enjoying it.

Let her went, I dident want her, & perhaps she guessed as much and thought if she couldent get what she would she would get what she could. The weather is cool to night + pleasant. The mosquitoes & flies & gnats *bother us terribly to say nothing of the fleas. I am one mass of flea bites and mosquito blotches. Good Bye & write to me again very soon. Give my love to Grandma & Mrs. Lyman's {unknown name} & {unknown name}. Kiss little Gracie when you see her for me and remember me to all the folks. I have not seen Geo. S. for about a month. He is {unknown word} and has a good place. Your Aff Son   Edward L. Cook*

Letter from A. Lyth to his Father and Mother

General Hospital Hilton Head S.C.
Sept 19ᵗʰ/63

Dear Father and Mother
   I received a Commercial Advertiser and a Harpers Weekly day before yesterday that had been down to the Regt and yesterday I received one of each again that came direct to the hospital here. I was very much disappointed when the mail arrived and there was no letter from home for me but as the mail steamer Arago is expected in to day or tomorrow I am in hopes of receiving a letter by her mail. The weather here is pretty cool just at present though I do not think you would consider it so up north but to us who has been accustomed to this hot climate for the past summer feel the cold more than if we had been in a northern climate. I like this kind of weather a great deal better than when it is hot yesterday and to day I took a walk down town and had a look round there are very few apples in this section at present and if you want a good apple you have to pay five cents for one you can get an orange for the same price. I got a letter to day from Tom Russell of our Co dated Sept 13ᵗʰ and he states there was great rumors of our Regt going somewere from this department and that had knapsack inspection on the 12ᵗʰ at four P.M. and again a 7 oclock in the morning but I think there is no truth in the rumor or we should have heard something of it here before this and the "New South" came out to day and there was no mention of it in the paper

Sept 22ᵈ The mail steamer Arago arrived yesterday and I received two newspapers one commercial and a harpers but I was disappointed having not received a letter and I begin to think that you must have stoped writing to me altogether for it is nearly two weeks since I received one. The weather here has never been below 65° or 66 degrees between the hours of 7 oclock in the morning to 7 at night though to us here it seams like November weather up north. but it is very seldom they have it even as cool as it is here in the middle of winter

Give my love to Sarah Ann and William and accept the same yourselves
From Your Loving
Son Alfred

P.S. Answer this and write oftener than you do.

Letter from E. Cook to his Friend

Office H.H. Q.M.
North End Folly Island S.C. Sept. 22/63

Mr. G. S. Lyman
Dear Friend
　　Your letter of July 13ᵗʰ 1863 reached me a few days ago. I am well and in good spirits. I have got to rejoin my regiment in a few days. Operations are suspended here for a short time to give the men a chance to rest. To day is quite a gala day. We have just received news that Genl. Gillmore has got his other star and is now a Major General. Every body is rejoicing and all the vessels in the Department have got all their flags & streamers floating to honor of the man who has shown such skill and good generalship in the campaign of this summer. I am of opinion that nothing further will be done down here until {unknown name} has moved down and threatens Savannah. When that time comes I think that there will be another move made on Charleston by way of Beaufort cutting off the line of communication between Charleston & Savannah. Perhaps at the same time we may make an attempt to gain Sulivan's Island by a landing & attack on the North End thus coming in on the rear of their strongest works. Such may be the plan of Genl. Gillmore but no one knows. He is a man who keeps his own counsel and whatever his plan may be no one will know it until he is ready to operate upon it. I believe the fate of Charleston and rebellion is signed & sealed by the Great Hand whose power moves

the universe. Time will work it out. This is not the day of miracles, God in these later years does not perform great works in an hour or a day, but brings them on in the natural way, in a way that the little mind of man can understand and his reason comprehend.

Sept. 24ᵗʰ 1863

I have delayed finishing this letter knowing that there was a mail for us on Morris Island and think there might be something for me. To day it came – a letter from Eliza. I will answer it at the first opportunity.
A grand review is taking place on Morris Island by Genl. Gillmore. A salute has just been fired by our batteries. The rebs have now got guns mounted that drop shell within from 40 to 80 rods of my tent but for some reason or other the shell do not explode very often and when they do it is far short of their range. If they succeed in timeing their fuses properly it will make our present quarters considerable warmer than comfort requires.

A fort is being erected within a few yards of our tent and as soon as the rebs discover it I think they will try and retard it completion as much as possible. The weather here at present is quite cool, and the nights are damp + cold but I think this cold spell will pass off in a few days & then we shall have it warm and comfortable again. Our quarters are right on the bank at the edge of high tide and we get all the wind & breeze from the ocean. In a warm day this is quite comfortable. But when it blows & storms it is impossible to sleep, and the occupant thinks every moment his tent is coming down on top of him.

I am a many times obliged to you for the stamps you sent me. We cannot buy them here as there is no post office nearer than Hilton Head.

I am going to rejoin my regiment in a few days if Capt. Walbridge cannot get me detailed from Genl. Gillmores H'd. Qrs. I am afraid that I shall be reported as a deserter and I would rather bear the hard ships of soldier than have the disgraceful name of deserter applied to my character. If I rejoin my regiment I may possibly stand a chance of being detailed to some duty on Morris Island. So the folks need not worry any on my account. Give my love to all the folks and all the little folks and believe me ever yours sincerely

Edward L. Cook

Please write to me again soon

Letter from A. Lyth to his Father and Mother

General Hospital Hilton Head S.C.
Sunday Sept 27th/63

Dear Father and Mother

I received your kind letter dated Sept 16th but I was very sorry to hear that Sarah Ann was not any better but I hope by the time this reaches you she will have recovered. I am very sorry to hear of Mr. Maharg death but poor Tom how will he bear it it will be a hard blow to him when he hears of it I am getting along very well at present and my health is very good I hope these few lines will find you all enjoying the same blessing The doctor here don't appear to be in any hurry to send me to the Regt and I am sure I won't ask him any more when he will send me as I have very good quarters here Our doctor is a very nice old man Just as I was writing these last few lines he is making his morning rounds and he was quite amused to see me writing so early in the morning but when I receive a letter I always sit down and answer it as soon as possible. Yesterday I had my hair cut and I got shaved so I feel pretty good this morning Our Regt are living pretty well now though they have a great deal of duty to do they have a large tent for every two men and they get fresh bread every day but as for duty first one day they have to go on picket then the next day they are relieved about 10 oclock and it generally take them the rest of that day to clean gun an accutrements and fix up the next day they have to go on fatigue duty then the next day they go on picket again so you see they are kept pretty busy

I am very glad to hear that your business is so good and that you will be able to get enough of draining to do this fall. I think it is a very good idea to raise the price of the socket pip when there is such a great demand for them and you can sell all you can make. I think if you can burn bricks in a clamp for 5 cts a thousand it is very little they cost burning and I have a notion that if you buy that peice of land you speak off and go into brick making on a more extencive scale that there may be quite a profit made out of bricks. If you make a bargain for that peice of land in the rear of your peice on puffer St let me know how much it will cost an acre. I have oft been wondering of late how Uncle Frank was getting along and I am sorry to hear he is making out so bad I think if his place is offered for sale two or three more times a fellow would be apt to make it a good bargain for he would probly get a few dollars if he would take the place. I think that tile making will soon be over as it is getting well on towards winter. I must close now with my love to you all and hope that you will have Sarah Ann better by this Give my best respects to all the neighbors

From Your Affectionate
Son Alfred

P.S. write soon and dont delay so long in writing to me any more AL

Letter from A. Lyth to his Father and Mother

General Hospital Hilton Head S.C.
Oct 1ˢᵗ 1863

Dear Father + Mother
     I received two newspapers by the last mail but no letter and I begin to think that you might write to me oftener than you do. I hope these few lines will find you all in good health and spirits and doing well as it leaves me at present We were paid four months pay to day and I shall express $40 of it tomorrow and keep $12 myself
     The weather here is quite warm there are no particular new here at present so you must excuse my short letter as I intend to write more in a few days. My Love to you all hope Sarah Ann is well again

Your Affect Son
Alfred Lyth

Letter from E. Cook to his Parents

Office H.H. Q.M.
North End Folly Island S.C. Oct. 2/63

My dear Parents
     I received a letter & three papers from Eliza yesterday. I have got just time enough to send you a line or two and no more. I have got Geo Clark's

247

things packed in a box ready to send to Mr. Comstock. In the box is a segar box containing some old letters and a few little trinkets belonging to me. I have rec'd 2 months pay and will send you 15 or 20 dollars in my next letter. Dont fail to open the box I send to Mr. Comstock + take out the segar box belonging to me. I am in first rate health and feeling well. The weather lately has been cool but not uncomfortably so. I go out oystering every 2 or 3 days and get about 3 bushels to a time. They grow in great quantities in these rivers and are a very good flavor. Two men could gather a boat load in 2 hours. Every thing down here is very dear. Butter is 50 cents per pound & cheese 40 cents. and every thing else in proportion. What is the news? We heard yesterday that {unknown name} had been reinforced and had fought Bragg the second time near Chattanooga and whipped him. Every thing is quiet down here at present. Genl. Gillmore has moved his head quarters to this Island, and no one knows what his plans are for future operations.

We are building a large number of batteries on Morris, Folly and other Islands for the purpose of defence. It may be that Gillmore will do nothing further toward the taking of Charleston until he can get a force in their rear and thus cut off their chance of escape when the grand attack is made from the front. The navy thus far has done very little toward the taking of Charleston. Even the naval officers admit this and say that the present admiral {unknown name} is not the fit person for the position he occupies. He is a middle size, thin, spare man, and his face and neck are as pale & white almost this paper. His looks are enough to place him on the retired list. It is rumored that Farragut is coming down here to relieve him and the navies are in high spirits at the news.

Both navy & army unite in the praises of Genl. Gillmore. Col. Turner, Chief of Staff & Chief of Artillery, has been promoted to a Brig. Genl.

I still have not seen Geo. Stoddard.

Letter from A. Lyth to his Folks at Home

Dear Folks at Home

The steamer Continental arrived here yesterday from the north and bringing a northern mail with her I received a Harpers and a commercial advertiser by her and as the mail steamer Arago is expected in today or tomorrow I expect a letter. I received a letter from the Regt from one of our Company who as been in the hospital here he say since he left here he has been up to fort Wagner twice on picket and one night they went in picket boats into Charleston Harbor for the harbor has to be picketed in the night he says there are two or three thousand men to work upon forts Wagner and Gregg night and day getting them ready for further opperations upon Charleston we get five or six men wounded every day as forts Johnson and Moultre keep up a steady firing all the time fort Sumter he say looks very well at a distance but when look at from fort Wagner she looks like an old brick kiln all bursted but the Rebels still keep their dirty rag flying upon it. but I think Gen Gillmore will not let it fly there much longer and I think it will not be long before he lets old Beauregaurd smell some of those barberous shells from our 200 pounders. The hospital boat Cosmopolitan went north last Saturday with a load of sick and wounded from the Beaufort and this hospital. Those that went were mostly sick cases of diarhoea who will have to go into the invalid Corps when they get to New York. if I had been like two of the men that went out of our ward I might have come north too but they will not get this child into the invalide Corps No sir'ee. those two men came into the hospital the same time I did with the same disease and have got along as well as myself but they would keep telling the doctor they never got any better and they would buy stuff to eat that would keep the diarhea on them so they were sent north. The doctor in charge of this hospital went north on the hospital boat on a 30 days furlough and our old doctor has got charge of the hospital untill he comes back so I think I shall not go back to the Regt untill the head doctor comes back as our old doctor don't like to send men back to their Regts he would sooner send them home if he had the power to do so. but you must not think him a sesesh for wishing to send sick men home for there ain't a better union man in the United States. The weather here is very warm days but the nights are pretty cool last night I sat up untill 10 oclock to read my newspapers and it felt so cold about 8 oclock that I went to work and built a fire in the stove then it felt a little more comfortable and when I went to bed I got an extra blanket to cover over myself. I was down town this morning and I took a notion to go in to a digurion gallery and had my likeness taken Just as I was in my shirtsleeves as you will see and I think by the looks of my likeness you will see that I ain't very sick for I am as fat now as ever I was in my life by the way I am enjoying very good health at present and I hope these few lines will find you all enjoying the same blessing. The envelop that I send this letter in came to me when I got my book on phonography it has been laid away ever since I got it in my knapsack in the baggage room but the other day I had my knapsack out and airing the clothes so I got out the book on phonography and I think I shall send it home when I got back to my Reg't. I have oft heard tell of the "Sunny South" before I enlisted and came down here and of its rich fruit its oranges and lemons and all manner of rich things but give me the north to live in here we have to pay five cents for an apple where we can now get two oranges for the same price as the oranges on this Island are getting ripe and to tell the truth I would sooner have a couple of nice apples now than half a dozen of the sweetest oranges you can scare up so it is with most all the soldiers and the niggers they think a great deal more of apples than oranges in the north you will see the rich fields of wheat and grain of all descriptions the nice patches of potatoes cabbages +c where here you will find swamps now an then a patch of sweet potatoes and a field of corn cotton or tobacco or a patch of peanuts I have heard the nigger say in the time of peace that down here they have to a pay 50 cents for a head of cabbage sometimes more Since I have been in the south I have never seen a stone not even as large as a pea but what has come from the north. the south is Just one bed of sand everywere you go it is either sand or swamps or marches even in the cities the streets are all sand or else a cordoroy road that is a road made of round logs hauled from the woods. in Charleston they say they have a few of the streets paves but the stone was imported from the north

Oct 7ᵗʰ this morning there was nine men arrived here from Morris Island they are going home on 30 days furlough they fetch the news that night before last the rebels got all the boat they could get a hold of in Charleston and started on an expidition into the harbor for the purpose of takeing the Ironsides by suprise and capture her but the Yankees were too wide awake for them they espyed them and got every thing in readyness for them. The rebels calculated to board the Ironsides but they were very much mistaken. Our gallent sailors let them come pretty near when they gave them a couple of Broadsides of grape and caneater which sent the whole of the expidition except two boats to a watery grave, so I think that the rebels had better stay at home and not try to catch the Yankees asleep any more. there was considerable commotion amongst the troops at the time the picket fired their muskets at the boats and the long roll was beat and all the troops turned out under arms now the rebs can blow all they have a mind too about our expidition to fort Sumter they have fared 50 times worse in their expidition to capture the Ironsides "big thing" My love to Sarah Ann and W^m and to you all

   From Your Affectionate Son & Brother   Alfred Lyth
write soon   write soon   write soon   write soon
write soon

Letter from E. Cook to his Parents and Sister

Office A.A. Quartermaster
North End Folly Island S.C. Oct. 10/63

Dear Parents + Sisters

   I rec'd a letter from Laura yesterday. I am glad the visitors have got home again all safe and sound. I sent a box to Mr. Comstock yesterday containing the clothes + other effects of George Clark. In the box is a bundle of letters and some few little trinkets done up together and packed in a cigar box. If you call on Mr. Comstock I think he will open the box and give you cigar box which lies just under the cover of the box. I am very well at present and enjoying myself first rate. We have all the oysters we want to eat for nothing. Every 2 or 3 days I take a boat & crew & go up the river & gather 3 or 4 bushels in half an hour.

   Fish also are very plenty but as it takes longer to get them than it does oysters I can not get time to go very often. I had some boiled cabbage the other day for the first time since I left home. I tell you it tasted nice.

Apples are plenty at 5 cents a piece. I am afraid operations are entirely suspended here for the winter. The weather now is lovely. Do you have to pay any additional postage on my letters when I put on such old stamps as I sometimes do. ~~Inclosed I sent you twenty dollars~~ *No I'll send it the next time I write. I send you two darts from the buck of the fish called the Stingaree. Dont prick yourselves with them for their wound is very poisonous. I am gathering some more sea shells. As soon as I have a sufficient quantity I will send them home by express. There is no news at present. A few days ago one of the North Carolina regiments stationed at {unknown word} mutinied and the rebs had to send up 2 squadrons of cavalry and a large force of infantry to quell its troops. They fired 30 or more rounds of cannon shot before the mutiny could be put down. This speaks very poorly for their cause in this vicinity The North Carolina troops every where throughout the South seem to be very disaffected and inclined to give up {unknown word} & Go Home. What is the news from Burnside? Is Meade making any head way in Virginia? Is it a fact that Sigel is again going into the field???*

The captain & I are going a fishing this evening so I must make a short letter I think on the whole I will send you $20 Give five to Eliza if she wants it. Write to me often. I will write you again soon.

from Your Aff. Son
Edward L. Cook
Co. H. 100th

N.Y. Vols

Mr. Lyman Cook
Box 1463, Buffalo N. Y.

Letter from E. Cook to Parents and Relatives

Office A.A.Q. M.
North End Folly Island S.C. Oct. 13/63

My dear Parents and Relatives
I wrote to you a few days ago sending you a $20# Bill. I understand the Spaulding leaves for the North tomorrow so I will try and get a letter off

in her. The weather along back has been very lovely but lately it has grown windy and I think before long our fall rains will begin then look out for lonesome hours and homesick sighs. I saw a paper of the 10ᵗʰ {unknown word} this afternoon but there was no news in it of any account. Everything everywhere seems to be on the stand still. I thought a few weeks ago that peace was near at hand, but now it looks as far off as ever. It is my opinion that the war is not going to end for several years. If we are fortunate enough to get the upper hand of Jonney Reb, it will only be the road for an opening of war in the precincts of Mexico. Mr. Louis Napoleon will find him self in the wrong man's lot if we can ever get through with this little squabble in our own family. Texas has already cost Uncle Sam too much treasure and too many precious lives for him to let Mexico pass quietly and without interference in the hand of those who are more powerful, scheaming, avaricious and relentless than its former possessors. I forgot to tell you in my last letter that the rebs had attempted to blow up the Ironside with a torpedo and almost succeeded. The rebs are concentrating their forces on James Isl'd and we expect an attack on this island every night.

Gen'l Gillmore is waiting for reinforcements but I do not think he will get any until {unknown name} has got through with his operations in the South west and by that time it will be too late for us to do any thing here. The rebs are fortifying their position more strongly every day and the longer we delay the attack the more difficult it will be to accomplish the final {unknown word}. There is a report a round here that negociations for peace are now going forward between the two Authorities at Richmond and Washington but of course the rumor is not believed although many anxious hearts are hoping that it might be true. Peace looks a long way off.

How is little Annie getting along? Is Flora S. going to be married this fall? How is Grandma at present? Does father have any work nowadays? Tell Henry Phillips I have never received his letters. I often think of him and all the rest of the friends of my school days. Tell him if he will write to me I will answer speedily with out delay. I inclose my address for you to hand to him when you next see him. Have any of you ever called around at "Scheffers"?

I am terribly at a loss for thoughts to night so you will not get a long letter this time. We pronounce "Arago" all kinds of was but the two most prevalent are <u>Air</u>'-a-go & A-ra'-go with the first sound of "A". Tell Laura to *remember me to E.S. when they meet. Give my love to Grandma & all the rest of the girls. Kiss Gracie and go to bed as I am soon going to do.*

Good Bye from Your Aff Son

Lyman Cook	*Edward L. Cook*
Buffalo N.Y.	*Co. H. 100th N.Y.V.*
	Morris Is^d S.C. .

Letter from A. Lyth to his Brother

General Hospital
Hilton Head S.C. Oct 14th /63

Dear Brother

I received your kind and welcome letter of the 4th inst and was very glad to hear that you were all enjoying good health and that Sarah Ann was doing well and getting better I never received the letter the letter that you said Sarah Ann wrote to me about a month ago containing some postage stamps. My own health was never better and I am getting along first rate. I take a tramp down town now every day for the boys that are wounded and cannot get up see you I am some use where I am the weather here now is very warm to what it has been but we have had no weather here yet that we could call frosty weather in fact the themometer has hardly ever been below 60 degrees. I had a letter yesterday from a friend of mine in the Regt but there is nothing of any importance going on up there at present and very little news of any description and there is nothing new going on here except they have opened a recruiting office for the Veteran Corps and they offer $40 to all soldiers who will enlist in it and I think they are getting quite a number of recruits but I am thinking it will be a long time before they will catch me enlisting again. anyway not untill I get out of this term of enlistment. not saying that I am sorry that I ever enlisted or that I am getting tired of the service for I think it is every young mans duty who can come as conveniently as I could to enlist but I think I will see this show out before I step into another one. Dear Brother the next letter you write to me write a good long one and let me know the particulars of how things are *progressing around Cold Springs now Give My respects to all the neighbors my love to you all*

From Your Loving
Brother Alfred

P.S. I enclose ten cents for Fanny
Buy some apples

Letter from E. Cook to his Parents and Relatives

Office A.A.Q. M.
North End Folly Island S.C. Oct. 21/63

My Dear Parents & Relatives

I suppose you are getting rather anxious to hear from me again. It has been about 2 weeks since I wrote to you and just about the same length of time since I received a letter from you. I received a good long letter from Mr. Lyman a day or two ago and will answer it in a few days. Did you get the $20# that I sent you a short time ago. I made out 4 sets of Returns for an Infantry Captain this month and he paid me $5# for it. I am now engaged in making up some returns of Clothing, Camp Garrison Equipage & Ordinance Stoves for our {unknown word} Provost Marshal and I expect him to pay me $5# more. If I hear that you have received the $20# all right I will send you this $5# & that 5# that I shall receive when my present job is done. I want you should keep it for your own use, and use it to buy any thing you wish or for any purpose that you like. I have worked very steady this month which accounts for my not writing to you before. I am in good health and feeling first rate & have plenty of out door exercise such as walking and rowing. Every few days I take a boat & crew and go up the river towards Seceshionville and get oysters. I generally pull an oar myself whenever I go any where. Once in a while a party of us go up to Black's Island which lies between us and Charleston. This is the extreme of Uncle Sam's possessions in that direction.

The Rebs used to shell the island very considerably but without doing much damage having killed only one man. They have ceased wasting their ammunition in that direction and have not fired on us for about two weeks.

The mosquitoes bother me so much and the evening air is so sultry that it makes me feel quite nervous and uneasy and not at all in a writing mood. The Captain thought I confined myself too close to the desk so he advised me take more out door exercise and told me to take any horse in the stable and have a ride whenever I felt like it. Last Evening Leigh Stevens and myself rode down to his regiment (the 112th – Westfield Regt.) and had a very pleasant visit. My usual hour of rising heretofore has been about 7 or 8 oclock but this week I have been up every morning before sunrise, and rowed with Leigh Stevens out onto the bar and gathered sea shells.

I have got some very handsome specimens that I am going to send home before long. I think I shall also send a branch of oranges and some green lemons + a green citron such as you put in cake.

I have taken a great deal of pleasure in gathering the shells and am quite proud of the collection and I hope they will reach home safely and that you will take care of them for my sake and I know you will. The first came from Florida and will be quite curiosities in "B". Especially the citron. The lemons and oranges will soon ripen and be quite palatable.

I have given up drinking tea + coffee since we have been getting in water from the sanitary commission. I bless the sanitary commission and thousands of other soldiers bless them for this great and almost inestimable luxury which they furnish us free gratis. I wish the newspapers would speak of what good the commission is doing and of the opinion that the soldiers entertain towards it for it would encourage the patrons of the commission to greater efforts, and make them happy to know that the soldier received and appreciated the good things that are sent to him. and learns that his wants and wishes are not forgotten by those at home.

A dispatch has just been handed to me for the gunboat that lies up the river towards Black Il'd. so I will leave off writing and take a row up there and finish the letter tomorrow.

Oct. 24th 1863. We have had a very hard rain storm today but it has cleared up and the evening deliciously cool and pleasant. I saw a sun rise a few mornings ago & I tell you it was magnificent. The sun dont rise here every morning. Sometimes it is foggy & the fog keeps the sun from rising but along about 8 or 9 oclock it crawls out of the fog & then looks out for a hot day. If you have not seen a sunrise lately I would advise you to get up about 4 o'clock some morning and wait for it to come up. I think it will repay you for the trouble. Capt Walbridge says he is going to get up some morning and see one. He got up two or three mornings ago & went fishing; he thought he was going to kill 2 birds with one stone viz catch a mess of fish + see the sun rise too; but as luck would have it the fish wouldent bite and the sun diddent rise so he got cheated out of both enjoyments.

One of my acquaintances in the 112ᵗʰ Regt has gone to Mayville on a furlough. He may call on you when he returns. If he does ask him to stay all night & use him well for if he goes to Buffalo he will have no place to stay. He is married and may take his wife with him if he visits "B".

Tell father to send me about 6 limerick perch hooks in the next letter if he has them about this size.

We can buy large ones here but none of the right size.

What is the feeling among the Buffalo folks in regard to officers in negro regiments? When I send my box it will reach you by express & you may pay the charges if you like. I think the fruit will be worth as much for curiosities as the charges will cost.

Another mail came in today so I suppose I shall get a letter from you tomorrow. Tomorrow is Sunday but I have got a good long job to perform that will take me all day so I suppose I shall not keep it a it was intended to be kept. It very frequently happens that we do not know when Sunday comes around & I have known Saturday & Monday to be kept for Sunday by officers in the Army. Good Bye. Write Soon from your Aff Son
Edward L. Cook
Co. "H." 100ᵗʰ N.Y.V.

Letter from A. Lyth to his Father and Mother

U.S. General Hospital
Hilton Head S.C. Oct 24ᵗʰ /63

Dear Father + Mother
I received your kind and welcome letter of Oct 10 and was very glad to learn that you were all enjoying good health as it leaves me at present I was very glad to learn that Sarah Ann is getting better and I hope by this she is entirely recovered. I am please to hear that business is good and I think as soon as you commence draining that your stock of small tiles will go off a

little more livly The weather here is very warm + pleasent. Yesterday though we had quite a rain storm. I was glad to hear that you have received the money all safe that I sent and I wish when you write again you will tell me what the Express charges on it were. I wish you would remember me to J. Robson and give him my best respects and tell him that I should like to have a letter from him. I was very sorry to hear that he was so sick and I hope he will be better when this reaches you if he is not better when his furlough runs out he will of course get it extended.

I have sent you Genl Gillmores likeness which cost me 25 cents it is an exact likeness of him as I have seen him a number of times Give my love to Sarah Ann and W^m and all the family and accept the same yourselves
From Your Loving Son
Alfred

P.S. I enclose 10 cts for Fanny.   Write Soon.

Letter to A. Lyth to his Brother

U.S. General Hospital
Hilton Head S.C. Nov 1st /63

Dear Brother John
I received your kind and welcom letter yesterday dated Oct 20th and to day I receive one from father dated Oct 18th and I was very glad to learn that you were all well and enjoying good health as it leaves me at present I also received two newspapers. the weather here is considerable milder than it has been for the last week or so past and the musquitoes are as troublesome as ever at night. There is very little news of any importance here except that last week there were quite a number of conscripts arrived here from the north and as you will see by the paper I have sent there are quite a number of them for our Reg't and they have gone up to Morris Island if they have to Join the reg't as soon as they get there they will have some pretty tough time for our Reg't has gone off from Morris Island to another Island nearer Charleston I am not sure weather it is Black Island or Balls Island where they have gone but I shall have a letter from there by tomorrows mail and I shall know how every thing is going on up there. All

day yesterday there was a continual roar of heavy cannonadeing heard in the direction of Charleston and I guess before long that we shall have some stiring news from there and I hope some good ones at that. I am begining to feel anxious to get back to the Regt again to see how things are going on up there and to see the boys again or at least what is left of them for John some of my best friend in the Co have gone to their last home. some are in the various hospitals badly wounded and waiting for the time to come when they will get their discharge and can go home to their friends by the way you speak of Edward Townsend now I can give you no positive information about him at present as in the letters I have received from the Regt some told me he was prisoner some say missing some say killed Now I am going to write to Tom Maharg this afternoon for information concerning him and if it is known or can be found out what became of him. Tom will certainly do his best to find out.

Since I have wrote the above there is more conscripts landed here they are for the 76 Pa Vols there are only 2 companys of that Regt on this Island and it takes nearly half of them to guard the conscripts which makes the boys awful mad the first lot that came here they put double guard over them the first night or two untill they got them assigned to the different Cos those that have arrived to day they have some of them under ball and chain for some cause or other. So much for staying to be drafted.
Give my respects to all the neighbors

> *My Love to you all*

>> *From Your Affectionate Brother*
>> *Alfred Lyth*

P.S. since I commenced writing I have received 2 more newspapers.
John I should like to have all your likenesses but I wish you would take fanny to town some fine day and have hers taken and send it to me

>> *Yours Truly A.L*

Letter from A. Lyth to his Brother
> *U.S. General Hospital*
> *Hilton Head S.C. Nov 1ˢᵗ /63*

Dear Brother William
> *When I get paid again I will send you a dollar for to spend for yourself*

but you must get your likeness taken when I send it. write to me as soon as you receive this and let me know if you will do it

From Your Big Brother
Alfred

P.S. I would send you a dollar now but I am getting short of money. Al

Letter from A. Lyth to his Brother

U.S. General Hospital Hilton Head
S.C. Nov 3ʳᵈ /63

Dear Brother

Having nothing of any importance to occupy my time at present so I thought I would write you these few lines hoping they will find you all enjoying good health as it leaves me at present. I have just been down town and I have found the mail steamer 'Fulton' sails for New York first thing tomorrow morning so I cannot send this letter by her and I guess by the time this reaches you you will have heard that our forces have got possession of Fort Sumter. John I want you if you can to send me a couple of five or a ten cent peice in silver as I want it to set a ring with that I am going to make. I am pretty busy nowadays a picking some small sea shells which I am stringing up for fanny a necklace and I shall send them home in a week or so and I want you to buy a clasp for them when I send them and then give them to her for a Christmas present I shall send you something or other for a Christmas present too. To day I have found out how much I am over my clothing bill last which is $54.84. so you see I have over drawn it to the amount of $12.85. but I have not drawn any thing on the second year and I have a new pair of pants and an old pair which with another pair will last me the second year I have two good shirts and my blanket over coat dress coat will last me very easy untill my time is out Now I think at the end of the second year I shall have quite a lot of my clothing money to draw as I shall not have to draw a Jacket this year which cost me $5.50

now I won't have to draw	*over coat*	*7.20*
any of these unless it	*dress "*	*6.71*
will be a over coat. for	*blanket*	*1.95*

the day before I came to this hospital I got my over coat wet and when I came here it was rolled up wet in my rubber blanket and put away in the baggage room and remained there untill I got well and went and got my knapsack and found that my over coat was all moulded. well I paid 25 cents for getting it washed and it looks pretty good but I think if I was coming north I should draw a new one and do away with this To day I have sent in a requision to day for a pair of armey boots and a couple pair of drawers the drawers will last me my next year out. Our Regt has got 137 conscripts and twenty of them are for our Co one of our boys here got a letter from the company and he says if I had been with the Co now the Leautenant would have give me a corporals berth but that I do not care about as I once refused it from Capt Dye now John I guess you think it is rather queer to refuse promotion but there are two or three in our Company have done it and now I will tell you the reasons first if a corporal has charge of a squad of men on duty and one of them does any thing wrong and the corporal does not report him and he is found out he has to be courtmartialed and probally he is reduced to the ranks and if he does report him he looses the good will of the boys. Then again the corporal does not have to stand post when on guard duty but he has to stay at the guard house and when any of the guards on post call out Corporal of the guard post No 1 or whatever number his post may be the corporal has to run and see what is wanted so if the guard wants to do a little Job for himself the corporal has to take his gun and stand his post untill he comes back and if two or three of the guards on post happen to take the diorea on purpose to bother the corporal they will keep the poor fellow running. then again if any thing goes wrong on a picket post the corporal in charge of the post is called upon to give is account of the circumstance and a good many more little inconvences he has to put up with which a private don't have to annoy him.

Nov 4th I have been down town again this morning and I see that the Fulton has not started yet as she was ordered not to start by Gen Gillmore but she will go out this afternoon. Gen Gillmore is at Hilton Head at present he came from Morris Island last night he paid a visit to the hospital

John I should like to know how uncle is getting along now if you have heard from them I wish you would let me know I should like to know how John Robson is getting along. I tell you must do John after you have read this letter you must take two sheet of paper like this and write them full and let me know all the particulars and news there is in that part of the country. I see that Capt Dye is running for city treasurer on the Union ticket and I think he will be elected any way I guess before this reaches you you will now whos elected Nov 7th I have got these shells put up in a small box and I shall post them with this letter and John I have sent you a pen and holder if you think you can make the necklace look any nicer you can string them over and have out the worst shells I could have sent quite a lot of those lose shells but I thought the postage would be more than they were worth if I could only get a lot of the shells we use to pick up on the beach in North Carolina I should send them home no matter what they cost as they far surpassed those in beauty that I have sent and were all shapes and sizes imagineable and from the purest white to the Jet black

To day there is very heavy cannonadeing here as it is Just two years to day since our troops took possesion of this Island and there are great goings on here to day with fireing salutes and the bands playing

Give my best respects to Robert Townsend, Cris and the rest of the men that I know tell Robert I have not got a letter yet from Morris Island but I expect one in a few days and probly then I shall be able to let him know something of Edward. Give my best respects to Mr. & Mrs. Newman and the rest of the neighbors

Give my love to Sarah Ann W[m] and all the youngsters and accept the same yourselfs

From Your Affectionate Brother, Alfred

P.S.

write soon and let me know if you have received those shell and a newspaper I sent you and how things is going on in that section of the country The mail steamer Arago
is here to day but I think she will not be in 'till tomorrow morning and then I expect a letter on her

A.L.

Letter from E. Cook to his Parents and Relatives

Office A.A.Q. M.
N. End Folly Island Nov. 3rd 1863

My Dear Parents and Relatives
I suppose you are having a very busy time up North in old York State today.

It is election day but us poor soldiers who are out here doing duties for our country are not allowed the priviledge of saying what men shall have a hand in propelling the ponderous wheels of government. If we could be allowed the priviledge of voting where you think would the poison copperheads stand? What would become of their party? But I believe there are enough true hearted patriots still left in New York State to carry the election against all the odds that vile treason can bring against it. The soldier longs for peace once more with a longing far greater than his friends at home for he knows how to appreciate the value of the blessing of peace but he does not want a peace disgraceful to himself + to the country for which he has periled his life. Peace still looks a long way off but still we do not want to return to our homes until we can do so with proud and thankful hearts that need not feel ashamed of the cause + country for which[ ]} they have been fighting.

Has Mr. Comstock received the box that I sent him containing Geo. Clarks things? If so did you get the little box of trinkets, belonging to me that I inclosed in the larger box?

I am going to send home another box as soon as I hear that the other one has gone all right.

Our batteries have again opened on Sumter and have already succeeded in knocking down the sea wall. There is a heavy smoke hanging over Charleston. But whether it is from shells thrown from our batteries or from fire caused by other means I do not know. We expect every night to hear that our men have stormed Sumter. The firing today is very rapid and heavy and chases away all thoughts of lonliness and fatigue. I had rather hear the firing of cannon and the bursting of shell than the song of the sweetest singer or the chords of the grandest organ. You have no idea of the lonliness that pervades our feelings on the days when there is no firing. It makes us feel sad and almost homesick, but as soon as the cannon begin to roar and the echoes pick up the sound and carry it from wood to cloud & from cloud to wood again, our hearts bound within us and chase away each gloomy thought and drown each homesick sigh. It is our music, and its melody is sweeter to our ears and more touching to our souls than the voice of the lute or the notes of the harp.

Our regiment has received between 1 & 2 hundred of the conscripts, but only one or two of them are from Buffalo. They are mostly fine looking men but some look thin + poor and illy adapted to stand the hard ships & exposures of the soldiers life. I am almost persuaded to go back to my company and try to win promotion in the proper and legitimate path of duty. I have been offered the position of orderly sergeant if I go back, but I do not think I am entitles to it and therefore I refused to accept it but the Lieutenant in command of the Company has not appointed anyone else still hoping to get me back. All that I want is your consent and blessing for I feel that I should not do right to go, back of own accord without your consent unless I am sent back in the same manner that I was detailed viz by an order from Head Qrs.

Dave White is well again and doing duty in the company. I do not hear from you as often as I would like. I think I receive all the papers that you send me. Does my {unknown word} magazine come now? I am sorry {unknown word} is removed. Did you hear Sigel lecture in "B"? How has the city election gone? Write to me soon and tell me all the news. Good Bye from your affection Son

Edward L. Cook
Co. "H." 100ᵗʰ N.Y. Vols.

Letter from A. Lyth to his Brother

U.S. General Hospital Hilton Head
S.C. Nov 11ᵗʰ /63

Dear Brother

I have Just received a letter from the Regt from Tom Maharg he says all they know of Ed. Townsend is that they have not heard a word of him since the charge upon Wagner so they have given him up for lost his clothes were sold to the boy in the Regt not long ago by Capt Topping. He found a testament in his knapsack & looking on the back of it he saw it was from his sister he gave it to P. Laforte our first Sergt and told him to send it home with some other little things that was found in his knapsack and Laforte sent them without telling his folks where they were from. I should like to give him such a good ducking I once before gave him when we were out in a boat in the river at Gloucester point bay for his carelessness. The Regt is still on Morris Island and have never been off Tom and the boys are all in pretty good health and are doing well

November 19ᵗʰ I received a letter from father yesterday and I was very glad to learn that you are doing well and are all enjoying good health as it leaves me at present and I expect to go to the Regt when the next examination come off by the head doctor in charge of the hospital. I spoke to our ward doctor about going back but he told to wait untill I was sent. The hospital steward was talking to me the other day and he wanted me to be detailed as nurse in this hospital but I refused. Because if I was once detailed I have to stay here and attend to the sick + and wounded and I could not go back to my Regt when I pleased.. then Mrs. Russell wanted me to go over to her department and assist the women all I have to do there would be to help and assort clothes after they are fetched in from the washhouse and take charge of the liquor that is used for the medicine in the hospital and deliver it out when the different ward doctors sent an order for any the reason that she wanted me to go was that as I did not drink wiskey Brany + wine myself I had a mind to take the situation I asked our doctor his opinion wheather I had better take it or not and he told me to please myself but he would advise me not to as he said Mrs Russell was an off kind of a woman and probly I could not get along very well with her and he said in a Jokeing was that I might take a fancy to the wine and Brandy. however I have considered not to take the situation

I cannot tell mother how soon my time will be out when we enlisted the Board of Trade told us our time would expire with the Regt's, but as we were sworne in to the service for three years the government may keep us untill our time is out if they need us. but it is said that we shall be discharged with the Regt which will either be next July or September but it is thought that the war will be over before that time and then we will be discharged. I might have got my discharge sine I have been away from the Regt if I had been like some cowards that have been in this hospital and abuse my body and 'play off' on the doctors but I would not have my name talked off as some for my discharge and a

    $1000 to boot. Dear Brother I must close now with my love to you all Give my best respects to John Robson

From Your Affectionate

Brother Alfred

P.S. Write soon and give me all the news in that section

Letter from E. Cook to his Mother

Office A.A.Q. M.

North End Folly Island S.C.

Nov. 19ᵗʰ 1863

Dear Mother

    Inclosed you will find five dollars which I wish you to devote to your own use for any purpose that you may see fit. I also return one of the darning needles that that I brought away with me more than a year ago. I still have one left but it is rather too fine and not as serviceable as the one I return. I make you a present of the needle and as it is impossible to put another "eye" in it I would be much obliged to you if you send me a new one to replace it of just the same size and proportions. I was in hopes that I should be able to send you ten instead of five dollars but I not not got so much just now, and will try and send the other five next time if I get it. The attack on fort Sumter has been put off again for a time. It was to have taken place last week and the boats and men were all ready and prepared to storm the fort, but again the navy failed to cooperate and the attack did not come off.

    The mail steamer from New York reached Hilton Head 2 or 3 days ago but I have not yet rec'd any letters from you though I expect I shall in a day or two more. There are two regular mail steamers now running between Hilton Head and New York, viz the "Arago" & "Fulton".

    The rebs have now got such perfect range of Folly river that our boats no longer dare to traverse it. The captain & pilot of the steamer were just in our office and said they would sooner lose their situations than to run the boat through the river.

Have you received all the volumes of my "Appleton's Encyclopedia"? Do you continue to take the Magazine? Do you ever have the interest figured up on my bank book? I should "kinder" like to know how much money I have got in the bank. Suppose you let Laura run up the account and tell me in the next letter how much I am worth. I wish I could see you all again. How I should enjoy a short visit or even an evening call. I would to hear the sound of the piano and see my dear old bookcase. I should love to sit in the old armchair and rock myself away as I told you of the scenes I have witnessed and the hardships I had passed. I wonder if the time ever comes when I can again enjoy the pleasures of home. I hope so & you hope so but how many "Hopes so's" have died in disappointment since this war began. Is Annie any better? Does Laura go to school now? If Aunt Grace should ever send a box to Geo. Stoddard I wish you would put a pound of smoking tobacco and a ¼ pound of magnesia in it for me and also 1 Dozen [ ] and I will pay part of the freight to George.

I am going to try and get down to the lower point and see George next Sunday if I can. I want to see him very much. I cannot get any good tobacco here and what I do get costs at the rate of about $1.50 per pound. The magnesia I want for the heart burn which does not trouble me near as much as formerly but once in a while keeps me awake at night. The weather is pleasant but the nights are rather cool. I am perspiring as I write so you may know that the days are not cool. I still continue to gather shells and will send home my collection by the next steamer I think. I do not think of any news to write that will interest you. Our Reg't. received a lot of conscripts about 2 or 3 week ago and are hard at work drilling &c.

We have heard from Capt. Payne. He is still a prisoner at Columbia S.C. He says his wound is getting along finely and that the rebs use him first rate but he does not like the confinement after having for so long a time been used to scouting and having his own way. Give my love to Grandma and all the folks. Write to me often.

Good Bye from your Aff Son
Edward L. Cook
Co. 'H.' 100ᵗʰ N.Y. Vols.

Mr. Lyman Cook
Buffalo
N.Y.

Letter from A. Lyth to his Father and Mother

U.S. General Hospital Hilton Head S.C.
Nov 23rd 1863

Dear Father and Mother

To day it is very windy and cloudy and we have an occasional shower of rain so upon the whole it makes out to be a very dull day so I though I would write you these few lines to pass the time away pleasantly for to tell the truth I always find it a pleasure to write a letter home and a much greater pleasure to receive one and I tell you I am greatly disappointed if I do not receive one with the weekly mail Steamer. The Arago will be in to morrow and I expect a letter as usal to day I posted a couple of "New Souths" and another newspaper with a speach of Henry Ward Beacher's in I think the speach is worth reading although he is an abolitionist Speaking of Slavery after this war is over slavery in this country will be over for if the slaves are not freed by the government they will free theirselves because since this war broke out they have learnt what it is to be free where ever our armies have penetrated the slave states there the negro has picked up a little education and have learnt that they need not be slaves if they wish to be free Take it in this department for instance every negro you come across has an A.B.C. book primer or second reader even old men sixty or seventy years old and they always carry them about with them and when they can steal a few moments from their work the sit down and open their books. Now around this hospital there are some ten or 12 niggers employed to scrub the floors and every moment they can hide away from the boss the stick theirselves in some corner and get out their books. I have asked them a great many times what they would do if they had to be slaves again. they would say 'I run away. or they can't make me slave any more. Here there is a nigger school and quite a number of the young ink stands go there. the other day I was down town and a five year old ink stand was counting over a roll of 'green $ backs'. when I said to him thats good for nothing. ain't it say he here you want and he offered it to me but when I reached out my hand as it to take it his eyes give one roll and he commenced to laugh Yah Yah Yah I tot dey was good for noting. it would be imposible to makes slaves of these nigs again particularly those that have been in the army.

Nov 24ᵗʰ There are very little news of any importance in this department at present on Morris Island there is very little going on except an occational shot is exchanged between our men and the rebels. There was a lot of sick came from there this last week and they say they will soon be doing something up there The Arago came in this morning and fetched a couple of hundred men of the invalide Corps from Washington and it is said they are going to do duty around this hospital they are armed with sabres and revolvers but I don't see the use of them around a hospital. I think if they do duty at this hospital it will be as nurses and other hospital duty Here in this hospital they have service every Sunday and prayer meeting four times a week and I make it a practice to attend them very regular. Now every Sunday I like to hear the sermon preached, but I sometimes get disgusted with the prayer meetings at the way some of them carry on and holler. The Chaplin of this hospital is a much better man than the chaplin of our Reg't but to tell the truth there are some of the chaplins in the army that are not fit to be private soldiers regular Government Robbers as they are called by the soldiers. I will soon be pay day again in fact I think the Regt will have been paid off before this. I don't know weather they will pay off in the hospital this time or not but if they do I shall have $12.85 clothing bill to pay so I shall not send any home but if they don't stop the clothing account this pay I shall send $10 home. I have just received a letter from Brother John and I was very glad to learn that you were enjoying good health and in good spirits as it leaves me at present for to tell the truth I dont remember the time I had better health than I am enjoying at present. I am very glad to hear that tile business is so brisk and that you have had good luck in your last kiln for the season. I often wish I was at home to help you but then I think again it is my duty to be here. Give my best respects to John Robson and tell him to write to me Give my love to Sarah Ann Wᵐ and the rest of the family and accept the same yourselfs

From Your Loving
Son Alfred

Letter from A. Lyth to his Brother

A Letter for William
U.S. General Hospital Hilton Head S.C.
Nov 24ᵗʰ 1863

Dear Brother William

I received your bully Letter for it was a bully letter the best letter I have had in a long time and I was very glad to learn that you were all doing well and were enjoying good health as it leaves me at present. You said you would send me your likeness in your next letter so I shall expect it. I am very pleased to see that you are such a good writer Jingo! if you keep on improveing so fast you will soon beat me in writing before another year is out you will beat me if you keep on. and then every word is spelt right which I am very glad to see A pig! that news and I tell you that you are well off that you have no secesh soldiers up there to come and steal it away from you the same as I have often helped to do to the secesh in Virginia and the same as the Union boys did when they first went on to Morris Island they capture and shot a great many pigs belonging to the secesh folks Give my love to fanny and accept the same yourself

From Your Affectionate Brother Alfred

Letter from A. Lyth to his Brother

U.S. General Hospital Hilton Head S.C.
Dec 1ˢᵗ/63

Dear Brother

The next letter you write you can address it to my Co for I am going back to the Regt tomorrow or the next day we have not been paid off here yet and I think they have in the Regt so I shall miss my pay this time but it makes no difference to me for when I get to the Regt if I need any I can get all I want in fact one of our boys wanted me to take five dollars but as he is in the hospital and may never go back to the Regt again as he was wounded so I did not take it besides I do not need it as I have a little and I have between two or three dollars coming to me by the boys in the Regt. I hope these few lines will find you all enjoying good health and doing well as it leaves me at present. The weather here is a little cold day before yesterday was the first time we have had frost and last night the themometer was 30 degrees 2 degrees below freezing but to day it is quite warm and it will be very warm to night

Dec 3ᵈ I received a letter from you this morning dated Nov 19ᵗʰ and I was very glad to learn that you were doing well and enjoying good health as it leaves me at present I think I shall start for Morris Island tomorrow or next day. I received a Harpers Weekly + a Commercial Advertiser also the silver + postage stamps you sent me you said you sent me John Robsons address in your letter but I have looked it over half a dozen times and I don't see it The Fulton came in last night and she fetched some pretty good news of Gen Grants victory but we had the news here five days ago from the Charleston Mercury of the 24ᵗʰ Nov the papers were got from the rebels pickets on Black + Morris Island as the pickets are on friendly terms again and the exchange various little comodoties same as we used to do on Folly Island

Give my respects to all my acquaintances my love to you all

From Your
Affectionate
Brother
Alfred

Letter from E. Cook to his Father and Mother

(printed stationary}

HEAD QUARTERS,
Co H, 100ᵗʰ Reg't N.Y.S. Vol. Infantry,
Camp, Morris Island S.C. Dec 21ˢᵗ 1863

Dear Father + Mother

I received your kind and welcome letter of Dec 2ᵈ and I was very sorry to hear that Sarah Ann is so sick again but I hope she is better by this time. I wish you would ask her if she received my last letter I wrote her when I was at the hospital for if she has not I want to write again to her. This morning Col. Dandy, Lt. Stowits and some more officers of our Regt have *started north on recruiting service beside a man from each company in the Regt if ever you come across Lt. Stowits you can introduce yourself to him he is a very nice man and he will tell you a good deal about the 100th Regt. I was on guard duty at fort Shaw this morning when they left or else I should have sent a message by the man that left our company. But when the recruiting office open in Buffalo if John goes there and inquire for Lambert S. Melvin he will find him and I should like him to do so. Melvin is a corporal in our company he is a Michigan man and an honest good hearted fellow by the way don't mention to him that Capt. Dye ever offered me a corporalship for Capt Dye not liked by any of the company On the 17th all the troops on this island had to turn out to witness the shooting of a deserter. he was a substitute and belonged to Co G 3rd N.H.V. he had got a pile of money as a substitute. All the troops were drawn up in line on the beach in the afternoon he was placed in a ambulance on his coffin at one end of the line and marched the whole length of the line the band playing the 'Death March' all the time he seamed as unconserned as if he was going to a picnic part of the way he lay on his coffin leaning on his elbow and part of the way siting up they came half way back up the line and stoped directly in front of our Regt about 50 paces from our company his coffin was placed close to the waters edge. he then stood on the side next the water the chaplin said a prayer. the he said something which we could not hear then he took off his hat and his shirt Just as if he was going to work then he knelt on his coffin a handkerchief tied over his eyes then the motions were given and they fired and he fell, he hardly had struck the ground when a large bird lit on his body and before he was shot there was not the appearance of a bird in the vacinity and they could hardly drive the bird away he was then picked up and streached out on his coffin and all the troops marched close past the coffin there were six holes through his body There is very little going on here at present I was on duty in fort Wagner one night and the rebels did everlastingly pop over the shell that night but did no harm our men fire an occational shot into the city my love to you all*

> *From Your Affectionate*
> *Son Alfred*

Letter from E Cook to his Sister

Office A.A.Q. M. *Tuesday*
N. End Folly Island S.C. Dec 22/63

My dear sister Laura

This is such a lovely day that I long to be out in the air and I almost begrudge the time that I shall have to remain in the office while I am writing this letter. If it were not for the look of the thing I would take my portfolio + writing materials out doors and and write to you under the genial influence of a Southern winters Sun. But the passers by would be apt to look inquisitively at such a scene and I would also be liable to interruption therefore the better ways is for me to remain where I am until I finish my letter and then go out & take an airing afterward provided it is not too late. I wish you could experience for a single days the lovely weather that is almost continuous in this latitude at this season of the year. It is not like our northern "Spring" although it approximates nearer to that season than it does to our "fall". I know of no term that will express the idea of the sensation associated with this weather so well as "Joyful". It is joyful weather. To be sure we occasionally have rains and cold days. Last Sunday morning the water in our basins froze ½ an inch thickness but such instances are very rare during the winter months. You spoke in one of your letters about having pancakes. We too have them but not made of Buckwheat. We form them by mixing flour & water with a little salt and frying them in grease. I do not consider them healthy and we do not have them very often on our table. I think you are mistaking about [   ]being killed. I am almost confident that I saw him at the regiment about 2 or 3 weeks ago. He could not have been killed on a forraging expedition for we do not have any such expeditions down here, as there is nothing to forage unless we go out hunting rattlesnakes & alligators and we have to much other work to do to indulge in such pastime.

You want to know who "Charlie" is that you? Well he our shipping clerk and belongs to the 47th N.Y. Vols. His name is Charles Deyo and he has got a sister Susan. I sent my compliments to her today at Fort Plains, Dutchess Co. N.Y. and I suppose I shall hear from about it some time in the future and if I do I will let you know.

Charlie has got a cousin named Maggie Deyo and I am going to send her a letter in a few days for she told Charlie that if he new any soldiers that wanted a correspondent she would fill such a position to the best of her ability, so I am going to open a correspondence with her in a few days and see what she has got to say for her self. 'Charlies' Regt. has gone to Hilton Head and he is ordered to join it. He leaves tomorrow. I am very sorry that he is going to leave us for we were about the same age and were first rate company for each other. He is a good fellow and has a good education & noble principles. His is a minister and like most all other sons of Reverend

[ ] he is somewhat wild but not much the worse for that. I am going to hear from him once in a while by letter & that will partly compensate for the void which his absence will leave in our little circle of messmates. You remarked in your last letter that "Eliza is working a blanket for a baby that is worth $15#. Now I have been puzzling my brain ever since I read that sentence to know which one of the articles is worth the amount mentioned and not being able, after a vast study, to determined the important question I am obliged to call on you for a solution, and in the interim I can only exclaim – How dear for the baby – and how cheap for the Blanket. I still have possession of my little

"[ ]" and often enjoy a smoke out of it. I am in hopes that I shall be able to bring it home with me when I return and keep it for an heirloom and memento of this war. I received three papers from home yesterday each of which contained a small wad of tobaco. I was pleased to receive this token of your remembrance and consider it as the next best thing to a letter from home not excepting a letter from any of my girls. How did you happen to think of this mode of sending anything I think I shall have to make use of this mode whenever I am in need of tobaco. It is a kind of underground railroad however and rather a risky institution to patronize. I wish you could send me a little magnesia by your underground railroad

So Flora is married. Tell me in your next letter all about the wedding and what the young couple are going to do. A deserter was shot on Morris Island last week. He was caught in the attempt to desert and sentenced to death by Genl. Gillmore. Some of our boys went over to see the execution. They said the man acted very cool and collected. He rode up to the place of execution in an open ambulance seated on his coffin. He leaned back upon his elbows and threw one leg over the other and looked out upon the regiments of soldiers drawing up in line to witness the scene of his moments on earth as composedly as if he were going to a fair and gazing on a crowd of visitors. Having arrived on the ground he bowed in prayer with some chaplain for a few moments, then deliberately laid off his coat & overshirt. His eyes were bandaged and the word was given – Fire! He died instantly and was laid out on his coffin. The line of soldiers were marched around the corpse and the ceremony of the execution was completed.

I went down to the south point of the island last Saturday and saw George S. for the first time in over four months although we are only 7 or 8 miles apart. I took my box of shells down there expecting to send them home by express that day but the express agent was not there and I had to leave it and trust to luck in getting it home. I would not have it missent for $50#.

I have got a citron in it but the other fruit was all used up before I had a chance to send the box. Mr. [   ] has left for "B" on recruiting service and perhaps he will take it along with him.

I wrote to Mr. Lyman yesterday and to "Lila" also. I guess she has forgotten that he has a brother in the army. I sent her a Christmas present of $5 Tell me when she receives it. Tell Mother that I have got a recipe for the Headache that I think will do her good viz. Take a piece of pure charcoal – remove all dirt by washing it in clear water or by brushing it. then dry it perfectly and pulverize it as fine as possible (The finer the better) take a table spoon even full of the fine charcoal and thoroughly mix it with a part glass of water and drink it. If this does not remove the headache in half an hour repeat the dose and either the headache will yield to its properties or else it may be considered incurable for if this will not cure it nothing will.

You can buy the pure pulverized charcoal at any druggists cheaper & better than you can make it yourself. Try this mother the first time your headaches and I believe it do you good. It always cures mine and I have tried it with others and always found it to work like a charm.

Inclosed is five dollars for mother to expend in buying Christmas Gifts for any of the little ones. It is a small amount and will only go a short ways but if all little children are the same as I was when I was 2 or 3 years old they will be as much pleased with a small gift as they would be with a larger one. But any how it is all I can send and you can use it while it lasts and then add some more to it if you want to.

There is no news in the department at present. Operations are suspended for a time and our men are going into winter quarters as fast as they can prepare them.

The rebs wake us up with their shells every time a steamer goes through Folly River but they do no damage other than scattering the marsh mud quite freely in all directions. I think I told you in my last letter that we were digging a canal through the marsh from Lighthouse Inlet into Folly River at a point where the rebs shells cannot come. The canal is progressing finely and in about two weeks we shall be able to give passage to steamers without their running any risks of being hit by rebel shot or shell.

I am in first rate health and feeling in good spirits. If Lieut Stowits does not call on father I should like father to call on him if he can learn his whereabouts.

Lt, Stowits, and a number of non. com. officers + privates have left the department and are on their way to Buffalo for the purpose of obtaining recruits. Give my love to Grandma and all the folks and tell them I hope to be with them before another year has drawn in its days & closed up its accounts with the past. Write to me soon and believe me ever your true and affectionate brother

Edward L. Cook
Co. "H." 100ᵗʰ N.Y. Vols.
Morris Island

Miss Laura Cook
Buffalo N.Y.

Letter from E. Cook to his Father and Mother

Office A.A.Q. M.
N. End Folly Island S.C. Dec. 25/63
Christmas Night

My dear Father and Mother

How many times this day have I wished you a "Merry Christmas" with all my heart I wish you a "Happy New Year" "Merry Christmas" all. One year ago this day we left our pleasant home *at Gloucester Point and embarked for this Charleston expedition. How little has been accomplished in this department during the long and dragging year.*

We are in the close vacinity of the vile city of treason and corruption but in a military point of view we are really but little nearer than we were a year ago when the largest portion this army of Gillmore's were in camps in Virginia + N. Carolina.

This Christmas has been a very quiet, but not a sad one. I have not passed it in a merry mood neither have I felt down hearted or dispirited, but it has seemed to me very like a Sabbath day because we have done no business in the office and every thing has passed off so very quietly since morning

I sent $5⁰⁰ in my last letter to Laura 3 or 4 days ago for the purpose of buying "Christmas Gifts" for the little ones but I am afraid you did not get it as the Mail boat was behind time in going north.

The day has been cold and windy but not very disagreeably so. I will give you a synopsis of my living for the day — breakfast, Oyster Soup Dinner, Fried Liver, potatoes, Coffee +c, with all usual trimmings, Supper, fried potatoes, coffee +c, Supper No. 2 (with Capt. Walbridge) Oyster Stew, fruit cake, Strawberry preserves, and Tea. I intend to have a lunch of raw oysters before going to bed. I wish father could be here to help me eat them. I think this is not a bad specimen of living for one day, but it is not what pleased most. – I have rec'd a Christmas present this evening myself – a letter from Laura, but that is not all, - a Rural New Yorker from Mr. Lyman (give him my thanks) besides these I received a very pleasant and agreeable letter from a young lady friend in "B" so you see that after all I have received quite a Christmas on my own account away down here in South Carolina where the birds still warble forth their songs at morn, and the flies and fleas our tents & beds adorn.

Dear Mother I inclose a small testimony of my Love (now dont laugh and say you are too aged for a great gawk of a boy like me to make love to, for I do love you) and remembrance, for your Christmas Santa Claus in shape of a $10⁰⁰ treasury note. You must wish me a "Happy New Year" and thank me for it in your own handwriting or I shall feel that you are indebted to me. Now Father you must not feel jealous and say that I am trying to curry favor with your wife by making her presents and not sending any thing to you, for there is only one thing that prevents me from remembering you in the same way, and that is my money is not elastic and will not stretch out; but it will be your turn next time that I get money and I will not fail to remember you. Dear Grandmother I wish you a "Merry Christmas" and "Happy New Year". I have thought of you many times *today and wished that I could see you. I have looked at the photograph of your dear self so many times and shown it to so many persons that it is beginning to show signs of ware. I would not part with it for any thing. I carry it with me day and night and often wish that I may live to see the dear original which the picture so faithfully represents. Nearly every one who looks at the picture says "What an excellent photograph" and "What a kind looking Old Lady." Yes, Grandma I wish you a* happy new year *and hope that every one around you will try and make the path of your declining years peaceful, pleasant and happy, and free from care and sorrow.*

Mother I have read the sermon of Rev. Mr. Smith that you sent to me, and was delighted with it. I have passed it around for others to read, and they all like it. I have also read & passed around the speach of Hon. E. W. Gantts formerly General in the Rebel Service.

If you want to read an excellent book get the Wifes Stratagem. My fire is going down & I will catch cold if I dont end my writing and go to bed so a "Merry Christmas" to all & to all a Good Night

From your loving son
Edward L. Cook
Co H 100ᵗʰ N.Y.V.

To My Parents
*Mr. + Mrs. Lyman Cook*Morris Island, S.C.*
Buffalo
N.Y.

Letter from A. Lyth to his Folks at Home

printed stationary
HEAD QUARTERS
Co. H., 100 Reg't NYS Vol. Infantry,
Camp Morris Island S.C. Dec 25ᵗʰ, 1863.

Dear Folks at Home

The mail arrived here to day but there was no letters for me so I was very much disappointed but it may be I shall get one in a day or two for it has very likely gone to the hospital this time. To day it is Christmas I was detailed this morning to act as corporal of a fatigue party for to day but orders came that there would not be any fatigue duty to day. I enjoyed this

Christmas a great deal better than the last one Tom Russell and his tent mate got up a first rate dinner and invited Tom Maharg and myself to take dinner with them. We had a large beef dumpling and apple dumplings and a large rich cake which we got baked at the Regt bakery + cheese. I wish you all a merry christmas and I hope you all enjoyed yourselves and I wish you a happy "New Years". I hope by next new years day I shall be at home to enjoy myself. I should liked very much to have been with you this year, but I consider I am engaged in a good cause so I make myself content, and am glad that enlisted when I did and did not wait to be drafted. But one thing I should like very much is that us Board of Trade men will get discharged when the old men do I wish you would make some inquiries and see if you can send me any information on the subject probaly Mr Pratt is one of the board of trade or may be you know some of them that would let you know how it will be. They are going to open a recruiting office in our Regt for recruiting for the veteran corps I dont think they will get me though for I want to be a free man again before I bind myself again. There is very little of any importance occuring here at present except that there was a pretty sharp engagement this morning at Stono inlet between our gun boats and some rebel land batteries no harm done to our boats but the rebels got the worse of it Our batteries throw an occasional shell into the city and the rebs return the fire from some of their batteries but do us no injury the other day I was up to the front on duty and I had a good spy glass with me I could see the clock on one of the churches in Charleston a very amusing incident happened that day Just as one man was stooping down to arrange something on the ground a ten inch shell from one of the rebel batteries past close in the rear of his stern and struck a sand bank near he mearly straightened up and commence scratching his rump and made some remark about the wrong breed of fleas. I will close this letter now hoping it will find you all enjoying good health as it leaves me at present and I hope you will not neglect writing to me on this God forsaken island

Give my love to Wm + Sarah Ann and all the neighbors My best respects My love and a happy new years to you all

From Your Loving Son + Brother Alfred

Letter from A. Lyth to his Father

{printed stationary}
HEAD QUARTERS
Co. H., 100 Reg't NYS Vol. Infantry,
Camp Morris Island S.C. Jan 6, 1864.

Dear Father

I received your ever welcome letter dated Dec 27th and I was glad to hear Sarah Ann was very well again and I hope she will continue in good health. I was glad to hear that you were all in good health as it leaves me at present. This letter is fetched by the orderly Sergt of our company. There is very little news here at present. occationally a little shelling from both sides which dont amount to much. yesterday there was a boat load of deserters came in here from the rebels but we have not learnt any of their statements as yet. General Gillmore is not at this post at present he is at Hilton Head fitting out an expidition but it is not known where it is going but it is expected they are going on to the main land and come in the rear of Charleston but that is one of the rumors but the most likly one a going

My love to
You All
A. Lyth

Letter from A. Lyth to his Father and Mother

Morris Island S.C.
January 9th 1864

Dear Father and Mother

I received your welcome letter of Dec 27 and I was very glad to hear that Sarah Ann was better again also that you were all enjoying good health as it leaves me at present There is very little news of any importance here at present except that day before yesterday a boats crew of men came in to our lines from Charleston harbor they belonged to the rebel navy. All the troops that could be spared have left this island and gone to Hilton Head and St Helenas Island and Gen Gillmore is at Hilton Head fitting out an *expidition it is not known where they are going but it is thought he is going on to the main land and to cut off the railroad communication between Charleston and Savanna and then come up in the rear of Charleston but that is only a rumor. There is a little shelling going on every evening here but it dont amount to much. The orderly Sergt and the fifer of our company are coming home on a furlough the Segt name is Peter Laforte he said if I would write a letter he would call and give it to you so I wrote a few lines. he came out with the Regt as Sergt and since that time he as been jumped four or five times that is others that were lower than him were promoted ahead of him but as he was the only Sergt that escaped the seige of Wagner unhurt he was nesserly promoted to orderly. he is a pretty good fellow in some of his ways and a little mean in others. but the boy in the Co abuse him a great deal and he has to take it for he is afraid to put them in the guard house for them then threaten to whip him We Shall get paid sometime this month and I shall draw four months pay but I shall not be able to send any home as I have $12.85 to pay for clothing and it is said we shall have to pay for our musquito nets which will be 2 or $3 more then I have bought a new over coat for $7 I bought it of a Sergt of our Co who had been to the hospital where he drew the coat which cost him $9½ but when he came back to the company they had the one he left when he went to the hospital so he offered it for sale. and I have run some little debts since I came back that I must pay as it cost me quite a little to get all fixed after I came back from the hospital and pass the holidays. after this next pay I shall try and save as much as I can and send it home I have not received my box yet but I shall get it before this reaches you as it will be here by the next steamer. Remember me to all the neighbors give my love to Sarah Ann and tell her to write to me my love to you all.*

> *From Your Loving Son*
> *Alfred Lyth*

P.S. Our Regt has received to splendid new flags to day from the Boarde of Trade a state and United States flag. They have some of the Battles marked on that the Regt has been through

> *AL*
> *Jan 10ᵗʰ 1864*

I received a letter to day containing the receipt for my Express box. it is at Hilton Head now I shall get it some time in the course of the next week you ought to have directed it to Morris Island you can send my letters directed Morris Island

AL

Jan 11ᵗʰ 1864

I had a good long talk with one of those deserters that came from Charleston and he says every thing is very dear there flour is $150 a barrell an apples + potatoes $75 a good pair of boot $50 and smoking tobacca 4 dollars a pound and every thing in proportion the rebel soldiers only get 11 dollars a month

12ᵗʰ

I was on Guard last night at fort Gregg and we fired a 100 pound shell into Charleston every five minutes

Letter from E. Cook to his Sister

Office A.A.Q. M. Vogdes' Division
Folly Island S.C. Jany 21/64

My dear sister Laura

The mail closes at 4 P.M. this day so I have got just time enough to write you a short letter. The day is most uncomfortably warm I am perspiring very freely indeed. There is scarsely any breeze blowing and the air feels sultry. The sun is shining bright & the sky is clear of clouds. so much for the weather. I am in first rate health. We have had a very healthy year in our regiment + I think the same may be said of all the regiments in the department. We have moved our office from the north end of Folly Island to about the middle of the Island. We are now at General Vogdes Head Quarters & you letters hereafter may be directed as follows Edward L. Cook. Care of Capt. C.E. Walbridge A.A.Q.M. Gen Vogdes Hd Qrs Folly Isld S.C. Capt Walbridge is now division Quartermaster for Vogdes Division. Has my box of shells reached you yet. Tell me as soon as you receive them. I received a letter from Laura containing a letter from Mother + Mary on the 18ᵗʰ This is the 2ⁿᵈ letter I have got this year. I should have answered it sooner but we moved on the 16ᵗʰ & I have been *very busy putting up my quarters & setting things to rights and have had no time to attend to writing. We will get thoroughly settled in a day or two more + then I promise you some long letters. I rec'd 2 more papers with tobacco on the 18th but I have not had time to read a word in them as yet. I am obliged to you for the tobacco I was just out. It is so much better than I can buy of the [ ] & goes a good deal further.*

Gen. Vogdes has gone home on a furlough and all the troops in his command are glad to get rid of him for a time. There was a grand review of all the troops on the island yesterday by Genl. Gordon who is in command. You have never told me if you received the $5[#] I sent home to buy Christmas presents. Another mail came in last night and I expect some letters from you to day. I am in hopes that the next time I write I shall be able to send you a longer letter and write some thing that will be interesting. We are going to sow some oats around our office and the office of the Adjt. Genl. so that by the time Genl. Vogdes comes we will have a nice grass plot all around his head quarters. We have had some very disagreeable weather lately but at present every thing is lovely. Our sawmill is in good working order and is ripping out the lumber at a great rate. The saw mill run through a log 16 feet long in just half a minute. Give my love to Grandmother & all the rest of the folks and believe me ever your most loving brother

Edward L. Cook

Miss Laura Cook   *Put the Loose papers in my writing desk*
Buffalo N.Y.   *or elsewhere + save them.*

Ed.

Letter from A. Lyth to his Folks at Home

Morris Island S.C. Jan 26th 1864

Dear Folks at Home

I received a letter from you day before yesterday and I was very glad to learn that you were all well and enjoying good health as it leaves me at present. I also received two Harpers Weekly and two NY Ledgers. We are having some fine weather here at present and likely to hold out so and we are having very good times in fact I enjoy myself a well as ever I did since I came sogering We have not been paid off yet but expect to be soon and the sooner the better for some of the boys are getting hard up Our first Sergt left here yesterday on a furlough for Buffalo and he took a letter for me that I have had wrote a good while and he says he will call and give it to you and if you have any thing you want to send by him you such as a likeness +c if father has an old vest that he dont want to wear any more if you have a mind to you may send it to me as we do not draw vests in the army Last night I was out to tea and it was proposed at table that every man should get his likeness taken after pay day and those that did not should each buy half a dollars worth of apples so and half a dollar worth of something else but we all calculate to get our likenesses so you see you will get my likeness again. Tom Maharg often makes me go and take dinner with him as he is in the commissary department and he has his pick of the stuff for cooking and a nigger cook to cook and set table and wait on us and when I am not on duty I oft go over to Tom Quaters to spend the evening. I then stay all night with him. January 29ʰ 1864 I have not received my box yet on account of it being marked Hilton Head you should have directed it to Morris Island and I should have had it long before this, now it will have to lay at Hilton Head untill some one goes from the Regt and fetches it or untill I write for it which I think I will do to day. For the last week there has been very little firing into Charleston but last night and to day our batteries fire a good deal at Sumter for day before yesterday a number of men were observed to work on Sumter so the officer of the day told the Capt in fort Gregg where I was to work to get his best marksman he had in the fort and elevate a peice and try his skill at them. he did so and he made his shot tell for there was a great scattering and some men were observed to roll down the outside of the fort into the water and about two or three hours after a body floated a shore right opposite Gregg and it was very badly hurt – the brest being all carried away. Two of the Negro Regiments have left this island and it is supposed they are to joine the expidition that Gen Gillmore is fitting out this morning one of our company tents was taken down to fix over again and in digging out the bottom a little we found some of the bones of a human body but we thought nothing of it for we are used to such sights here the first three weeks I was here most every morning up near fort Wagner the bones of a human would be lying on the beach. I think I will close now with my love to you all Give my respects to [   ] and the rest of the Neighbors My love to Sarah Ann and Wm + family

From Your Son
Alfred Lyth

Letter from E. Cook to his Parents

Folly Island S.C. Jany 28/64

I was much pleased to receive a letter from you about a week or {unknown word} ago. It came just about to time that as moved our office to Gen. Vogdes head quarters and I was so busy that I did not have time to reply to it by the return steamer, so I will answer it now and have it in good time for the next steamer. I wish I could receive a letter from you much oftener than I do, but I suppose your time is fully occupied in daily duties and leaves you little leisure to dip the pen and write the lines. I think that the soldier will know how to value the services of a wife or mother when he returns to his home, for his experience down here is a lesson that will not soon be forgotten. He will know how to value her ceaseless industry and tireless energy. What better lesson can be taught him than the lesson of experience. The soldier has to cook, wash, mend clothes, darn stockings, and in fact perform for himself all those little things which his wife or mother used to do for him & which we would never have learned to appreciate if he had not turned himself into a bold volunteer. Anxious wives and loving mothers bless the day when your sons + husbands joined the army, for when they return to your pleasant homes and cherished society they will value your love and the blessings of home far more than they ever could if they had never been separated from them. An absence of 3 years from every thing we hold most dear is a long time to look forward to, but how precious will be the hour when we are again permitted to join them. I think that the happiest day of my whole life – past + future – will be when I return to my home and find all there whom I have left. But if one should be among the missing whether sister, parent or my dear old grandmother I think the happiness should be destroyed. How many hours I have spent in thinking of my reunion with the loved ones at home? I almost fancy sometimes that I am on the point of meeting them, and my happiness is almost complete but alas the dreams of day do not last and my happiness is soon destroyed.

I am glad Laura has got such a nice warm cloak and I can wish as you do that I was there to go out with her when she wares it. I am glad too that you are so well supplied for the winter. I wish I might be permitted to help you dispose of the Codfish + good sweet butter. We dont know down here what it is to have good sweet butter although we can get plenty that is not *fit to eat by paying 40 cents per pound. I enclose $10# which if you dont want to use you may deposit for me.*

The weather is perfectly lovely just like a warm spring day at the north. I am in first rate health but the heart Burn has troubled me a great deal this week. George Stoddard talks of going back to his company but if I can see him I will try and persuade him to remain where he is. Give my love to all the folks and kiss little Gracie for me. Send her pictures + fathers' to me as soon as you get them. I will write to Laura today or tomorrow. Good Bye from your loving son – Edward

Letter from A. Lyth to his Brother

MD
Parole Camp Annappolis
Jan 30th/64

Dear Brother
I arrived here safe and sound last night we had a few stoppages on the road for we had hardly got six miles out of Buffalo before the train came to a broken rail and we run half the train over it before the train was stopped but they soon fixed and we went on again but soon got stuck in a snow drift and was sometime in getting through it which made us to late to catch the 8 o'clock train at Elmira so we had to take the 4 o'clock train next morning, but on account of the delay we had the good fortune to meet Tom Maharg and some more of the boys bound to Buffalo on furlough We also missed the evening trains at Baltimore so we put up in an hotel to wait the Sunday evening train we spent Sunday in walking around to see what might be seen in the famous city of Baltimore not forgetting to visit the Washington monument in that city we took the ½ past three o'clock train and arived at 5 o'clock and found Tom Russell well nothing was said to me about staying over my time but some of that stayed over say they got their seven dollars and a half ration money stopped. so I suppose I won't get mine but I don't care for I had the worth of it in staying at home

There is some talk of them giving us all another furlough some time soon and it is also reported that we will not be exchanged untill next May Give my best respects to Lewie and his folks and all the neighbors

My love to you all from
Your Affect Brother, Alfred

Letter from E. Cook to his Sister

Office A.A.Q. M. Vogdes Div.
Folly Island S.C. Jany 31/64

My dear Sister Laura

I have just received a letter from you + one from Lila, a paper from Mr. Lyman and 3 papers from home (one of which contained my long expected magnesia. I should think that fruit cake was about spoiled by this time but I presume it is so rich that it will keep a long time and the older it goes the better it gets. I have not yet heard from Maggie Dayo but I presume I shall though by the next mail. And I expect also to hear that you have received my box of shells for I learned yesterday that it left by the Arago on the 14th of this month and you have no doubt received it by this time. I would like to know if you ever received that dust of "Sumter" that I sent home in a letter on the 11th day of November last. Two men from my company went home on a furlough this week and one of them took a little package for me. It contained some very pretty little shells, a small piece of "Fort Sumter" some specimens of my handicraft at whittling with a jackknife and I guess that is all. The boy who took it is our Company fifer. His name is "John Moisinae" If he does not call and see you, you can find him by inquiring of "H Stillman" fur dealers on Main Street. If he says he will bring back a small package to me from you I wish you would fill the little tin can which he has received from me (containing the trinkets) with smoking tobacco and return it to me. It is my tobacco box and I have nothing now in which to keep my smoking tobacco. Dont send me any thing that will inconvenience him to carry for he is small and I do not like to impose on good nature. If you could buy me a good military cap that will fit me I should like it very much. Mr.[ ] in Stillmans used to know my measure but I presume he has forggotten it. I think it is 6¼. My head is very small. I guess though you had better not send many as warm weather will be around again in a little while and then I shall not need it. I used to be very well acquainted with Mr. {unknown name} the lumber dealer of whom you spoke in your last letter.

The "Fulton" & the "Arago" are the two regular mail steamers between this point & New York. They leave alternately every 8 days. When the Arago leaves here, the Fulton leaves New York & vice versa. They remain at each place 4 days & consume 4 days in making the passage from place to place. If the Arago arrives in N.Y. on the 4th she will sail on the 8th + the next steamer will arrive at New York on the 12th and sail on the 16th and the next one will arrive on the 20th & leave on the 24th. This will guide you in sending letters for this coming month. Always be sure and have your letters in the mail at least two days before the steamer sails. I hear that the Arago has been ordered to make a trip to New Orleans but if she goes some other steamer will take her place and it will not alter the dates of leaving New York. Is Eliza as much struck with Young {unknown name} as he is with her. I will answer Eliza's Letter by the next steamer. I am a little afraid that this is too late for the the next mail. Five or six deserters from a rebel gunboat in Charleston harbor came inside our lines a few days ago. They represent the affairs in seceshdom in a most deplorable condition but did not communicate anything of importance. They say our shells make terrible havoc among the buildings in Charleston. General Beauregard has erected long rows of temporary shelters for the poor people just outside of the City. Affairs are just the same here as they were a month ago. The rebs fire but very little. I went down to the 112th Regt. last evening with Sergt. Stevens + they treated us to some first class bread + honey. I am very anxious to receive your next letter for I am in hopes to hear in it that you have received my box of shells. Father's picture look as natural as life. I am very proud of it. I went up to the north End last Monday and while we were up in the river after oysters our batteries on Folly Island opened on Seceshville. the shells went whistling over our heads and we could hear them explode in the vilage almost as distinctly as we could hear the report of the gun that fired them. The weather is lovely. The birds have commenced their spring songs. I am very thankful for that magnesia. Tell me as soon as you receive the little box of trinkets from {unknown name}. I wrote to mother a day or two ago and sent home $10#. Give my love to Grandmother and all of the folks and remember to Annie + Lillie. Tell them that in their little nightly offerings of prayer they must not forget their soldier uncle. Tell Gracie to kiss you for me. I shall expect a letter from Mother by the next mail. I have now got to go to the north End of Folly Island to issue ration to a lot of our men working up there so good bye for the present.

from your loving brother
Edward L. Cook Co H 100th N.Y.V.

Miss Laura Cook
Buffalo
N.Y.

Direct in Care of Capt. Walbridge
A.A.Q.M.
Folly Island SC

Letter from E. Cook to his Sister

Office A.A.Q. M. Vogdes Division
Folly Island S.C. Feby 3rd 1864

My dear Sister
    I will give your letter the preference of four letters which are now lying in my desk waiting to be answered. You write to me so seldom that I think I must encourage you by giving your letter my earliest attention and see if that will not produce a change in your behavior for the better and recall your wandering thoughts to a renewed sense of their duty. The letter from you was rather unexpected for I have not received a letter from you in so long a time that I had about given up all hopes of hearing from you for 2 years or during the war. But I am going to trust in your promise and believe you will be a better little girl in the future and write to me regularly and always send me good long letters. I think you take too much pains with your letters to have them just right and most immaculately proper, and therefore it takes you a long time to write a letter and you get discouraged and make up your mind that writing letters is a great bore and you will occupy your time in some other way more profitable & less troublesome. Now Lila you must write more naturally & not spend so much time in your composition. If you cant think of some big word to fill in a sentence dont let you letter stand waiting until you do think of it, but put in some smaller one, and let it go at that. Remember you are writing to your brother and not to any one who is going to show your letter around among his friends and have a general laugh if a slight mistake is made in the rhetoric, composition, or orthography. A sister's letter is sacred property and is read only by the eyes for whom it is intended.
    Write free, write easy, write naturally, write news, write pleasantries,

write any thing that you think will interest one who has an interest in your interest and I promise you that your letter will be interesting and most heartily welcome to the recipient. I suppose I have misspelled a dozen or less words already in this letter but I am not going to run all around the department to try and borrow a dictionary to prove them. I will leave that for you to do & tell me in your next letter and correct them so I will not make the same mistakes again.

Do you ever see Alice Smith Is she any nearer to being married than she was five years ago? How is Frank -Wilder – eh! How often does he call around? Dont get excited Lila because it is your first beau.

I assure you my dear sister that you do not look forward to my reunion with my relatives in B with more interest and anxiety than I do. I often think that I can date my real <u>existence</u> from the time of my return. I believe the time of my return will be the happiest hours of my life and from that day I shall begin to <u>live</u> for I will know how to appreciate and enjoy the comforts + luxuries which this world contains. How often I have repeated the familiar words "There is no place like home" but now I feel the full force of the six little words as I never understood them before. There <u>is</u> no place like home for the heart is there, the thoughts are there, the affections are there, every thing that makes life loveable is bound up in the associations connected with that little word 'Home'. I shall be there one of these day – I hope. But if I never am permitted that happiness, then pray to the Being above that I may meet you all as an unbroken & undivided family in that world of endlessness, when, meeting once, we shall never again be disconected, but dwell on in heavenly love and pure spiritual enjoyment in the presence of our sainted Savior and all the host of bright robed-ones before the throne of that God whose love is infinite.

He may be a little inclined that way but my opinion is that he might more appropriately be classed with the Egotists. He talks a great deal about himself and thinks a great deal of himself. He is all "Big I; little U."

{unknown words} for George the place which he now occupies for I got it for him myself, but I will give him credit for putting in a good word for me {unknown words} detailed a year ago last January at Carolina City N.C.

Lottie {unknown name} and myself still correspond. The last letter I received from her she complained of your long silence and wondered and thought it strange you did not write. I told her that it was not very strange that you did not write to her for you had not written to me for six months or less and I supposed you had forgotten her and myself and, for ought I knew, all the rest of mankind besides.

A blockade runner went ashore a few nights ago in trying to run into Charleston harbor. She had successfully passed all of our gunboats but owing to the dense fog which prevailed at the time she missed her course and went ashore on Sulivan's Island under cover of "{unknown word}." As soon as our boats discovered her they opened a heavy fire on her and I hear that they have today succeeded in setting her on fire but I am a little inclined to doubt it. It will be seen by this that all our land batteries, our {unknown word}, our Ironsides and a score of wooden vessels all clustered around the entrance of one harbor cannot prevent blockade runners from successfully running in and out of the port.

Thursday, Feby 11ᵗʰ 1864
I paid a visit to my regiment yesterday afternoon. The boys are all well. Dave White inquired about "Grace". The weather for the last two days has been quite cool, and the nights have been correspondingly and most decidedly cold.

We have sowed oats around our Head quarters and they are now springing up and we will soon have a crop of oats, but we don't care for the oats if we can only make our {unknown word} cook nice and green. Remember me to Mr. + Mrs. Lyman, and give my love to Annie & Lily. I recd. a rural New Yorker from Mr. Lyman last week for which he will please accept my thanks. He owes me a letter. I have not yet heard from my box of shells. It left Hilton Head on the 14ᵗʰ of January and I shall be disappointed if

I dont hear, in my next letter from home, that they have recieved it all right. Write to me

soon. Give my love to father, mother, grandma + the children and tell them to write to me as often as possible.

Good Bye
Miss Eliza G. Cook   Your Aff Brother
Buffalo   Edward L. Cook
N.Y.

Letter from E. Cook to his Sister

Office A.A.Q. M. Vogdes Division

Folly Island S.C. Folly Island Feby 6/64
Evening

My dear sister Laura

    I have just this moment received your letter No 74. Unless you count the one that Lila sent to me I am short one letter for I have not received No 73. I have not been so pleased in a long time as I was to hear by this last letter that you had received my box of shells. But now that I have heard I am more anxious than ever to know if you received all I sent. I presume by rights I ought to have taken a list of what was sent as they sometimes open boxes at Hilton Head but you can tell me if mine looked as if it had been open and any of the shells extracted. As near as I can recollect I sent 3 or 4 cigar boxes in the large box and about a dozen conchs then there was a little bottle partly full of small shells and 3 or 4 pen boxes with some scroll shell in them and one or two {unknown fragment} boxes filled with sea urchins (a kind of round shell with a little round hole in the top) Some of them had quills in like a porcupine. Then I sent a string of conchs eggs and some horse shoe crabs tails and I dont recollect what all. Nearly all of the small shells were packed inside of those flat cockel shells and paper tied around them. Did they all go safe without breaking?

    Did the large pearl shell oyster go safely? It was packed inside of a Cigar box at one end of the large box. I think a great deal of it and should be sorry to lose it or have it broken. When I said I would not take fifty dollars for the shells I did not mean to say that they were really worth that but I had the pleasure of gathering them myself and I would not take a great deal for them. The only name I know for that 4 cornered or 4 pointed thing is "Sea Pod." They grow sometimes much larger and the boys use them for tobacco pouches. They also make cigar holders out of those Crabstails. The 5 pointed fish is a starfish. It is not a shell at all. When first taken from the water it is perfectly flexible but when it becomes dry it also becomes hard + stiff & takes the appearance of a shell. There is another shell which I sent home that is called a star fish. It is perfectly flat on the bottom and a little bit rounding on top with the form of a star on top. What do you think of the sea grass? Are not those scroll shells very pretty? Did you count those little bits of shell in the small glass bottle? How much was the freight on the box? Did the box still have a rope around it when it got home? If there any shell that you would like to know the name of, you can make a drawing of it on a piece of paper and send it to me. This will be a very pretty amusement for you and will also give you some experience in drawing from nature. I will give your letter a more careful perusal and more complete answer by the next mail.

I have sent you one letter today and had entirely given up all hope of receiving a letter from you in time to answer it by this steamer. You must excuse this miserable scrawl and poor composition for I assure you I have written it in very much haste so as to have it in time for the mail.

Answer all my questions and more too in your next letter. Tell me all about every thing. What did Grandma + Lila say about the shells? If Mr. A.M. Clapp put any in the paper about them you must send me the piece or tell me what he says. Dont fail to answer me as soon as you get this. I had to laugh and I did hold my breath when I read what you called the most curious thing in the collection, viz the "Packing."

In reading that sentence there were half a dozen different things ran through my mind but when I came to "packing" I burst out laughing. I dont believe you can half read this letter for I dont think I can myself, but you must excuse it for I am all excitement & nervousness. I dont think it would agree with me to receive such news every day. Good by my love to all.

To Miss Laura Cook　　　　　　　　　*Edward L. Cook*
Buffalo N.Y.　　　　　　　　　　　　*Co H 100 N.Y. Vols.*

Letter from A. Lyth to his Father and Mother

Morris Island S.C.
February 11ᵗʰ, 1864

Dear Father + Mother

I take the present oppertunity of writing you these few lines hoping they will find you all enjoying good health as it leaves me at present. We were paid off day before yesterday so that all the Regt are in good spirits I have sent you a picture with this of our camp at Gloucester Point Va if you look to you right hand when you look at the picture and pick out the third tent in the second row you will see the tent that I used to boarde in and I don't know but you may find me out in one of those companys that are drilling I dont know. But I will leave it for you to find me out

There is very little news here at present only that I forgot to mention in my last that the expidition had started south in the direction of Savana. Orders were read of at the dress parade of all the Regt on this island last night sentenceing

3 men of the 97th P.A. who are stationed at Florida for to be shot. I enclose a dollar for Billy and I want him to get his and Fannys likeness taken with it he must get them taken together then when I get the likenesses I will send him some money to spend for his self. Give my love to Sister Sarah Ann to Wm and the children. I must close now with my love to you all so no more at present

From Your

Loving Son

Alfred

Letter from E. Cook to his Parents

Office AAQM

Vogdes Div. Folly Island S.C.

Feby 14/64 Sunday

My dear parents

I rec'd a letter from Laura No 75 and 2 papers with tobacco yesterday. I wrote until Midnight last evening so as to finish my monthly papers for January. My head aches this morning to pay for it. I enclose some envelopes already directed in which you will send my letters until you hear from me again. Gen. Gillmore has gone to Florida on an expedition and the Captain + I are going down there next Tuesday or Wednesday and as we do not know where we will stop you will have to direct my letters the same as the inclosed envelopes until I know where we are going. I send you this little line for fear I may not have time to write to you at length. I have got to work all day but if I can steal time enough before the mail closes I will write again.

Good By

Your Aff Son

Edward L. Cook

Mr. Lyman Cook

Buffalo

N.Y.

Letter from A. Lyth to his Brother

Morris Island S.C.
February 23rd 1864

Dear Brother

I take the present oppertunity of writing you these few lines hoping they will find you enjoying good health and in good spirits. I guess you must be having some gay times now sleigh riding and skateing. You never told me weather you were going to school this winter or not. I think if you are not you should be improving your spare time at home for I assure you cannot learn too much. I have often wished since I have been in the army that I had improved my time better when I went to school but I always think of the old maxim 'its never to late to mend' and I assure you if ever I get out of this I shall do my best to better my education. Since I have been in the service I have made two or three attemps to study but although having so much spare time it is very difficult. But I think that by and by I shall have an oppertunity to do some thing for my self in that respect and I calculate to try and learn phonography as there is one of the boys in our company knows it and he had promised to assist me. Now John if you have an old Practical Arithmatic throwing around the house I wish you would send it to me. Since I last wrote there has been some stiring times on the island one night last week all the troops on the island turned out under arms the 100th NY Vols as usal being the first to get in marching order when the long roll was beat. I was reported that the rebels tried to drive our garrison from Block island and that they open from all their fortifications in our front to call our attention but in the morning all was quite and very little damage done except the flag staff being knocked of the Battery yesterday being Washingtons Birthday there was quite a roar of cannon firing salutes and the Batteries in the front fired shot and shell at the city and at Sumter. Fort Moultre open out and threw a quantity of mortar shells on to the island and in the afternoon there was a man buried that was killed with a shot from Sumter. It was suspected that the rebels were fixing a little sand battery inside of Sumter and we realized the truth of those suspicions yesterday but since we have found their position there is no danger to apprehend from that quarter except at such times as our pickets are releiveing one another. To day our Lieutenant got a letter from St. Helenas island from a man named S.M. Barbarow inquiring any particulars of Edward Townsend or if he knew of his where abouts for he said it would be confering on both him and his afflicted family a great favor. Now I had to go to all the boys in our company and find out if any of them knew what became of him that night of the charge and to write the answer to his letter. I found out all I could and it is quite evident that he was killed that night near fort Wagner. He was last seen a few rods from the fort and it is supposed that it is near there where he met his fate but it was so dark at the time that the boys could hardly could recognise one another Dear Brother I have not received my box yet but I wrote up to Hilton Head to a friend to go to the express office and inquire about it he went and he wrote that the company were unloading a schooner of express matter that had been on the way some six weeks and I am pretty sure that it is amongst the lot so I shall get it pretty soon. There is a good many rumor about here as to the preformance of Gen Gillmore and his expidition there is no use me telling you all the storys there is afloat here about his fight he has had for you will get a more reliable reporte in the papers. I must close now. Give my respects to all the neighbors and my acquaintances my love to you all and write soon and let me know how things is going are going on at Cold Springs

Your Affectionate Brother

Alfred Lyth

Letter from A. Lyth to his Folks at Home

Morris Island S.C.

February 28th 1864

Dear Folks at Home

I received my box day before yesterday and I was glad to see that the names of you all were marked on some little article It has been so long in coming that of course the two pies were completely spoild and the two cakes were a little mouldy on the outside but all right in but the best of all is those usefull articles that Mary and the handkerchief that Mother sent. The cake Mrs. Yates sent was very nice. The salve that Mr. palmer sent I have not had any occation to use any of it yet and I hope I shall not but I suppose it is very usefull in some cases I am very thankfull to the neighbors for thinking of me

There is very little news here at present but I tell you our Regt came near *going on an expidition to Florida to reinforce Gillmores forces there Gen Terry who is in command here sent in for the Medical report of the Regt the condition of the men and how soon it would take us to get ready to go but as luck would have it another Regt was not needed or we assuredly would have been the one Feb 29th Since I wrote the above the 3rd New Hampshire Regt has left this island and gone home on a furlough for having enlisted over and the few of them that did not enlist were to be sent to florida. The duty now is very heavy on the men left on this island the men are on duty 24 hours out of every 36 and sometimes more and there is no likely hood of it being any liter for a month or six weeks to come when Gen Gillmore has promised to relieve us It is thought the rebs if they should attack this island now they could drive us off from it. but of course they could not hold it. we were mustered in for two months pay to day and we probally will get paid about the latter end of March. There is a good deal of talk of the Regt coming home in the spring. but I should prefer staying in the field if I have to stop my time out. of course we should enjoy coming home and seeing our friends and relatives. and getting amongst civilization again but soldering is too lazy a life for me if we were at home and. I should not like it I must close now with my love to you all*

Your Affectionate
Son + Brother
Alfred Lyth

Letter from E. Cook to his Father

Office A.A.Q.M. Seymours Div.
Jacksonville Fla. Feby. 29th 1864

Dear Father

I received a letter from you last Wednesday enclosed in one of Laura's letters. I think this is the first letter, ~~I think~~, which you have written to me since leaving home and to pay you for the honor you have conferred upon me by addressing a letter to your unworthy son I shall give that letter the preference of 4 or 5 others which are now lying on my desk awaiting my august pleasure to be answered. I am very glad indeed to hear that you were all in such good health at the time you wrote and I can assure you that your wish that it might find me enjoying the same blessing was not in vain for I am in good health and have been, ever since I entered the service of "Unckle Psalm", with the exception of one or two little pull backs which lasted only for a few days. Your letter was handed to me just as I stepped from the gangway of the "Maple Leaf" onto the wharf at Jacksonville, it having preceeded me in its arrival at this place. You do not wish for my return to your fireside any more earnestly than I desire to be with you again. I long for the time when I can once more be with you all – at home to stay. I want to see you all and see the old city of Buffalo but still I do not want to go home until my time is expired and I can go home to stay.

My time is just half gone. If it has passed as quickly with you as it has with me, then it does not seem very long; and I hope the last half may roll round just as quickly + as pleasantly as the first. I am in hopes that I may not have to remain during my full term of enlistment. It is very probable that the war will find its close during the present year, but if it does not, then I am willing to stay until my time is out and in the interval render to my country any service which it may be in my power to offer in the line of duty, be its nature what it may. I have now been in the Q.M. Dept. upwards of a year. I know that I have been of service to this Gov't. in this department and I like the duty very much better than being in my company (although by my absence from the company I lose all chance of advancement in the line of promotion) yet whenever my commander sees fit to recall me I shall return willingly & cheerfully to any duty which may present itself for my kind regard. I think I can almost see the picture of the "Peep into the Sitting room" which you described in your letter. I can imagine dear old grandma sitting in the arm chair reading her bible {unknown word} sitting quietly looking at the fire and twirling her thumbs thinking of Edward, George, David, Harriet, Eb, Eliza, Grace all in rapid succession and wondering what each and all of them are doing and thinking how she should like to see them all. Alas! some she will never see again and some will never again see her.

Then next comes yourself sitting at the table & for the first time in a year writing a letter. This is the most difficult part of the picture for my weak imagination to paint. I can see you sitting at the table with your specktacles under your nose and your eyes peeking over them onto the newspaper in your hand intensely engrossed in the perusal of the presidents message or the telegraph column; or I can see you lying down on the lounge, *or nodding over the sleepy proceedings of the City Common Council but I cant see you writing a letter. Then there is mother, away off in the dark of course, straining her eyes to make out some outlandish and unintelligible word that has puzzled her brain ever since she received the letter. Laura is writing to me. I wonder if she knows how I appreciate her sisterly kindness. She has been very good to me and very faithful in keeping her promise of writing to me often and she will be rewarded some time or other for her kindness and be glad to think that she has contributed so much towards making the life of her brother pleasant & happy, by keeping up a communication between him and his cherished home. Then there is little roguish Gracie and Annie + Lilie just come in + by & by the august parents – Steve & Mary – come poking along and then the room is full and the picture is finished but not complete. I am not there but I hope to be one of these days and then wont there be oh grand old jollification and happy hearts for a little while, I dont care how soon this war is ended and we are dismissed and paid off and allowed to return to our homes.*

Tell Lily that she owes me a letter and I want her to write it and send it to me {unknown word}. Have her tell me about her music lessons & her scholars. If she has not time to write a long letter then tell her to write a short one and like Mary's a sweet one. I think she is a little bit vexed with me but I dont care. If she is going to play that kind of a side game then I will get vexed too and I will write to her in spite of herself and bore her with letters until she will be glad to write me for the sake of getting rid of my letters.

Our troops captured a small quantity of salt, turpentine, rosin & cotton at Camp "Finnegan", about 8 miles from this city, & also 7 cannon where we first took the place but on 20ᵗʰ {unknown word} in the fight at "Alustee" we lost 5 cannon so are not much a head in that line.

Give my love to all of the folks and write to me again as soon as you can for your letters are very welcome and cheering when I feel at all sad or despondent.

To Lyman Cook *Good Bye from your aff Son*
Buffalo *Edward*
N.Y.

Letter from A. Lyth to his Father and Mother

Morris Island S.C.

Feby 29ᵗʰ 1864

Dear Father + Mother

    I received two letters from you to day dated Feby 15ᵗʰ and 21ˢᵗ and I was very Glad to hear that you were all well and enjoying good health as thank God it leaves me at present I have Just finished a letter and posted it when the mail came so I wont have much to say in this. I received my box. I think the reason you did not hear from me in so long a time is because the mail was held back Enclosed find five dollars. and you must draw all that is in the bank and use it and I will send you five dollars in my next. and I will contrive to send you all I can but it takes me a little more than it used to live now for of us have a mess together and of course we have to expend a little in extras. You ask me if I get any more pay for being company clerk, but I assure you I consider myself a lucky dog. I had sooner be where I am than a sergt in the company for I have much better times
Your Affect Son

Alfred Lyth

Letter from E. Cook to his Sister

Office A.A.Q.M. Seymours Division
Jacksonville Fla. March 1/64

My Dear Sister Laura

    I own that I have been very negligent lately in writing to you, and yet I must say that my comparatively long silence has not been owing entirely to negligence. If I had known precisely where we were going when we left old Folly Island I should have written to you before and had you direct your reply to this place. Hereafter you may direct your letter to me in care of Capt. A. J. Dunton A.Q.M., Jacksonville Florida, and then I will be sure to get them. I have 3 letters from you, now lying on my desk unanswered, so I have just been reading them through again + I think the first thing I do will be to reply to them and then I will write about the news.

    The 100ᵗʰ Regt is not going home. A number of the men have reenlisted and are therefore entitled to a 30 days furlough. This may have been the cause of starting a report that the regiment was going home. I keep an a/c of all the letters I receive from you and all other parties + also an account of all letters that I write. I am not acquainted with my {unknown word}

300

.

named Charles Prentice; perhaps he is writing over a false signature and if you reply to his letter you had better be very guarded in your expressions. You can use your own judgement about writing to him but I would advise you not to do it. No I wont either – do just as you choose.

I have received an answer to the letter I wrote to Maggie Deyo; but she would not have replied if I had not received a kind of distant introduction and informal passport to her acquaintance through her cousin + my friend Charlie Deyo. I received your letter containing a statement of my bank account. If the amount of interest mentioned your last letter, viz $9 ^{85}, was the computation for the whole year, I think there must be some mistake or else my money is not drawing as much interest as I supposed it was. I am sorry father was so sick I wonder how he would like to come down here and work at joiner work for the Quartermaster Department at $3^{00} per day. I think the climate might agree with him and restore him to his former strength. There is no very heavy work and he would not be always hurting his back. I had not heard, until I received your last letter, that Uncle Ebenezer had enlisted. I am very much obliged to you for your opinion of my opinion, and your estimate of my estimation. I think when I said I did'nt take Ma's sugar, I didn't take Ma's sugar. As for the speedy close of the war I can only say that I think the war is not ended to day & will not end tomorrow or the next day. A civil war is always long lived and far more bloody and revengeful than a war between separate nations.

The magnesia you sent me was just the thing I needed. It has almost entirely cured my heartburn. That Piece of poetry "Brother Come Home" is beautiful. I commenced to gather a box of shells for Mr. Lyman but being ordered away from Folly Island S.C. has knocked that project in the head. There are no shells around here except Iron ones (by the bye we expect to hear plenty of those tonight or tomorrow) but if we can get down to the sea shore I can gather some splendid specimens. I am glad those pearl shell oysters went safely. They are the ones shaped like your drawing in your last letter. They grow on rocks & stand up on their small end. From their upper edge there grows a kind of beard or hair. In the Mediterranean Sea this hair attains such length + fineness that the natives use it for weaving stockings & which very much resemble silk.

I dont know what you mean by a petrified wasps nest among my collection – explain! I wish I could have attended the masquerade at Mary's house. How I should have enjoyed myself in the costume of one old long coated & short breeched Yankee. My paper is nearly out so I will leave off until tomorrow morning. Our Cavalry has a fight this morning with the van of the enemy's forces. They are marching upon us 20000 strong. Our cavalry retreated to within 2 miles of the city. We will probably have a severe fight tomorrow. I will try and get up time enough to finish this tomorrow morning.

Morning - It rained last night & is raining still so the fight will most likely be delayed until the rain ceases. All our men are under arms. I hear that Seymour will not wait for the enemy to attack us but will go out to meet them. I do not expect to be in the fight but if our men are driven {unknown word} the entrenchments, which are only 5 minutes walk from my office, it will be necessary I presume for every man to turn out & defend the city. We must hold it's place at all hazards and I am willing to give what little aid I can, or my life if it is necessary for our cause. I hope for your sakes that it may not be necessary for me participate in the fight, but if it is I cannot in honor or in duty hold back a single step. I speak thus at length in order that you may not think that I am possessed with a spirit of bravado or false courage, whatever I do, I shall do it under a powerful conviction of my imperative duty and in accordance with my idea of man's most sacred attribute – honor. Give my love to Grandma Father + Mother and to all the rest of them. Tell them that my time is now on the down hillside and each passing month will bring me nearer to my home. Good bye – write soon and believe me ever your aff. Brother

Miss Laura E. Cook	Edward L. Cook
Buffalo	P.S. I wrote to Mr. Lyman & to Father yesterday
N.Y.	Co H, 100th N.Y.V.

Letter from A. Lyth to his Father and Mother

Morris Island S.C.
March 7ᵗʰ 1864

Dear Father + Mother
    We recieved a mail here yesterday and there was a couple of Harpers + Ledgers for me but not letter now I want you to write to me so that I can receive a letter every mail any way if not more. Pete LaFort arrived here all safe and fetched me the vest you sent so to day I went and had my ambrotype taken in it the likeness is a good one except the collar I had on did not set on my shirt as it should have done and in my eye it has spoiled the looks of the picture. There is very little news here at present. the rebs fire at us once in a while from their batteries but do us no harm and our men keep throwing shells into Charleston To day there was some 18 or 20 recruits came to the Regt + one Joined our company I must close hoping that these few lines will find you all enjoying good health as it leaves me at present Give my love to Sarah Ann and Wᵐ and all the family My best respects to all the neighbors

From Your Loving
Son
Alfred Lyth

Letter from A. Lyth to his Brother

Morris Island S.C.
March 13ᵗʰ 1864

Dear Brother John
    I take the present oppertunity of writing you these few lines as I have nothing else to occupy my time. On the 9ᵗʰ there was an order came from 1,000 men from this island and all that could be spared on Folly Island for to get ready with three days rations for to go on an expidition. We only recieved light marching orders. which means to take no knapsacks or tents only our rations overcoat + rubber blankets. I was ordered to stay in camp and take charge of the company property and the few men that was left of the company. The boys started away after dusk they went from here

in small boats to Folly Island then from there they embarked on board of steam transports. over half of our Regt was on the expidition when they got aboard of the boats only 2 or 3 hundred were allowed to go on each steamer and they were all of them ordered to remain on the decks so that the rebels might think there was an awful big expidition coming against them the fleet started early in the morning and entered Balls Bay which is a few miles from here adjoining Sullivans island They made a big show and commenced landing a few of the troops. The motive of the expidition being to make the rebs think that there was a great force coming in that road to take Charleston so that they would call some of the troops back from Florida so as to give Gen Gillmore a chance down there. When our boys were ashore they found that the rebel pickets had put for the main land. well our boys staid there all night and were ordered to build fires all over so that the rebs might think there was lot of campfires which they did they staid there two nights without molestation. then they came back again after having a first rate time of it. Night before last there was eight men came on to this island from Charleston as deserters one was a soldier the rest citizens in the Government employ. They said the reason they came away was because Jeff Davis was going to draft all no matter weather they were in the Government employ or not They said they were willing to work for the Government but they were bound not to soldier for them. They were all well dressed & when they came they fetched five old fashioned muskets with them for they said if they were chased they were going to sell their lives dearly for the had double charges in them They say that lately there has been two or three steamers with cotton aboard run out of Charleston unobserved by our fleet

March 15th 1864

Dear Brother I calculated to have sent this letter before this time but I put it away in my port folia and completely forgot it. So I will add a few more lines and close. I guess you have heard through the newspapers of Gen Gordon who has been in this department all last summer and this winter and had his head Quarters on Folly Island has been put under arrest. and he is being Court Martialed at present for communicating with & giving information to the rebels. and it is said that it is his fault that Gillmore has been defeated in Florida. If the charges brought against him are proved and he found "guilty" he should be strung up by the neck or fetched on this island and set up for a target for the soldiers to shoot at. To day there was a *man shot himself in Fort Shaw he took a musket and placed the muzzel in his mouth and pulled the trigger the reason he had got some bad news from home about family affairs he was a conscript and belonged to the 52ᵈ P.V. Dear Brother I will close now with my love to you all. Give my love to Wᵐ & Sarah Ann and the rest of the family*

> *From Your Affect*
> *Brother*
> *Alfred Lyth*

Letter from E. Cook to his Sister

> *Camp Co H 100ᵗʰ N.Y. Vols.*
> *Morris Island S.C.*
> *Tuesday March 15/64*

My dear Sister

    As you will perceive by the heading of this letter I am again with my company. I presume you will fell a little disappointed when you learn that I have rejoined my regiment; but it is from no wish of mine that I am here. I was ordered to return and orders are imperative. I look upon any unavoidable occurance as a decree of an overruling Providence and feeling this I must say that I am as contented & happy in one place as in another; and it is my wish that you will not murmur or feel sad at any change that may take place in my situation or affairs for you must remember as you have often told me that God is present every where, and always takes care of his children wherever they are. My only hope is that I am one of his children and I desire your {unknown word} prayers that I may be such and that I may have faith in his promises for then I need have no fear & you need have no fear for me, for what ever may befall me I shall be sure of a mansion in heaven. I have been promoted to Sergeant this day, so you see they are determined to keep me here now that I have returned. I did not desire the promotion and I did not think I deserved it & in fact requested my commanding officer not to {unknown word} but I guess he was afraid that if he did not that I would be detailed again very soon. It is rather a difficult matter for any Quartermaster to get a sergeant detailed and I think that is one reason why I was promoted.

I think I told you in my last letter we had sent up an expedition to St. John's about 60 miles from Jacksonville to capture some stores supposed to be there. They landed there without any opposition but found no stores. They took 1 prisoner. Up to the time of my leaving the city they had not returned. I expected to have left Jacksonville last Friday morning but the boat left before her appointed time & I did not get up early enough to go on it, but I was glad afterwards that I did no go for the boat carried a lot of veterans and most likely was very crowded. It was rather an unlucky Friday for me, for I took a horseback ride in the afternoon and lost my {unknown word} pipe. I believe I never knew who gave me that pipe and therefore never had the pleasure of thanking them for it but if any body should make a present, through the mail, of another one of the same kind & quality carefully packed & prepaid they would have the pleasure of receiving my most heartfelt thanks through a letter of acceptance, and if I ever return they shall receive my thanks in person. If anybody with funds to spare thinks such a recompense sufficient for the outlay, let them improve this opportunity.

I left Jacksonville at 8 oclock on the morning of Saturday March 10/64. We arrived at Mayport & crossed the bar between 10 + 11 oclock A.m. Gen. Foster + Capt. Dunton went down on the same boat (Maple Leaf) with me. We arrived off Hilton Head about 12 oclock Saturday night and in attempting to cross the bar we missed the channel and struck on the bar; we pounded there for about half an hour before we could get her off the bottom. At daylight there were breakers all around us & if it had blown any thing of a wind we would have gone to pieces. We crossed the bar & went up to the wharf about 8 oclock Sunday morning. I walked up to the quarters of Gen. Gillmore's boat crew, with whom I am well acquainted, & had a nice piece of bread pudding for dinner. I left Hilton Head on the Mary Beuton about 2 oclock Sunday night. We had a schooner in tow so we did not make very fast time. We arrived at the Inlet about 1 o'clock Monday afternoon. We stopped at the dock for a few moments and I had an opportunity to see George Stoddard. Then we steamed up Folly River & disembarked at Pawnee Landing. From there I got a ride in an ambulance to the north end of Folly. I visited our old boat crews for a short time & took a parting supper with them and then I crossed the Creek and rejoined my regiment at about 6 o'clock on Monday afternoon. I think Geo. S. has given up all idea of returning to the regiment and I can assume that he *will not come back if I can say any thing to prevent him. I reported to my commanding officer for duty early Tuesday morning and within an hour thereafter I was promoted to sergeant.*

Wednesday March 16/64

There was a general infraction this afternoon but as I had no gun I did not have to go on. I was busy all the morning helping my tent mates to fix up their traps preparatory to inspection.

A mail arrived at the company this evening but of course I got nothing by it. My letters having all gone to Jacksonville but they will be returned to me in two or 3 days & then I will write again.

I received the package you sent to me. I am very much obliged to you for it but I am sorry to say that I have nothing but a common clay pipe in which to smoke the tobacco. That square package is the very best kind of tobacco but I am afraid it is too costly & you need not send me any more of it. If costs 10/_ ($1²⁵) a package out here. The little tin can looked like an old friend. I have often wished for it since I sent it home and now that I have got it again I intend to keep it. Tell Lili I will write to her tomorrow. It is awful cold this evening and I know I shall sleep very little tonight. I was in agony the first night I slept in camp on account of the fleas which are innumerable. Give my love to all. I have rec'd your letter No 79. Good by ~from your aff. brother Edward L. Cook

Miss Laura M. Cook	*(Direct) Co. H 100ᵗʰ N.Y. Vols.*
Buffalo	*Morris Island*
Box 1463 NY	*SC*

Letter from A. Lyth to his Father and Mother

Morris Island S.C.
March 18ᵗʰ 1864

Dear Father + Mother

The mail arrived here yesterday and there was nothing for me but a couple of Harpers Weekly's. I was very much disappointed for I had expected a letter from home. However I write you these few lines and send you one of my photographs with it I send two or three of the company and

I want you to keep them for me. In a week or two I shall get some more of the boy's pictures and I shall send them also. and wish you to save them for me. when I come home which I hope will not be long though I dont expect it for the next 12 months. I shall send Sarah Ann one of my photographs and one to cosin Wm Eyeington. There is no new here worth mentioning so I will close with my love to you all

From Your Affect Son Alfred Lyth

Letter from E. Cook to his Sister

To Miss Eliza G. Cook
Box 1463 Buffalo
N.Y.
Morris Island S.C.
March 20/64

My dear Sister Eliza

If I do not commence a letter to you this evening I am afraid you will think that I have forgotten you. I shall write you a very short letter for I am tired & sleepy and my neck aches. I was on picket last night with gunshot of Sumter and what with the cold & the myriads of fleas I had a wright time of it. After we came in this morning we had to clean ourselves up & go out on Dress parade. This afternoon I took a short & restless nap and this Sabbath has passed and I have accomplished nothing of any account. There is no news from this district. We are all looking with much anxiety towards the district of Florida for some movement of importance.

When Mr. Seymour writes to me I wish he would give me his idea of who will be candidates in the coming election and also the one of his choice for President. If they allow soldiers to vote I think I shall electioneer a little myself and I will be thankful for any papers he may have an opportunity of sending to me.

The weather here now is generally warm but we have some very cold days and all of the nights are cool & damp.

Mr. {unknown name} the superintendent of the sawmill on Folly is dead. He died yesterday morning of congestive chills after an illness of about 10 days.

While at Jacksonville I was vaccinated but it did not take effect on me.

I have been promoted to sergeant.

The duty is very severe especially on the privates who do not average more than 5 nights in bed during a month. They are on picket or camp guard 5 or 6 nights hard running; and when on picket they have to walk 3 or 4 miles to get to their posts or stations. It is just as bad for the corporals but only ½ as severe for the sergents who are in bed every other night. The drum has just beat for roll call so I will finish this in the morning.

Monday afternoon March 21/64

I enclose herewith a package of papers relating to my detail. I wish you to hand them to Laura and request her to put them someplace where she can find them if I should require them at any time. My pay is now $17^{00} per month with the same allowance of clothing & Rations as heretofore.

Tell Laura I will answer her last letter in a few days or as soon as I get time. I had a friend named Corp. Wm Becker who belongs on Folly Isld. come to see me this A.M. He staid to dinner with me, and as our "company dinner" consisted of only been soup, which is so common in the army, I did not like to ask him to partake of it so I went over to our {unknown word} & bought a pound of sausages, 30 cents, & 5 doughnuts, 25 cents. I fried the sausages & steeped a cup of black tea & made out a very good dinner. I think when I return home I will hire out to father for his barber & to mother for her cook & to the family generally for a housekeeper & Jack of all work. How is Grandma? I have not heard from home since leaving Jacksonville. It will take some time for my letters to get straightened around again. The last letter I rec'd from Laura said Grandma was very sick. I hope my worst fears are not realised. Lili you must excuse this short letter & write to me very soon wont you. I sometimes think you dont think of me very often but this I know you do and I know you will write to me very soon & send me a good long letter.

Your loving brother Ed

Letter from A. Lyth to his Brother

Morris Island So Carolina
March 24 1864

Dear Brother John

 It is a long time since I received a letter from home so I have made up my mind to write and give you a good blowing up, so here goes. but I guess I had better wait untill I get a letter and see what you have got to say for yourselves. We expect to get a mail tomorrow or next day and then if I don't get a letter from some of you you'll have to look out. The weather here for the past two day past has been very windy and stormy and rained in torrents. yesterday it did not rain but the wind blew a perfect hurricane and quite a number of the tent in the Regt were blown down and the sand drifted same as the snow does in old Buffalo on a windy day. if a poor cuss put his head out side of the tent he was sure to get his neck ears eye + hair filled with sand In the tent that I stop we have got quite a nice little stove which an officer of the 3rd New Hampshire found missing one day when we set it outside for to get his chimney fixed and all I could do yesterday was to go out and steal a few wash tubs boxes or anything in the shape of wood to keep a fire going and keep ourselves comfortable but to day it is a very pleasent in fact – the sun shines pretty hot Day before yesterday one of the men belonging to our Co fell overboard out of one of the picket boats as they were coming in from the harbor he lost his gun which he had in his hand at the time. They soon hauled him back into the boat again. but he had to leave his shooting iron behind. I guess there is a great deal of talk up north now about who will be nominated to run for the presidency this coming fall I think if they nominate Gen Grant and let the soldiers vote he will get elected if not and "old Abe" is nominated again he will get it. The copperhead party is I believe completely played out now it is in the army one man in our Regt that used to side with the copperheads said the other day that he was a Lincoln man to the back bone for he said in the charge upon fort Wagner the rebs fired as much at him as any the rest of the men and would have killed him if they could so he would not be copperhead any more There is very little news here at present and a great many rumors the rebels have fired a great deal to day from the Bull of the wood but done us no harm. The gun that we have used to fire into the city of Charleston all

through this seige burst last week having fired over four Thousend charges
out of her. they say that it is the largest number of charges fired out of any
one gun on record it was a 100 Pound Parrot.

March 25ᵗʰ 1864

Yesterday the mail arrived and I received a letter from Father dated
March 10ᵗʰ/64 and I was very glad to hear that you were all enjoying good
health as it leaves me at present. I was glad to hear that the letter with
the $5 and the check came safe for to tell the truth I do not like the idea
of sending money by mail. We expect to be paid off again in a couple of
weeks. but I shall not send any money home for I want to let the pay after
run and not draw it so that I may draw four months pay all at once and I
think I will save more by it

There is a great deal of talk now about the old men being discharged in
June but I cannot tell how true the report is. but I hope it is so for it is a long
time since they have seen any civilization and to be three years in the field
is too much for any man. I believe that the Boarde of Trade men would
have been discharge with the old men if Col Dandy had not been against
it. but as I have got used to soldiering I dont mind it much. I should like
if you hear any thing conserning the Regt in old Buff. I wish you would
let me know The conscripts in our Regt expect when they have served nine
months they will be discharged but in my opinion they will be very much
disappointed for I think they will have to serve "three years orduring the
war". The conscripts in our Regt as a general thing are pretty good soldiers.
But the conscripts in the 52ⁿᵈ and the 104ᵗʰ Pennsylvania Regts are a lot of
green horn as soldiers in one Regt they were with the Regt 4 or 5 months.
before they would trust them with arms at all and even now they dont trust
them on out post duty. I will give you a little instance which happened a
few days ago. One of our corporals got a conscript of the 52ᵈ on his post.
when he posted him the sentinel he gave him the countersign or watch
word. then he went away. but in the course of half an hour returned to see
that all was right he goes up to the conscript who was the sentinel on post
and asked him if he had the countersign. he answered no did you give it to
me. yes answered the corpl. Well I must have lost it answered the sentinel
upon which he commenced to feel in his pockets and look around on the
ground as if looking for the countersign. The corpl could hardly keep from
laughing out right but at that moment he observed an officer coming along

the picket line so he told the sentinel to halt him as he came up. when the officer got near enough Mr Sentinel call out 'Who comes there". The officer answered "friend with the countersign". Fetch it here says the sentinel I Just lost it a short time ago. Then the Corporal steped forward and told the officer to "advance and Give the countersign" which he did. then he asked what kind of a man that was on post the Corpl told him a conspt of the 52^d the officer gave orders for him to put another man on the post.

Dear Brother I will close this letter now, as I have Just got some writing to do for the company. Give my love to Sarah Ann + W^m and accept the same yourselves.

Your Affect
Brother
Alfred
Co H 100th N.Y. Vols Morris Island, S.C.

Letter from A. Lyth to his Brother

Morris Island S.C.
April, 1864

Dear Brother John

I received your kind and welcome letter of the 23 of March and I was very glad to hear that you were all well and that you were enjoying the winter season by having a jolly sleigh ride now + then I think if you could find 2 or 3 frenchmen every day that wanted to enlist you would be doing well but I advise you never to show an old soldier a recruiting office or you may get what's not quite agreable I hear that the veterans of the 100th are disgracing the Regt by their goings on in Buffalo. But it is just as a great many of us expected for those mostly that have reenlisted are the roughest caracters in the Regt all that our Co has I am glad to say is one amongst the lot that have come home For the last month past there has been a great many robberies commited in the camp and around Head Quarters since four weeks ago some three or four men were caught rolling off a safe with about $15,000 in it from a building near the Head Quarters. as soon as they were discovered they run and all escaped except a man named John Ross of Co F of our Regt who was to drunk at the time to run he is one of the conscripts he has been in the provost Guard house ever since awaiting *his trial by Court Martial There has been quite a number of watches stole and amongst the rest our Chaplins gold watch was stolen some one cut his tent and reached in and took it off the nail it was hanging on week before last a couple of men went into Col Dandys tent and took out a box of money belonging to the sutler to the amount of $1300 but they found the box buried in a tent over at the Provost Guards quarters so the occupants were put under arrest and the money recovered There is very little war news here though for the last week back there has been considerable firing from both sides*

The statement about Geo Barnum being reduced is false and I don't see how such a thing could have come to Buffalo for George is liked by most every body in the Regt and as for James Pixley he would never write such as thing home if it was not so for Jim is a pretty good fellow and one of my chums as we say in the army

I must close with my love to you all

From Your Affect
Brother
Alfred Lyth

Enclosed you will find another of the boys of my Co picture put it with the others I sent in my next I shall send two or three more

No 13
P.S. I enclose $10# for Mother

Letter from A. Lyth to his Sister

Morris Island April 9th 1864

My dear Sister   *Saturday Evening*
You must not expect a very fancy looking letter from me this time and I am in a hurry for fear that if I do not get this letter in the mail tomorrow morning it will not go north until the next Steamer. So if you feel inclined to find any fault with the appearance of this sheet just remember that it is with the intention of affording you a little pleasure that I forego the desire of writing neatly, and in place of neatness will present you with haste & dispatch. Before answering any of your many letters which are now lying

313

*before me let me proceed in my old style of Journalizing, commencing where
I left off in my last letter to you*

Monday April 4ᵗʰ 1864 Weather quite damp & terribly rainy. The wind
blow'd very hard from the rear and as it is just about the time for our high
spring tides it played the deuce in our part of the town. The sand bank – a
kind of natural sea wall at our end of the Island is only about 3 or 4 feet
above high water mark and when you cross over that you find your self
in a kind of hollow basin. This basin is always dry in ordinary times &
tides, but if the tide is a little higher than usual & the wind blows rather
briskly from the sea it will carry the water right over this bank in one long
continued sheet, and fill up the basin to a level with the sea. The basin
is somewhat concave and when filled with water is in many places over a
man's head. Thus it was this afternoon; the water came pouring in upon
us in a perfect cataract. The occupants of about 50 tents were driven out of
their quarters. The water entirely surrounded the little hill on which one
officer stands and we were left on an Island with the water a foot & a half
deep all around us. The water about reached the level of our 3ʳᵈ step & the
waves came splashing their foam right into the doorway. I tell you it was
a grand sight to see the long sheet of water come pouring over the seawall,
and to watch the waves as they rose & sank and moved onwards until they
came right up to our doorstep. Yes it was fun for us who knew that the
tide would not rise high enough to drown us out, but it was not quite so
pleasant for those poor fellows who were forced to leave their quarters and
stand out in the rain until the tide went down. The only inconvenience
I experienced was being obliged to pull off my stockings & take off my
shoes and wade through the water to the supper table. Our stables were
completely inundated and the poor horses & mules about 200 in number
were compelled to stand up to their haunches in the cold water for about
two hours. Some of the tents that were drowned out were built on frames
& had board floors laid in them. These were lifted from their foundations
by the force of the waves, and sent floating off in all directions at the mercy
of the water & the winds. It was laughable to see them floating around
here & there with 2 or 3 fellows holding on to them for dear life almost, to
keep them from being washed out to sea. A party of drunken sailors who
were ashore this afternoon on a kind of spree were surprised by the tide
which cut them off from their boat and there was no way for them reach it

except by wading up to their middles which they did after much hesitation. How we laughed to see the drunken fellow go pitching & rolling through the water. Now I have given you the pleasing side of the picture, but there are some sad and grave features connected with it. Do not think that the inundation was allowed to subside without producing some very disastrous results. It becomes my painful duty to chronicle the death of more than one poor creature. Alas what will be the feelings of their fond friends & relatives in Buffalo when they hear of it. It was high tide about 7 oclock P.M. When the water began its backward march, the waves sighing the requiem over the departed, the night was {unknown word} dark and at 7 o'clock the next morning the tide was high again so that it was not until about noon the next day that the bodies were discovered. Passers by looked on with horror yet no one touched them and, with shame be it spoken to those whose duty it is to attend to such matters they were allowed to remain untouched during the afternoon when a little boy with his dog came along and cried out r-r-r-r-ats! r-r-r-r-a-t-s! r-r-r-r-a-ts!!! Rats!

Tuesday
~~*Thursday*~~ *April 5/64   Pleasant*

We have had a very pleasant day after the rain & storm of yesterday. Many of the bodies of our poor soldiers who were killed in the charge on fort Wagner were disentombed by the rain & tide yesterday but were reburied today by some of the boys of the 3rd R.I. Artillery. I enquired of one of the party if the rebs buried our dead deep enough he replied that the bodies were buried deep enough but every wind that blows is constantly shifting the sand, making hills of the hollows & hollows of the hills, and a little rain completes the work & reveals the partly decayed bodies of our poor boys. Such is war.

Wednesday April 6/64   Pleasant

Friday April 8/64   Lovely Day I rec'd your letter No 82 and {unknown word} photograph. I did not like it at first but the more I look at it the better I am pleased. I wrote to Eliza today & sent $10.00 for mother. The last letter I send to you also contained $10.00.

315

Saturday April 9/64   Rainy   I was particularly favored by the mail today. It brought me a letter & paper from Mr. Lyman, a letter from Mary, a letter from Mother, a letter from you and a letter from Ella Halsey.

Our Veterans returned today and I had the pleasure of receiving a package containing a pipe, a pound of smoking tobacco & a cake of maple sugar, for all of which I hope you all will accept my very grateful thanks. The pipe was not just what I expected & if I had seen your little note about sending it back without smoking it if I did not like it, I think I should have done so, but fortunately I was so anxious to try it that I had it filled with tobaco and was smoking it before I had proceeded to peruse any the notes or letters; and now I am glad of it for I would not part with it or exchange it for anything. I have been offered another that cost considerably more money than mine did but I would not trade. I am much obliged to all of you for this kind memento of your love and regard and I shall always think of the donors whenever I take it up for a smoke.

There is no necessity for my praising the tobacco, its name "Big Lick" tells the story and speaks the fact. The praises of the maple sugar I must extol in my letter to mother. But you all know I dont like it much. I am glad Gracie is getting so much better & all the rest of you are recovering from your late illness. I am very much pleased with the promotion of General Grant. I had much rather see him Lieutenant General than to see him president. All the army is much pleased with his promotion and confident of his success in the operations he may have in view. I think that matter of interest on my money is all straight. I received your letter No 77 and all of the rest of your letters up to No 85. I am glad you did not give Henry Phillip one of you photogs. I dont think he deserves one. I feel as though he had not treated me as he should have done after our former friendship and daily. It is not the way I should have treated him if our positions had been reversed. I have answered all of the letters that I have received from Aunt Lydia. I have raised whiskers 2 or 3 times since I have been away from home. I dont need any cats & cream. We have got cats, dogs & kittens down here of our own & we buy condensed milk instead of cream. Tell Aunt Grace that I dont think George plays cards for money. He has been away from his regiment and for a long time has not been paid. He has not been able to draw any clothes from the company and has had to buy every thing he wears of the {unknown word} who charge about twice as much as Uncle Sam does. I think George tries to do the best he can under the circumstances, and I do not think he has the best kind of luck. In fact he has been quite unfortunate in having things stolen from him while he was away from his quarter attending to business. I believe George is a good boy and a loving son, but like all the rest of us he sometimes gets down hearted and discouraged and that will make any body cross.

Sunday April 10/64 There I suppose I have wrote & waited until this letter will miss the steamer and be laid over until the next boat, but you must excuse me this time for I got <u>so</u> sleepy last night that I <u>could</u> <u>not</u> write any longer and had to leave my letter unfinished. We have had a very pleasant Sabbath. I went over to the company this AM and had quite a visit with Dave White. I told him what you said about the shirts and he was surprised for he did not expect to get them on such easy terms. As soon mine arrive I will show them to him & then write immediately and let you know what he says. Corneal looks as natural as a pea. I guess he was used pretty well in Buffalo for he has fleshed up considerable since I saw him last. I almost think that if I was sure that I would have to stay my 3 years out that I would reenlist and go home but I have some slight hope of being discharged before that time. Nearly every body in the army seems to think that this war will have been used up by this spring & fall campaign.

I am in hopes that it will, not only for my own sake but for the sake of our country and all who are interested in her best welfare. It seems though too much blood has been spilled and to much money spent & wasted already on this rebellion and I think that our Government is henceforth going to push the war to its speedy close. I think we have fooled and played with the rebs about as much as we can afford and it is now about time to wake snakes and call the lizards up, or else cave in and acknowledge ourselves whipped. There is no reason in the world why our government should not whip Secession and drives it to its vile den & utterly demolish the whole scheme & structure. I think this if the feeling of General Grant and I hope he will continue to feel so until his purpose is accomplished and the war is ended and we are once more allowed to return to our homes and the bosoms of our families. Wont that be a happy time though when this war is ended and we go marching home. Wont our eyes light up with joy and our hearts kindle with gladness as we approach the city & hear the hills ringing & the guns firing and the people shouting because this cruel war is ended and we have reached our home. *Give my love to Grandma and tell her when I get through our hurry of making out our monthly papers I am going to write a letter wholly to her dear self. Tell Mother I will answer her letter by next mail. Good Night Your*

Miss Laura M. Cook	*loving brother*
Box 1463	*Edward L. Cook*
Buffalo, NY H 100 N.Y. Vols.	

Letter from E. Cook to his Brother

Morris Island S.C.
April 9ᵗʰ 1864

Dear Brother

To day it is raining or I should have said "pouring down" I have been writeing all this morning for the Company making our monthly returns and have just got them done so I thought I would write you these few lines to pass away the time. I have a tent all to myself for an office and it is rigged up nice and comfortable for me. I think I never told you how we were troubled with fleas here. they are so thick that on a fine day if we look close at the ground we can see them play tag and having batallion drill. to keep the bloody things away as much as we can we have to put plenty of black pepper on our blankets and on our stockings drawers +c. Yesterday the Regt all had to take up their tents and set them further apart. for it is coming hot weather and we had to move the tent to make it more healthy.

The veterans or at least some of them have just arrived. And a mail has come in on the same boat I got 2 letters from you dated March 25ᵗʰ & 31ˢᵗ I was glad to hear that you were all well and enjoying good health as it leaves me at present. Dear Brother I must close now for since the mail has arrived I have got plenty of work to make out some clothing accounts of men that have been transfered to the Invalide Corps so you must excuse my short letter Enclosed you will find some more of the boys Photographs and the 2ⁿᵈ Lieut of our Co

Your Affect
Brother Alfred Lyth

Chapter Nine

Virginia Campaign
Operations around Drury's Bluff, Bermuda Hundred and Richmond, VA

April, 1864 – July, 1864

"Thank God we have left that desert called Morris Id On the night of the 13th after half our Regt had gone on picket we got orders to get ready immeadately to leave the island. The boys were called back off picket and were up all night packing." A. Lyth letter dated 4/15/1864

"After I was taken prisoner to Petersburg, I wrote you a few lines to let you know that I was well as thank the Lord I am at present." A. Lyth letter from Andersonville, Georgia dated 6/10/1864

"Genl. Grants Hd. Qrs. is at City Point just across the Appomattox. He was on this side to day and I had a very good sight of him. He is very plain and unassuming and attracts no notice. He came from City Point to this place in a little tug while Gen. Butler has for his private use the largest and fastest river steamer in the Department. He wore no sword or other outward trappings except his buttons and plain shoulder straps. His pants were tucked inside a pair of long dusty boots and his whole attire looked dirty and travel stained. His shoulders are very broad, and from his habit of carrying his head slightly inclined forward and looking downward he has the appearance of being a little round shouldered. He walks with a long slow stride and slightly emphasizes his left foot step. I associated with his appearance the idea or similee of a huge ponderous Iron roller (on a very slightly inclined plane) which though hard to start yet once fairly underway by his momentum carries every thing before it and is almost impossible to stop." E. Cook letter dated 6/14/1864

"Mr. Lyth you must not worry yourself to much about him for I am pretty sure that he is only a prisoner + that is not so bad as it might be we have boys come back almost every day that we had taken at the charge of Wagner they have been gone almost a year + they look fresh + good so you see there is a good sight for Alfred to get back all wright." T. Maharg letter 6/19/1864

"In the early spring, the regiment with most of the troops of the department were embarked for Virginia, and rendezvoused on our old camping ground at Gloucester Point. From there, as the Army of the Potomac started to fight its way southward through the Wilderness, we were embarked on transports and hurried up the James river to take Richmond or Petersburg if possible. Failing in these objects the Army of the James was at least to occupy the attention of the enemy to the extent of preventing reinforcements being sent to Lee." Lt Col Charles E. Walbridge address at the first Annual Reunion 7/18/1887

Letter from A. Lyth to his Brother

On Board of the U S Transport Cannonicus
Port Royal, S.C. April 15ᵗʰ, 1864

Dear Brother
 Thank God we have left that desert called Morris Id On the night of the 13ᵗʰ after half our Regt had gone on picket we got orders to get ready immeadately to leave the island. The boys were called back of picket and were up all night packing up The next morning crossed over to Folly Island and marched to the landing. I had come up the night before in charge of the Co baggage on board of a ferry boat In the morning we embarked on board the Cannonicus and came to Hilton Head. This morning the Regt went ashore but I was left on board with three men in charge of the Co property but I left the men to watch the things and then went ashore to see some of my acquaintances and get some breakfast. I went up to the hospital and saw my old doctor. he was very glad to see me so well and in good health. I had a good time ashore, then I came on board again found all right then went up to the Co and got my mail but did not get a letter from home came a board again then the steamer put out from the dock and anchored in the stream so I sat down and wrote these few lines but I guess we shall come north as far as Fortress Monroe on the same steamer that this letter will come on which is the "Arago" We don't know exactly where we are going but it is thought into Virginia again. we shall probly go to Annapolis Maryland to fit out. I will close now and write as soon as I get a chance at the next place we stop. We shall probly not leave here in a day or two. From Your
       Affectionate Brother
        Alfred R Lyth

Address my letters

   Co. H 100ᵗʰ N.Y. Vols

George Barnum's Personal Notes

"*We are very glad at this time to get orders to go North and three regiments were loaded on the steamer Arago which boat was the last large side wheeler on the ocean. The captain was given orders to sail in a certain direction 24 hours when he received instructions from our Colonel. Fortunately the sea was calm and we had a pleasant voyage.*

Soon after starting the Colonel called the captain and the Chief Steward to his office and asked them if there was any liquor aboard. They said they had and the Colonel told them under no circumstances were they to either sell or give it away. The next day a chum of mine who had enlisted with me came to me and asked me to loan him $5.00. I said that I did not have 5 cents and that as we had not been paid for 14 months, there wasn't $5.00 in the regiment. Sometime previous to this he came to me one day just before we were to be engaged in a fight and handed me his gold watch. I declined to take it and he said he thought my chances were better for coming through the fight than his were. I was then acting as Adjutant of the regiment whose duty it was to carry orders from the Colonel to the different Captains during the fight and told him I would be more exposed than any men in the regiment but he insisted and I took the watch.

Then I said, "Well, Tom, what do you want the $5.00 for, I know you don't drink." He at first refused to tell me what he wanted the money for but I persisted and at last he said he could buy a pint of whiskey from the steward for $5.00. Then I said to him that I could get the money. I was attached to the Colonel's staff at this time who by the way could get him the money. You may know the Government did not provide the officer in the Army with rations the same as to the men but they had to buy them when and where they could. I told that Colonel I had a chance to buy a pint of whiskey from the steward for $5.00 and asked him to loan me the money which he did. I gave it to my chum with the understanding that when he got the whiskey I was to have the first drink. Shortly after he returned with the whiskey. I soon found out that it was fully as much water as whiskey and then told Tom he could kiss the flask good-bye as he would never see it again and took the flask to the Colonel. We immediately sent for the steward and accused him of selling liquor to the men. At the same time, he sent word to the boys of the regiment that they who had bought whiskey *from the steward could get their money back from him. The Colonel made the steward refund all the many he had taken in. He was a fine looking German with a full head of hair and a fine beard. It was a pleasant warm sunshiny day and he ordered the barber to come and pout the steward up on the top of the big wheel house where he shaved off half of his hair and half of his beard and set him up there for 24 hours."* [21]

Letter from A. Lyth to his Brother

Gloucester Point Va
April 20th 1864

Dear Brother

 We the 100th Regt arrived here yesterday morning after having a most beautifull passage we left Hilton Head on the 16't. after having had quite a little muss there with the negro soldiers the night before we embarked one of the negro patrol attempted to take one of our boys that was making a little noise well the boys did not like to be hauled up by negros so they rescued him from the guard then a whole company of niggers came with loaded fire arms and the boys commenced throwing broken bottles brick bats and what ever they could pick up and leveled two or three and severely wounded half a dozen. then the niggers took aim and fired at our boys and wounded one then the boys made a rally for their muskets which were in a building but the officers locked the doors and stood with drawn swords beating the boys off. The negros left then and I tell you if they had not there would have been great slaughter for the boys were determined to have their guns and there was two Regts of us besides the rest of the white troops on the island even the Artillery boys who were ordered out with their peices to quell the riot turned on our side and swore they would spike their cannon before they would fire at us. Our Major then went to the provost Marshall and told him if he did not put on white troops to patrol the town he would not be answerable for what the Regt did. the Provo Marshall then put on white patrols and then the boys cheered them and then the boys kept every thing quite and peaceable. well we got on board of the steamer "Arago" on the afternoon of the 16th and put to sea the same evening. On the 17th some of the men got wiskey of the hands on board of the boat and got drunk

and fighting and I guess they will have to suffer for it Well yesterday the
19th we arrived here and I tell you we were glad to get to such a good place
we should have chose this very spot if we had had our choice before we left
Morris Island I wish you would write to me without delay and Address

Alfred Lyth
Co "H" 100th N.Y. Vols
Gloucester Point, Virginia

You can address the first two letters you write as above and by that time if
you do not hear from me you can Address Co H 100th N.Y. Vols

Washington D.C.

We are likely to stay here about 3 or 4 weeks probally more. They are fitting
out an expidition here by all appearances to move on to Richmond but it
will take quite a while to get ready in the meantime I am having good
times as I don't have any duty but the clerking of the Company to do. I
will close now with my love to you all. Give my love to Sarah Ann + W^m
and the youngsters

From Your Affectionate
Brother Alfred

Letter from E. Cook to Parents

Gloucester Point Va. April 23/64
Wednesday

My dear Parents

Here I am at dear old Gloucester again. I would as soon {next 7
lines are illegible} {unknown word} {unknown word} after dark. We
remained at Hilton Head two days & one night. While there some of our
boys got drunk and raised a disturbance so that the authorities ordered
out a company of negro soldiers to disperse our boys & drive them to their
quarters. This only made matters worse & our boys instead of going to their
quarters only defied the negroes until they fired on us & wounded one man
so that he lost his leg.

<u>Wednesday Evening</u>

The affair would not have ended here if the officer in command at Hilton
Head had not immediately ordered the negro companies back to their

quarters and sent in their place a company of white soldiers. I will write you more particularly when we get settled and have more conveniences. At present I am stretched out on the ground and leaning on my elbow. It is not the most comfortable or convenient position for writing and therefore you must excuse the appearance of my letter. We have no idea what we are going to do in this summers campaign but every one seems to agree in the opinion that we are in for some hard fighting. The weather during the passages was lovely; we could not have enjoyed a more pleasant passage in that respect, but on the boat every thing was confusion. I never in my life passed through such an experience as I had on that boat. The hands employed on the boat had a quantity of Whiskey which sold promiscuously at the rate of 6 dollars a quart. Some of the men spent upwards of a hundred dollars in whiskey during the passage. Every body nearly was drunk even the guards and at one time I thought blood would be spilled without a doubt. One man was threatening to shoot another. One was flourishing a sword which he had wrenched from an officer and daring any body to take him alive but no one approached him. On the third day they detected one of the boat hands selling whiskey & they seized him & shaved half his head & put him up on the wheel house where every body could see him. This had the effect to stop the sale of the whiskey & then things gradually got sobered down & when we landed at the Point nearly every one was all right.

I have not yet received my shirts but I suppose I will by the next mail. I got a letter from Lilie while I was at the Head. I will answer it as soon as an opportunity presents itself. You must excuse this short letter. The drum has beat for roll call and I must stop writing & spread my blankets so good night. Write soon + oblige your loving Son
Edward L. Cook

Letter from A. Lyth to his Sister

Gloucester Point Va
April 25ʰ 1864

Dear Sister
I received your kind and welcome letter dated April 3ʳᵈ and I was very sorry to hear that Emma and Willie were sick but I hope they are well by this time I guess you have heard before this of our Regt having left Morris

Island and I tell you the boys of the 100th Regt were mighty glad to leave that desolate island were we have lost so many of our comrades. You will probaly have heard of the fuss our Regt had with the negros at Hilton Head so I will not mention it We left Hilton Head on the evening of the 15th on board of the steamer "Arago" but we did not know where we were going and I tell you the boys were mighty glad on the morning of the 19th when we tumbled out of our bunks and went on deck and found our steamer plowing the waters of the York river bound for Gloucester Point the place where I first joined the glorious 100th Regt and where we passed so many pleasant weeks some 15 months ago. The secesh on this point were very pleased to see the 100th Regt back for they say that there has not been a Regt here since we left that treated them or paid them so well for eatables as the 100th. And I belive them for the other day when 2 or 3 of my chums and myself were at the house of an old widow lady taking her our washing a couple of soldiers of another Regt came along and commenced to tear down her chicken pen for to make themselves bunks of but we made them stop and talked a little to them 'till we made them ashamed of theirselves.

Dear Sister we are in a very pleasant camp now and are having pretty good times but we cannot tell how long we will stay here there are 12 or 14 thousand troops here now and more arriving every day and when the expidition is formed we might expect to move on to Richmond but it is certain we shall not move untill next month and then I guess we shall have a few hardships to pass through but as soldiers we do not mind them if we come out victorious in the end Dear Sister I must close now with my love to you all and the young ladies There are plenty of nice young ladies down here but the color dont suit me for the ink that I am writing with would make a white mark on them.

When you answer this Address
Alfred Lyth
Co "H" 100th N.Y. Vols
via Washington, DC
PS give my best respects to Mrs. Collins

Letter from A. Lyth to his Father

Gloucester Point Va
April 27ᵗʰ 1864

Dear Father

I take the present oppertunity of writing you these few lines not knowing how soon they may reach you for I believe that our mail is stopped at Fortress Monroe and will be retained there untill this army is on the move. It appears certain that we shall move on to Richmond and I sincerely hope we shall be succesfull. As to the direction we shall take it is not known by the troops so of course there are a great many rumors and surmises about it some think we shall go up the penusala again but from appearances I should judge we are going to take the main land through Gloucester County. however I think we shall know for a certainty soon for the preparations are going on here very rapidly. Yesterday seven transports came in loaded with troops and all the Regts on the Point drew shelter tents to carry on the march and they have to turn their large tents to the Quartermaster for storage. Gen'l Terry issued and order on the 25ᵗʰ that all the troops should reduce their stock of Clothing to one Blouse. One good pair of trowsers. two shirts. two pair of drawers. three pair of Socks. two pair of government Shoes one woolen Blanket. One rubber Blanket. and one Over Coat all other clothing is to be packed in a Co box and turned in to the Quartermaster to be sent to Norfolk for storeage

The 100ᵗʰ Regt N Y Vols went on picket yesterday with three days of cooked rations. The picket line is about 4 miles in front of our camps and when a Regt goes on picket they take three days rations with them and remain out that length of time. I was left in camp to make out the Companys Muster of Pay Rolls and the other Co writeing

George Barnum will get his commission as 2ⁿᵈ Lieut this week and he is trying his best to get Tom Maharg in his place as Q.M. sergeant So Tom was telling me this morning but told me not to mention it as he might not get the position James Pixley's father is trying to get his son a commission in another Regt and a great many of the boys in different Companys in the Regt are getting a commission through the help of their friends at home. Now I was thinking if I had some one to put in a word for myself I might do as well as a great many of the boys if I only had any one with influence at home I could get a reccommendations from officers in this Regt I am now in a very easy office now as Co Clerk and our Lieutenant told me the other evening only that he would make me corporal the very next vacancy and I should stand my chance with the rest of the corporals for promotion. But in my place I do not wish for any vacancys for I do not like to see a non commissioned officer reduced to the ranks or killed in battle and it is only through one of those occations that a vacancy occurs Now if you inquire into the matter you might find a friend to put in a good word for me. As to my being competent to fill such an office you need not question for I understand the drills much better than some of the officers in our Regt take the 2nd Lieut of our company for instance some times when he has had the company out at drill and when I was at the head of the company I would have to tell him half of the moves.

Day before yesterday 7 men all (substitutes) deserted across the lines and have gone to the enemy one belonged to our company. We also lost 9 men from the Regt by their enlisting in the navy. One of them also belonged to our company and I made out his discharge and Descriptive List + Final Statement to day

I will close now with my love to you all and my respects to all my acquaintances

Your Affectionate Son
Alfred Lyth

Alfred Lyth Presentation

"On the morning of May 5th, 1864 . . . transport Thomas Leary, containing the 100th Regiment, arrived off Fortress Monroe from Gloucester Point, Va. Those fortunate enough to witness that magnificent spectacle of transports laden with troops – crafts containing military stores, river steamers fitted up as hospitals, the whole flanked by an enormous array of gun boats of every description, small steamers, darting about carrying dispatches, and launches manned by jolly tars, conveying commanding officers to and from the shore; the arrival of transports loading with troops continuously being greeted by cheers long and loud; flags flying, the sparkling and glistening waters under the bright sun of the May morning and, beautiful beyond description, the splendid and magnificent display of lights from the fleet at nights off the mouth of the James River – is a scene never to be forgotten and which represented the gathering known as the Army of the James , so soon to participate in the active operations against our enemies.

Early in the morning of the 6th the regiment landed at Bermuda Hundred, on the west side of the James, above the mouth of the Appomattox River, destined for a dig at the rebel capital by way of operations against Fort Darling and Petersburg, under the command of General B. F. Butler. On that warm May morning, the march in a scorching hot sun, and how the roadside was quickly lined with shoes, socks, shirts, coats, blankets and surplus baggage, the flanks literally carpeted with cast-away clothing, etc., by the lightening of knapsacks."[22]

Letter from Ed Cook to his Parents

[May 5, 1864]

I have only an opportunity to let you know that I am well. I am now on board of the "Thos. A. Morgan" en route for "Fortress Monroe" & from there to "Bermuda Hundred" on the James River. I am still in the Q.M. Dept. but do not know how long I will remain in it. You can direct your letters to the "100th Regt., 10th Army Corps, Washington D.C." and I will get them all right. It has been a long time since I heard from you. Are the folks all well? We have heard of Gen. Grants successes. I cannot as yet call them victories. Time & the end of this campaign will decide that. Our Corps left the old site of Gloucester Point last week & the 100th of course was in the advance. I have not heard from any of the boys since then but it is reported that Gen. Butler in whose army we are has had a fight and the probabilities are that the 100th was in it.

The last I heard of Geo. Stoddard he was at Fort Monroe. I dont know where he is now but I dont think he is with the Regt. Those shirts you sent me are just a fit. I am very much pleased with them.

I have worked very hard since I saw you last. I have drawn clothing & tents for our whole corps & helped to issue the same to the brigade, Regts. & batteries. Our Corps is about 15 or 20 thousand strong and it is no small job to clothe and equip such an army.

I think this campaign is going to end the war either one way or the other. If our side wins – then the south is no more but if the South wins – the North must give up the struggle.

The campaign has opened most gloriously, and if Grant has the same ability to meet and overcome unexpected reverses, that he has to plan the first opening of the campaign, then our victory is certain and you may expect me home by next Spring. Our cause is most evidently in Gods hands and he is on the side right & liberty. We cannot fail.

I dont give Grant praise for I feel that it is Gods goodness & power manifested through him that our present successes are owing to. Give my love to Mr. Lyman & family.

[Ed Cook]

Letter from A. Lyth to his Father and Mother

Here Enclosed find my Photograph which give to Brother John in return for the one he sent me last summer
In the Field Va. near the Petersburg and Richmond Rail Road
May 8th 1864

Dear Father and Mother
I should have a good deal to write to you if I had the time at presant but as I have not I will give you hasty discription of our proceeding since we left Glou Point. On the 3rd the 100th drew four days rations and orders to move at a moments notice. On the morning of the 4th we were got out of our beds at 1 o'clock in the morning but we did not leave camp untill afternoon. we marched down to the landing at the York River where there was a very large fleet of transports awaiting the troops going aboard some Regts were already aboard and all the troops got aboard of the transports at dusk. They having been embarking on both the Yorktown + Gloucester sides of the river. The fleet got under way at 2 o'clock on the 5th and arrived at Fortress Monroe at day break Gen'l Butler and Gen'l Gillmore were runing around the harbor in their little steamers giving orders and they got the whole fleet under way for the James river in a short time. Our Regt gave Gen'l Butler three hearty cheers when he ordered our transport forward. When we got up the James

river as far as New Port News we found that a fleet had left there loaded with troops up the river. It was a beautiful day and a most splendid sight to see the whole fleet making their way up the river with their flags flying and the gun boats for escorts we past Harrisons Landing at dusk in the evening and arrived off Bermuda Heights at eight o'clock and anchored in the river. the troops commenced disembarking but our Regt did not get ashore untill morning the 6th. The only houses near were a group of half a dozen one being a church. I went over to them but found no inhabitants except in one and he was an old infirm Negro. he said the people of the houses run away at the first appearance of our fleet. they belonged to the rebel signal corps. The army got on the move before nine o'clock and such a sight I never saw in my life and never want to see again. Most all the troops had a good knapsack and the best new clothing but the day was so intencely hot that when we got on the move we could not carry half our load for three miles the roads were lined with blankets overcoats rubber blankets shirts drawers stockings pants caps portfolias whole knapsacks with all their clothes in them even pocket books were thrown away razors and trinkets of every discription. It is a fact that over ¾ of the army threw away their woolen blankets. Thousands of them bran new Just before we started there was a Gen'l order that each man should have two pair of army shoes and the men drew them but hardly any of them carried their extra shoes a mile. They threw them away shoes that they had never even tried on. Some few pulled of the shoes they had worn a little and put on their new ones but they had to suffer for it for the new ones were not broke into their feet. I threw away my rubber blanket 2 pair of drawers one pair of socks and other things of no value. we marched some 6 or 7 miles and piched our camp for the night but were not allowed to pitch tents. Just at dusk Gen'l Butler came along the lines of the army and they all cheered him heartily. he is a noble looking man to tell the truth he is the only Genl that I have seen that I think capable of commanding an army leaving out Genl Gillmore. As soon as we had got some supper they dug entrenchments in front of the whole line of troops and cut down about 100 acres of woods in front of us to keep the rebels from coming upon us in a suprise party. On the morning of the 7th we were got up at 3 oclock having slept on our arms all night and were got ready to move. we made 2 or 3 attempts to move but did not get started they got some coffee cooked we then sat down + had some breakfast but had hardly got commenced to eat the orders came to "fall in" but the boys were bound to finis their breakfast and did by swallowing scolding hot coffee. We got under arms and ready for the march when we were ordered to take off our knapsacks and pile them in a heap and leave guards over them. then we began to suspect there was going to be some work and not far distant we were well supplied with ammunition and got started but had only got a few rods when the Co Clerks were ordered back to straighten up the Co papers + accounts. I tried to get some one to do my work for me so that I might go with the Co but it was no go so I had to go back. There were two Brigades started out. They had not been gone over an hour and a half before we heard firing and then it increased I got through writing about noon and the papers sent off to Washington when the firing got to be awful. I was half crazy then as I wanted to be with my chums so I buckled on accutrements took my gun and started for the front to try and find the Regt and I run on to a line of pickets who would not let me outside so I cut into the woods and came to an old barn where they were cutting off legs + arms pretty fast and dressing wounds. I then struck off into the woods again to try and get round the pickets and got to where the bullets were flying pretty thick in the woods when I run across one of the 100th boys coming in with a finger shot off. I stoped and dressed his finger and we both then started to find the Regt he to look after his cousin an me to find my Co but we run on to the pickets again and they would not let us past but gave us only ten minutes to get to the rear out of sight. We turned back and got into camp about four oclock and found some of our boys in camp wounded. Shortly after that the firing ceased and the Regt came in about ½ past five o'clock. we had coffee cooked ready for them so they sat down and drank a cup of coffee and eat a couple or so of hard tack with no meat and made a supper then we fell in and moved about a quater of a mile to the rear where we stacked arms in a field an slept under the heavens for a roof all night. What battle they call that which we fought yesterday I do not know but all we had was in was 8 or 9 Regts of Infty and a few peices of artillery there was more rebs than there was of our men. the object of our men was to tear up the Petersburg + Richmond R Road which is a bout two miles from our presant camp the rebels were in a gully on the opposite side of the rail road and had a good many peices of artillery planted. see P.S.

P.S. the rebs kept our men in check a long time and made two or three flank movements on us but could not drive us at last our Regt + the 49th

331

M.S.N. + 48th N.Y.V. and another Regt made a charge on the track and drove the rebs tore up about ½ a mile of the track and telegraph line set fire to the rail road stays having piled them in a pile and then fell back Just as reinforcements were coming to the rebs This morning we fell back ½ a mile further to the rear and other troops took the line in front we drew rations a some were nearly famishing I made a good hearty breakfast out of 4 hard tack + about ½ a pound of raw salt pork and a cup of coffee. In the engagement I could not tell you how many either side lost but our Regt lost only between 50 + 60 killed wounded and missing Our Co only had two wounded in the hands and I have been very busy this morning making out their descriptive lists and papers to send them to the hospital we had 4 officers wounded but none killed there was one of our Colonels killed in the fight but I don't know what Regt he belonged to. The Regt is all out at work now building a fortification in front of our camp about ten rods from where I am writing. there is an artist taking a sketch of the work and I have got to go and look after drawing some rations for the Co so I will close with my love to you all. I forgot to say a small mail arrived this morning and I got two Harpers Address Gloucester Point Va. but there is some of our mail laying back some where which we shall get soon. Enclosed you will find the photograph of our 1st Lieut and Co Commander he would have been our Capt when Capt Walbridge left us but he wont be promoted for he wants to go home when his time is out which will be in the fall but if he accepts a captains commission he will have to swear in for three years more and he dont want to. he has been in every battle that the 100th Regt has been in and was never wounded but has had balls give him close calls often Yesterday a ball passed through his coat.

I will write soon if I have a chance and write to me often. Give my love to Sarah Ann + Wm from your

Loving Son
Alfred Lyth

Alfred Lyth Presentation

[May 16, 1864]

"Many of the Regiment were taken prisoners, not having a chance to leave the rifle pits before the rebel line was upon them, and were sent on to Richmond. When captured, I was taken with several others to the stump lot, and guarded by a couple of Rebs, one of who soon started to gather plunder and trophies, the remaining soldier's attention being occupied in watching the field in the distance and the success of his comrade. Embracing a favorable opportunity, I darted behind a stump near by, and taking advantage of circumstances made good [my] escape to a piece of woods to the right and rear of the open field in which the Regiment was at the opening of the fight. In running across a corner of the field to gain the wood, a bullet struck the cap off [my] head, a loss very much regretted at the time – the head-gear being a very fine cap, presented to [me] by Lieut Jas. H. French a few days before. While hurrying through the woods [I] came across a soldier severely wounded, being shot through the arm and the bullet penetrating his side. The wounded soldier was Corp. Stark, Company A of the 100th. He begged so hard for help and we stopped to bind his arm with a handkerchief to stop the flow of blood. Then, urging him to follow, we started again to find a place of safety. At the edge of the woods to our left, we came to an opening descending to what appeared to be the bed of a creek, the banks overgrown with underbrush. Upon the slope on the opposite side of the creek were stretched, as far as the eye could reach a line of infantry wearing the Union blue. On the crest of the hill above, their infantry and field guns were planted, showing that our troops had formed a new line of battle, or reserves were preparing to meet the foe. On reaching the creek, which proved to be dry, musketry firing from our left and rear was quite rapid, and glancing in that direction, a line of rebel infantry was seen advancing. The Union line opened up with volley after volley, and the cannon above sending their greetings in rapid succession, the confederates withdrew. During a lull in fighting, a number of Union soldiers, including several from the 100th, lying low in the bed of the creek, ran for the lines, passing on to the rear making inquiries for a field hospital. Being directed to a small grove on the Weldon Railroad, we found a large number of wounded congregated in the vicinity indicated, some severely, others more or less injured. No surgeons or commissioned officers being there, no one with authority to direct affairs, we were at a loss what to do next. A soldier passing said the field hospital was now located at the junction, a mile further on the railroad. Assuming to direct affairs, we ordered the worst cases to be placed upon two flat cars, conveniently at hand;

all who were able lending a willing aid to push them along. About 120 or 30 crippled and wounded started down the track at the junction. Half a mile from the starting point had been gained. A soldier walking in front of the moving cars on the look out cries out a warning, "Rebel cavalry ahead, boys!" Immediately several ran out to the front of the cars to ascertain, and coming to the conclusion it is a false alarm , that the horsemen in the distance are Unionists, we proceed, but only, in a few moments, to be hailed by mounted rebels on the banks of the railroad cut above us, to throw down our arms and surrender. Many instinctively turning to the rear for a chance to run, we find a troop of Confederate cavalry coming down the track. Hemmed in on all sides, with no possible chance to escape, the only course was to cast aide the weapons we possessed and submit to the inevitable.

The flat cars containing the severely wounded were continued moving along the track in the direction for Petersburg, Va., the others are directed to march on behind the cars. Proceeding in this manner nearly a mile, a halt was ordered. Soon, however, those on foot were directed to fall in, and proceed towards the city. Our wounded on the cars, it was said, would be given surgical and necessary assistance at once, or sent to hospitals.

Many wounded, other than those mentioned, requesting the same consideration were refused, being told they would be taken care of in the city. Reaching Petersburg at night-fall, weary and tired – in fact, completely exhausted – we were crowded into the city jail, a stone structure similar to many others in southern cities, used to confine criminals. Entering the portals the detachment we were marched into one room, soon realizing that there, we must remain at least for the night. No rations were issued, most everyone being provided, having well-filled haversacks.

That night, in Petersburg jail, its horrors, its suffering, the agony, groans, shrieks, moans of sick and wounded men, crowded so thick together that there was not room for all to lie down upon the floor, in one corner of which there were two buckets for use to answer nature's calls, many suffering from diarrhea." [23]

[May 17, 1864]

"Some of the worst among the sick and wounded were sent to a hospital; all were taken to an adjoining room and searched for valuables, knives and money; their name, rank, Company and regiment recorded, being told that all taken from us was entered on the register to our credit, and would be returned to us when released   Some of the worst among the sick and wounded were sent to a hospital; all were taken to an adjoining room and searched for valuables, knives and money; their name, rank, Company and regiment recorded, being told that all taken from us was entered on the register to our credit, and would be returned to us when released. During the search those who were suspected of trying to conceal anything, were stripped naked and every particle of clothing thoroughly inspected; under the arms, in the hair, shoes and stockings, or where suspicion might dictate that a stray greenback was allowed.

That day several embraced the opportunity to pencil short letters to the dear ones at home, trusting that they would reach them and relieve their anxiety regarding our fate. Then follows another night in jail, to some the suffering worse than the previous night. The next day we were transferred from the jail to more commodious quarters in a tobacco warehouse nearby. Suffering from the wound in my foot and diarrhea for several days following, I was too ill to note passing events." [24]

[May 27, 1864]

"At the end of the week we were glad to get orders to be ready to move, any kind of change being agreeable. In the early morning we were marched to a train of box freight cars, in which we were all crowded like so many sheep – not enough room for all to lie down at once. Thus the journey of seven days and nights, from Petersburg, Va. to Andersonville, Ga. began. During that time we were only out of those closely packed cars one night, and during the removal from one train to another."[25]

Letter from E. Cook to his Parents

Office Asst. Q.M.
Bermuda Hundred VA May 24/64

My Dear Parents

I spose you think you am forgotten but you am not. I have been very busy and when I have not been busy I have been very tired. Work fatigues me very much. It is a pain for me to walk a few rods to my meals. I am so fat that I <u>cant</u> walk I have to <u>toddle</u>. I feel as though I weighed about two hundred and eighty pounds. All the boys laugh at me. I am coming home one of these days to try weights, capacities, and measurements with "Phelps".

Our regiment has lost a great many men since they came here. It has been complimented for bravery by Gen. Butler, Gen. Gillmore and by Col. Plaisted our Brigade Com^{dr}. When the 11th Maine (Col. Plaisted own regiment) sent out to the advance he (Col. Plaisted) told them that if they only did as well as the 100th N.Y. he would be pleased. I sent home a box about two weeks ago containing some of my surpluss articles. Did you receive it? In the box was a package within a large envelope I wish the package to remain inclosed until you receive orders from myself or some other party to open it. I received a letter from Laura a few days ago. I also received a letter from her about 3 or 4 weeks ago containing some postage stamps for which I am very much obliged. There has been no fighting for the last two or three days. I see Geo. Stoddard every day. He says he answered Laura's letter but he will write to her again.

I think we will be paid off before long and I can then send you some money. I have been very prodigal with my money since last pay day. I have borrowed 7 dollars. There have been a number of days when I drew no rations and therefore had to board myself at the rate of 50 cents per meal. I still have 10 dollars which I want to keep for any emergency as we can never know in the field and in an exposed position what will happen to us. I am in good health and our troops are in the very best of spirits. Things looked a little bit gloomy when we heard of Lee's stand on the south side of the Po. where he kept Grant at a stand for a short time but we have just heard that he is again retreating and Grant has crossed the North Anna. There now remains but one line of fortifications between him & Richmond and these are reported to be very weak but I hope Grant will take the course which has been his plan thus far, viz, to flank their works instead of storming them. We have every confidence in him as a general and have no doubt of his final success if the Great Ruler sees fit to bless our cause by permitting the Elements to favor the operations & plans which he has formed. But if God in his wisdom withdraws his favor who shall find fault if we again fail. Good Bye

Write Soon	*Your loving Son Edward*
Direct to E.L. Cook	*Edward*
Co. H 100 N.Y.V.	

Alfred Lyth Presentation

[June 1, 1864]

" . . . On the first day of June the train arrived at Andersonville. Leaving the railroad station, fifteen hundred prisoners from Richmond and Petersburg were marched to the headquarters of the commandant of the prison, Capt. Wirtz. Our names, rank, Company and Regiment taken, and a search for valuables was commenced but soon abandoned, all having been searched at Richmond or Petersburg. While standing in the ranks a very heavy shower of rain poured down upon us, and being in the front rank we stepped to the rear that a comrade might receive part protection from the rain by sharing our piece of oil cloth blanket. . . .Our names being taken we were marched into the prison camp, or stockade as it was called. The walls were formed of large hewn pine logs, planted in the ground, side by side, about twenty feet high above ground and enclosing a square of about twelve to fourteen acres. Passing through the gate men from every state were gathered about the entrance anxious to see if any of the new-comers were from their regiments or were acquaintances. The sight there spreads out before our eyes was horrible beyond description – hundreds, and it seemed to us thousands of men appeared to us as if they were walking skeletons arisen from the grave. Many almost naked, with what was once a shirt and pants to cover their nakedness; pants tattered and pieces torn from the legs to patch the seats; shirts ragged and all covered with filth and vermin; hair, long and unkempt; eyes, sullen and lusterless; men with swollen limbs and raw sores on their bodies, was a spectacle to strike us with terror, and almost freeze the blood in our veins. . . . There can not be a worse hell than this. Standing and viewing the strange and horrible sight, a familiar tap upon the shoulder causes us to look aside. We are greeted by comrade Chas. R. Moss of Co. H, who informs us that James Pixley, Thomas Russell and Albert Tombers are there with many others of the Regiment captured in the trenches on the 16th of May, and taken to Richmond, having arrived at Andersonville two days before. No shelter whatever was provided for prisoners by the prison authorities. Drenched and wet by the afternoon rain, late at night, we lay down, wet and weary, sharing our piece of blanket with a comrade. Early the following morning, rising heartsick and nearly discouraged at the prospect before us, our daily routine of prison existence begins.

On the first of June, when we entered the stockade, it contained about 10,000 prisoners. Recollect, all those were collected in a space of about thirteen or fourteen acres, out of which space, taken of by the dead line and the swamp and creek running through the center, was to be deducted. The dead line was a line of demarcation all around inside the enclosure, and located twenty feet from the stockade, and was composed of posts three feet high, ten feet apart, on top of which was nailed a light board railing. To pass beyond this line was instantaneous death. The sentinels were posted on platforms arranged inside the stockade at regular intervals, having strict orders to shoot any one trespassing over this line, without warning. It was said that guards killing a Yankee were always rewarded with a furlough for thirty days. The swamp in the prison was a horrible place. Along the edge of all the sink arrangements of the prison were located, and through this swamp ran a stream supplying the prison with water. At the edge of the swamp in the slime, mud, and filth, maggots by the millions were constantly crawling, and thousands of these maggots, with wings, were dropping on the sores of men lying asleep and exposed, and stinging them like gadflies. On the left side of the prison and close to the railing of the dead line there was a road across the swamp. At this point the water was deemed to be pure, the creek here entering the stockade and passing on through the swamp. Those wanting water would go to this point, and reach as far up the stream as they could to get water as pure as possible. It was here that many a poor fellow reaching beyond the dead line a little too far was shot, which at one time was almost of daily occurrence." [26]

Alfred Lyth Diary

June 1, 1864: Rain

June 2, 1864: Heavy rain shower; wet all night

June 3, 1864: Hot sun in the morning; arrival of more prisoners; showers.

June 4, 1864: Prisoners from Sherman's army; rain all day; cleared upon the evening; lay in wet clothing all night. Two escaped prisoners turned back into stockade, and compelled to wear ball and chain six days.

June 5, 1864: Rain in showers; rumors of an exchange

June 6, 1864: Hot in the morning; rain in the afternoon; cleared up in the evening.

June 7, 1864: Early in the morning cloudy; tremendously hot at noon; very heavy rain storm in the afternoon. Comrade James Pixley very ill.

Letter from E. Cook to his Sister

Office Asst. Quartermaster
Bermuda Hundred
June 7th 1864 Tuesday

My dear Sister
I received two letters from you yesterday, one of them was mailed May 9th just a month ago and the other was of a shorter date. I have been very slack in writing of late but I will try and make amends in the future. I cannot write long letters {missing word} there is nothing of importance to write about.
Last Friday evening we listened to the most rapid and terrible

cannonading that I have ever heard. There had been firing all day but it was not until evening that it sounded as if every gun in the army of the Potomac had opened simultaneously. Grant cannot be a very great distance from us for the firing sounded very distinctly. We have not yet learned the course or the result of the fight but we are waiting patiently & anxiously for yesterdays papers for they will most likely contain some account of the battle & its results. Since Friday night there has been no cannonading except a few occasional shots on our own immediate front. The rebs charged on our works a few days ago but were driven back with heavy loss. Some colonel from chivalrous Georgia with a regiment of little boys had command of the storming party. He was very confident before the charge and boasted quite loudly (so prisoners say) that he could take our works; but instead of his taking our works we took him, but he was not of much account as both his legs were off and his body was pierced in a number of places. I have this story from men in our own regiment and I presume it is true. We are very anxious to hear from Grant. There is a rumor that he is coming down this way and intends to make an assault on Richmond from this direction. I presume it can be done but it will only be by a terrible loss on our side. I believe we have about 70 pieces of cannon in the short space of 5 miles and we consider our position almost impregnable, but the rebs have even more cannon than we have and whenever we assault their works we can only take them by walking over our own dead. But I consider Grant a great strategist, and as strategy seems to have been his most powerful & successful ally in this campaign we are in hopes that if he comes here he will call into action the same power and give us victory without a loss great enough to dampen the joy & gladness which the news of a victory always produces. My breakfast is ready so I will eat & then finish my letter.

Well I have finished two or three ordinary men's breakfast so I think I can manage to subsist until dinner time. My breakfast was coffee without milk, bread without butter & fried salt pork but I was hungry and relished the meal first rate. We had a heavy rain last night but it was not stormy. This morning is most deliciously cool & pleasant but it looks as if it was going to rain again we have had considerable rain since last friday but if it is, it is also giving our poor boys a chance to rest. Hereafter I will try and write oftener. You need not send me the commercial but if you came across any {unknown word} in the local column that you think I would like to see, you may cut it out and send it to me in a letter. I should also like the *deaths & marriages so as to keep posted in the changes going on at home. I rece'd the Post Stamp you sent me some time ago. The diarrhea is beginning to make its appearance among the troops. If you have any opportunity to do so, I would like you to send me a little stick cinnamon. If it does not cost too much and you can pack it safely you might send me 2 or 3 ounces by mail but do not send it if it costs very much, or more than the cinnamon itself. Write to me soon & give my love to all.*

Your Affectionate Brother
Edward L. Cook

Direct to
Co H 100ᵗʰ N.Y. Vols
> *Bermuda Hundred*
>> *VA*
Via, Fort Monroe

Letter from E. Cook to Parents

Office Asst. Quartermaster
Bermuda Hundred VA
June 7ᵗʰ 1864

Dear Parents

I sent a letter to Laura this morning. And now I have the pleasure of informing you and all the rest of my friends that unexpectedly and unasked I have received a commission as 2ⁿᵈ Lieut. in the 100ᵗʰ N.Y. Vols. I shall return to my regiment tomorrow and try to perform my duty to my country and to my friends. I trust that neither may ever have cause to blush for my conduct on the field. Pray for me that I may always be blessed with courage to stand up to my duty to God, to my country and to my fellow man. Until you hear from me again you may continue to direct to Co "H" 100ᵗʰ N.Y. Vols. Do not attach any rank or title to my name but direct simply to Edward L. Cook. I do not fear to face the enemy, but on account of my comparative ignorance of military matters I should have preferred to be with my company as sergeant.

I have this day borrowed of Capt. Walbridge (82) Eighty-two dollars and given him an order on you for the amount. You can fill out one of the blank checks that I left with you when I came away and draw the money

341

and hand it to the person who calls for it. I presume Capt. Walbridge's brother will present the order. I have drawn the order in favor of Mrs. W. C. L. Walbridge or order so that she will have to endorse it before you pay it. You had better go up and draw the money as soon as you receive this for the order will reach Mrs. Walbridge as soon as this reaches you. I have borrowed the money for the purpose of {unknown word} my uniform +c. I presume Mr. Lyman will want to buy me a sword but Capt. Walbridge has got the start of him for as soon as he heard that I had rec'd a commission he immediately wrote to his brother in New York to buy a sword for me. Mr. Lyman must not feel disappointed for I may sometime have the pleasure of receiving an acknowledge of his kindness and good will towards me in the shape of something fully as acceptable as a sword – say a suit of civilian clothes – or a cradle   Give my love to everybody and write soon.

Good Bye
Your loving son Edward

Letter from Ed Cook to his Parents

Friday June 10th 1864 The force sent out Wednesday night advanced to within two miles of Petersburg but finding the enemy too strong for them and fearful that if they delayed another night then retreat would have been cut off, they immediately returned & arrived in camp last evening. They did not succeed in destroying the bridge, but without any proportionate loss on our side the cavalry took between 40 & 50 Prisoners, who had every appearance of belonging to the rebel militia force. Many of them had on clothes of a far finer quality than are worn by the rebs and some had on Hats looking as if they had left their daily avocations at a moments notice and rushed to arms for the purpose of defending their city from the assault of our troops.

Saturday June 11th 1864 A larger regiment of 100 days Ohio troops arrived to day and more are coming. It is reported that between 30 & 40 thousand troops are soon expected at this {unknown word}.

Sunday June 12/64 This morning I went in company with Bell Mason & Ken VanHusen a short distance up the James River, and had a most delicious bath in its fresh waters. On our way we stopped several times at the foot of some of the many cherry trees that shade the roads & paths through the rich plantations, and had our fill of their delicious fruit. The whole country instead of having orchards as we do with, plant their fruit trees by the rodeside & bridle paths and wherever you go you will be sure to ride beneath the branches of cherry, apple, peach, pear & mulberry trees.

Monday June 13/64 I was making preparations to day to go to Norfolk tomorrow for the purpose of buying my uniform +c but this evening I have heard that Gen. Smith is coming back to this place with a portion of Grants army tonight or tomorrow morning and will make a move on Petersburg tomorrow, so I am not going to Norfolk tomorrow but will remain and learn the success of this move. If we had had the force last week which is coming tomorrow we could have taken Petersburg with little loss but I am afraid that it has now been reinforced too strongly for us to assault and take without great loss of life. I am well and hope you are all the same. I have not yet been mustered in as Lieutenant and still remain with Capt. Walbridge. I receive all the papers you send me & also those which Mr. Lyman sends me and am very much obliged to both of you for your favors. Dont wait for me write but write to me as often as you can conveniently. Tell Mr. Lyman to write to me again. Give my love to all and all pray for me. Pray that I may never act the part of the coward, that I may always be where duty calls me, and that I may always do my duty to the honor of myself & my friends & to the Glory of God. Pray that if in this war it is God's will that I should fall, you may have courage to bear the affliction and faith to look forward to another life where I may meet you all in the presence of our Maker in the new Jerusalem. Pray that I may live and die a Christian & have a home in Glory.

Your Loving Son Edward

Letter from A. Lyth to his Father and Mother

Prison for Federal Troops
Andersonville Georgia
June 10th 1864

Dear Father + Mother

After I was taken prisoner to Petersburg I wrote you a few lines to let you know that I was well as thank the Lord I am at present. Since I last wrote they have fetched us all here to Georgia where most all the prisoners are now located our prison is a large camp surrounded with stocades Our Regt lost very heavy the day I was taken there is between 120 + 120 of us here as prisoners there is 12 of our Co here and Jim Pixley is one of them he wishes you would let his folks know that he is well We both try and intend to keep up good courage and hope for the best and that we may not have long to remain here the weather is very hot you can write me a few lines if you chose enclosed you will find a confederate stamp which if you write you can use if you write

Address

Alfred Lyth

Prisoner of War Andersonville

Georgia

Via Flag of Truce boat

and do not seal the letter Give my respects to all the neighbors I send my love to you all

From Your Loving Son

Alfred Lyth

Alfred Lyth Diary

June 8, 1864: More prisoners arrive, and report Grant closing around Richmond. Rain after sunset.

June 9, 1864: Lay in pool of water all night.

June 10, 1864: Scorching hot part of the day; rain in the afternoon, Tombers helps carry out the body of a dead comrade.

June 11, 1864: Rain again. James Pixley very sick.

June 12, 1864: More rain; rations one-half pint of sour rice; one ounce and a half of meat which the maggots are contending for.

June 13, 1864: Cold, raw day; rain in showers; rations one-third pint of rice, three ounces of coarse meal; rumors of parole and exchange.

June 14, 1864: Rain most all night; no wood today; Pixley much better.

Letter from E. Cook to Parents

Bermuda 100 Va. June 14th 1864
Tuesday

My dear Parents
I know of no better way and surer plan of keeping you informed of my whereabouts and whatabouts than to write you a short article each day and mail a letter whenever my sheet is full. The 18th Army corps returned to this place today and there is a rumor that the whole of Grants army is coming after him. The move of course is to be on Petersburg.

Wednesday June 14th 1864 A large number of 100 days men have arrived this week. Grants army is crossing the James river on a pontoon bridge about 6 miles below us and are marching towards Petersburg tonight. Genl. Grants Hd. Qrs. are at City Point just across the Appomattox. He was on this side to day and I had a very good sight of him. He is very plain and unassuming and attracts no notice. He came from City Point to this place in a little tug while Gen. Butler has for his private use the largest & fastest river steamer in the Department. He wore no sword or other outward trapping except his buttons and plain shoulder straps. His pants were tucked inside of a pair of long dusty boots and his whole attire looked dirty & travel stained. His shoulders are very broad, and from his habit of carrying his head slightly inclined forward and looking downward he has the appearance of being a little round shouldered. He walks with a long slow stride and slightly emphasizes his left foot step. I associated with his appearance the idea or similee of a huge ponderous Iron roller (on a very slightly inclined plane) which though hard to start yet when once fairly underway by its momentum carries every thing before it and is almost impossible to stop.

Thursday June 15/64 We sent a train of 70 Wagons to City Point this AM for the purpose of supplying the Army of the Potomac with ration until their teams arrive. Capt. W. went with the train and will probably see

Petersburg before he returns. There was a hard fight in front of Petersburg last night. Our army was successful. Over 300 prisoners were brought to Bermuda Hundred today. I went down to the James river this afternoon to take a bath but the tide was so low and the water so muddy that I did not venture in. I was repaid for my walk though by the quantities of blackberry bushes in our immediate vicinity. The fruit is already turning red, and if I do not rejoin my regiment too soon I shall have a rare feast of rich ripe blackberries. Dont you wish you all were here to go blackberrying with me. I suppose though that you would prefer to have me in "B" to go blackberrying with you.

Friday June 17ᵗʰ 1864 Gen. Grant was on his ride again to day. There is fighting going on again in the vacinity of Petersburg. We can hear the booming of cannon and the rattle of musketry. The enemy in our immediate front fell back yesterday & our boys now occupy the rebs old earthworks. We took a number of prisoners some of whom were asleep. The rebs fell back in such haste that they did not draw in their pickets and left many of their men behind who did not know (until our men were in their lines) that their friends had deserted them.

Saturday June 18/64 Every thing is comparatively quiet at present but it will not remain so long. I have no heard from you for more than a week; What is the matter! I am glad to learn that Corneal {unknown name} is at home and getting along comparatively well. I have not yet been able to get mustered in as none of the companies are large enough to muster a 2ⁿᵈ Lieut. it requiring 80 men in a company to admit of commissioned officers.

Sunday June 19/64 Nothing further has been accomplished as yet. The pontoon bridge across the James river has been taken up. Our lines (The Potomac Army) are advanced on one flank to within ½ mile of Petersburg. No news from our immediate front. An officer in a "nigger calvery" regiment and a {unknown word} got into a quarrel yesterday & the {unknown word} shot the Lieut. in the head and some of the officers men retalliated by shooting the {unknown word} who died to day. The Lieut. is still living and is expected to recover. The ball entered near the ear and came out of his mouth.

Monday June 20/64 We are going to throw a pontoon bridge across the James river to night & two corps will cross onto the peninsula between here and Richmond. There was heavy firing heard yesterday in the direction of the white house in the[   ] and it may be possible that our cavalry has succeeded in drawing out some of Lee's army and Grant expects to capture it by a flank movement.

Good Bye Write soon

Your Loving Son   *Edward L. Cook*
Co "H" 100ᵗʰ N.Y. Vols.

Alfred Lyth's Diary

June 17, 1864: Commenced to rain at 3 o'clock A. M. ; heavy showers all day; Three men from our detachment who went outside for wood with a rebel guard, when in the woods, tied the guard to a tree, and taking his gun, started for "God's country.

June 18, 1864: One of the men recaptured, placed in stocks all night; blood hounds hunting for others; showers in the afternoon; arrival of prisoners from Sherman's army.

June 19, 1864: A well being dug caved in last night; a poor fellow lying near slipped in and was smothered; guard on post 14 near our quarters, fired at a crazy prisoner who had wandered across the dead line; failed to hit him, but badly wounded others lying near by; more prisoners from Grant & Butler.

Letter from T. Maharg to A. Lyth's Father

Camp 100ᵗʰ N.Y. Vol
Bermuda Hundred
June 19ᵗʰ/64

Dear Sir
I rec. your letter for information yesterday in regard to Alfred being

missing but as I am not in the company + therefore not in the fight I am a fraid I will not be able to satisfy you but I will tell you what the boys of the company sayes They told me that he got off the battle field all wright + was crossing the Rail Road when they seen a car loaded with our wounded coming down the track + Alfred went to help push it so as to get it out of the way as the rebs was chacing them up but they faild in geting it out of the way + we think that Alfred was taken with it. He was taken on the 16th of May he had nothing with him but his haversack + cantene but the Ordely will take care of his knapsack as long as we stay hear now if you would like to have his things sent home. Mr Lyth I have just been over + seen the Ordely + he said that there was an order from the Col. to look over all the knapsacks belonging to the wounded + missing + if there was any thing in them that was worth any thing to take it out + burn the rest for after the 16th of May we did not know how soon we would have to leave + we could not carry them, he told me he thought that some of the boys had some trinkets belonging to Alfred + as soon as they get in off picket I will hunt them up + see what they are, + tell you. We have had two or three Battles cince but have not retaken the ground where they fought when Alfred was taken but I hope we will before long. The Lt. did not want him to go with them this day they left camp as he was company clirk + his place was in camp but he would go for he had never seen a fight + he thought if he stayed back the boys would think he was afrade + I guess you know that he was a boy that would not have that said of him.

Mr Lyth you must not worry yourself to much about him for I am pretty shure that he is only a prisoner + that is not so bad as it might be we are having boys come back allmost every day that was taken at the charge of Wagner they have been gone almost a year + they look fresh + good so you see there is a good sight for Alfred to get back all wright.

From Your Humble Friend Thos Maharg

Letter from E. Cook to his Parents

Asst. Quartermaster's Office,
Bermuda Hundred Va. 1864 June 20/64

My dear Parents

It has been more than two weeks since I heard from you. What is the *matter? I am very fearful that some one is sick and you do not write and tell me. I have been much worried with this thought for the last few days. Write to me immediately. Direct to Edward L. Cook Care of Capt. C.E. Walbridge A.Q.M. Bermuda Hundred Va. I will write to you again today and tell you what news there is though that will not be much. Dont wait to receive another letter from me before you write but write immediately. I inclose a few trinkets &c. which I would like to have preserved among them is a small piece of the rebel flag staff of Wagner.*

Your Loving Son, Edward L. Cook

Alfred Lyth Diary

June 20, 1864: Joseph Achuff, one of the men that escaped on the 17th, came into the stockade, having been in the stocks for thirty-six hours; he says when they tied the guard to a tree, he separated from the others and started off alone, and in his own way search for liberty; soon he heard the deep voice of the blood hounds, and he took to the swamp, thinking they could not track him there. In a short time, however, the hounds and their yelling owner were upon him. He turned at bay with his back against a tree, and a dry limb in his hand. His only clothing was a ragged shirt, pants, shoes and cap; five dogs attacked him; his stick broke, and for ten minutes he fought the hounds with his fists; the owner orging them to fiendish and hellish work with yells; when at last overpowered, he was torn and bit until the brutish owner was satisfied. He called the dogs off, catching one by the hind legs and tearing him off with part of his pants and some flesh following. When brought back, Wirtz ordered him put in the stocks, exposed to the hot sun and rain. Bloodly, wounded, sore as he was, he was compelled to suffer, and when Wirz was appealed to during his torture, he swore at him and told him to shut up or he would blow his damned brains out.

Letter from E. Cook to his Parents

To Lyman Cook	*Direct to E. L. Cook*
No 59 Oak Street	*Care of Capt. C.E. Walbridge*
Buffalo	*A.Q.M.*
N.Y.	*Bermuda Hundred*

Asst. Quartermaster's Office,   *Va.*

Bermuda 100 Va. June 22ⁿᵈ   **1864**

Wednesday

My dear parents

   Nothing of any importance has transpired since I wrote you last. Petersburg is virtually in the possession of Grant for he can take it any time he chooses but the opinion seems to prevail here that he does not wish to occupy it at present, but chooses rather the course of investing, instead of invading, thereby detaining in a position favorable to his plans a large portion of the enemy's force while he operates in with much greater effect upon some distant point when his blow is least expected.

Thursday June 23ʳᵈ 1864 Uncle Abe has paid us the honor of a visit at this front but we unfortunately did not know of it until he had gone. There is almost continual fighting along in line either at one front or another but very few casualties occur. The regiment has crossed the James river, in company with several regiments, at a point 10 mils this side of Richmond and have commenced fortifying. This is a new and {unknown word} move on the part of Gen. Grant. No one can conjecture its meaning or significance. At the same time that my regt. and the others, all under command of Brig. Gen. Foster, crossed the James, another, and a much larger body of troops crossed the Appomattox in an exactly opposite direction.

   What do these moves mean?

Friday June 24ᵗʰ 1864 In company with Capt. Walbridge I rode out to the pontoon bridge this afternoon and crossed over to where the regiment is. They have been working on fortifications ever since their arrival there but had been relieved that day and were just going on picket when I arrived. There is no chance at present for me to get mustered in as a Lieutenant, so my commissions for the time being is worth just about as much as the parchment is worth. The boys all looked tired and worn out. Co. "K", commanded by Capt. Granger did a very gallant little deed yesterday. The evenings skirmishes supposed to be only a few in number never drawing most too close to the scene of our operations and it became necessary to force them to retire. The officer in command requested Col. {unknown name} to send out a couple of companies from our regiment to dislodge the enemy and drive them beyond a house in front of our line and then to occupy the house. Company K, and the sharpshooters of Co 'H' were detailed for the job. The sharpshooters occupied a slight eminence & deployed on the right while Company 'K' deployed on the left. This gave them quite an extended line though they were really very few in numbers. When they were ready they gave a h-lish yell & started at a charge double quick. The rebs saw them coming in a long line but did not wait to assure themselves in regard to numbers but skedaddled with them. So that every thing was accomplished that the general desired. This is one of the most brilliant little feats of the war. The rebs instead of being only a few in number as was supposed were a regiment upwards of 250 strong. The affair is much laughed at by our boys. Only one man was injured. We have heard that some of our troops have made a long detour & are now 19 miles in the rear of Petersburg and moving towards the Danville Railroad.

Saturday June 25/64 I have not yet received a letter from home. What can be the reason? I am afraid some of you are sick. The heat here is most oppressive. I never before experience the like of it. Not a breath of breeze from morning to morning again. Rest at night is almost impossible and comfort during the day is quite so.

Sunday June 26/64 I despatched of few little trinkets to you this morning including a piece of the rebel flag staff of fort Wagner and a {unknown word} received of a seceshionist when were at Gloucester Courthouse in 1862. Please preserve them. I went blackberrying with Smith, Mason & the cook yesterday afternoon and gathered 5 quarts in a very few minutes. We had blackberry dumpling for dinner. The crust was made by a Negro wench and our cook say he borrowed one of her childs diapers to boil it in. We have lived quite well lately. We have had string beans, cabbage, squash and a number of other little articles.

Yesterday we had some fried Eel fattened on the carcass of a horse.
Good Bye Write soon   *Your loving son*
I have not heard from you in nearly 3 weeks   *Edward*

Alfred Lyth Diary

June 21, 1864: Very hot morning; afternoon, rain; a man leaning on the dead line was fired at, but not hit; another is wounded, however, and not expected to live.

June 22, 1864: Very hot; average deaths in stockades about sixty a day; many go out to hospital and die there; first day this month no rain fell.

June 23, 1864: Very hot; rebs filling up tunnel discovered; two ounces of fresh beef to-day.

June 27, 1864: Scorching; sand almost hot enough to cook rations; about five hundred more prisoners arrive, among them some of the 100th New York, taken at the charge upon Fort Wagner.

June 29, 1864: There is a gang of rowdies organized in the prison, who plunder prisoners, especially new arrivals on their first night in prison, and take from them money, watches, blankets, and any property they may have been fortunate enough to keep from the rebels, frequently knives were used to enforce their demands. One night they surrounded some men belonging to our regiment, searched them and took a watch from one. A police force was organized among ourselves to arrest the raiders, as they were called, and a great many arrested were thus made. The rebel authorities gave permission to us to arrest raiders, and those known to be guilty were captured. Twenty-four were sent to be held for trial by a jury, which, being selected from among the new comers, they were tried on July 1, and six of the number, being found guilty of murder, were sentenced to be hanged. The balance were turned into the stockade and made to run a gauntlet of enraged sufferers, ranged in two lines, with clubs ready to mete out such punishment as they could by striking them as they passed through the lines. Many were fearfully punished, some escaped lightly and two or three, it is said were killed... Digging out through tunnels was frequently attempted, and had it not been for the many contemptible traitors in our midst who, for some favor or an extra ration, would betray any attempt to escape, many

352

would have gotten away. *These sneaks and traitors were generally traced to the raider gang.*

Alfred Lyth Presentation

[July 1, 1864]

"The prison pen is enlarged at the north end and an addition of some ten acres being added and stockades were erected, the partition between the old and the new part was allowed to be torn down by the prisoners, which was a godsend in the shape of fuel to cook rations. Our little family, by industry, secured a good supply. It would be curious if among so many prisoners there were not at all times many brains concocting schemes for freedom. Digging out through tunnels was frequently attempted, and had it not been for the many contemptible traitors in our midst who, for some favor or an extra ration, would betray any attempt to escape, many would have got away. These sneaks and traitors were generally traced to the raider gangs."[27]

July 14, 1864: An alarm among the Rebs. Wirtz has discovered another tunnel; All sentry platforms overlooking the stockade are filled with soldiers, each having forty rounds of ammunition. Three or four hundred march into the stockade and take position inside the dead line where the tunnel is located, ready for action if necessary. A gang of slaves, with teams, are set to work filling up the tunnel, and Wirz had several men arrested, suspected of being connected with the project. They are to be placed in the stocks and rations reduced to two ounces of corn bread per day Oh! I hope that I may live to see the day when this fiend, Wirtz, will swing.

Chapter Ten

Virginia Campaign
Operations around Petersburg, VA
July, 1864 – August, 1864

"Our orderly (messenger) went out to Peterburgh last week with some messages, and he represents the state of the troops as very critical They are complaining bitterly of their condition and are almost cursing the officers who are high in authority, and vowing that they will never charge on the rebel works at Petersbough. They (our troops) are dirty, poor, tired, desponding and care less both of their own fate & the fate of the country They have to watch incessantly day and night and if they get any sleep at all they have to catch it during the day when the sun is so scorchingly hot that the rebel gunners are glad to cease firing & leave their guns to seek for themselves some shelter from the scorching sun rays. Our poor men are in danger not only on the battle field and in the zigzag trenches but even their camps and of little shelter tents the fatal bullet finds its way and picks off many noble sons and fathers. . . . The men say that they have been hurled into battles and urged on to charges and have lost 80,000 of their comrades and they ask "What have we accomplished by it?" "Nothing!" "We are no nearer to Richmond than when we started and we will no fight any more, all the officers in the army shall not compel us to charge again." E Cook letter dated 7/18/1864

"After the repulse at Drury' Bluff there followed in quick succession the fighting along the lines of Bermuda Hundred, the battle of "Ware Bottom Church", the operation at Deep Bottom, and the taking of the "Grover House," by the brilliant dash of the company under Major Nash, Captain Grander and Lieutenant Stowits. During the operations of the Second Corps, under Hancock at Deep Bottom your capture of a battery of four rebel guns under the immediate observance and by orders of General Grant, was accomplished in a manner of which any regiment might well be proud and when, after a week of continuous marching and fighting in that intense August heat you returned to camp, it was with many losses, among them Captain McMann wounded and Captain Warren Grander captured. "After these events, we settled into winter quarters and waited for the spring campaign to open. It was evident that the end was approaching and that "if things were pushed", the war would soon be over. In the later part of March, after your division had been reviewed by President

Lincoln, General Grant and other officers of high rank, you marched across the Appomattox, and took your place in the lines in front of Petersburg in readiness for the final struggle. Colonel Dandy assumed command of the brigade and Major James H. Dandy was in command of the regiment." Lt Col Charles E. Walbridge address at the first Annual Reunion 7/18/1887

"You need not be reminded of the days spent in the trenches in front of Petersburg, where the firing was incessant, and a man could not stand erect and expose his head above the earthworks without at once attracting the fire of a dozen sharp shooters, nor of the operations in September and October, north of the James." Lt Col Charles E. Walbridge address at the first Annual Reunion 7/18/1887

Letter from E. Cook to his Sister

Bermuda Hundred Va. July 18/64

My dear Sister

Your letter No 99 written on the 10ᵗʰ {unknown word} (Sunday) has just reached me. I was weary of waiting for a letter, and yours was very welcome as I had not received a letter or papers from any person since the 6ᵗʰ {unknown word}, nearly two weeks. I expected a letter from you two or four days ago and when this mail was brought to the office without numbering one for me I was much disappointed. Last Friday & Saturday were, I think, the "bluest" days I have experienced since I entered the service of "Unkle Psalm". I felt sad, very sad, during both the days, and it seemed to me as though some of my friends at home were sick or about to be visited by some calamity. Your letter partly verifies this experience, but I am happy to learn that matters are no worse. I am glad that mother is recovering from her attack of Cholera Morbis, but fearful that your next letter may not convey the wished for intelligence that she is fully well again. I hope to hear from you again very soon and learn that you are all well once more. Poor Father is down again. I wish with all my heart that the time had come when I could be with you all once again and in a position where I could earn enough to relieve father and mother from any more hard work. I hope that none of you are denying yourselves any of the comforts of life on account of prices of produce. While what little money I have lasts you are as welcome to it as the earth to rain; and there is no time when it will do any more good than the time when it is needed; so if you want it, use it, and use it freely. How is Grandma getting along? I have not yet received her letter. I guess it is more of a task for her to write now that it used to be a year or two ago. I should dearly love to receive a letter from her in her own handwriting – even if it was but a few lines, but I will not exact it, for I know it is far more of an undertaking for her dear old finger to travel with a pen over a sheet of paper, than it would be for me to pick my self up and travel from here to Washington; but I should like to receive a letter from her for all that, and you, Laura, must choose some idle hour (if you have any such, and if you have not you must make one) and while she furnishes the thought and moulds it on expressions you must catch it up and trace its meaning on the paper and then it will still be her letter and I shall be very glad to receive it and to answer it.

Our orderly (messenger) went out to Petersburgh last week with some messages, and he represents the state of the troops as very critical. They are complaining bitterly of their condition and are almost cursing the officers who are high in authority, and vowing that they will never charge on the rebel works at Petersburgh. They (our troops) are dirty, poor & ragged, tired, desponding, and care less both of their own fate & the fate of the country. They have to watch incessently day and night, and if they get any sleep at all they have to catch it during the day when the sun is so scorchingly hot that the rebel gunners are glad to cease firing & leave their guns to seek for themselves some shelter from the scorching sun rays. Our poor men are in danger not only on the battle field and in the zigzag trenches but even their camps and of little shelter tents the fatal bullet finds its way and picks of many noble sons and fathers. They are safe nowhere and at no time. They cannot feel thankful, when after lying 48 hours in the dirty, dusty trenches, they are received and sent back to their camp for the same length of time, because they know that even there they are not safe from the enemy's death dealing missiles. While our orderly was passing down the camp of his regiment a bullet came whistling towards him and fell at his feet. If he had been advanced a few steps farther it would have entered his body. The men say that they have been hurled into battles and urged on to charges and have lost 80,000 of their comrades and they ask "What have we accomplished by it?" "Nothing!" "We are no nearer to Richmond than we were when we started, and we will not fight any more, all the officers in the army shall not compell us to charge again" Thus they talk, and those who do not know the hearts of soldiers, or are not soldiers themselves, are alarmed and fearful that something dreadful is going to happen if another battle occurs. But God only can penetrate the hearts *of men and understand the mysteries that there lie hidden. The noblest work that God ever made is man & the noblest man is the soldier. He (the soldier) may make rash vows and use idle words, he may swear that he will not fight, but let the drum beat "to arms" and the bugle sound to "charge" and his officer say "Come boys!" and every man, but the coward at heart, forgets in a moment all his idle threats, and with his bayonet at a charge rushes on to meet his unknown fate. God! have pity on the soldier for no one else will pity him. God! have mercy on the soldier, for no one else will show him mercy. God! pardon him his sins and forgive his transgressions for he is thrown into the midst of great temptations and he knows not what he does; for Jesus' sake forgive-amen.*

Have you any fears for the result of the war? I have not. With such men as our army contains to fight for us and with such a cause as ours to fight for, we must succeed – there is no such word as fail. I still have every confidence in Grant and trust that my confidence may never appear to have been misplaced.

The raid up North has excited no particular interest in the army, and if it had been for the great scare which it has produced at home, and the great sensation which it has caused among the "newspaper dailies" I should not even have deigned to mention it. It is all over now and the rebs have got back with whole skins and unbroken organisation just as I bet they would when I first heard of the raid. Nobody wanted to check their depredations or catch them when they offered our people a good opportunity to cut them off and use them up. One of the screws in the machinery of our government has been loose a long time and I am forced to believe the thread is worn off and it can never be tightened up again.

I saw Sammy {unknown name} to day. He called on me and took dinner. He is looking first rate and has improved in character very much since he came into the army. He visited with me all the afternoon and is going to call on me again very soon if he does not move out of the department. Do you ever see Dora & Bertha nowadays? If you do, just remember me to them. One of our clerk from Co "C" 100th has gone to the hospital. He went yesterday. His name is Wm. Mason. I think he will recover and be back with us again in 2 or 3 weeks. There is a great deal of Typhoid Fever in this vacinity but it is mostly among the few days men (100 days men)

Give my love to everybody and write again very soon.

Your Loving brother
Edward

357

Miss Laura M Cook
    No 59 Oak Street
        Buffalo
            N.Y.
Tonight is the anniversary of George Clark's death at the charge of Fort Wagner.
Direct your next letter as heretofore.

Letter from E. Cook to his Sister

Bermuda 100 Va. ~~July~~ Aug 4/64

My dear sister Laura

    I received your letter 2 or 3 days ago but as I wrote Grandma two days ago I thought I would wait a short time before answering yours. I received a letter from Lottie McLane day before yesterday and answered it last evening; it is the first time I have heard from her in over three month. She is well and enjoying herself amazingly I guess from the tone of her letter. She has been to New York this summer and expects to go again this winter. She says she has not heard from Lila in nearly a year.

    I have not heard from the {unknown name} boys since they went away. They are now at Wilsons landing and I suppose are having good times.

    I went over to the regiment with Bell Mason to day and had a pleasant time. They have not lost many men lately and are in pretty good spirits.

    How do the people North feel about the Petersburgh affair. Everybody here is down on the niggers. Our loss was very heavy but a large portion of it was caused by the white troops firing into the retreating niggers. We had Petersburgh in our power that day if the nigs had not been seized with a kind of unusual panic or if we had followed up our success, in taking the first line, by an immediate charge on the remaining line. The rebel force was very small in compassion to our own as it is proved that only 1 corps was in Petersburgh.

    I have received notice that Co 'B' has men enough to muster a 2ᵈ Lieut so I am going back next Monday or Tuesday if the Captain returns by that time. We are very busy just now, but as Strobridge is well again & Mason has returned from the Hospital it takes a {unknown word} of work off from my shoulders. I saw Dave White today he is looking well. I see by one of the papers that you sent me that Bill Goffe; Shelton, and a number of other Co H. Boys are in the Sisters of Charity Hospital. Shelton used to be a tentmate with George Clark, Geo. S. & myself. Geo Stoddard went over to the regiment with us today. If you visit the Sisters Hospital (& I wish you would) you must remember me to all of the boys. Tell Bill Goffe or any one else of my company that Mike has got back from Rikers Island.

I think Grant is going to give up the hope of whipping the rebs at Petersburg for the present. I can not imagine what will be his next move but I believe he will leave only troops enough to hold the works and withdraw the main portion of his army to some other point. He has failed in this attempt but it was not from any fault in the plan (which seems to have been a good one and promised complete and prefect success to our army, and a most terrible & telling and decisive blow to the cause of seceshion. Man proposes & God disproves. A short delay of an hour, of a single hour, or the unaccountable panic that seized the niggers, lost us a battle, which if it had been gained, by us, would have proved to be the most important and decisive one of the campaign either in this department or any other. But we have failed and must submit for it is the will of God, and He doth all things well. It will only prolong the war for an additional length of time, but perhaps each delay will only serve to make our peace more lasting & complete when it does come.

I am getting tired of the service and if the war continues another year & I do not get out of it honorably at the expiration of that time I think I shall be in favor of Peace on any terms.

I wish you would send me 50 cents worth of Postage stamps as I cannot buy any here and you can take your pay for them out of the first money I send home. Give my love to all the folks and tell them all to pray for me, that I may do my duty manfully, suffer any pain patiently, and if I die that I may die hopeful of life here after, where I can meet you all, where there will be no more parting, no more pain, and where sin and death cannot enter. I do not dread a battle field except for your sakes. Life is sweet to me only that I may some day add happiness to the lives of those who have done so much for me. And whenever I think of death, I remember only the sorrow that such an event causes in the fond loving hearts around the home circle. If I could be assured that you, all of you, could look on death only as a temporary parting, and all feel that there was no need of mourning

& sorrow, for soon we all would meet again around our saviours throne, I could go back to my regiment with a far lighter heart for a heavy burden would be lifted from my thoughts. Try and feel this way and then if it is my lot to be a sacrifice to this struggle for freedom the blow will not fall so heavily on you, for you will know & feel & realise that your Edward is not dead but only sleeping, only gone before.

Miss Laura Cook   *Edward L. Cook*
Buffalo N.Y.   *Co. "H" 100th N.Y.V.*

Alfred Lyth Diary

August 7, 1864 The rebel Quartermaster informs the detachments that Winder has received orders to parole all prisoners and send them to Federal lines as soon as transportation could be procured. On the 9th of August heavy rains washed away the earth supporting the stockade in four places. Double lines of troops are placed before the openings, the guns manned and three shells fired over the stockade as a warning. This action is greeted with laughter on our part, and I believe many were anxiously praying that firing amongst us would begin in earnest. The many determined faces and set lips foretold the fire that lay slumbering ready to break forth. Lumber is sent into the prisons to build shelters dispelling all ideas of exchange.

Letter from E. Cook to his Sister

Bermuda 100 Va. Aug. 14th 1864

My dear Sister
I received two papers this evening from home. I shall not try to write you a very long letter as the time is late and I am sleepy. We have just received a very refreshing little shower just enough to lay the dust for tomorrow. We need a good rain very much to cool the atmosphere and refresh our weary troops. The 2d Corps and the balance of the 10th Corps crossed the James last night and made an advance towards the City of Richmond this morning. I do not think it is a genuine attempt to take Richmond but merely a diversion to weaken the rebel force at some other point. The 2d Corps embarked at City Point yesterday and then dropped down the river

a short distance until night, when they steamed up, and about 10 or 12 oclock, they all sailed past Bermuda 100 in sight of an our office. I sat up until very late watching them pass. It was a pretty sight but it was saddened by the thought that before the same hour next morning many of them will have {unknown word} their last journey and fought their last battle. Yet all are unconscious of their fate, and many are passing their last hours on earth in sweet untroubled sleep, on board the boat that carries them toward their graves. There is no reliable report from the scene of operations, but we have heard quite heavy firing in the direction of the troops that would indicate some severe fighting. I feel as though I ought now to be with my regiment, yet I cannot but think that it is through a kind providence that I have been kept were I am and I have no inclination to rush into danger when duty does not call me.

You speak of having fast day at home, and ask me if we kept it here. I recollect to have heard that the president had appointed a day of fasting and prayer but had forgotten all about it, and when the Captain told me how universally it was kept at home I was surprised for it has slipped by us without even eliciting a single remark that I am aware of. You speak of Capt. W. as being so universally liked. He is indeed a fine young man and of very promising aspects. I like him very much but, although I have allways stuck up for him in every other respect yet I have always said & still say that he is like the large majority of others offices, viz, he has no honor or respect for us enlisted men farther than it will advance his own interest in some cases (like my own) to treat a private with a little more than the usual portion of "Regulation" courtesy meted out by officers to the men under their command. I suppose he said that he thought very highly of me. Of course he would tell you so because he could not or dared not clothe his thoughts in any other words. If he has truly said what he meant he would have said "I value his ability, his knowledge of my business, his services" but any other enlisted man that could fill my place would do him just as well. It is a prize to a man to have a clerk who can take charge of his business for thirty day and keep things straight while he is home enjoying comforts & luxuries; and any where else, except in the army, such a clerk might have a claim on the affections and indulgence of his employer, but here it is not so. An enlisted man is no better than a dog – he can come when he is called and go when he is sent, without a murmur or a question. If a "valuable clerk" is enlisted he must ask for none of the priviledges & conveniences that are furnished to the civilian clerks. If an enlisted "valuable clerk" is sick, no matter how dangerously, and it comes under the notice of his employer, he is told to go to the doctor and get a dose of quinine. Perhaps the man is unable to walk there but that makes no difference, he must go & and return as soon as possible to resume his work. The case is different with the civilian clerk. If he is ailing slightly he must go to his quarters and have the doctor sent to him and the enlisted clerk must do his work while he is away. The ability of the one is no greater than that of the other, his services are really not so valuable. What then constitutes the difference? Simply this, one works in a uniform and draws $13 a month and is a slave, subject to orders; the other is a Civilian, wearing his own clothes, draws his $100 a month and is either his own master or else is master of his employer. I dont often grumble do I? I generally look on the bright side, but I must still declare that are enlisted mans experience is that of a dog or a slave.

In one of your letters you spelled asylum with 2 S^{es}. It only has 1 S.

Don't run down Genl Grant yet. He was not the one to blame for the Petersburgh failure. Abraham Lincoln is the man for next president.

Good Bye write again soon + direct as heretofore.

Your Loving brother
Edward L. Cook

Letter from E. Cook to his Sister

Deep Bottom Va. Aug. 23^d 1864

Dear Sister

I have at last got seated to answer your letter of the 16th I am in my company at present an in command of it. you will know how to direct. But I would rather not have you put on the Lieut. at present. Merely say as here-to-fore Edward L. Cook, Co H. 100th Regt N.Y.V. 10th Army Corps, Washington D.C. I received the stamps you sent me all right but they will be gone by the time you can send some more in your reply to this. The plural of sky is spelled skies. If you know where Robie Henderson lives I wish you would call and see him and tell him that all the boys in the company feel very sorry for him in his affliction and we all hope he will recover and live to see us return to meet him in Buffalo. I always felt a kind of pity for Robie because he is so young and he always appeared so kind and *affectionate and never flinched from doing his duty. You speak of Capt. Walbridge rejoining his regiment. Capt. W. has no regiment now. When he received his appointment from the president as A.Q.M. he was mustered out of the 100th Regt & now belongs to no regiment. I joined my company yesterday. I met Geo Stoddard on the pontoon bridge as I was coming over. He was looking well. He thinks some of coming back to the company but I advise him not to. We had a hard rain last night so that this morning was quite cool but it is decidedly warm this afternoon. I go on picket tomorrow morning. There is no news that I know of. I send you a copy of part of a letter that I wrote to a young lady in reply to one she sent to a young fellow in the employ of Capt. W. named Dan Sherman who advertised in the Waverley under the name of Fred Sommers for correspondents. I dont feel a bit like writing to day so I will only give you a short letter this time and write you a good long one the next time. I have gone to keeping house on my own hook. I bought some potatoes, onions, salt Pork, hard tack, sugar, tea & coffee; and I have detailed a man out of the company to cook for me. Give my love to Grandma and to all the rest of the folks. Write to me as soon as you receive this and send me a good long letter like the last. Write me all the news about the boys in the hospital. I have never said any thing to Lottie about my promotion. Good bye.*

Miss Laura M. Cook
Buffalo N.Y.

Your loving Brother
Edward

Alfred Lyth Diary

August 31, 1864: It is just two years ago to-day since I enlisted for three years; where shall I be when that third year has expired? None can tell; perhaps in the grave yard near here, where Union soldiers are going at a rate of eight per day.

Letter from E. Cook to his Sister

Miss Laura Cook
    Buffalo   *On picket Near Petersburgh Va*
    N.Y.   *Sept. 3ᵈ 1864 Co. H. 100ᵗʰ N.Y.V.*

My dear Sister Laura
    Your letter of Aug. 22/64 No 106 was received last evening with two papers the Christian Advocate & the Commercial. I received a day or two ago a letter from you and one from Lila but your letter No 106 is the oldest date. I will answer it first. I have been quite busy lately making out the muster rolls of my company. I made out the first copy one day when I was on picket last time and during the two days and nights that I was in camp I made out the other three copies. The illness of one of the Captains of our regiment places me to day in command of two companies on the picket line. There is not 1/10 part as much shooting to day as there was when we first came to this vacinity. Scarcely a shot is fired along the whole line during the day and not near as many at night as there used to be. Once in a while if we explore {unknown word} too much and too long they will send us a couple of bullets as reminder of our proper positions. The rebs are very anxious about the Chicago Convention. They want Seymour or Fillmore nominated. They think that McClellan is somewhat to be feared as being too much of a war democrat. But the nominations are now made and we are anxious to hear what the {unknown word} say about it. There has been no exchange of papers on the line today but perhaps there will be before night. There is a rumor that Sherman has Atlanta and, if it is true, I think very likely the rebs will allow no communication between the pickets for a day or two. There were no particulars rec'd of affair but the general impression seems to be that Hood has evacuated and is coming up to assist Lee in retaking the Weldon road. I fear for Grant but trust he is prepared. We have received a few reinforcements within a day or two and they have all marched to the left towards the Weldon road. I have never yet lost confidence in Grant and I am not going to despair now. If he had only had 50,000 fresh troops at the time of the Deep River affair and when he took the Weldon road this war would today be 6 month nearer the end than it is now, and if we can only get a few more troops to enable us to hold our ground against the combined forces of Lee & Hood we can perhaps do

as much good we could by a fierce battle. We have now fortified ourselves so strongly at this point and have so many guns mounted that our artillery can hold our position here with a very small force of infantry for picket duty and I think it is very likely that if Hood does attempt to reinforce Lee, our corps will be ordered to the Weldon road to assist in defending our position there. I think Lee will have a hard task to drive Grant back from his present line of works. Things are coming around all right by & by and I hope it will be very soon. I would like to see a peace but I dont wish to see such a peace that in a few years we shall have to fight it over again. I dont wish to see a dishonorable peace. What will our once glorious country be worth if we acknowledge the right of any state to withdraw herself from the union whenever any measure is adopted in the general congress, for the general good, that does not suit the wishes of any one state. Why our country would not be worth living in and I should be ashamed to own it and should want to live in Canada or South America or some other place where they had a government worthy of respect. I dont know what to think of McC's nomination. The idea of nominating a War Democrat on a peace platform is to me very ludicrous. And then what a platform. It is so very ambiguous that almost any party could nominate a candidate on it and then he the candidate could put any contrivetion on its meaning that he saw fit. If the war faction of the democratic party can succeed in keeping the name of McC before their faction and hiding from their supporters the principles of the platform and if the heads of the peace faction can succeed in keeping before their supporters the platform and hiding the candidate they may unitedly elect their McClellan but if the eyes of two factions can be opened to see this sharp political intriguering for the reins of government and the handling of hundreds of millions of money then good bye to their pretty acheive & success to old Abe. I have every hope that if Abe is reelected he will push this war to speedy end and let us have an opportunity to see our homes again.

Mr. Stowits sends his regards to all of you and requests as a particular favor that you will speedily pay a visit to his wife and family and cheer them up. Go by all means. Mr. Stowits has the name of being the bravest man in the regiment. I wish such could be said of me. Dave White will not go home this September. Charlie Deyo is in the 47th N.Y. I think his time expired last month and he is very likely on his way home. Who is Emma {unknown name}? Give her my love and send me her picture. I have not heard from Ella H. since I was at Gloucester Point. I received a letter from her while I was there but it was such a tardy reply to my previous letter that I never answered it. It is too bad you have dropped the acquaintance of Nellie S. I used to think much of her but she is out of mind now.

Give my love to Grandma and to all the rest. I will send you a Richmond paper if I can get one tomorrow. Tell Mr. Lyman he owes me a letter. Goodbye

> *Your loving brother*
> *Edward L. Cook*

Letter from A. Lyth to T. Maharg

Camp Sumter, Andersonville
Sept. 3rd, 1864

Dear Friend Tom

I send you these few lines to let you know that Jim Pixley and myself are in good health, also that Tom Russell is doing well. When we first came to this prison there was about 130 of the Regt but 15 of them have died since. There was 12 from our Co. mainly T. Russell, C.R. Moss, C. Fone, A. P. Cushman, T. B. Reynolds, W. Bishop, A. Tomes and myself and Jim. We are also doing well except W. Phillips who is in the hospital with the scurvy. We oft wish we were with you and the old Salt Junk again. Give my best respects to all the boys. Sergt. Maj. Jones is well. Jim sends his regards to you all.

From your old friend,
Alfred Lyth

Alfred Lyth Presentation

[September, 6, 1864]

"There is a great ecstatic thrill pervading the whole camp. Eighteen detachments were ordered to be ready to move at a moment's notice. At last! At last! This last rumor really looked as if it would really amount to something. Some said, "We have been lied to so often and believe there is no truth in the rumor." However, the next morning a line of men from the hospital were seen moving towards the railroad station, and five detachments go out to the cars, and we really now believe they are off for our lines and "God's country."[28]

Alfred Lyth Diary

Sept 6, 1864: Eighteen detachments were ordered to be ready to move at a moment's notice. At last! At last!

September 12, 1864: When my regiment got orders to go to the cars, I am unable to accompany them. [swollen and inflamed foot] Comrades J. Pixley and Al Tombers urged me to make the effort and undertook to lead me, but it was of no use.

September 14, 1864: All who left the stockade the day previous returned, the train bearing them having run off the track; several were killed and about forty were wounded. One of Company B, of the 100th, was killed and two badly wounded.

September 15, 1864: All the sick that could walk to the station were told to get ready. I determined to make one grand, determined effort. Having reserved our tent saplings, I got some men to make me a couple of rough crutches. By this aid I got through the gate past the guard, where I sank to the ground completely exhausted and unable to maintain an upright position any longer. Determined not to give up, however, seated on the ground, the lame foot elevated in the air, I propelled myself to the cars, crab fashion, and being assisted into an old baggage car by comrades my spirits soared to the skies, and the happy, blissful contemplation of being homeward bound, seemed to fill the world with sweetness, and for the time being made me forgetful of pain and hunger.

Alfred Lyth Presentation
[September 16, 1864]

"The train which bore us from Andersonville arrived at Macon, Ga., early in the morning of the 16th of September, and reached Augusta the same afternoon, where we changed cars for Charleston, S.C. Late in the evening, the train stopped at a place called Lawrenceville, and it dawns upon us that we are not going to Charleston to be exchanged, but are going to some other prison. On the afternoon of the 18th we are ordered off the cars a few miles above Florence, S. C. and commanded to get in line to march to another stockade, two or three miles away. Oh! The agony of that keen disappointment! Can these fiends of rebels have hearts at all, to deceive suffering, dying men in the systematic manner! Many of our poor fellows lay down beside the railroad track and died. All that could walk were taken to the stockade. Those unable were told to get there as best they could, no means of transportation at hand. My wound was very painful. I, however, began the slow crab-like process toward the prison, in the hope of receiving some attention for my wound, and something to eat. It rained during the night, the weak and sick being scattered all along en route from the railroad to prison, the whole line being covered with dead; the poor fellows, becoming exhausted, stopped and died, many expiring on the spot where they were lifted off the cars.

The 20th was a dull, heavy day and showery; the sick and wounded are gathered together under some trees outside the prison, which is a stockade similar in construction to the one at Andersonville. My foot is now in a very bad condition, gangrene getting in its work in fine style, the suffering from pain being intense, and that dread affliction, scurvy, is causing my gums to swell and bleed. The collection of sick and wounded under the trees is classed as being in the hospital, and rations for the time being are far better than at Andersonville – rice, sweet potatoes and corn bread- but having no means of cooking, it is eaten raw. No medicine for the sick and bandages for the wounded for several days.

E.V. Austin, a Massachusetts soldier, on the 23rd cooked some food for me. Otherwise, in my helpless condition, I would have to go hungry. On the same day, a farmer brought in some milk and biscuit. I received one biscuit and one gill of milk, having begged it to make a poultice for my foot, but I was so hungry that I divided with my foot, eating one-half and using the other for poultice. Up to the 26th, no medical treatment whatever had been received and rations were cut down to so small an allowance that there was not even enough to sustain life, many actually dying for want of food.

September 27th will ever be a day to be remembered. Having suffered such intense pain during the past week, and acting on the advice of a rebel doctor, I consented to submit to an amputation of the foot; in fact several days previously I had myself requested the operation and then backed out. This day, however, several operations were to take place, and the surgeon in charge, with several young men, medical students, was on hand to assist in the operations. I was laid on a couch of pine boughs, covered with an old blanket, awaiting my turn. A young man named Dr. Clark, who was a hospital steward in our navy when taken prisoner, and under parole as an assistant in the hospital department, happened to be passing where I lay. Noticing my forlorn and dejected condition, he stopped, asked a few questions and examined the foot, then gazing upon the prostrate and helpless figure before him he shook his head in a sympathetic manner, at the same time muttering his thoughts, which were not intended for my ears. I caught part of his words – "Poor boy! Poor boy! I believe I could save that foot."

Ah, how the blood thrilled through my veins as I caught those joyous words that to me meant life.

"Dr. Clark," I cried, "you shall have the chance."

"Too late," he replied, and passed on. Soon my turn came for the operation. I said to the doctor, "I have changed my mind and will not have the operation performed."

"Tut, Tut, young man," replied the Chief Surgeon, "There is no use; it must come off; there is no other help for you.

Besides, I understand you have requested this yourself." Rising to a sitting posture, I said "Doctor, I have changed my mind. If you cut that foot off, you will have to kill me first. I might as well die fighting for life as in any other way, because if you cut the foot off I will die anyhow."

The young fellows gathered about the couch on each side, grasped hold of my arms and laid me down, one having hold of each arm and one of each leg. I began a desperate struggle, and wrenching one of my arms loose and swinging it blindly with all the force possible, I struck the doctor in charge a terrific blow in the face, drawing blood. Two of the students immediately grasped clubs and were about to strike when the good old fellow who had received the blow stopped them saying: "Well, that boy's got some spunk left; we'll attend to his case later on," and passed on. It might be said here that I never heard of a single amputation either at Andersonville or Florence that did not prove fatal.

The next day Dr. Clark burnt the gangrene from the wound with a blue powder, and, as I was afterwards informed, it took six men to hold me while the burning process was under way, and that I was raving all night; however the following day when the wound was washed, it presented a very good appearance, fleshy parts looking red, the ligaments and bone being rather dark or black looking, the foot a little swollen. The results of the treatment gave me considerable relief from pain and an opportunity to get a little sleep at night, although it was very cold. The rations for several days were one and one half hard tack and four spoonfuls of molasses for 24 hours."[29]

Chapter Eleven

Virginia Campaign
Operations around Petersburg, VA
September, 1864 – February, 1865

"Your letters always do me good for they are full of Christian faith and holiness. My trust is in the Lord. Without him I should be weak indeed. I have a hope that if God sees fit to deliver my body unto death during this war my soul shall live to find a home & {missing word} in heaven. It adds much to my present happiness to know that my friends pray for me, and that they have strength & faith to put their trust in God and permit Him to shape the course of events and {unknown word} to submit unto Him all the ways of life and all the future of our friends. Still continue to think and pray for me for I need a mothers prayers. Temptations are many & powerful and it needs the strength & faith of a true Christian to withstand them."
E. Cook Letter dated 10/6/1864

"Grant does not make a move until he is ready to make it. His army lies apparently inactive for a time, everything seems to indicate that the campaign is closed, and men and officers begin to build their winter operations, but all the time Grant is not asleep - he is cautiously and silently working in some unexpected quarter – adding weight to the vast mass that he intends to move, concentrating every thing towards the complete success of his plan and when every thing is ready, when a move is least expected and where it is least anticipated, he puts the mass in motion and it rolls on and on and over every obstacle until the design is accomplished and the plan carried out completely & effectually in all its points. This is Grant. He is now apparently inactive, engaged merely in {unknown word} up defensive work, but in reality working out beneath this calm exterior a plan of stupendeous proportions – a mighty storm is brewing + soon it will reach its proper temperature and then it burst over our enemy and overwhelm them in its onward flood working ruin in their army and destruction to their hopes". E. Cook Letter dated 10/25/1864

Letter from E. Cook to his Sister

Camp of 100th N.Y. Vols.
Near Petersburgh Va. Friday Sept. 23/64

My dear Sister Laura

 I am sorry to see that I have allowed myself to get so far behind times in answering your letter. I received your letter No. 111 last night so that I am now 3 letters behind hand in answering. I am glad to hear that you have commenced to attend the seminary and are in the Collegiate department. I hope you will try and improve your time and study hard. I enclose ($50[00]) Fifty dollars. You can use as much of it as you wish and whenever you want any more just let me know and I will send it to you, or if you want to use any before you could have time to get it from me you can draw it out of the bank. The bill I send you is a fifty dollar compound interest bearing note, so you had better not break into it if you have any loose change lying around for your immediate necessities. It is better to keep these bills than to deposit them in the bank provided you do not want to use the money for three years to come as they draw much more interest than the bank can afford to pay. But after all I will not advise you. I make a present of the Fifty dollars and I wish you do with it just what you please and never tell me any think about it. Tell Eliza that I will remember her the next time I am paid. There is no news of any importance. The weather is damp and disagreeable. I have to go on picket again to night and be gone 3 days & nights. The last time I was on picket I was placed in charge of Co "J" on the left of the skirmish line. There is no continuous trench on the left skirmish line and, therefore, as the rebel lines and ours are in close proximity, they being on the top of a small rolling hill and we at the base, it is extremely hazardous in relieving the men which can be done only at night when they cannot see us, and very silently that they may not hear us. The rebs have the advantage of us at that point for they have a trench all along the front and can relieve without danger to themselves. I was never on this line but once before and that was the first time we ever went on picket here. Then the rebs and us were on the very best terms and we used to expose ourselves in open day, and even went so far as to meet half way between the lines and exchange little trinkets. At that time it was the best part of the line for there was no picket firing either day or night but now it is the very worst part of *the line and the only part that is fully exposed to the fire of the enemy and that has no protection or approaches. Well when I took my relief out I was given a small number of shovels to complete the pits & form a continuous trench. I was told that the work had been commenced and was nearly finished and that I could finish it with my men in one night. I moved my men forward down a ravine until I approached the right part of the left line. Here I found the officer (belonging to the 10ᵗʰ Conn. Vols) who had charge of the line the night previous. I tried to get some information from him about the number of posts +c but he was crouched up against the side of his pit and all the information I could get from him I could put in my eye. He said he had not been along the line and kept begging me to come in the pit out of danger and send my men along the line alone. My orders were to halt my men at some safe point and send them out in squads of threes to relieve the old pickets. I might have done this if I could have obtained any information from the 10ᵗʰ Conn officer, but as I could not, I had to go along the whole line and find out where the posts were and how many they were and how many men it required before I could post my men on a post. This I did within stones throw of the rebel line. I relieved the old picket and posted my men all right and to my own complete satisfaction and never lost a man or had a man struck. I think I hear you say "brave boy" "courageous act" "wonderful preservation" +c. All this would have been true under certain circumstances, but it happened on this particular occasion that the Jonnies did not fire a single shot which probably accounts for the fact that nobody was hurt. Well when I had my men posted I tried to start them at digging but the ground was so hard that the shovels would make no impression on it. I then went away back to the rear and tried to get picks but I could not get them and returned to tell the men to use their bayonets as far as possible but, during the interval that I was gone the moon arose and the firing commenced. I started to go along the line again but the bullets came ahead of me & over and behind me and when I got about half way I dived into a pit until the moon got behind a little cloud and then I started back for the pit where I staid for I knew if I got to the end of the line I should not be able to get back until the next night unless the sky clouded up so the rebs could not see me. I told the men in the pits as far as I went what to do & then left them to themselves. The next night when I went round with new relief I told the officer in charge just what was wanted and gave him instructions so that he could make twice the headway that I did the night previous. I came in all right and brought all of my men in safely but you can judge whether it was a hot place or not when I tell you that the men fired from 100 to 250 rounds of cartridges each and the rebs fired full as much as we did if not more. But I must close for I have 2 or 3 more letters to write to day. I was down to Bermuda Hundred day before yesterday and saw Capt. Walbridge and the boys. The Captain did not even invite me to stay to dinner but perhaps it was because he had no conveniences. I had dinner with the clerks and was well satisfied. The Captain looks well and received me very kindly. Give my love to Grandma and tell mother that I have received her letter and will answer it soon. I will also write to Aunt Harriet the first opportunity. Good bye.*

Write as soon as possible. Some poor soldier has gone to his last home – I hear the band playing the doleful "Dead March"

Your affectionate brother
Edward L. Cook
Co. H. 100th N.Y. Vols.

Miss Laura M. Cook
  Box 1463
  Buffalo
  Erie Co.
  N.Y.

Letter from E. Cook to his Sister

Camp 100th Regt. N.Y. Vols.
Near Petersburgh Va. Friday Sept. 27/64

My dear sister

 I received three papers from home to night. The last time I wrote to you we were on the point of marching. We broke up camp that same night and marched to the rear a distance of 2 miles or so. We were relieved by the 2^d Corps. We are encamped in a field between two woods. We are out of range of bullets and out of line of shells. The rest of our Corps is encamped in the same field. We are altogether again the camp of one regiment joining right on to that of another for the distance of nearly a mile. Oh! it seems so good to be once more out of range where we can sleep above ground and not *have to live in holes and have {unknown word} and proofs and earthworks built above and around us. I never experienced such a perfect feeling of relief as the first day we pitched our camp in this position. In our old camp we could not step out of our tents without hearing a bullet go ping or pish or burr, over our heads & then chug as it struck the ground. Our men are feeling as merry as crickets & happy as birds. The reversion of feeling experienced for us all on account of the sudden and unexpected change from a position of constant danger to one of perfect safety is almost miraculous. I cannot describe it but I can realize it and one must needs be placed in the same situations to rightly understand it. It was not fear, that in our other camp, kept down our spirits and destroyed our natural flow animation. It could not be fear for we never for a moment hesitate to go from tent to tent or lounge about in the company tents and talk and transact business even when the bullets were flying the thickest. What was it then? It certainly was something – a constant knowledge of our danger and a knowledge that at any moment we might be called to face our Maker, and give an account of our stewardship. There certainly is such a change in the feelings of the men that they seem like a different set of individuals. I only hope that we may continue in our present camp for some length of time but I fear not. We are reorganizing for another campaign in some direction or other. My belief is that we are going to North Carolina to fight during the winter as long as the weather will permit. Our corps is being reorganized in as complete a manner as it was at Gloucester Point before the commencement of this present campaign. If we were going to Bermuda or Deep Bottom to make a move there we would not wait here to fit up the regiments with clothing +c and instruct men in drill of company & Battalion as we are doing here. In the morning we have company drill & in the afternoon battalion drill with knapsacks on. It is reported to night that our division has received orders to be ready to march but even if it has it may be several days before the final order comes to strike tents & get up & git. I see George Stoddard now every day. I took dinner with him on the day after we arrived here. George is looking first rate. He has been ordered back to his regiment but as the order emanated from Division Hd. Qrs. and he is detailed from Corps Hd Qrs. I do not think they can get him back. I told him not to come back on any account if he could by any possibility manage to remain where he now is. He is having first rate times in comparison to what he would have if he was to come back to the regiment. When you write again I wish to know* *all about how you are getting along with your studies and how you like the institution and its associations. Have you formed any acquaintance with Capt. Walbridge's sister or sisters. Whenever you want any money for books or clothes or tuition just let me know and I will get it for you if possible only you must pay attention to your studies and not let dress or other such influences draw your attention from its proper direction. Feel above the low minded, the bad dispositioned and the haughty-aired persons who will surround you; and do not let their taunts & slurs or sneering looks and insulting acts deter you from pushing straight forward and showing your own vast superiority over such dispositions by your excelence in deportment, character & studies. Learn too to love your country – learn its plans, its principles, its design, its laws, its government, the foundation on which it stands, the material of which it is built and then you will not have to <u>learn</u> to love it for such knowledge of such a country can only conduce to love – a love almost divine and second only to our love for Him who has given us life & being.*

Let our <u>young</u> girls acquire such a love and let it grow with them, and then when they have become mothers and a new generation is born, let them instill it into the hearts of their sons and daughters, and what power on earth think you would be strong enough to wrest our country from its people. <u>Union</u> is strength, but the great <u>power</u> of a country to sustain herself against the machinations of traitors at home & enemies abroad lies in the "Amor Patria" of her people. Love your country!

I have still three letters remaining unanswered. Two of them are yours & one Eliza's. I answer them in the order of their dates so Lili must not pout and think I am neglecting her for if her letter had been dated before your letter No 110 I should have answered her first. Give my love to your friend Em – something – (the blonde with yellow hair) I dont admire yellow hair, but I love the rosy cheeks & pearly teeth and dont object to the blue eyes. If she had red lips and a pretty mouth you may pick out a good looking fellow to kiss her for me or if she object to that I will come home and kiss her myself. This cruel war is almost over. I know it. – I feel it. and we are coming home 300. Then lookout girls for we are like wild men & with our heads unshaven & unshorn are enough to {unknown word} to flight about. Eleven hundred & Eleventy-Eleven young ladies. I wish they would send some of our regiments back for a home guard; we would take care of the miserable traitorous Copperheads and put them where they would never bother this country again or any other country. Dont they want this war to end? If they dont we do and we are going to end it, if He *will permit and surely He is on the side of the right, and end it so that it will stay ended and we will never again be bothered with the sentiments of nullification and secession. Give my love to dear old Grandma and tell all the folks that I should be pleased to hear from any & all of them.*

Has Col. Dandy arrived in 'B' yet? Pardon the look of this letter. I am awful sleepy and am going to bed immediately if not sooner so good night. My Love to All.

Your Aff Brother
Edward L. Cook
Co 'H" 100ᵗʰ N.Y. Vols.

Miss Laura Cook
Buffalo
N.Y.

Letter from E. Cook to his Sister

On Picket before Richmond Va.
Oct. 6ᵗʰ 1864 Thursday

My dear Sister
    The weather to day is warm and pleasant but has certain indications of approaching rain, so I will try and finish a letter to you before another rainy season sets in. If a rain comes at this time of year it is sure to last at least 3 day and as a general {unknown word} even longer. I will give you a short sketch of our moves up to the present time as taken from my diary.

Saturday Sept. 24/64 Our regiment & brigade were relieved from picket this evening after dark by troops belonging to the second corps. On arriving in camp we found every thing packed up and ready for a move. While lying off at my case & waiting for marching orders to march, who should come along but Dean Wilson – he is Lieutenant in the 155ᵗʰ Regt. He looks as natural as the day I last saw him in "B".

Sunday Sept. 25/64 We marched about 2 miles to the rear last night but instead of moving in a direct line we took a very circuitous route of nearly 5 miles. We stopped, and after breakfast we went into camp near where we stopped last night. The weather was lovely and the men are feeling in the best of spirits for we are now out of range and for a time out of danger. I have been and am now on duty as officer of the day.

Monday Sept. 26/64 I came off duty this morning as officer of the day & had company drill this afternoon. I took dinner with George Stoddard yesterday.

Tuesday Sept. 27/64 Had company drill this morning and battalion drill this afternoon. It was the first battalion drill I had taken part in for about two years and of course I was quite green but I got along without making many mistake and did very well considering my want of practice.

Wednesday Sept. 28/64 Had company drill this morning and received orders to be in readiness to march at 3 P.M. Broke up camp & were in line at the appointed time. There are many rumors as to our destination. Some say we are going to the rear to receive pay – some say we are going to Bermuda to relieve the 18th Corps but the large majority think we are going to North Carolina and there is some foundation for such a rumor as all our preparations seem to indicate a move by water.

Thursday Sept. 29/64 After a very fatiguing march last night through woods and over bad roads, crossing the Appomattox & then the James river on pontoons we found ourselves at 2 ½ oclock this A.M. halted at Deep Bottom. This does not look much like going to North Carolina. We stacked arms and laid down in our places with orders to fall in again at 4 oclock and continue our march.

A little after the appointed time we were under arms and moving forward towards the enemy's works. Just as we entered the woods we were surprised by a sudden and continuous rattle of musketry on the left. Our regiment which was reduced by straggling to less than half its proper number yes! less than 100 men was deployed as skirmishers on the extreme right. We advanced slowly, cautiously but surely until we came out in front of the rebs forts. We were not opposed as we expected {unknown word} and it was fortunate for us for we were in a perilous position skirmishing through a wood where they could have raked us with artillery if they had known of our approach & chosen to do so. We afterwards fell back to a position on the road. Here we rec'd a few shell from Jonny but they did us

no damage. Soon the cheers on the left announced to us the fact that the
storming party (Negroes) had been successful in their charge and carried
the enemy's position. Then the order came to forward and we forwarded
driving the enemy before us for 4 or 5 miles where he made a stand having
been reinforced from the city of Richmond. We could not dislodge him by a
direct attack so our division moved to the right up the Darbytown road to
within 3 miles or less of Richmond while the 2^d Division charged their line,
but did not succeed in taking the works. We then fell back about 3 miles
where we turned the last line of the rebel works taken by us and entrenched
ourselves.

Friday Sept. 30/64 Our position remains unchanged we are about 6 miles
or so from Richmond. We have been strengthening our line to day and now
we have no fear of being obliged to fall back before an attack of the enemy
unless they flank us which they cannot afford to do unless they have more
men than we give them credit for. They did try to take back the works
we took at Chapins farm on the left but they lost most heavily – charging
three times without accomplishing their object. It is beginning to sprinkle
so I will close now & try & write again tomorrow. I rec'd the combs you
sent me. I thank you for them but I wish now you would send me a pair
of wooden ones. My stockings are holey & sole-less. I wear them with the
heal up on top of my foot. The next change will be to sew up the leg of
them & wear them in that manner. Our baggage is all at Deep Bottom &
we cannot get at it. Send me a few more stamps & if possible a clean shirt.
The shirts you sent me before lasted well but they faded the first time I wore
them. There is no news of any kind. I am on picket to day and have no
overcoat. Mine was stolen from me two or three {missing word} when I
was out of camp on fatigue. I have not yet heard from the 50 dollars that
I sent Laura. Did she receive it?

The rebs here are very friendly. They exchanged papers with us to day
and wanted to trade tobacco for coffee but I would not let the boys trade
such material. I sent you an old Richmond paper today and will send you
a later one if I can get it. I am well and feel first rate. If the rain does not
last long I will write another short letter to mother and enclose it in this.
Give my love to all the folks. I dreamed the other night that Grandma was
dead but I trust my dream is not true and was not true for a long time yet
to come! Remember me to Grandma & tell her I often think of her. My

respects to Mr. Lyman & family & my love to all the girls including your friend "Em".

Write to me as often as your studies will permit for I always love to receive a letter from my sisters & once in a while one from somebody's else sister. I wrote to Eliza day before yesterday or the day before that Good Bye

Miss Laura Cook	*Your loving brother*
Buffalo Erie Co N.Y.	*Edward L. Cook*

Letter from E. Cook to his Mother

On Picket before Richmond Va.
Oct. 6ᵗʰ 1864 Thursday

My dear Mother

I ought to have answered your letter sooner but I had no good opportunity to do so and indeed I am even now writing under difficulties. I wish you would write to me much oftener. Your letters always do me good for they are full of Christian faith and holiness. My trust is in the Lord. Without him I should be weak indeed. I have a hope that if God sees fit to deliver my body unto death during this war my soul shall live to find a home & {missing word} in heaven. It adds much to my present happiness to know that my friends pray for me, and that they have strength & faith to put their trust in God and permit Him to shape the course of events and {unknown word} to submit unto Him all the ways of life and all the future of our friends. Still continue to think and pray for me for I need a mothers prayers. Temptations are many & powerful and it needs the strength & faith of a true Christian to withstand them. I dare hardly think of the many sins that I commit but I pray God in that all powerful name "Christ Jesus our Redeemer" to forgive my sins and strengthen me against the hour of temptation. If truly good works and the obedience of the commandments could make us whole and give us the everlasting life where would our salvation be and who among the Sons of Men could hope to find mercy at the {unknown word} of God. But may the Great {unknown word}! be forever praised – He has opened unto us a way where by we may be saved even through the blood of his own dear precious Son.

And we though sinners vile as earth may hope for {unknown word} at His throne for sinners fallen from their birth, his precious blood will full atone. His precious blood His sacred blood – each drop is worth a thousand lives – 'Twas spilled for all – the bad the good & for every soul that seeks & strives. Great God be praised that he has given to ev'ry man that hateth sin a way of entrance in heavin by which the good may enter in

> *Thou precious One, thou sainted One*
> *To Thee give we our holiest love*
> *Thou suffered for the sins of men*
> *Prepared for them a home above*

Adieu dear mother until I write again and pardon this ill looking letter and I hope that the next time I write it will be under circumstances where I can have more & better conveniences.

> *My kindest love to all*
> *Your Affectionate Son*
> *Edward L. Cook*
> *Co H 100ᵗʰ NYV*

Mrs. Lyman Cook
Buffalo
N.Y.

Letter from E. Cook to his Sister

> *Camp 100ᵗʰ N.Y. Vols.*
> *In the field before Richmond Va.*
> *Oct. 25ᵗʰ 1864*

My dear Sister

It has been almost a week since I rec'd a letter from any person, but I cannot find any fault for of course I cannot expect to receive letters if I do not write any myself. I am in good health but my cold still hangs on a little though it is gradually winding up and I am in hope that it will soon make its final farewell and leave me to enjoy the blessing of perfect good health. The weather is quite cold generally though we have some beautiful, warm & sunshiny days but the nights are always cold. We have received nearly 200 recruits at our regiment they have as shelter tents or rubber blankets so that they will be apt to suffer very much if the rainy season sets in before they are supplied. I have now 50 men present in my company and almost

30 absent sick, wounded or prisoners of war. The regiment now has men enough to entitle us to our full set of officers and I understand that Col. Dandy is going to make some promotions. Perhaps he will see fit to give me a lift and make me 1ˢᵗ Lieutenant though I rather doubt it as I do not think he is very favorably impressed with my appearance as an officer. I do not cringe and humble myself to him as some of the other officers do in order to gain his good will. I am too proud to pay homage to a man who possesses so much of the brute nature as Col. 'D' – it is against my principles and ideas of honor, and if I do not gain promotion until I force it from him by flattery and other equally degrading means that I shall always remain in my present grade. If the Colonel reforms, as he says he is going to, and gives up some of his beastly habits and tries to make a man of himself then I will try to honor and respect him and give him my support heart & hand but I <u>cannot</u> *respect a drunkard even if he were my best friend. I have promoted Dave White to 1ˢᵗ Sergt. and have recommended him for a commission. He will make a splendid officer and will do honor to his straps. If Geo. Stoddard was here now I could give him a good lift but I advised him to remain where he is. If I had my choice now between commission in the line and his situation with a chance of retaining it until my time expired I would throw up the commission and accept his place. He is not only comparatively free from danger but he is his own master. He does not have to be up and under arms every morning before daylight. He can go to bed when he get ready & get up when he sees fit. He is always sure of having a place to lay at night. he has no guard or picket duty to perform, he can go when he wishes and come when he will. His work is all done during the day and when it comes night he can lay down to quiet slumber, undisturbed to rest and dream of home and friends till morn nor think of danger nor start up at night to hear the loud drums roll or bugle call to arms. He now is safe, secure from every danger incident to war with prospects fair of seeing home and friends once more. There let him stay nor shall an act of mine do aught to call him back again to duty in the ranks. The position that we now hold is being made very strong. We have a continuous line of breast works, and good ones too, from the right of the line to the left and in front of each brigade they are building redoubts to contain from three guns upwards. This will be one of the strongest positions in the whole cordon that Grant is throwing around Richmond and Petersburgh. When it is finished a few men can hold it against a vastly superior force and thus enable Grant to remove the bulk of his army to some other point either to assail the enemy's position and force an entrance into the City or to take and hold another position towards the completion of his vast encircling chain of forts and breastworks. The works goes forward almost imperceptibly, but like a vast moving body its momentum cannot be resisted. It carries every thing before it. Grant does not make a move until he is ready to make it. His army lies apparently inactive for a time, everything seems to indicate that the campaign is closed, and men and officers begin to build their winter operations, but all the time Grant is not asleep - he is cautiously and silently working in some unexpected quarter – adding weight to the vast mass that he intends to move, concentrating every thing towards the complete success of his plan and when every thing is ready, when a move is least expected and where it is least anticipated, he puts the mass in motion and it rolls on and on and over every obstacle until the design is accomplished and the plan carried out completely & effectually in all its points. This is Grant. He is now apparently inactive, engaged merely in {unknown word} up defensive work, but in reality working out beneath this calm exterior a plan of stupendeous proportions – a mighty storm is brewing + soon it will reach its proper temperature and then it burst over our enemy and overwhelm them in its onward flood working ruin in their army and destruction to their hopes. This is my conviction and my prayer is that I may not be swallowed up in the flood but live through it all to raise my voice in thanks to Him who giveth victory to the righteous and causeth desolation to swallow up the wicked. Give my love to Grandma and all the rest. Write soon your Affectionate brother*

Edward L. Cook
Co H 100ᵗʰ N.Y. Vols.

Miss Laura Cook
    Buffalo
    N.Y.

Letter from E. Cook to his Parents

Camp 100ᵗʰ N.Y. Vols.
Oct. 28ᵗʰ 1864

My dear Parents
    I can write you but a few lines for the mail is about closed and I wish to send this to night. I received Laura's Letter just as I arrived in camp.

We have been out in the field since yesterday morning at four oclock. It was the hottest place for a while that I have yet been in but I thank God that I am safe. The regiment lost 15 men & 1 officer Lieut. Stowits who was wounded in the right fore arm. If you have not yet sent my shirts then do not send them with Lieut. Stowits for it is likely I will not receive them as he is in the hospital. If you have sent them then you had better send right up to Lt. Stowits house and if they have not sent his valise then take them out and send them by mail. Laura's Letter contained 15 P.O. Stamps which came very opportune as I was just out & needed them. I need some undershirts very much. If I left any in my trunk that are not in use I wish you would send one with the other shirts and also a pair of stockings. I send you the Law about postage on clothing but if you have lost it then you can inquire at the P.O. and they will tell you all about it.

I have not got a change of shirts or stockings and it is so long since I put on the ones that I am wearing that I cant recollect when it was.

Tell Laura to thank Em Anthony for me and kiss her to pay for the picture she sent me.

I did not lose a single man out of my company. When Lieut. was wounded he was acting as Asst. Adj't. General on Col. Plaisteds Staff he having been detailed just the day before. Give my Love to Grandma and the Girls and keep a good by share yourself. Thank God for my preservation. Surely he has been kind this far in keeping me safe from harm. I will try and write more at length tomorrow.

Good night
from your Aff Son
Edward L. Cook
2ᵈ Lt 100ᵗʰ NY Vols
Camp Co H

Mr. Lyman Cook
Buffalo
N.Y.

Letter from E. Cook to his Sister

Monday October 31ˢᵗ 1864

My dear Sister
This campaigning in the field in all kinds of weather skirmishing through woods & [ ] and bivouacking under an autumn sky all tend to

take the polish off from a soldiers garments and accoutrements. You speak of Miss Ida Haven as your seatmate. Has she not a sister of about her own age. I used to know, quite a number of years ago, two Misses Haven who lived on west Genesee Street below Franklin. They were then little girls and dressed in mourning. I always felt an interest in them because they seemed to feel an interest in each other and I seldom saw one unless the other accompanied her. They carried with them, although so young, an air of refinement and their looks, actions and deportment betokened an intelligence and experience far in advance of most girls of their age. I predicted for them a future high in the status of society, and from your estimation of Miss Ida I doubt not that my prediction will be verified. I am glad you select such characters for your associates. Ascertain what has become of the sister if they are the two that I have spoken of.

I did not notice that the outside of this sheet was so dirty until I had written one page. But I must let it go now by merely remarking that it is almost impossible to keep any thing clean out here. I think I shall commence to put up another log house in a few days. It does not seem possible that Grant can keep us moving much longer. We must go into winter quarters before long though if I put up a good house it will be with no expectations of remaining in it any length of time. I suppose that our business will be to keep the picket line established this winter and wherever the James come out and drive in our cavalry {unknown word} we shall have to go out and drive {unknown word} Jonny back to his place again.

I closed my letter last evening by saying that we fell back across the field at dusk and bivouacked in the woods. It rained nearly all night and I got wet through but each company kept up a rousing big fire of fence rails so we managed to keep warm if not dry. In the morning my company & three others were detailed to go on picket. It was dangerous work but I would rather do it then lay out in the field where we did the day before. I think that I forgot to say in my other letter that the first day closed by a charge of one of the brigades of the 2ᵈ Division in which our skirmishers advanced. The rebs poured shell & cannister in the charging party and drove them back in less than ten minutes but our skirmishers held the ground over which they advanced and during the night a picket line was established in our front. This was the line that we were to relieve the morning of the 2ᵈ Day. We expected to be shelled in crossing the field where we lay the day before the Jonnies did not see fit to open on us. The only danger therefore was from Sharpshooters. *No that was not all for while a party was advancing to relieve the extreme right of our brigade's picket line the reserve on the left of the line belonging to the brigade on our right fired 3 volleys over our boys that completely {unknown word} part of our line. They mistook us for rebs probably though I do not see how they could have done so as most of us had overcoats on. The only injury they inflicted was to wound 1 man in the head & shoot another man in the haversack & canteen. Rather poor firing I should say. About 10 oclock a colored boy came out with my breakfast. Soon the news came that the troops were falling back to camp and the picket was to be drawn in. My heart leaped up into my throat for to draw in a picket line from before an enemys work in open daylight is no easy matter or enviable task for it must be done silently & secretly so that the enemy cannot know of it and follow us up with bullets, shot & shell. However we accomplished it without the loss of a single man though the rebel sharpshooters fired at the men every time they showed their heads. We fell back out of range and there formed as fast as the men came up and then marched to Camp where I was surprised to find it was about 5 oclock when I did not suppose it was more than 1 or 2 oclock.*

The first day when we were lying out in the field seemed as long as two days because we were in active but the next day seemed to be greased it slipt away so quickly.

The next morning the rebs advanced & drove in our Cavalry Pickets so about noon we received orders to fall in under arms and advanced again. Arriving in dangerous proximity to the enemy's bullets skirmishes were thrown out, the troops formed line of battle in their rear and when every thing was ready the Cavalry charged across a field & the skirmishes advanced along the whole line. The Johnnies did not stand at all but skeddadled into the works. We held the position until evening when we retired and left the Cavalry occupying their old position. None of our regt. were hurt. God's own hand seems to be over us to protect us from all harm and shield us from all danger. I feel more thankful and prayerful than I can tell you and as God knows my heart I attribute my preservation thus far to faithful prayer & divine providence.

Now Laura I am going to ask a favor of you and if you grant you will never regret it. There is a young man, an officer in our regiment in whom I take a deep interest. He is an orphan. His experience is a romance in real life. Before he received his commission and for 6 months afterwards he never used an oath or tasted liquor but bad associations from which he could not flee although he struggled for a long time gradually had their evil influences bind themselves around him and ever since then they have been drawing him down, down into the abyss of ruin. Two or three times he has tried to rally, but no kind hand was stretched out to aid him, no kind letters came to cheer him, no thoughts of a warm welcome could comfort him for he has no home. On the day of the terrible battle of "Fair Oaks" he fought in three different regiments remaining with one as long as it stayed on the field and when it retired he moved into some other that was still in action. On the day when we lay out in that field with the pieces of shell tearing through our ranks, when every other man was lying on the ground and hugging mother earth for dear life I looked up and saw St. Nichols quietly sitting on a stump and composedly eating a dinner of fat pork and mouldy hard tack and telling his men to lie still and not be afraid as long as they saw him sitting there. When the regiment advanced in line of battle he did not get behind them and say go on men but went before and said come on boys. He is the bravest boy I ever saw and one of the noblest men I ever knew. Speak in your note of your deep interest in the soldiers welfare and tell him that the divine hand of God is in this war and his protection & love is for the faithful soldiers who are fighting in our cause. If some person would kind and christian like letters such as my sisters and mother write to I would leave off his bad habits and forsake the enticements of his false associates and become what he was a year ago an ornament. Now what I want of you, Laura, is to enclose a short note to him in your letter to me and I'll correspond with you. Do not mention any circumstance I have cited but merely request a correspondence as he is a dear friend of your brother! Do your request as an exemplification of nobility in man. Do not do this. Request him as a friend of your brother to write to you and he will do it, and you will never regret it. it will be the means of redeaming a fallen & backslidean fellow creature. Speak in your note of your deep interest in the soldiers welfare and tell him that the divine hand of God is in this war and his protection & love is for the faithful soldiers who are fighting in our cause. Make him know that God has an interest in those who are fighting our cause. Now, good bye, to pray for both of us. Give my love to Grandma andtogether with a splendid sword belt before I left to father + mother & all the rest. Write soon & tell May I will write to her next. Lili his office,

387

but they do not look as fine as they did owes me a letter. Direct your note
inside of mine to Edwin Nichols Co 'Co. H. 100ᵗʰ N.Y. S. Vols.
     Your loving brother Edward L. Cook

Alfred Lyth Presentation

[November, 1864]
     "In November the nights became so cold that many could not sleep,
and they would walk up and down the path ways trying to keep warm;
towards morning, becoming exhausted, they would lie down on the
ground almost anywhere and die. There was plenty of wood outside near
the prison, but none was allowed for fires, only one small stick for each
100 men to cook with. In the hospital corner we were furnished plenty
of wood and fires were lighted and kept burning during cold nights.
The fire over which I was accustomed to crouch nightly was located
near a railing dividing the hospital from the prison, and rebel guards
paced their beats along the line of the railings to prevent prisoners of the
stockade coming into the hospital section. During several severe cold
mornings, just about dawn, a poor little fellow would come crawling
near the line watching an opportunity when both guards' backs were
turned, to snuggle through and lie by the fire until the sun arose, with
a favorable opportunity for flanking out occurred. He was bare footed,
bare headed, having only a pair of ragged pants and part of a flannel
shirt in the shape of clothing or covering for his body. One morning,
coming rather late, there were five, including myself, waiting, expecting
his visit, and as was our custom, ready to help him get past the guard
by going to the ends of their beats and attracting their attention, while
others were ready to cover the little fellow with a piece of blanket as
soon as he dodged under the rail. But alas! "The red-headed devil" of a
lieutenant, having come in early and walking near by saw the boy get to
the fire. He rushed up and grasped him by the hair of his head and the
seat of his pants, raised him as easily as a feather and kicked him in the
stomach, beat him, then carried him and threw him over the railing,
jumped after him, dragged him away quite a distance and left him to
die. The five comrades at the fire sat down together after witnessing
this brutal fiendish act, talked the matter over, and each took a solemn
oath, that if ever it should be their good fortune to live to be released,

and they should meet that "red-headed devil", they would kill him on the spot."[30]

Letter from E. Cook to his Sister

Camp 100th N.Y. Vols.
Before Richmond Nov. 8/64

My dear sister

I know you think I have forgotten you because I have not written in so long a time but it is not so. I have made so many excuses lately that I am not going to make any more but I will say, lest you think that I have given others the preferance to yourself, that I have now on hand six unanswered letters besides your own, I answer all letters in the order of the date that they were received and we have been moved around so much and been so unsettled during the past month that I have got way behind hand in my correspondence.

I am going to try and catch up now & if I do I will keep up after this if the thing is possible. We are not even now what you may call settled for we do not know what hour we may be ordered to move. There are rumors floating about camp all the time and every 2 or 3 days we get orders to hold ourselves in readiness to fall in under arms at any moment. Every morning we are under arms at a quarter to five & formed in line of battle where we have to remain until daylight. Sometimes we receive word that an attack is expected & then we have to march out to the right of our entrenchments and remain in line until day light to prevent a flank movement where we have no breastworks. I dont hardly think that we will be ordered to advance on the enemies works this winter as he is too strongly intrenched but he may take a notion to drive in our Cavalry pickets every little while and then we shall have to advance out and reestablish them as we did the other day.

I think if the Jonnies let us alone that Gen. Grant will be satisfied to let them alone until the next spring campaign. Well this is election day. I tremble almost for the result. We are all fearing a fight at the north between the Unionists, and Copperheads. If there is fight I pray that father may take no part in it. Let him not compromise himself in any way. He does not know the horrors and terrors & trials and humiliations of a soldier's life and I pray God that he may never learn them.

I think nothing would ever tempt me to enter the Army again unless it was the imminent peril of my country. There is not wealth enough in the whole world to induce me to bind myself for another three years but then what is wealth compared to the salvation of one's own native land. Tell father not to enter the service on any account or to take any part in the deathly struggle that seems to be now threatening our homes at the North. I will answer for our family and surely one is enough where there are only two. I will do my duty – I have done it thus far and been well spoken of and I hope I may continue to do it well and nobly, but let one suffice from our family. Lilie why dont you write oftener. I will answer all of your letters when I get to them the same as I do Laura's and everybody else's.

I am now acting asst. of the regiment so I do not have any picket duty to perform but my duties are more arduous in other respects. I still have command of my company and have all the company papers & returns to make out & also have this responsibility on my hands. I must close this letter now in order to get it in the mail tonight. So good bye for the present.

Write soon
Your Loving brother, Edward L. Cook

Letter from E. Cook to his Sister

Camp 100th N.Y. Vols.
Before Richmond Va. Nov. 10/64

My dear Sister

All here is now on the {unknown word} to hear the returns from the elections of day before yesterday. I want you to write me all the news about how the election went and how it was carried on in City of Buffalo. Were there many fights and riots. I hear the 10th Conn. Vols is now in Buffalo. It is a good regiment and belongs to our brigade. We had another scare last night. The news came in that the enemy were massing on the Charles City road. We have only one fear and that is that the rebs may flank us on the right as our breast work extends only a short distance from where we are encamped and the distance from our right flank to Deep Bottom (about 3 miles) is guarded only by two or 3 scattering forts and in case of an attack in that section we should have to fight as we did on the 7th in the open field or woods without the protection of Abattis & breast works. In such a case, as our line is very long, if the rebs should mass and strike that one point in heavy force they could turn our flank and perhaps capture some artillery but I hardly think they can drive us from our position. Last night a fatigue party of 1200 men were working all night throwing up entrenchments at this weak point and by another 24 hours our line will be upwards of 2 miles farther extended to the right & rear and protected by good substantial earth works. Then if Jonny takes a notion to come down why let him come we will be ready for him.

Delays are dangerous. If they had attacked us last night they might have accomplished something but to night it will be doubtful and to morrow night there will not be much chance for them to break through any where but if they come down upon us they may make up their minds to get terribly cut up & decidedly whipped. Our regiment has never yet had the priviledge of fighting behind the many breastworks that they have built and helped to build, so many of them are really anxious to have Mr Jonny come down and give us a trial for once. It has been the lot of our army ever since this war commenced to have to attack the strongly entrenched position of the enemy and we hope that we are now in a position where he will have to come out and attack us. I was up nearly all night & I do not feel much like writing to day so you must excuse the look of this letter. My pen is also very poor and my ink not good. We are having very rainy weather at present but just the sun is shining and the air is warm and pleasant. We are edging off into our indian summer and if we do not have a move pretty soon I think we are good for the winter here. I should be kind of sorry to leave here now for I have got good quarters again. I have got a log frame built about 4 feet high and 9 feet square. Logs are set up endwise like posts in front of the tent & an opening left for a door which is made by nailing cracker box boards to a couple of pine poles & hung on leather hinges. The cracks between the logs are closed up with mud, the back end is closed with a double thickness of an old flag and the whole is covered with 6 pieces of shelter tent. I have a fire place & chimney of brick and really every thing seems quite homelike & comfortable. I hope we may stay to enjoy these luxuries for some time at least and not have to leave them as we generally do just as we get them finished. I am waiting anxiously for a letter from you in hopes that it will contain a note for Ed. Nichols. I shall be disappointed if it does not. I *don't think he has touched a drop of liquor since I wrote you. That letter of Mary's that I read to him exercised a deep influence over him and if I could only get some one at home to take an interest in him I think he would entirely reform and become what he was a year ago. I do hope your next letter to me will contain a note for him. Is Emma Anthony going to write to me? The next time I write to you I will enclose a letter from a Miss Mary C. Stauton a young lady with whom I correspond but whom I have never seen. She lives in Yorkville and writes a very good letter.*

I am sorry you have trouble with your algebra but I dont think I could help you much for it is so long since I had any practice that I suppose I should experiance considerable difficulty in stating problems. I wish when you come across a real hard problem you would copy it and send it to me just to see if I could solve it. We received news to day that Pennsylvania & Vermont have gone for {unknown word} but I dont believe it. We are waiting anxiously for the reliable reports to come in. There seems to be but little doubt here even among the democrats that Lincoln will be elected. I wrote to Lili a day or two ago. I have received several papers from home & among them a Christian Advocate containing {unknown word} in Memory +c. I heard from Lottie McLain a few days ago she has not yet gone to New York. Her mother is quite ill. I have never written to Elle Halsey. Do you ever see her & does she ever say any thing? Give my respects to Miss Emma & ask her if she is going to write to me. I have received the

Wooden Combs & they are "Bully". The horn combs are broken already. Give my Love to Grandma & father & mother & all the rest. I rec'd a letter from Lily a few days ago & also from Mr. Lyman. Good night Write soon

To Miss Laura Cook	*You Loving brother*
Buffalo	*Edward L. Cook*
N.Y.	*Co H 100th N.Y. Vols.*

Alfred Lyth Presentation

[November 4, 1864]

"One of the incidents of our prison experience at Florence should not pass without notice, and that is the interest the Rebels seemed to manifest regarding the coming presidential election at the North. McClellan was their universal favorite and they built high hopes on his success. "If McClellan is elected," they would say, "we shall have peace in a short time." On election day a quantity of white and black beans were sent into camp to be used for ballots, and all were given a chance to deposit a bean in a bag hung upon the stockade inside of the dead line, and a detachment marched up to the bag, each man being given both a white and a black bean, and allowed to vote which he chose, the white beans representing McClellan, the black ones President Lincoln. The result chagrined the Johnny Rebs very much, the Lincoln votes being considerably in the majority, many democrats voting with republicans for Lincoln."[31]

Letter from E. Cook to his Sister

You may send me a few sheets of good note paper if you wish
Camp 100th N.Y. Vols.
Before Richmond Va. Nov. 20/64

My dear Sister
I have not any news to write but as I have a little leisure that hangs like a dead weight on my hands this evening, I thought I would write to you although I mailed a letter only yesterday or day before.
You spoke in your letter of the funeral of Genl Bidwell. When I think of the pomp displayed at home over the body of one who has died in his country's service of how he is laid in state – how the flags are lowered at half mourning and droop as though they were intelligent and understood that they were mourning over the last remains of one who had poured out his last drop of hearts blood in their defence and to their glory and honor – how the people come to take a last look of him on earth and then follow, sad and mournful, the hearse that bears him to his last resting place. And then contrast all this respect, and honor, pomp & display with the contempt and sneers and abuse and ignominy that is cast upon the soldier who still lives to peril his life yet again & again for those who remain at home to dispise and shun him in society if he returns and to breath out treason & curses on his deeds if he remains, I feel as though a nation of such people were scarcely worth fighting for because they can never attain nobility of mind sufficiently to appreciate the blessings of a good home and the value of a country instituted & based on free & democratic principles and organizations.

The proper escort to a soldiers funeral is a fife & drum, and his mourners are his comrades, his shroud is his uniform and his blanket is his coffin. I rejoice that the result of the late election has shown us that all do not think that we are fighting for a vain, useless and unworthy cause. There are many still left who are proud to take a soldier by the hand and tell him "Welcome to our hearth stone" Thousands still left who are not ashamed to receive and assist the poor fellows who have become maimed & disfigured for life in the struggle to build up a name and a sure foundation on right principles for this country the best that had a name and recognition. You speak in your letter of Mr. Stowits resignation. Laura if you ever deserved a scholding in your life you merit it now and I never felt more like scholding any body than I do you now. I told you that Mr. 'S.' was the bravest man in the regiment & I still think so yet you say "Is this your brave man" +c Laura make it a point never to talk about anything that you dont know anything about. It is not on account of cowardice that Lt. 'S' would resign. It is on account of motive far more powerful & pressing than that. The only reason why Genl. Plaisted selected Lt. 'S' for his Adjt. Genl. was because he knew that Stowits would go any where that he was sent and could be trusted at any and all times for the speedy and proper execution of any order that might be given to him. He received his wound in crossing an open field in view of the rebel sharpshooters to deliver an order to the skirmishers who were posted in rear of a line of earthworks. I could tell you of instances of his personal bravery that would almost make you love the man for his courage. Why the meanest man in the regiment and Stowits own worst enemy would not say of him what you intimated in your letter. Every man in the regiment will tell you just what I have. Even the Colonel who once said (because Stowits showed a little leniency to his men) "Damn him he (Stowits) is enough to demoralise any company" always selected Stowits to go to any position of the field where he was afraid to go himself and yet must go himself or send some one to carry his orders. I dont blame Stowits for wishing to resign neither does any of the officers blame him and those who know all the facts & circumstances attending his case only wonder that he still remains in the regiment. Dont ever judge harshly in a matter about which you are wholly ignorent.

Mike who was wounded in the arm Oct 7/64 returned to the regiment to day. His wound is not quite healed but he will be able to do light duty. His time is out so he will not have to go to the front any more and he is pretty sure of returning to his home again but he cannot get discharged until the 9ᵗʰ of January I suppose. He is looking well & hearty. He was home for 5 days at Election time and says he very much hated to return.

Henry Phillips has never written to me once since I left home. I guess he feels ashamed to write and I should think he would for I know I should if I had a friend in the army with whom I was as intimate as Henry + I were and had neglected him for so long a time.

You say 'Em. 'A' sends her respects. I have no objections to respects but I should like to receive a letter along with them. Give her my <u>love</u>. I wish you would copy those line to "Addie" in that old composition book of mine where all that "<u>Alburn</u> <u>trash</u> is written. (Lines scratched out and marked "Private".) I dont think that Gracie look much like she did when I left. I dont believe I should have know her if she looks like her photograph. Those 75 men who went off with Ed Nichols on the morning of the 18ᵗʰ have not yet returned. Their 2 days rations ran out last night and they must be without any thing to eat. We have not heard from them and do not know where they are so we cannot send them anything. I feel very anxious about them but hope they are all right. I hear that the people of New York are going to send the soldiers a lot of turkeys for Thanksgiving. Wont that be old gay if they get here all right without spoiling. It has rained for the last 2 or 3 days & I pity those 75 men who have doubtless been exposed all the time with nothing but overcoats & Rubber blankets. I am in good health. The mail has just come so I will go over and see if there is any thing for me. Yes a letter No 120 & 2 papers. Give my love to father + mother + Grandma + everybody else. Good by write soon

Miss Laura M. Cook	*Your Loving brother*
Buffalo	*Ed L. Cook*
N.Y.	*Co H 100ᵗʰ N.Y. Vols.*

Letter from E. Nichols to his Friend

Camp 100ᵗʰ N.Y. Vols
Before Richmond Va.
Nov. 29ᵗʰ 1864

Dear Friend

Your welcome letter dated Nov 20ᵗʰ was received yesterday morning + pleased I was to get it. You were correct in supposing that speedy answers would be acceptable. indeed they are + I have reasons to believe they always will be from you, + so you imagined I should think you presuming. I am sorry you entertained such a thought, I knew your letter of kindness + as such I appreciate it & thank you. Ed was right in saying I had no father or mother + might have said no brother, + I might almost say no sisters. I had those once but have seen but very little of them since I was a boy. It is as you imagine lonely. Yes little do some people think how sad & lonely it is to be without Father, Mother, brother + without a home how few those are that know the real value of a good home & the love of a kind father + mother, when those are gone then + not {missing word} then do they know what they have lost; still it is enough to be thankful for every day of my life. I am blessed with good health a few kind + true friends + I am not wanting for a home. A person has no Father or Mother and they have no home. "If it is ever so homely there is no place like home" how happy a person must feel when they know that kind + anxious hearts are watching + waiting for their return; the last day of this month I have been thirty eight months in this Regt & have never received a leave of absence or been from my command a day but after the troops go into winter quarters I intend going North if I can for a short time + then if I do not change my mind I shall remain a Soldier until this war is over or until I get either killed or wounded. Day before yesterday was thanksgiven day + the soldiers had lots of nice things sent them such as fowls, Ducks, turkeys +c not in large quantities but sufficeint to let them know that they were not forgotten by the kind people North, they would have had much more but I am sorry to say a great deal that was intended for the Soldiers was appropriated by those whose duty it was to see justice done, a week ago, a week ago yesterday morning your brother Ed {missing words} to go with a party of men on fatigue for two days as was supposed but instead of the fatigue we found ourselves at Bermuda Hundred the same night a cold rain set in + continued incessantly until the following Tuesday morning + the men without the least particle of shelter + no help for it, all I could do was to have fires burning night + day + keep the men huddled together, as {unknown word} them, it would have made any ones heart ache to see the poor fellows sitting + lying in the mud trying to sleep, we were on picket Sunday + relieved at night to take up our former position behind the breast works in the mud + rain all that night + the following day the rain came down in torrents, Tuesday after the storm was over the men had their shelter tents sent them since I have been

a soldier I never saw men suffer more. Thanksgiven day we were on picket + as soon as we were relieved we received orders to return to the Regt. + in a few minutes without even waiting to get supper we were off + a delightful time we had wading through the mud, it being very dark every few minutes some poor fellow would fall + then there would be a general laugh at his expense. I never saw men in better spirits or enjoy a night march better. We arrived Home about 11 oclock the same night + since then I have done no duty thanks to a certain person you are well acquainted with, I had almost forgotten to tell you the reason we were sent to Bermuda Hundred. The night previous to our leaving the Regt. the Rebels made an attack on our picket line at B.H. + captured quite a number of men + held possesion of the center of the line, + still hold it + the troops that left here was to have taken it back again as near as I can learn
Sunday

but for some reason unknown to me it was not accomplished, the greater part of the troops stationed at B.H. were new men + as I am told slept on picket by mutual agreement + were surprised + captured as might have been supposed on the center of the line our pickets are within fifty yards of the Rebs.

there was considerable firing the first two or three days we were there but I am pleased to say only one man as far as I could learn was wounded in our detachment. I think I had better stop scribbling or I am sure you will not have the patience to read it I know this will be a very poor return for your interesting letters perhaps I can learn to do better in the future. I know I ought not to tell tales out of school but I must tell you your Brother Ed is 1ˢᵗ Lieut + please I am not only on his account but also his friends at home, if he knew I told you I presume he would not thank me excuse all <u>blunders</u> for I suppose I have made about ten thousand.

from your friend

Ed Nichols

You will plainly see by this half a sheet of paper that I do not stand on ceremony. You must do the same, that is always do as you please. write soon + oblige

E.N.

Letter from E. Cook to his Sister

Camp 100th N.Y. Vols. Before Richmond Va.
Dec. 2/64

My dear Sister

I suppose you are waiting anxiously to hear from me and I have been waiting just as anxiously to hear from you. Last night I received a letter from you and a paper containing 4 envelopes for which I am very much obliged. Before I go any farther I am going to answer a question that has been asked of me 7 or 2 times and one that I think I have answered 11 or 8 times or less viz: <u>I</u> <u>did</u> <u>receive</u> <u>Gracies</u> <u>picture</u> and if it is a good picture then I think she has changed very much since I left home for I do not believe I should have known her if I had seen her previous to receiving her picture. I received Shirt, Stockings & handkerchief that you sent me. I have had the checkered shirt washed once and it has shrunk a little but not very much. If you ever make any more you must allow about 5 yards for shrinkage. When I wrote you last I expected to be in a fight before this time and indeed we are still expecting it daily and I think it can not be long delayed. The troops are all going into winter quarters but they have had no orders to do so and therefore they cannot blame any body but themselves if they have to break up again and move. I thought at one time that Grant would remove from here all the troops that were not actually needed to hold this position and open a winters campaign farther south, but I have come to the conclusion the General's going to fight it out in this line of it.

I was mustered two or three days ago as 1st Lieut. The mustering officer said I would have to stay 3 years from my last muster but I do not believe it. I trust that when my original three years is up I can come home. St. Nichols has been promoted to Captain and right nobly has he earned it. I never saw such an improvement in a person as has taken place with him since you commenced your correspondence with him. I trust that God will some day bless you for your instrumentality in this reformation. St. Stowits has been promoted to Captain but as he is at present away from the regiment he cannot be mustered. St. Baker was mustered as Captain at the same time that I was mustered as 1st Lt. 1st Segt., Dave White Co H 1st Segt. Albert York Co 'J' 1st Segt., J.E. Head Co 'A' 1 Sergt., Mansfield Cornell Co 'C' (He used to live near where aunt Grace did on Prospect Hill) have all been promoted to 1st Lieutenants. Dave White is in the hospital at Fort Monroe *and cannot get mustered until he returns. 1st Segt. Saml. Eley Co K.. Segt. Connolly Co 'C', Sergts Heimeus & Skeldon of Co B. are promoted to 2^d Lieuts. When we get them all mustered in we will have a pretty good number of officers and our regiment will pick rapidly under their exertions and we shall soon have a first rate lot of men & a good regiment. We had a dress parade evening before last and the regiment looked first rate. I am still acting Adjutant and at the same time retain the responsibility of my company although the company is no longer mine as Capt. Baker is on my rolls & the company is now his. Col. Plaisted of the 11 Maine Vols. our old brigade commander returned last night and will assume command of the brigade to day, this will bring Col. Dandy back & he will relieve the Capt. of the Com^d of our regiment. Perhaps this will oust me out of my place. I hope it will for it is a position that I do not like and I have asked to be relieved once but the Col. would not let me go at that time.*

If we do not make a move pretty soon I am going to day and get detailed somewhere and perhaps I will any hour. Since I wrote the above I have been to see the Colonel. He intimated to me that he would appoint me adjutant if I wanted it but I most respectfully declined. I see Corneal Adriance has resigned and his resignation has been accepted. I suppose Corneal has got tired of soldiering and so have I. I dont blame him for getting out of the service for he has had a long seige with his wound and I presume it troubles him even yet but all those who are acquainted with him here, very much regret to lose him from among them. Very many of the incidents and associations of a soldiers life are very pleasant and I think if it were not for the horrors & hardships of campaigning very few would ever leave it after once entering it especially if they hold any position above that of high private. I believe that no firmer friendship can exist between man and man than that which each soldier feels for his comrades. There seems to be an influence similar to that of secret organizations which binds one to another with an inseverable tie.

I run entirely out of money this week and borrow $5[#] of Lieut. Gilbert Gaum. I lent my overcoat to one of my company who had neither blanket, rubber overcoat or change of clothes. He naturally enough became infected with Uncle Samuel's clothes and I did not dare to wear the coat after him so I made him a present of it and bought a new one of Capt. Walbridge which cost about $11[#] but I did not pay him for it. I think the Greenback Man will be around here about the middle of this month so you need not send *me any money unless I speak about it again. You may give my compliments to Miss Em. Anthony and tell her that I appreciate her good taste in not wishing to write to me if she cannot write a* <u>sensibleish</u> *letter but I opine from her very refusal that she is far from being one of those most ridiculous of all persons – a simpering young lady. I do really think that if I had my choice between a life of toil and poverty, with one of the above class for a life companion, and a life of comfort, happiness, & prosperity, with a noble and loveable woman for a companion, I would choose the latter nine times out of ten. I must begin to stop or else I shall not have room. Give my love to Grandma and father + mother + Lilie & Mary & Stephen & Gracie & Lillie and Aunt Gracie & everybody else including 'Em'. I feel so sorry for father who is troubled so much with his back. I wish he would not do any thing that will have a tendency hurt him in that region. He is getting on the down hill side of live and he must remember that any illness, injury or excess will have a far more deleterious effect on him than when he was younger. I am going to have 2 or 3 hundred dollars coming to me next pay day & then I will send home some money which will help to carry you through the winter. How many sisters has Capt. Wall ridge got? What are their names? If they look like Charlie they can not be very handsome. But I must say Good Night and pleasant dreams, Beneath branches and beside streams mayst thou in sleep appear to rest. And this I pray may emblematic be of life's bright close when having sailed the stormy sea, you sleep to wake among the blest.*

Your Loving brother

Miss Laura M. Cook   *Edward L. Cook*

Buffalo N.Y.   *Co H 100ᵗʰ N.Y. Vols.*

Alfred Lyth Presentation

[December, 1864]

"The latter part of November, we were told that we were going to be paroled, that an exchange had been agreed upon and we should soon all be sent home. As usual, a few were sanguine to believe; the majority shook their heads and muttered "another rebel hoax.

"On December 4, however, a number from the hospital were taken out and told to sign a parole. It seemed like a pleasant dream, and many expressions of joy were manifested; still it was impossible to remove all doubts from the mind. The day following we marched down and boarded a train for Charleston. The train rolled away amid cheering by ourselves. A happier lot of men never started on a journey. We were going home; that was enough to make us bright, happy and cheerful.

"On the 6ᵗʰ we were marched through the streets of Charleston to the wharf where two steamers were moored. One was the flag of trace boat, containing Rebel officers, the other a large flat deck streamer of transport for the prisoners. On board the steamer, we began to feel like free men again, breathing the pure air coming in from the sea – those dirty, ragged, disease-racked skeleton frames seemed to drink in the inspiration of freedom and joy.

". . . the trip through the harbor of Charleston, passing closely the tumble down walls of old Sumter; after I took part in that long siege on Coles, Folly and Morris islands, (had much interest to me) as one who had been . . . helping to batter down the defenses he now was passing. Reaching the outer harbor towards our fleet, the transports of the Union were waiting to receive us. From the rigging we descry the stars and stripe. To cheer? An attempt was made. Overpowering joy was too much; we could not cheer. It was a touching sight to see upturned faces, gazing upon that flag so dear to their hearts. Passing from the Rebel boat to the deck of the transport New York, it seemed like our cup of happiness was full.

"On Board, we stripped off all of the wretched garments and threw them overboard, gladly witnessing them float away, lice and all. Conveniences for a thorough wash were provided, and though the water was cold we were glad to be clean once more. We were then given a full suit of Uncle Sam's blue, with underclothing, shoes – in fact a full "rig-out". On board the New York we received our first meal of army food. Ah, boys; never again do I expect to partake of such a feast. Salt beef, hard tack and coffee; a pint of hot coffee! . . . We sang, we danced, and every man was full of happiness and contentment. Thus ended our prison life, only to be recalled in our dreams and imagination, or when in after years the seeds of disease there planted in the system would ever be reminders of our terrible experience."[32]

Letter from E. Nichols to his Friend

Camp 100th N.Y. Vols
Before Richmond Va. Dec. 9th 1864

Dear Friend Laura

Your letter dated Dec. 4th was received last evening & pleased I was to get it. I was expecting one so you see I was not disappointed. You say it is only an appology for a letter.

I think we have bid a final adieu to the beautiful weather we have been enjoying lately judgeing from present appearences last night & to day was very cold + froze quite hard + I for one am glad to get near the fire, as I am writing this the ground is white not snow but hale & the storm still continues. What a long, dreary, & sleepless night this will be for the poor fellows on picket. I think myself very fortunate in not being on duty this cold & stormy night but we are liable to be called up at any moment through the night. I expect before this reaches you you will hear some important news a great many troops left here for some place or other. I think you will hear from them in the direction of Savannah or Wilmington unless they return again in the dark + move for the Danville railroad, but it is useless for a soldier to speculate concerning Genl. Grant's movements. he deceives his own soldiers as well as the Rebels, Our Regt. fell in the other morning with three days rations & expected to move every minute but after waiting for two or three hours the men were sent to their quarters.

Your brother Ed, has just left my quarters + has gone to bed + I think I shall follow his example + finish this tomorrow, good night.

10th Last night was the roughest one we have had I think + remind us of what we are to expect this winter. You ask a question that I can readilly & willingly answer. I have no home, no Father, no Mother, no brothers & I really do not know if I have any sisters now it has been a very long time since I heard from them, I have seen them three times in fifteen years & then only for a day or two each time. I have no relation whatever in this country of course you must know I am English & came to America with the intention of making it my home + never have I once regretted it. When first I came to this country I did not know a single person but now I am pleased to say I have some good, kind + true friends & some perhaps that will be glad to welcome me should I be permitted to return North. You say excuse you for asking so many questions, to be sure I will but only on one condition, + that is whenever you feel inclined to ask any question no matter upon whatever subject it may be I shall always be pleased to answer them if I can, so in your next letter ask me ten thousand if you wish.

Evening, this is the third attempt I have made to write + now it is about 9 oclock this morning our cavalry pickets were attacked + driven in but not far. The men in the different Regiments were under arms in a few minutes + ready + I believe anxious to for the Johnies to make their appearance & after waiting & watching patiently for them until nearly seven oclock this evening we came to the conclusion they had changed their mind + the men were allowed to go to their quarters, but if we are not called up before morning I shall be very much mistaken, the guards are in a horrid condition a mixture of Virginia }, snow + the men were passing the time to day away by snow balling each other + appeared to enjoy it very much. This afternoon I saw a specimen of a Rebel soldier taken past our camp, to one of his own cavalry he was a little thing not over 5 feet in height + almost as thin as the stem of a tabacco pipe, how in the world he could carry a gun is more than I could imagine. I actually felt ashamed + mortified to think I had to fight against such children, he certainly could not have been over 15 years of age. I heartly wish this dreadful war was ended it is fearful to think of the blood + treasure that has been sacrificed & merely to satisfy a few ambitions, miserable, miserable wretches. If the war continues much longer the country will be one vast hospital + then to think of the poor widows & orphans who are left to mourn for those who are sleeping their sleep in a soldiers grave. Well I must change the subject for it makes me feel bad every time I think of it.

I am not at all supprised that you should think so much of your brother Ed + if you had seen him where I have I know you would think still more of him, You know a person in the Army shows themselves in their true colors it is the best place in the world to find out what a man is made of. Ed has <u>proved</u> himself a brave man + a good kind hearted boy. Now do not {missing word} that I say this to flatter him or because he is your brother, neither must you ever let him know that I have said anything about him.

You know what Ed is when at home + it is right that you should know what he is when away from home & all the influences. I guess I had better bring my scribble to a close + go to bed for in all probability Mr. Johny Reb will have the imprudence to call us up bright & early in the morning + perhaps before that time.

I have received several newspapers accept my thanks for them. After the troops go into winter quarters I shall try to go north for thirty days + so will visit Buffalo if nothing happens to prevent it. I have scribbled this in a hurry so dont notice all the beefstakes I have made. It is a soldiers you know.

> *hoping to hear from you soon I remain your friend,*
> *Ed Nichols*

Letter from E. Cook to his Sister

> *Camp 100th N.Y. Vols*
> *Before Richmond Va. Dec. 12/64*

My dear Sister   Laura
Your letter is the next one on the programme and I am going to answer it although I can give you only a short letter in reply. I have received two shirts from you and 2 pair of stockings and one handkerchief all of which come very acceptable. I have no objection to another handkerchief if you have one to spare. I find too that an undershirt would come very acceptable this very cold weather and I am not particular about the kind, color, age or quality as long as it is of warm material and of any color that will contrast with the color of Uncle Sams "body *guards" if you know what they are. I think I sent home a pair of Soldiers two legged mittens; if father is not wearing them I can appropriate to an excellent use out here by wearing them every morning when we have to fall out in under arms and stand in line of battle until breakfast call. The Jonnies came down here day before yesterday and we were under arms all day and standing at our works waiting for them to attack us but they moved about a half mile to our right and attacked in one of the worst places that they could have selected. Of course they were driven back with some considerable loss on their side and very little on ours. We took a very few prisoners. I do not know the*

particulars and of course never will unless see an account of the affair in the New York Herald. You have read of the little interest that a soldier feels in what occurs around him. Here we were waiting and if it were wrong I would say devoutly wishing that the Jonnies would come on and attack in front of us. Our cavalry pickets were driven in a fight occurred on our right and within half a mile of us and yet none of us has the energy or interest to walk down the line half a mile to ascertain the particulars of the engagement. I received a beautiful pair of shoulder straps this morning and greatly obliged to some kind & loving friend for the chaste present. I expect to wear them on dress parade this evening if we hold one. I hate to put them on my blouse and I almost think I shall buy a fine deep coat to correspond with the straps. I shall take great pride in telling my brother officers that they are a present. No class of persons love to display and brag over presents so well as a soldier and none know better how to appreciate them. The straps are <u>beautiful</u> and I am very thankful to the donor.

I have not yet received Miss Em. Anthony's promised letter is she going to write to me. I send you a few lines to copy into my old composition book. They will make you a good composition some time or other. I actually received by mail all the items mentioned in the bill of fare.
Good Bye
To
Miss Laura M. Cook
Buffalo
N.Y.

Write Soon
Your Loving brother
Edward L. Cook
Co H 100ᵗʰ N.Y. Vols. 24ᵗʰ Army Corps

Letter from E. Cook to his Sister
Camp 100ᵗʰ N.Y. Vols.
Before Richmond Va. Jany 2/65

My dear Sister
I wish you a happy new year. The weather? it is very cold. My health it is good and every thing goes along well. I wish Lili you would not write just such gloomy letters Every day around a soldier is gloomy enough without their gloomy letters from those who should try to enliven & cheer him up. When a person cannot take a short walk in any direction without coming across the grave of some fellow soldier and {unknown words} are right in

the midst of camps & companies I should think his life might be dismal enough to merit a little syrup {unknown word} & cheer from this friend at home who are surrounded with blessings that they do not know how to appreciate. You are growing up to fasy and second (I wont mention name) wishing you were dead. Any body that did not know you would think you were an old maid dying for love & a husband. When you have been disappointed in Love as many time as I have you will learn to look upon such matters FilliSoffiCallie and not mourn your self to death over a slight change in the would be programme. Just think, of the many losses I have sustained Abby Stone, Alice Smith, Mary Clemmens, Mary Adams, Nelli, Fannie Porter, Nellie Sherman, Ella Halsey, Mattie Butter, Susie, Nellie Hines, Lottie McLane, Sadie Lyons, Em Anthony and a million & two others too numerous to be mentioned.

I suppose you think because I write in this lively strain that I am not in earnest but I am. I have taken each one of these disappointments deeply to heart have grown so that now I dont weigh anywhere near 280 pounds. Alas!

Your Loving Brother
E. L. Cook

Letter from E. Cook to his Sister

Camp 100ᵗʰ N.Y. Vols
Before Richmond Va. Jany 14/65

My dear Sister

I have just returned from a trip down the {unknown word} River to start off our regiment. They left fort Monroe and I suppose they are now in old Buffalo. I saw the old settlement of Jamestown the home of Capt. John Smith + Pocahontas. I send you enclosed a sprig of willow which I wish you to plant. I send home some relics which I wish have preserved. You would walk down to his house on Niagara Street and get them of him. There are three plants the smallest one was cut from the old Churchyard + all the rest + write soon

Your Loving Brother
E. L. Cook
Co H 100ᵗʰ N.Y. Vols.

Letter from E. Cook to his Sister

Camp 100ᵗʰ N.Y. Vols
Before Richmond Va. Jany 22/65

My dear sister

I guess you will think I am writing in my old style of Journal form. I wish I might but my time is so uncertain that it is scarsely worth while to commence such a system for am afraid I could not carry it out.

The weather to day has been a kind misty, foggy, mixed up day. We had a regimental inspection today together with the other regiments of this brigade. The regiment that was found to be in the best order is to be excused from our weeks picket duty. I hope it may be our regiment but I am afraid that such will not be the case. I regret that I could not be the means of realizing your expectations on Christmas. I should have liked very much to have been with you during the holliday but we do not always get out likes. For instance I liked Mattie Butler but I didnt get her and I think my <u>heavy</u> *loss (how much does Mattie weigh) ought to afford you some relief and consolation for the disappointment you sustained is not having my horrible personage with you during the holliday.*

Lambert Melvin has not yet returned to the regiment and I am going to send him his descriptive list so that he can get mustered out of the service at the hospital when his time is out without coming way down to the regiment. I guess that those chestnuts that you sent to me by him will never have the exquisite pleasure of being passed between my saffron colored lips to be munched and crunched by my grinders. But I suppose they will taste just as good to Melvin as they would to me and perhaps better. I dont begrudge him the chestnuts half as much as I did the big sweet potatoes that he stole from me at Gloucester Point when I was there the first time. But after all I am glad he eat my sweet potatoes for it will serve as a reminiscence. The hire officer had a meeting tonight condemning the City of B for not giving a proper reception to the old men of our regiment. We are going to send copies to the Buffalo Papers so you will have an opportunity to learn our views on such matters. I do think that the way in which those men were received who had served faithfully for three years in the defence of their country's rights and in protecting their own and the homes of those who gave them no welcome was a shame to Buffalo and a lasting disgrace to the former magnanimity of the board of trade. What have we who remain to expect any more than they received. Poor encouragement for us to go on rough it through another campaign with the hope that our fellow citizens and friends are watching us with interest and wishing us well & patiently waiting for us to return that they might prove to us their friendship by receiving us with manifestations of welcome and good will. I hear that the board of trade is going to try and make the amends honorable by inviting the old boys to a well spread board on some future occasion. This is very well but it is not like a reception offered to returned soldiers at the time of their return. The soldier feels all these things more keenly than you think for he is accustomed to doing things rightly and he know what is right in such matters and any departure from a proper just & honorable course is more quickly perceived and more keenly felt that by any other class

P.S. A rebel ram and two rebel iron clads came down last night to try and get through our blockade of the James and cut off our supplies. We have been under arms all day expecting an attack as the rebs were in line of battle ready to make a move as soon as the ram got through but our batteries struck one of the rams and the other two got ashore and were abandoned under the fire of our guns so the rebs have ground quiescent and abandoned the instruction of driving us away from the place.

   Ed Cook

P.S. I had the regt. line and we gave three cheers for the old flag.

The colonel is on a courtmartial and I am in command of the regt. about half the time.

Letter from E. Cook to his Sister

     Camp 100ᵗʰ N.Y. Vols Before Richmond Va.
           Jany 23ʳᵈ 1865

My dear Sister

The day has been damp and drizzly and terribly wet and muddy under foot. I long for pleasant weather again. Are you having such rainy times up north or is it briskly cold and good winter weather. There has been a great deal of shelling going on down to the left. I could plainly see the flashes but could not see the shells. I think it must have somewhere near Dutch Gap from the length of time it took the sound to travel.

I am sorry you worried so much about me during the long interval that I did not write but I think I am making up lately for the delay and hope to be able to do better in future.

I am glad that Capt. Nichols letters please you but I guess his letters do not please you more than your letters please him. You say you think he writes like me but I think he writes and composes much better than I do. For when I sit down to write a letter I write just what comes into my head first without stopping to think of the fact that it may be inappropriate and out of place. Tell ma she must not cry when she thinks of me for I would rather that she would joy to think that I am in the army of the right fighting for a good cause and in the hope of a speedy and glorious victory. This war is soon going to end and I hope to see you all again in the full blush of health and prosperity. Matters are now looking more brightly than ever and God is smiling on our cause and promising by the success which he is giving us to lead us to happy close and a more perfect reunion in which the accursed institute of slavery shall have no part or foothold.

If I knew that you all desired to see me home before my time of service expires which is now but little more than 7 months I would try and obtain a leave but if I consult my own wishes and inclinations I shall not return until I return to stay. Wont that be a happy day when we meet again and not to part until some power stronger and more terrible than rebellion summons us to our last long home beneath the clay upon which we now tread in the full vigor of life & manhood. What do you mean by your other house on Delaware? I dont understand you? Please tell me immediately and dont keep me in suspense. I think you did right with him.. I did not take offence at the Psalms sent to me how could you harbor such a thought I am glad to receive them. They are such good comfort but I never did like to read them so well as I like the new testament except when I feel in low spirits or when I feel peculiarly happy and wish to give vent to my feelings then the Psalms are indeed welcome but for beauty of expression and interest I do like the new testament. But I must close I will try and write again soon.

Your loving Brother
Miss Laura M. Cook   *Ed L. Cook*
Buffalo   *Co H 100ᵗʰ N.Y.V.*
N.Y.

Letter from E. Cook to his Sister

Camp 100ᵗʰ N.Y. Vols
Before Richmond Va.
Jany 25/65

My dear Sister

I have just got around to your really welcome note of Dec. 30/64. I have got one more of your letters besides this to answer and then I shall be even with you and after that I hope I shall not keep you waiting for an answer whenever you see fit to write to me but be able to answer immediately. At one time I was about 20 letters behind hand but I have caught up so fast lately that I am now only 4 or 5 behind.

I wrote to Laura yesterday and told her about the rebel rams coming down. There is no more news about them but I think they must be a heavy loss to the confederates. There are not many desertions from our lines at present but the rebs come into us by squads and I never saw the rebels look so poorly as those do that come into our lines now. None of them have overcoats & very few of them have blankets. Some of those who came in yesterday said that the late rains had washed away the Dansville Road and they could not get up supplies and the rebs were coming down to try and get some of us. They did come down on our right but did not show fight, and this morning there was not one of them within three miles of us so the Cavalry said.

If their rams had succeeded in breaking through our wooden gunboat fleet they would have hurt us more than a little and if it had not been for our shore batteries they would have broken through for what could our wooden boats do against iron clads. All but one of our monitors have gone down the coast. The design of the rebs was to get their Rams below dutch gap and shell our rear from the river and then move a large column on our right & front & try and gobble us and our eatables but they couldent come it and if this is the way in which Jeff was going to astonish the natives than he succeeded in the accomplishment of his design for the world will be astonished to learn that his rams did not go through.

(Private) You need not return the wreath at present. Who told you that I was the best looking officer in the regiment? They were to flatter you for it is not so. I am one of the most {unknown word} figures in our

whole brigade. I am glad that you feel as you so about my coming home. You need to stay home when I do come and that is just the way I feel myself. When I get home I shall never want to {unknown word} again but I hope that that time may not be far distant when I shall be permitted to be with you all again. I long to see you to be with you once more, once more to sway back & fro in the old arm chair to read" Literature" Hugh Miller "Spakespook" and +c, to roll on the the old carpet with Gracie little spoodoodledoodle and dive in the old basement. Yes I wish with a sigh that I were there. Clouds would appear like sunshine sorrows like joy and pain swallowed up in pleasure would be forgot.

Good Bye
Your loving brother
Ed Cook
Co H 100th N.Y.V.

Lili Cook
Buffalo, NY

Letter from E. Cook to his Sister

Camp 100th N.Y. Vols
Before Richmond Va. Jany 27/65

My dear Sister

I have a little time to spare to day and as I am at present in command of the regiment I am my own master and therefore no one can blame me for employing my time as I see fit. It commenced about five oclock this morning to rain and freeze and has continued steadily all day but the cold has somewhat decreased in intensity and now it is raining without the freeze. I think you are about right in regard to the class of young men left at home. I dont think it would be possible for me to remain at home in active while my country was pouring out her life blood in a terrible struggle for freedom and existance. It is the duty of every man to come forward at his country call and offer his arms and his life if need be for her salvation and support. I have never regretted that I joined my country's cause and if I live to get through this how I shall bless God that I was permitted to lend my fickle aid to the cause of liberty and union.

You speak in your letter of Addie Barker. Do you know if she is married yet or is she still vanily waiting for me to return. How is Em Anthony? I never received that promised letter I think I have waited quite patiently for a long time without finding any fault but I am not going to wait any longer and now I want her to write to me as she has promised or else I shall think she is a story teller. By the time I receive her letter I shall have answered all letters now on hand and will be able to devote all my time and abilities to a studied and appropriate reply. Tell her to write.

I wish I could have been home at the time Uncle Ben & Aunt Susan were there for I would have given a great deal to have seen them. Uncle Ben used to be the personification of my {unknown word} ideal of an uncle. I used think that every thing good was intimately connected with his name – that is every good thing in the shape of turkey, pigs, geese +c. In my boyish imagination he was the next grandest + best man to Santa Claus. And then you had a goose for dinner my favorite fowl. I think I could almost {unknown word} a whole goose raw. If am ever again permitted to get in the vacinity of a table where goose is served up I think the host will have to thank his stars that all his borders are not such men as I am. So you are anxious to learn about my thanksgiving dinner are you well I will tell you that it was sent to me by Miss MaryC. Staunton of New York with whom I am acquainted only by letter. The bill of fare came with the dinner and every item on the bill was appropriately represented in dinner. The fish were of candy and so was the fowl. The potatoes and onions were genuine but of course were very good. The wine was claret put up in a little homeopathic vial. I think all the rest was of candy. No the cranberries were genuine and the cake also. I wrote Miss Mary a {unknown word} effusion for her donation but she never received it and now she wants me to send her a copy of it. If you will write me a copy I will send it. Give my love to Grandma and all the rest of the folks. Write Soon.

Your loving brother

Edward L. Cook

Co H 100ᵗʰ N.Y.V.

Miss Laura M. Cook
  Buffalo
  N.Y.

Letter from E. Cook to his Mother

Camp 100ᵗʰ N.Y. Vols

Before Richmond Va. Jany 28/65

My dear Mother
  Lili said in her last letter that she wrote for you while you were over to

Aunt Grace's quilting so I am going to consider it as coming from you and write the reply to you. First I will answer the questions asked in the letter. I do not know all the caused that combined to induce Dave White to leave home. He was always reserved on that front and as he never offered to recite his history I never questioned him. I learned at different times during our acquantance from various expressions and short sentences that he would occasionally let fall that he loved and was loved by some young lady who was not in favor with Daves father and some of his relatives. Therefore he could not obtain the consent of his parents to marry her and as he did not wish to take upon himself the vows of matrimony & gain the ill will of his relatives he concluded to wait a time and let matters take their natural course. But as a natural consequence a discord arose between father and son and in a passionate moment Dave left his fathers home and went to Buffalo and in a hasty thoughtless moment he enlisted. He regretted the act next day but resolved that in as much as he had promised to faithfully serve in Uncle Sams army he would make the best of it and do his duty. Right manfully did he keep his resolve doing duty even when he should have kept his bunk; and only yielding when disease had obtained a vital hold upon his system pressing him on towards the grave. Yet no one thought when he left the regiment that he would never return and I do not think that he entertained the idea himself, for when he was at the field hospital he wrote and told me that he was getting better but the next word I had of him was that he was dead. What a strange philosophy is death. None can foretell his coming and none can divine his shape – he cometh in his power to the strong man and like a whirlwind cutteth him down, he {unknown word} his step from the presence of the invalid who lyeth at the brink of the grave and straightaway the man is restored to health and strength. O death! how strange thou art how multiplied thy {unknown word}; war, accident, disease thy agents are, from whom no man escapes. How much then it behooves us all they messengers to meet – to be prepared when summoned hence by agents strong and fleet – to stand before our Saviours throne and offer to his love the record of our worldly deeds and claim a life above. Sweet thought that when the good shall die their souls will live again no perfect happiness in heaven where Christ & glory reign.

I receive all the papers you send me I think. I have several times been the thankful recipient of papers containing envelopes & not paper in acknowledgment for which I can only say do so some more and I wont get *mad. Lili spoke of Emma Lovejoy – does the family still live Cor. Swan & Michigan and are any of the girls married yet. I still correspond with Lottie McLane. I received a letter from her to day she is now in New York. She said she did wish Lili would write to her again but supposed that Lili's letters were more acceptable to <u>her</u> than <u>her</u> letters were to Lili. She said she used to enjoy the letters that Lili wrote very much. I received a letter from Laura to day containing some stamps. Tell Lili to do just as she pleases about writing to her but if she does write dont mention a word about me. I enclose her address which is as follows "Miss Lottie L.McLane, care of Northrup, Taylor + Co New York. I never told her that I was commissioned and I dont want any one else to tell her for me. When I get ready for her to know it I will tell her myself. She sings in a Catholic Church in New York. Her teacher gives her great praise but I suppose he would do that whether she was deserving of it or not. Tell Peter S. Lyman that his turn comes next in order as the recipient of a letter from me. I will try and do him the honor tomorrow evening if business will allow me but as it is drawing towards the close of the month I think I will close this letter and draw the clothes over me. Good Night dear mother & father and Sister and Grandma. Give my love to all and believe me ever*

Your Aff Son
Edward L. Cook
Co H 100ᵗʰ N.Y.V.

Mr. Lyman Cook
    Buffalo
    N.Y.

P.S. Please send me a little black silk thread.

Letter from A. Lyth to his Brother

Annapolis Md. Feby 6ᵗʰ 1865

Dear Brother

I take my pen in hand to write you a few lines to let you know how I am getting along here. well for the last few days I have been on the lookout for a letter from you and I hope I will get one before this reaches you and I want you to be very punctual in answering my letters you receive.

The most of my time so far I have spent in reading novels but I get tired of the nonsence and wish I was with my Regt then I think of the nice little songs that the "minie balls" sing and the very unpleasant noise of shells bursting also how I would look with but one leg and then I come to the conclusion I am better off here. though to tell the truth I should like to have a chance to pay the rebels for a few of those pints of corn meal that they were so kind to give me while I was pay a visit to "Dixie's Sunny Land" last summer.

The weather here is very pleasant we have light frosts at night but warm pleasant days, there was a few inches of snow on the ground when I first arrived here but that has all disappeared Tom Maher has got charge of a cook house where they cook for over 400 men so of course Jim and myself suit ourselves as to what we eat in the shape of grub and Tom says if there is an exchange likely to come of soon he will have us detailed in his cooking establishment if we wish it and I have no doubt but we will accept the offer.

I wish you would write as soon as convenient and send me cousin William's directions as I have forgot them and I wish you would send me a Buffalo paper occasionally also a few postage stamps as they are very hard to procure here

In my next letter I can tell you how I come out on my furlough but I think now I shall very likely get my ration money however I cannot tell for certain. Let me know how father is getting along at the oil well I must close now, hoping these few lines will find you all enjoying good health as it leaves me at present thank God.

Give my best respects to Lewis and his sisters also to Jim. My love to you all

Your Affect Brother
Alfred Lyth

Chapter Twelve

Virginia Campaign

Final Operations around Petersburg, Appomattox and Richmond, VA and Muster Out

February, 1865 – August, 1865

"Then came your last battle. To your division was assigned the bloody work of assaulting Fort Gregg, manned by its garrison of desperate Mississippians. After an impetuous attack, which lasted twenty-three minutes under intense fire, the crest was gained. As you hugged the slope, Color –Sargeant John Goodfellow was killed, but Corporal Charles H. Waite, of the color-guard, caught the falling flag – the old battle flag which we have with us to-day – and planted it in triumph on the parapet. Your brave young commander, Major James H, Dandy, was killed just before the parapet was reached. With the sacrifice of many other precious lives, the fort was taken, thus gloriously and victoriously closing the record of the 100th New York. Three or four days of forced marching in which you were urged by the impetuous Sheridan in the very brink of human endurance, brought you to Five Forks, and the surrender at Appomattox.." Lt Col Charles E. Walbridge address at the first Annual Reunion 7/18/1887

Letter from E. Cook to his Sister

Reply to No 133
Camp 100th N.Y. Vols
Before Richmond Va. Feby 23rd 1865

My dear Sister
Your letter is at hand. Tom was home on a furlough at the time he married but has returned to his duties again I think I should prefer to wait until I went home for good before I tied to a piece of calico. The honeymoon of such weddings is most to short to pay for the anxiety and fear of the following seperation.

I received the shirt you sent me and am highly pleased with it. How are Mr. Sees children getting Did Horace Riley say anything about them. I wonder if Cornelia See has got over her mad at me. I received Emma Anthonys letter and answered it but no reply has yet been returned. I have got my Captains straps. I think that bar is worked in splendidly. The bullion of which the straps are made is not gold but is simply galvanized on a silver base but then they are good enough for this climate and where it rains all day + freezes all night.

I think I have got now as high as I wish to go for if I am mustered again I shall have to serve another three years and I do not wish to do that for I want to get out of the army when my time is out. I am beginning to count the months. By time you receive this I shall have been in the service nearly 2 years + a half and six months more will see me on my way home if God spares my life and preserves my body from injury + illness. I received the silk thread you sent me and now I should like a few threads of red silk to sew up my sash which is commencing to unravel in several places. I will also intimate that I always have to borrow when I want to sew on a button with <u>white</u> thread. I received those last envelopes with my initials to day. They are very neat indeed but the back of them does not run up high enough to prevent the mucilage on the flap from adhering to the letter. The note paper is most excellent but you fold it the wrong way when you wrap it in the newspapers. If you would double it lengthwise instead of crosswise it would be much better. I am not acquainted with Edgar Benson. I will call on Horace Riley if I ever pass through New York. I am glad that Uncle Eb has got such a good situation & hope that he may be able to remain in it until his time is out. I suppose you have heard the news about Charleston and Columbia. We gave three cheers on the color line day before for the victory I hope the news may not prove a chimera like some other reports that have been circulated. There was a wide spread rumor through the camps yesterday that Petersburgh had been taken by our troop after several hours hard fighting but as there is no confirmation of it this afternoon I take it to be unfounded. The mail is ready to close so I must stop. Goodbye

Your aff Brother

To

Ed L. Cook

Miss Laura M. Cook

Co F 100th N.Y.V.

Buffalo

N.Y.

Letter from E. Cook to his Sister

Camp 100th N.Y. Vols
Before Richmond Va. March 11/65

My dear Sister

I commenced this letter to you on the eleventh and now it is the 14th I have been busy during the day & have not had an opportunity and at evening for the past week or more I have been one of a committee appointed to examine applicants for commissions previous to recommending them to the governor of the State for appointment. As each examination occupies nearly two hours and as there are upwards of 20 applicants it takes some little time to get through the job. Whenever we have battalion drill or inspection I have to go out and we generally have one or the other about every other day which occupies about 3 hours each time it steal away very many valuable moments that I would like to devote to corresponding with my friends. I expect to go on battalion drill this afternoon and if I do I must cut this letter short. We were reviewed by Genl Grant this last Sunday. He was accompanied by a large staff & numerous ladies. Our division at a review last week was reported to be the best in the army of the James and that probably is the reason why Gen. Grant came over to see us as he did not review any troops on this side but our division (the 1st Div. 24th A.C.) We did look splendid & no mistake and marched like clock work I tried hard to steal a look at the ladies who were seated in ambulances but the dust was blowing toward them and they were compelled to keep their veils down I was extremely sorry of course at this heavy disappointment but I bore it like a hero. Genl Grant is of a very ordinary appearance so much as that the presence of ladies attracted all attention from him. Of course up north where you have lots of ladies & few Lieutenant Generals the case would be just the reverse.

I think this review is precursory to a move indeed an order was circulated yesterday saying that as this army was liable to move at any moment no more Leaves of absence or furloughs would be granted except in very urgent cases. I received my straps, bars, stockings, slippers, valise & stockings all right. What did you pay for the valise? It is a splendid one and will last a person his lifetime. The weather is lovely. Tell Mary +

Laura I will try and write to them to night if I dont get too sleepy by the time I get through with the examinations. I received the red silk thread you sent me. There goes the call for drill so I must stop writing. Give my love to all the folks. We are going to get paid off this week if we dont move and then I will send you some money. Write soon and tell me all the news about every body.

Your loving brother
Edward L. Cook
Co F 100th N.Y.V.

Miss Eliza G. Cook
  Buffalo
  N.Y.
  Camp 100th N.Y. Vols

Letter from E. Cook to his Parents

Before Richmond Va. March 21/65

The day is rainy and it continues so for 11 hours it will again make the roads so impassable that artillery will not be able to get through and our move will be put off until the weather is more {unknown word}. I send you enclosed $100[#]. I sent home $50[#] last week. Do you know if it was received? I think I enclosed it in a letter to Laura & directed it to her {unknown word} on the numbers of the P.O. Box.

We are in good condition for the coming campaign which I hope to pass through safely and {unknown word} I for a happy welcome from the loved ones at home. I have only got about 2 1/1 more months to serve and those will pass quickly by. When we have once commenced on our summer movements. Except an occasional rain the weather is mild & balmy. I think I shall be tempted to come down south & live after this war for it is so much pleasanter & inviting than our cold home north. Tell the folks to take out what money they have paid out for things for me and then if they do not want to use any they can do what they please with it. Ask Laura if she has had my bank account settled since the first of Jan. and if she has let her tell me how it stands. I think if a person does not want to use money for two or three years it is better to keep the compound interest notes on hand than it is to put it in the bank. We have had no news from Sherman lately though I believe him to be doing well. Sheridan was at the White house a day or two ago + had a fight with Picketts Division of the rebel army. We do not know any thing about where we are going and we do not care much for in the army one place is about as good as another. I have not yet received my boots +c. I wish I had them here now for they would be just the thing to go on a march with. I saw Geo Stoddard a day or two ago. He has not been paid off. I have given all the money that I do not want to me to Bill {unknown name} and Dr. Mr. Segeant & if any thing happened to me he will turn it over to Capt Walbridge who after deducting what I owe him will sent the balance to you. But I hope to come out all right & then I can send it to you myself. Give my love to Grandma + mother + all the rest of my relatives + friends and tell them to write me soon. I must close now for I have got to mend some stockings +c and I need all my spare time if we move in the morning.

I am in command of my company and have the colors to escort being the third ranking officer present. Lt. Henry Conry takes my place in the Adjts Office.

Good Bye

Your Aff Son

Edward L. Cook

Co F. 100th N.Y.V.

To
Lyman Cook
    Box 1463
    Buffalo
        Erie Co. N.Y.

T. Maharg, Personal Notes

"When we were chasing Lee to Appomattox where he surrounded, the roads became so bad that our horses and mules drawing our supply wagons became exhausted and one after another would drop, thus threatening the loss of our supplies. I being the Comm. Sergeant of the Regt. became anxious and learning that the planters along the line of the march had run their horses into the woods for safekeeping, I got permission to see if I could find a few of them. So with my assistant, the band master of the 24th Mass. (colored soldiers) who volunteered to join us, we started out taking a cross road and following it to a point about a mile from our own line of march, *then took a course in the direction of the army's line of march and parallel to it.*

"*The first building we came to was an old empty barn and about a mile or so from this barn, we came to a planter's house with its slave quarters, fine barn and (UNKNOWN WORD), but not a human being around. Everything was in order and we judged that they all had fled through fear of the yanks. We killed a lot of chickens, tied them together, threw them across the back of the horses, told the Negro soldiers to lead him back to the empty barn and await our return 'cus we intended to return.*

"*We continued our hunt, shortly after leaving the planters home, we entered thick woods. As we ere plodding along over fallen trees we heard some one whistling a tune, we scurried to cover, we had not to wait long before a man came into view dressed in the confederate uniform, whom we forthwith captured. He became much excited, and then told us that he had deserted from Lee's army and was on his way home. When we asked him if he knew of any horses hidden in the woods, he said no whereupon the sole purpose of having a little horse play with him, the band master called to me to set him up and he would have a shot at him which I proceeded to do. Then he told us if he would let him go he would show us where there were eleven horses hidden in the woods. Enough said, we gave him a certain number of minutes to find them and started off blushing from excitement. We followed with our revolvers in hand, telling him that if he led us into trouble he would be the first one shot. After struggling through the woods until his time expired and not having the horses, we put him up again for a shot but he begged so pitifully for a further try that we allowed him more time but he became so confused that he admitted he was lost. He told us if we let him go to a house that we could see in a clearing, he could return with the horses (he had admitted he was one of the men who had hidden them) His proposition seemed to us pretty risky as there might be other confederates at the house. However we were in such stress for horses we decided to take a chance. When we moved to the house, we saw a man sitting in the front porch, a typical rebel. We stepped quickly passed our guide and asked him where those horses were that he had hidden in the woods. He said he didn't know. When one of his slaves chopping wood a short distance away where upon hearing his master say he didn't know, wanting I suppose to be of service to his master said "I knows where they is massa", we lost no time getting a grip on the nigger and sent him with my assistant for the horses. Tad (for that is what we called the band master) and I settled down for a heart-to –heart talk with the planter. We told him that we were authorized to give him a receipt for whatever we took from him and if at the end of the war he could prove that he had been loyal to Uncle Sam he would be remunerated by our government. It goes with saying that we kept our own eyes anxiously fixed upon the road where those sent for the horses had disappeared. Finally we saw a cloud of dust I assure you our anxiety reached its limit to know whether it was friend or enemy but friend it proved to be our comrade with the slave riding the finest two horses with the others following at a mad gallop. We ran and opened then barnyard gates and they rushed 11 of them we looked them over found a few among them not fit for our use, receipted for the rest bid goodbye to the planter and his family and started for home in passing the empty barn we saw nothing of colored soldiers or his charge and never saw or hear from him from that day to this."* [33]

Letter from E. Cook to his Parents

Camp 100 NY Vols
In the Field near Appomattox Station Va
I think it is April 12th 1865

My dear Parents

I have lost all track of days + dates. Genl Lee surrendered his command last Sunday just one week after we charged fort Gregg. I have received no letters since I left before Richmond except one from Laura in which she acknowledged the receipt of $50 #. Since I sent the 50 dollars I have sent 100 more but have not heard that you received it. We have had some hard marching + were well paid for our work. Our brigade fought the last battle but out regiment was not in it as we were selected as rear guard two days before the fight.

Our regiment is in the 3rd Brig 1st Division 24th Army Corps,
Col. Dandy commands the brigade
Gen. R.S. Foster " " Division
Gen. Gibbon " " Corps
" Ord " " Army of the James to which our corps belongs.

Our corps has done good service in this campaign. It is said that Genl. Lee made the remark that he surrendered to the 24th A.C. for the Army of the Potomac could never have whipped him but when he made a dash expecting to fight only Sheridans Cavalry he always found the infantry of that Gd d-d. 24th Army Corps.

When we took fort Gregg the rebs inside asked us what we belonged to when we told them the 24th A.C. they said they thought + knew we were not the Potomac Army for they never stuck to a thing as we did.

We are again under marching orders but we do not know where we are bound for. The war is not yet ended but I think it soon will be. One more good hard battle will finish up everything. Johnson will soon have to surrender or be cut to pieces. I enclose herewith an article clipped from the herald it will give you a better idea of our movements up to the 2d April than I can write you.

Please send me any article that may appear in any of the papers about our brigade or regiment. Col. Dandy has shown himself to be a trump in these late movements. He does much better as a brigade commander than he does as a Regimental Comdr.

Grant has sent reinforcements to Johnson who will probably operate adversely to Johnsons wishes.

It is said that Grant intercepted a dispatch from Johnson asking Lee to send him reinforcements at once. So as Grant has Lee a prisoner and Lee could not comply with Johnsons wish, Grant out of courtesy and by military etiquette relieved Lee from his embarrassment by sending Sheridan + the 6th Corps to aid Johnson in holding his ground. I am in good health + spirits + ready for another month except I have nothing for the men to eat. Some of them have not got a mouthful of any thing. Not even an ear of corn. I never knew the army to be so short of rations. If the men could only get corn it would keep them from starving until we can get rations up to us.

We can get fresh beef but that is poor fare without any thing else. There is not a single hard tack to be had for love or money. I would like to hear from you but I suppose the guerrillas prevent the mail from coming through. I have not yet received my boots + hat but I guess it will be all right.

> *Good Bye*
> *Write Soon*
> *Your Loving Son*
> *Edward L. Cook*
> *Co F. 100th NY Vols.*

Letter from A. Lyth to his Brother

Richmond Va
April 15th/65

Dear Brother

Before this reaches you I shall be with my Regt We left City Point yesterday afternoon and came up the James river on a steam boat Just below this city the river has been blockaded in 8 or 9 different places. In coming through one place where our men had just opened it large enough for a boat to pass through our steamer struck and nearly capsized and in the excitement 15 men jumped over board and got a shore when the boat righted again and got through they were left behind and had to walk to the city. we landed after sunset and marched through the city to Head Quarters and we went through the part that was burnt down which is about 30 of the finest squares in the city in marching through the streets the boys sung a lot of patriotic song such as 'rally round the flag boys' 'Red White + blue' John Browns Body +c Our Regt is somewhere outside this city part of our Brigade is doing provost duty in the city and they tell us just before Lee surrendered our Regt was in a fight and lost heavily. My headquarters are now in a tobacco wharehouse on Franklin Street I will close now with my love to you all

Alfred
I have sent a Richmond paper

Letter from E. Cook to Parents

Camp 100 NY Vols
In the Field Va near Appomattox C.H.
April 16/65

My Dear Parents

I wrote you two letters since the charge on fort Gregg and today I received a letter from Laura. This is the first mail that has come through since we took Petersburgh just two weeks ago today. Laura's letter was written on the 2d of April and perhaps at the same hour that I was in the hottest of the fight. In her letter she wonders what I am doing but she little dreams what scenes were at that time being enacted around me. Thank God I lived through that awful battle one of the most desperate of the war. We fought at the parapets of the fort until not more than twenty of the garrison were left alive and then we fought inside the fort. Such a desperate resistence is seldom met with in the history of any war.

I received Anthony's letter but shall not answer it until we go to Richmond or some other place to stay. Our men were starving for a few days but they managed to get rations through at last and to day a train of wagon came in from Lynchberg with lots of Bacon Flour + smoking tobacco all of which were issued out to the officers + men free gratis. And now there is a good feeling manifest every where. Nothing like food to eat to make a soldier feel good. The war is virtually at an end and I hope soon to be with you again. The army was shocked to day at a telegram from the north stating that Lincoln + Seward had been assassinated. If the news is true (and every body here believes it is) all that we want is to be let loose and we will go through the parties who instigated such a deed with a vengence that rivers of blood only will wash out. Thousands will swear war to the death under the black flag if they can be allowed to avenge the cowardly deed.

My God must our country become another France. Can not the lives of our Presidents be safe in the Capital of our country.

God will avenge such work.

Give my love to all.

Did you get the $100 # I sent home to father?

Your Loving Son

E L Cook

George Barnum, Personal Notes

"The 100ᵗʰ New York were in the First Division of the 214ᵗʰ Army Corps and the charge of Fort Grigg was the last battle fought by the 100ᵗʰ regiment and its record on that terrible occasion is enough to have earned for it all the honor and glory that can attach itself to any body of men in the accomplishing of so sanguinary work and crowning the dead with glorious victory. This fight occurred on Sunday.

"As soon as Fort Grigg was taken, Lee abandoned Petersburg and started

on his march South. General Sheridan followed on a road leading in the same direction and cut down trees and did everything possible to obstruct and delay Lee's army, but the obstructions were soon cleared away and the retreat continued only to meet further obstruction. In the meantime, the 24th Army Corps of which our regiment formed a part followed as close after Sheridan as they possibly could until Monday morning on the 9th of April when our corps got ahead of Lee. When Lee surrendered the Army of Northern Virginia he had about 25,000 men.

"Printing presses were set up to work printing paroles. A regiment of our troops would be drawn up in line opposite a regiment of Confederates. The Confederates would stack their arms and leave their colors and march away. There were mutual congratulations that the war had ended.

"At the height of our rejoicings, in the rain and waiting for orders, along the wires which followed the army in all its movements, came the thrilling and astounding intelligence that President Lincoln had been assassinated. It could not at first be believed. But, as reports settled into fact, and there seemed to be no doubt of the sad news, a cloud of gloom pervaded the entire army. Our victories paled in their glory, and for the moment all our fightings and successes were apparently of no significant value. But in the loss of a martyr President, we had the inspiring thought of a saved and united nation."[34]

"The news of the assassination of President Lincoln seemed to affect our Confederate brothers in different ways. Some of the men expressed their joy in hearing of the death of Lincoln and made it known in a very objectionable way, but it was not long before several of these men had a rope around their neck and were hanging from a tree. This soon put a stop to any more hilarity ."[35]

Letter from A. Lyth to his Brother

Camp 100th N.Y. Vols.
Richmond Va.
Apr 27th/65

Dear Brother

I received a letter from you last night dated Apr 16th and I was very glad to hear that you were all well and enjoying good health. We left Petersburg day before yesterday and marched to City Point which is 10 miles to get transportations for Richmond again where we arrived that same day about 6 PM and we stayed in old Libby prison until morning when started for our corps Head Quarters. From there we went in search of the Division then the Brigade and we got to the Regt about 5 o'clock P.M. where we were welcomed back by a few of the old boys. First Tom Maharg asked us to take supper with him which we did then Capt Cook wanted us to have supper with him + the boys in the Co got a supper ready for us. Our Regt is camped in a grove a couple of miles outside of the city and it is a very pretty place. The capt of our co is a bully feller and things are lovely. What pleases us best is they have not got any guns for us so we don't have any duty to do. Capt Granger is back to the Regt and he will have to take charge of it. As Col Dandy has command of the Brigade.

I will write soon again and let you know how things go in a day or two and I want you to write to me without delay and let me know if you have received any letters from me since I left parole camp Give my respects to all

My love to you all
Alfred Lyth

George Barnum, Personal Notes

"The march of a victorious army for Richmond was a rest of mind to the veteran soldiers. The best of discipline was observed. The people were evidently surprised at our appearance so orderly, well clad and respectful of the rights of the enemy.

We entered the city on the morning of April 25th, after a night's bivouac at Manchester, two miles out. We were received by General Devin's division with music, cheers, and salutations of an exultant soldiery. The colored population was jubilant. The succession element was sullen, and dispirited. The grand appearance of our army in contrast with ragged rebel soldiery, told the enemies of the nation with what a power they had dared measure arms, and that they could not but reap what they had so recklessly sown- death, ruin and destruction."[36]

"When our army entered Richmond, many remarked that the statute, in Capital Square of Washington, pointed in the direction Lee had fled with his army; a significant index of the great desire of the Father of his country that it should remain one country and one people, and that treason and traitors should be secured and punished. The people seemed friendly and thought the "Yanks" a fine looking people and did not expect to see such "heaps" of them, and a right smart lot, too."[37]

Letter from E. Cook to his Parents

Camp 100th NY Vols.
Outside of Richmond VA
May 3rd 1865

My dear Parents
My box has at last come to hand. The cookies were pretty good and the maple sugar first rate. The boots fit me rather tight + the hat fits me a little too much. I bought me a suit of clothes in Richmond the day I received my box

Blouse	*$30.00*
Vest	*7*
Pants	*20.00 Total $57.00*

So with my hats + boots I have now a complete outfit. I expect to be home before long.
I could get a leave of absence for 20 days if I desired it but I think it would be scarcely worth while for it is my belief that the whole army will be discharged before long.
Give my thanks to Mr. [ ] for his portion of the contents of my box. I

have not got much time to devote to letter writing as I have lots of company writing + business. I am just getting over an attack of the dysentery and ague. I kept up first rate on the march but as soon as we had halted where we were going to stop I was taken sick. I should have written to you before if it had not been for this. I am almost well now and feel better to day than I have before for about a week. We came through Richmond and marched about 3 miles + encamped where we now are within about 2 miles of the city by the shortest route. Our camp is in a very pretty spot near a farm house and in a very pretty little grove of oaks + hickorys. I have lost the key to my watch. I wonder if [ ] has got one that will fit it. There are all kinds of rumors about our going home. Now that the war is over I am awful lonesome and homesick and I want to get out of the service. I hear that Charlie Wallbridge is Colonel to Chief Qr. Mr. of the 10th A.C. at Raleigh. Write to me as soon as you get time and tell me all the news. I have not seen Geo. Stoddard since I left the north side of the James.

Our whole loss since we started is about 80 killed and wounded perhaps a little less than that. Col. Dandy is going home on a leave of absence tomorrow.

> *Good Bye*
>> *Write Soon*
>>> *Your Aff Son*
>> *Edward L. Cook*
>> *Co "F" 100th N.Y. Vols*
>>> *3d Brig. 1st Div.*
>>>> *24th Army Corps*
>>>> *Richmond Va.*

To
Lyman Cook
No 59 Oak Street
>*Buffalo*
>> *N.Y.*

"The tents of the various staff officers were pitched in front of the house, much to the annoyance of this loyal lady to the lost cause. She had three little children, aged respectively, six, eight and eleven years…. This peaceful military life was not without its delights; regular duties imperative, the music of bands, parades and reviews, all gave stimulus and excitement, differing from the fears of expectant danger and battle. The little girls mentioned became quite familiar and presented Capt. Stowits daily with bouquets of choice flowers, and insisting their disbelief that he was a Yankee, since how could he be and treat them so kindly, for had they not been taught that the Yankee was a savage, a creature of untold monster characteristics? Yes, thus even had childhood been perverted in its notions of that large number of enterprising, industrious and loyal men had rescued a nation and saved an element of it from its self-destruction and the destruction of a government that had given them existence and untold blessings. Said the mother to Capt.Stowits: "You have won my children and their favor; such are the impressible natures of the young." The Captain responded and said: "It is not strange. My life has been spent among children, and I have learned the way through the doorways of their frank and usually unsuspicious natures."³⁸

Letter from E. Cook to his Parents

On Picket near Richmond Va.
May 9ᵗʰ 1865

My dear Parents
I suppose you all think that now the war is ended there is no use in writing any more to your letter boy. What does he care about hearing from home now that there is no more fighting? I have received just one letter from home since we came here. I received a weekly express yesterday I sent home 2 or 3 papers a few days.
Two corps of Genl. Meade's army of the Potomac passed through here two or three days ago on their way to Washington. We expect two corps of Genl. Sherman's army through here in a few days. The rebs say that they do not wonder any longer that Genl. Lee surrendered to Grant. They think we have got all the men we wanted to whip them out. It took upwards of 7 hours for the soldiers of the 2ᵈ + 5ᵗʰ Corps to pass a fixed point let alone to supply baggage + ammunition trains. We supposed we were going right on to Washington but things look now as if we were going to stay in Virginia

until our time is out. What do you think about my coming home for a couple of weeks? They are granting furloughs + leaves of absences to go out of the Dept. for 20 days. I suppose it would cost between 50 + 100 Dollars to go home whereas if I wait 4 months longer I can go home for good, but if you all really wished me to come home on a short visit I think I would try and accommodate you. I wish they would muster us out of the service tomorrow. I am 10 times more anxious to get home now that the war is over than I was while we were fighting all the time. Col. Dandy starts north on a leave of absence tomorrow. Every thing is awful dull around here at present. Capt. Nichols is well and takes matters very easy. Capt. Granger has been exchanged and is now back and has command of the regiment. Capt. Payne our Lt. Colonel has given up military and I suppose we shall now see him again very soon.

There are now vacancies both for Lt. Col. + Major. I suppose Capt. Granger will get one of them and I don't know who will get the other. I would not remain in the service for a Brig. Gel's commission.

I received the box you sent me. The hat, boots + maple sugar were all right as were also the things Mr. [ ] sent me. but the cookies were spoiled. Capt. Nichols took a taste of the cookies for little Gracie's sake as she said one of them was for him. If Laura should see one of the Walbridge girls I wish she would ascertain his address and send it to me as I wish to write to him about some business matters. Where is Geo. Stoddard now? I saw Henry two or three times on our march but I have not seen Geo in a long time.

How does Flora get along, and Aunt Grace. I went to St. Pauls Church in Richmond last Sabbath. I heard some fine music + singing but the preaching did not amount to much. The minister talked so much like a nigger that I could not understand more than half what he said. When I come home for good would you like to have me bring my nigger along with me to do chores + cooking. He is a splendid cook + a good chamber maid. Can make delicious buckwheat cakes out of wheat flour + water and improvise a mellow feather bed out of rails + oak leaves. Can milk a horse, drive a cow, feed canary birds tend the pigs, build tent houses split kindling wood and make himself generally useful besides eating all of his own rations and not leave any of his comrades' to waste + spoil. If you think such a specimen of negroality would be of service to you I will bring him along with me.

To L. Cook   Good Bye   Your Aff Son   E.L. Cook
Buffalo N.Y.   Write Soon   Co F 100th NYS Vols

"Picketing, provost duty in the city, inspections and reviews were the several duties of the regiments, brigades and divisions. The city of Richmond, and its surroundings, at this season was beautiful to behold. It is situated on the James river, at the head of the navigation, with all the exhibitions of modern taste in the designs of its public and private buildings."[39]

"The temptation to visit the city of Richmond was to be expected, being so near and the conscious knowledge that war had ceased, and the old habits of civil life coming vividly to thought, there had to be some method in the way of enjoying that coveted boon. Furloughs were granted to officers whose companies on inspection presented an almost faultless appearance in cleanliness of person and equipments. A certain number of passes were given to enlisted men to go to the city, daily, after inspection of clothing, guns and other accoutrements, at brigade headquarters, by Act. Asst. Adjt. Gen., Capt. Stowits."[40]

Letter from A. Lyth to his Brother

Camp 100th N.Y. Vols near
Richmond Va May 19/65

Dear Brother

    Having a little spare time on my hands at present I thought I would write you these few lines to let you know that I am well and in good health. We are having very pleasant times here at presant and by all appearances we are likely to stay here for some time yet. Last Saturday all of our corps had to turn out in light marching order and go to the city to receive the 2nd and 5th army corps as they passed through here on their way to Washington. They commenced to pass at a little after 8 o'clock in the morning and were passing all day untill dusk in the evening before the last passed through and I tell you it quite astonished the rebels to see so many troops but when they were told that all they had seen that day was only two army corps some of them would hardly believe it for they thought it was the whole of Genl Grants army. I went to town to see them and I came across a good many of the boys I was acquainted with and I had a good time of it as I did not have a gun to bother me and I could go where I pleased. Yesterday part of Shermans army commenced to pass through here on their way to Washington Sheridans Cavelry were passing all day and the infantry and Artillery commenced early this morning to pass through the town and I guess if they march all day to day they will not get through then It is thought that our corps will be kept here untill they get the 25th corps which is all negros well drilled then it is said they will releive us Some think after Shermans army has all passed on to Washington that we will follow them up to be on the big review there. if we do I shall be home in the course of a couple of months with my discharge in my pocket if we do not I am good to remain here untill my time is out which is only a little over three months now

I with three or four more boys of my Co went to the theatre night before last in Richmond but when we got there we found it was a negro minstrels had the theatre and was going to preform we were very glad of that so we bought our tickets and went in to see the fun.

We are having very fine weather here and the farmers crops are looking nice wheat is heading out fine popatoes are 6 and 8 inches out of the ground peaches are hanging thick on the trees about the size of plumbs. early cabbage is begining to head up and we have had lettuce + onions three weeks ago I forgot to tell you that just across the river here there is a large brick + tile yard in the city of Manchester. We went past it when leaving this city for Petersburg a few weeks ago. Next week I am going to apply for a pass to go to Manchester to see the place and their machinery. Dear Brother I must close now hoping these few lines will find you all well and in good health. Give my best respects to Lewie and Miss Kepplar and the rest of the folks

Your Affectionate
Brother Alfred Lyth

P.S. write soon

At the review, Maj. Gen, Gibbons issued his parting words to the heroes of the 24th army Corps. Headquarters, Twenty-Fourth Army Corps Review Ground, Richmond, Va.

June 10th, 1865

Soldiers of the Twenty-Fourth Corps:-

This probably is the last occasion upon which you, as a corps, will be assembled. Many of you are about to re-enter civil life, to resume those domestic duties which by your service in the great cause of your country, have been so long neglected.

Before we separate I desire to thank you, in the name of a grateful country, for the service you have rendered her.

By your discipline, long marches and hard fighting, you have established for yourself a name second to none in the army.

Your badge has become an emblem of energy, valor and patriotism, and is a source of just privilege to all who wear it.

Those of you who are entertaining civil life should still wear it, on all occasions, as an evidence to your brothers who remain in service of your pride in a badge made sacred by the blood of so many brave men, and your disposition, should your country ever again call you to arms, to again assemble under that proud emblem, and revive the glory of the 24th corps.

To our comrades who are leaving the service we pledge a kind farewell and a wish that their career in civil life may be a successful and prosperous one as their military life has been alike honorable to themselves and beneficial to their country.

John Gibbon
Maj. Gen., Vols. Commanding Corps.[41]

Letter from E. Cook to his Sister

Hd. Qrs. 100ᵗʰ N.Y. Vols.
Richmond Va Aug. 19 1865

Dear Sister Laura

I received your letter several days ago. I do not recollect the name of the young lady I met on the boat but it was not Miss Smith. I had to wash my haversack to get the victuals out. I am sorry I did not know then Morris was so near me. You need not send my shirts for I expect to be home in two weeks. Our Regt. is ordered to be mustered out. We expect to go to New York and get a big reception we would go to Buffalo but it is such a mean stingy place that it cannot afford any show superior to a Lager beer picnic in a Dutch garden.

I am glad Mary + Frank Sharp are getting better. Return my warmest thanks and best wishes to Helen for her kind remembrance. Tell Em Anthony that I shall be home so soon that it will be hardly worth while to write as I am so very busy making out discharge papers that my hands are full and I will tell her all the news vis-à-vis the first time I see her. Write me as soon as you get this and send me Mr. Sprague's address in New York if you can get it.

Good By
Give my love to all
Your loving
Brother
Edward L. Cook

Adj't. 100ᵗʰ N.Y.V.

Richmond Va.

The old brigade, Division + Corps is broken up

"After consolidation, and order for muster out, from some unexplained cause, the regiment was ordered to Albany for muster out, instead of Buffalo, where a majority of the regiment desired to be sent. As most of the officers were of the original regiment, and about two hundred of the men, composed of re-enlisted veterans and what were termed "Board of Trade men, it was hoped that they, at least, would come to Buffalo in a body, that the honor of a reception might be given them, as their services merited. The Board of Trade was ready, waiting any action on the part of the members of the regiment, to fulfill their obligations, and pay their respects to the remnants of a body of men aggregated under their auspices, after have done such valiant service for country, a pride to Buffalo and an honor to the nation. But it was otherwise ordered, and on the 28th of August, 1865, at Richmond, the regiment was discharged, left for Albany by the way of Baltimore and New York City, and was noticed by the New York press in terms of the most flattering character."[42]

George Barnum, Personal Notes

"The pay master made his appearance before we left Richmond and soon after on August we left for Baltimore and were then transferred to a lot of cattle cars and taken to Albany, New York where we were mustered out.

" The Board of Trade at Buffalo with other citizens had sent word that they were going to entertain us on our arrival at Buffalo. As I did not care to make a show of myself marching up the street of Buffalo, I left Albany a day ahead of the regiment and stood on the sidewalk and watched them pass".[43]

CIVIL LIFE

The Close of the War and the Start of Civil Life

After over three years of "soldiering", the boys from Company H are home. They arrive as heroes but are facing the post-war reality of finding jobs. There are no benefits or services to ease their transition to "civil life". Ed Cook secures a position in the plumbing business. Alfred Lyth rejoins the family business of manufacturing tile. Tom Maharg becomes a clerk in his Uncle's soap manufacturing business. George Stoddard takes a clerk position in a local drug store. Tom Wharton becomes a janitor in an armory. George Barnum knows he doesn't want to remain in Buffalo and finds a job in Minnesota. Ed Nichols leaves Buffalo as well. George Stowits goes back to teaching in the Buffalo school system. Charles Walbridge becomes a buyer for a hardware store. Despite the fresh memories of war, they seem to be "picking up the pieces". As the years go by, they must long for opportunities to reminisce about the part that 100th Regiment played in the war and want to reunite themselves with their old Comrades. More than twenty years after their return, they formed a Veterans Association for the 100th Regiment and held their first meeting in 1887. Excerpts for the published proceedings of selected annual reunions detail the "boys" thoughts and perspectives on their civil war experiences.

Veterans Association of the 100th Regiment N. Y. State Vol.– Proceedings of the First Annual Reunion – July 18, 1887

"The 18th of July (the 24th anniversary of the charge on Fort Wagner) was selected as the date, and Sour Spring Grove as the place for holding the reunion.

"Although rain fell until 8:30 A.M. on the 18th of July, the majority of those living in the city began to assemble at No. 40 Niagara Street. The meeting was more interesting to the survivors of the Regiment from the fact that some had come long distances, and Comrades met and clasped hands that had not looked in each other's faces for very many years, in some instances not since the close of the war.

"At 9 A. M. the line was formed under the command of Capt. Chas. H. Rauert, and headed by miller's band, marched to the Buffalo library and received their regimental colors – the shreds of famous flags that were borne by the brave men in many a hot and bloody conflict. The line of march was again taken up, and the little band of veterans, representing a regiment that when it first left Buffalo for the seat of war numbered over 1,000, passed through Lafayette street to Main, to North Division, to Washington, to Exchange, to Main, to Seneca, to Pearl, to the terrace, to Main and hence to the dock, where they embarked on board the Periwinkle, and after a short trip up the lake were transported to Sour Spring grove. On arriving there line was formed, the roll called and the command dismissed for dinner.

"At 2 o'clock the formal exercises of the day were held, Capt. Rauert presiding. The band played the "Stars Spangled Banner," a prayer was offered by the chaplain, Geo. M. Booth, and the orator of the day, Lieut Charles E. Walbridge, was introduced to the audience and met with a cordial reception. His address is a comprehensive and graphic epitome of the history of the organization of the regiment and the signal performances in various engagements which gave it great fame"[44]

"Corporal Tanner, being invited to address the assemblage, made one of his characteristically brilliant and forcible addresses. He had attend many –reunions, he said, and it was no undeserved compliment for him to say that the address of Col. Walbridge was one of the most graphic descriptions of the experiences of a regiment to which he had ever listened. A glowing compliment was paid to the old soldiers for their bravery, fidelity and honor in the war for the Union.

" Corporal Tanner said that army life stripped a man of all disguises. If he had any meanness in his character, if there was a streak of a grand characteristic or any attribute that goes to make up a true man, it was certain to be noticed. Many a man, who was a little god at home, left for the seat of war with great acclaim, but his character, shriveled up when he got there. Again, there were others who, in the ordinary walks of life at home were not deemed remarkable or of any consequence. But when they go to the front and were put to the grand crucial test, how they blossomed out! In concluding, Corporal Tanner said that the old soldiers are a little sore because they think that the world is forgetting them; but the fact remained that they had done that which would put an end to an internecine war in the future; the men of this nation would stand in a solid line for one country and one flag, and this was something that was truly appreciated when once the hearts of people were reached. The speaker exhorted his comrades to hold their personal character as high as they did their country's honor and their country's flag in the hour of peril; to live as true to their God as they had to their country; and then when they had all crossed the line of this life they would have a grand re-union, which would never break up."[45]

Veterans Association of the 100th Regiment N.Y. State Vol. – Proceedings of the Second Annual Reunion held at Buffalo, N. Y. on July 18, 1888

"Comrades, I want to introduce to you Mrs. James M. Brown of Jamestown, New York. There was a moment of perfect stillness and as the woman stood with the eyes of her husband's old comrades fixed upon her reverently, her lips began to quiver, and their faces grew blurred and dim to her eyes. Comrade Lyth, with a chocking voice and tears springing from his eyes said: "Boys, you know what you'd do if you're old Colonel was standing here before you to-day; you'd salute him. By heaven, you would boys! Comrades, let's salute our Colonel's widow". As one man the sixty-eight veterans rose, and silently made the military salute. The widow was overcome and many of the men were moved to tears"[46]

"The principle orator of the day was Major George H. Stowits. He spoke on the great and important services of Colonel Lewis S, Paine,

Captain, Company D as a "scout" in front of the army of occupation and before Charleston, from the time of the landing of the regiment on Cole's Island March 27, 1863, to his capture, wounded and a prisoner in the hospital in Charleston, and subsequently Columbia, S. C., and until his release and restoration to his family and friends at the close of the war. His record is not given to magnify the services of Colonel Payne above the glorious record of that body of noble men and officers. . . . No! Colonel Payne would scorn any attempt to seek notoriety to the detriment of any one of his associate suffers on those sandy isles. As the character of his duties were unlike in kind to those in the camp of the Regiment, hence, as individual officers and men, we have one and all desired to know more of that life of daring risk and exposure in the silent watches of the night, beneath the stars, in the swamps and inlets of those desert isles of South Carolina."[47]

"The President next introduced Mr. George S. Hazard, who was President of the Board of Trade of Buffalo at the time that body did so much toward furnishing the One Hundredth Regiment with recruits, thus keeping the Regiment and its history intact." His address, in part, follows:

"More than twenty-six years, almost a generation, have passed since the regiment was organized. Memory, however, carries me back to the day it marched out of Buffalo, numbering nearly one thousand strong determined men, in all the grace and beauty of youthful manhood, bidding farewell to fathers, mothers, wives and sweethearts. It was an interesting and touching sight, for with that strong body of loyal men went out the hearts and hopes, and fears and prayers of other thousand. But that patriotic Regiment had well considered the situation and object upon which it had entered, and there were no regrets or allurements to divert the loyal here from its purpose.

"The change from the independent go-as-you-please civil life to that of military obedience and discipline was not easy to conform to, but necessity and patriotic emulation soon made your good soldiers, You did not volunteer your services to gratify personal ambition; there was no malice or hatred in your hearts towards those you were going to meet in deadly conflict. You went not for conquest of any portion of this fair country, neither for the abolition of slavery, but simply and purely for the purpose of defending, if necessary, with your lives the laws and institutions of your country against one of the most formidable and unjustifiable rebellions which history has recorded. In this noble and self-sacrificing undertaking, after three years of untold privations and perils by sea and land, toilsome marches, bivouacking, without shelter, and often without bread, exposed by night, and by day to the shot and shell of a vigilant and remorseless enemy, but always ready, regardless of rest or food to "fall in" at the tap of the drum or the bugle call, to go forward even to the point of the bayonet or the cannon's mouth.

" In looking over the ground, the attention of the committee was attracted by the meritorious and gallant deeds of the One Hundredth Regiment. Not, perhaps, that it had distinguished itself more than some others but in its new and inexperienced condition had been placed in dangerous positions, and although fighting with all the bravery and steadiness of veterans, were sadly cut up in losses of officers and men. The condition of the Regiment appealed so strongly for assistance and the sympathy of the committee was deeply enlisted in its favor, and its recommendation the Board of Trade lost no time in passing a resolution adopting the 100th regiment, and making arrangements for recruiting men to fill its ranks. A recruiting office was opened on Main Street and salaried agents were employed. I will not enter into details, but simply state that from the month of August, 1862 to the latter part of 1864, 511 men were enlisted and bounties paid each enlisted man. These men were all forwarded from time to time to the Regiment in squads of 20 to 50 men each.

"During the later part of 1864 men became scarce, in fact, if I use a commercial phase, the "market was bare," and still the Regiment, after the assault on Wagner required more men but none could be found. The Board of Trade appealed to the secretary of war for help, begging for a detail of three hundred men. After considerable correspondence, a detachment of some two hundred men were sent from Washington to the regiment." [48]

Veterans Association of the 100ᵗʰ Regiment, N. Y. State Vol. – Proceedings of the Third Annual Reunion held at Buffalo, N. Y. July 4, 1889

"And now we may ask, what are the results of this Great War of which the nations of the civilized world gazed with wonder and astonishment?

"A million of human lives were sacrificed and thousands of millions of treasure lost, but in the providence of Almighty God the infamous curse of slavery, which for generations had remained a blot upon the escutcheon of a free country, was by an inevitable sequence swept away forever. The doubtful and often disputed problem of permanence of a constitutional republic has been solved for all time, showing by a living example to all the Nations of the world that the people are not only capable of governing themselves but fully competent to create and perpetuate the best form of government of the people and for the people that the world has ever known.

"Furthermore, the power, resources, inflexible courage and superior military qualifications so suddenly developed on both sides in the late War practically demonstrate the ability of the country to take care of itself under any emergency which is ever likely to occur.

"The heavy clouds of war which so long hung over us dispersed and peace and prosperity under a wise and beneficent government are assured to all. May we not hope and soon realize that reconciliation and friendly intercourse which already seem largely established in the heart of those recently engaged in deadly strife will so increase that the imaginary lines of North and South will become blended and forgotten, and the people, firmly cemented in the bonds of a common nationality, kindred, and commerce, will remain for all time an independent, free and united Nation

"For all the blessings of peace, let us given fervent thanks to Him, the Supreme Ruler of the Universe, who directs the destiny of nations, and to those men who, inspired with a brave and noble patriotism, gave up all, even their lives, to preserve the existence and integrity of the Constitution and Law of their beloved country. To them, the noble and patriotic dead, and living heroes may the hearts of a generous and loyal Nation to the latest posterity even turn in grateful remembrance."[49]

"Mr. Hazard's interesting remarks were attentively listened to and frequently applauded."[50]

"The GAR quartette sang several more patriotic songs, after which the President introduced Comrade Alfred Lyth, of Company H who had been designated by the Executive Committee as the Orator of the Day. . . ."

"Comrades: Two years ago, at the first annual reunion of the 100th Regiment Veteran Association, Col. Walbridge, in the course of his admirable address on that occasion, in a brief reference to the battle of Drury's Bluff, May 16, 1864, mentioning the loss the Regiment sustained in that engagement, used these words: "Of the dreadful trials of those who were captured in this and other engagements how can we speak in adequate terms! The 100th Regiment was represented in the prison pens of Andersonville and Florence, in Libby and on the Belle Isle. There are some of you gathered here to-day to whom the memories of that experience must come back with horrible and startling distinctness.

"Those words prompted a request on the part of the executive committee to have the experiences of prison life made the subject of a talk at some of our annual gatherings, representing to us from personal observation, the sufferings of comrades in these "Hells upon Earth" Rebel Stockades and Prisons. During the year 1863 many desperate and bloody battles were fought, but how many realize that during that time there were more Union soldiers killed by exposure and starvation in the prison pens of the South than were slain by rifle and cannon in many desperate engagements of the war in the same time! This may seem incredible to some, but history will bear out this fact.

"You have heard much of the heroism of the men who fell in battle

443

and met death in active combat before the guns of the enemy; little is ever heard about the heroism of those who sacrificed their lives in rebel prisons, and died, sooner than accept life and liberty at the expense of treason to their country. Talk of patriotism, and reflect upon thirteen thousand patriots buried in the cemetery at Andersonville, every one of whom offered the opportunity of earning good wages, with abundant food to eat, if they would go into the workshops of the South. Reflect, comrades, upon the sublime firmness with which they endured unto death, all the neglect, the ingenious cruelty and barbarity their foes could inflict upon them while in captivity.

"The 100ths, with its usual luck being in the vanguard, took an active part in the fighting at Port Walthal immediately after landing. The 7th was a day of stirring events; digging rifle pits, supporting the movements of a battery, and participating in a movement upon Richmond and Welden R. R., and successfully repelling the enemy in their attempts to drive us from our position. This class of movements was of daily occurrence up to the 13th when the regiment was brought in direct conflict with the enemy. The troops, in our immediate front having driven the rebels from their fortifications, we pushed on; entering a line of works on a hill-side the rebel were seen in full flight on our left. Below and in the distance other forts and breast-works confronted us. The 100th was here selected and ordered on alone to charge a fortification in our direct front. The command "Forward, the 100th," we started down the hill-side in line of battle, eyes eagerly strained watching the works in our immediate front; half way down, again the command, "Forward" being repeated, several enthusiasts, privates and non-commissioned officers, several yards in advance of the line yelling "Come on boys, let's give 'em hell." The bottom of the hill is reached; we cross a small stream, and men in our line begin firing.

"Rebel cannon diagonally in front to the right and left are pouring a destructive fire into our ranks, men are falling like ten-pins, one particular shot taking off five legs, still the ranks closed up; a rising knoll in our front reached, and for the first time the guns we are charging belch forth their flame and smoke, the instant those several puffs of smoke were seen on the line of the breast-works before us, every man in the battle line, without a word of command, drops to the ground. The experiences of the siege before Charleston on Morris Island, S.C., where the flash of smoke of the guns on Rebel fortifications prompted men to drop into trenches, came here into play. As the shells go whistling and screeching over us, the line, as if by impulse, seems to rise as one man, and the command "Charge bayonets!" is answered by a yell and cheers as the ranks rush madly onward, every man, it would seem, intent on being the first to reach the line of works; but, alas!, the distance is too great. Grape and canister and the Rebel infantry pouring destructive fire into our line from the left, the ranks are broken and, falling back a short distance, are reformed under direct fire from the enemy. Preparing to renew the charge, orders are received to move off towards the right.

"We crossed Proctors' Creek into a low, swampy field, and lie down behind a small ridge, directly in our front being a line of skirmishers firing into the woods where Rebel sharp-shooters are giving us constant and painful reminders of their presence. After dark, the Regiment was ordered to re-cross the creek and placed on picket duty. The painful remembrance of that night on picket will be recalled by many – the cool night air, the benumbing influences of cold and wet; the continual double-quick on beat to prevent giving out altogether, and finally how gratefully before morning we quietly vacated that picket line to a relieving party and, retiring to the rear, lay on our arms the balance of the night. At eight o'clock on the morning of the 14th an advance was ordered. The 100th in its position in line of battle as part of the front line moving the enemy's works is waiting the command for action. Companies H, and I, are thrown forward to skirmishers, and enter a wood through which Rebels are retiring. Beyond this line of woods is a board fence, then an open plowed field about 400 feet across; then a rail fence; beyond the rail fence a pasture and stump lot; then a slashing and the Confederate works.

"The enemy retired across the plowed field and took a position in rear of the rail fence, ensconced behind which they had a fine range over the open field at our boys when showing themselves at the edge of the woods on the opposite side. For an hour or more, behind the trees, we kept up continuous exchanges of shots with the enemy, protected by the rail fence. As the advance of the line was urged, but to leave the protection of trees, scale of board fence and enter an open field, was an undertaking which required considerable fortitude, particularly as the trees behind which we were sheltered were being literally stripped of their bark by Rebel bullets. Company E, coming to our assistance, a break is made. With a cheer the line moves forward, vaulting, tumbling, climbing over the board fence and charging across the open field; the rail fence is ours; the enemy retiring into the stump lot and their works beyond. Many will remember the laughable instance of the capture of a Rebel prisoner by reaching through the rail fence, and catching him by the hair, dragging him through between the rails. For the balance of the day the position at the rail fence is held, and a deadly fire between our men and the enemy sustained. During this day's work we can remember that Lieut. Hoyt, of company I. was killed and Lieut. Pratt wounded.

"Men were generally shot in the head, and fingers and thumbs were lost while firing in crouching positions. [I], while kneeling at the rail fence to fire a musket, was hit by a bullet striking the breast-plate on the cartridge-box belt over the heart, deeply denting the plate, and knocking the breath out of [my] body temporarily. Being picked up by [my] comrades as a "goner", [I] rolled over, regained [my] breath and [my] place behind the fence, firing that day one hundred and twenty rounds of ammunition from muskets being loaded by comrades lying on the ground beside [me]. About nine o'clock that night the enemy made a desperate and exciting charge on our line to dislodge us from our position, but were repulsed, with considerable loss on both sides. After the charge the 100th was relieved from the skirmish line, and rifle pits were dug all along the in rear of the fence. On the 15th the Regiment lay in the woods occupying its position in line anticipating attack, though no enemy is in sight. The men began to look anxiously, expecting momentarily to be called into action, and some began to fear inaction on our part was giving the enemy an opportunity to concentrate his forces and get reinforcements. At three o'clock on the morning of the 16th the Regiment got up under arms and moved forward near the line of rifle pits by the rail fence, occupying the same positions as the skirmish line on the 14th.

"A dense fog, obscuring the sky and completely shutting out objects a few feet distant, we awaited the expected onset. Shortly after four o'clock firing was heard both to the right and left of our position. First it was the pulsations of artillery that grew stronger and more regular; then it was followed on the right by cheering and discharges of musketry. Our regiment was awaiting orders, but no orders came. The tide of battle on our right indicated that our forces were being driven from their position. On our left the battle rages and the fog obscures everything. Presently the mist began to rise; we notice on our left the line has broken to the rear, and in our immediate front, the enemy are advancing out of the fog. The regiment sprung forward to the rifle pits, and by a well directed fire check the advance of the rebels. Again the enemy advance. [I], loading a musket by placing the ram-rod against the rail fences in front, pushing the cartridge home and hastily firing ram-rod with the charge at the advancing foe, am hit in the foot by a piece of shell, cutting the shoe at the instep and slightly wounding the foot, at the same time being struck in the hip by a fence rail, which undoubtedly was thrown against me by the bursting of a shell I fell into the rifle pit and in a few moments am ordered to crawl out, a prisoner of war. Lieut. Col. Langdon says in his account of this engagement: "But for none it was more critical moment than for Dandy's 100th New York. After having prepared to join the assault it received no orders to fall back. The regiments on both flanks had retreated, and the gallant Dandy, believing that it has been designedly left as a forlorn hope to hold the enemy in check and give them time for the retiring regiments to take up a new position, held his ground till overpowering numbers, threatening to envelop his command, compelled a retreat to avoid capture." Among the last to leave was Col. Dandy himself. First Lieut. A. Wayne Vordes, then of the 100th New York, though wounded only two days before while fighting on the skirmish lines, and with his Colonel, narrowly escaped being made prisoners. This regiment, which had suffered severely during the fighting of the 7th, 13th, 14th and 15th, lost in this affair 191, rank and file killed, wounded and missing. Many of the latter were undoubtedly killed.

"Many of the Regiment were taken prisoners, not having a chance to leave the rifle pits before the rebel line was upon them, and were sent on to Richmond. When captured, I was taken with several others to the stump lot, and guarded by a couple of Rebs, one of who soon started to gather plunder and trophies, the remaining soldier's attention being occupied in watching the field in the distance and the success of his comrade. Embracing a favorable opportunity, I darted behind a stump near by, and taking advantage of circumstances made good [my] escape to a piece of woods to the right and rear of the open field in which the Regiment was at the opening of the fight. In running across a corner of the field to gain the wood, a bullet struck the cap off [my] head, a loss very much regretted at the time – the head-gear being a very fine cap, presented to [me] by Lieut Jas. H. French a few days before. While hurrying through the woods [I] came across a soldier severely wounded, being shot through the arm and the bullet penetrating his side. The wounded soldier was Corp. Stark, Company A of the 100th. He begged so hard for help and we stopped to bind his arm with a handkerchief to stop the flow of blood. Then, urging him to follow, we started again to find a place of safety. At the edge of the woods to our left, we came to an opening descending to what appeared to be the bed of a creek, the banks overgrown with underbrush. Upon the slope on the opposite side of the creek were stretched, as far as the eye could reach a line of infantry wearing the Union blue. On the crest of the hill above, their infantry and field guns were planted, showing that out troops had formed a new line of battle, or reserves were preparing to meet the foe. On reaching the creek, which proved to be dry, musketry firing from our left and rear was quite rapid, and glancing in that direction, a line of rebel infantry was seen advancing. The Union line opened up with volley after volley, and the cannon above sending their greetings in rapid succession, the confederates withdrew. During a lull in fighting, a number of Union soldiers, including several from the 100th, lying low in the bed of the creek, ran for the lines, passing on to the rear making inquiries for a field hospital. Being directed to a small grove on the Weldon Railroad, we found a large number of wounded congregated in the vicinity indicated, some severely, others more or less injured. No surgeons or commissioned officers being there, no one with authority to direct affairs, we were at a loss what to do next. A soldier passing said the field hospital was now located at the junction, a mile further on the railroad. Assuming to direct affairs, we ordered the worst cases to be placed upon two flat cars, conveniently at hand; all who were able lending a willing aid to push them along. About 120 or 30 crippled and wounded started down the track at the junction. Half a mile from the starting point had been gained. A soldier walking in front of the moving cars on the look out cries out a warning, "Rebel cavalry ahead, boys!" Immediately several ran out to the front of the cars to ascertain, and coming to the conclusion it is a false alarm , that the horsemen in the distance are Unionists, we proceed, but only, in a few moments, to be hailed by mounted rebels on the banks of the railroad cut above us, to throw down our arms and surrender. Many instinctively turning to the rear for a chance to run, we find a troop of Confederate cavalry coming down the track. Hemmed in on all sides, with no possible chance to escape, the only course was to cast aide the weapons we possessed and submit to the inevitable. Being provided with an elegant seven-shooting Spencer rifle and ammunition, a revolver and other traps hastily gathered from the battle field after our escape in the forenoon, we quietly slipped the Spencer rife under the slowly moving wheels of the train cars yet in motion and threw the ammunition in the ditch. While in the act of disposing of equipments, a rebel on horseback rode up and presenting a cocked revolver said "You Yankee son of a gun, what did you spoil that gun for?" Trembling and stuttering forth a reply, "S-s-so it wo-wont be used to kill a Ya-Ya-Yank." Was greeted on the part of the rebel with a frank remark: "Bully for you, I'd have done that myself."

"By our captures, we were treated fairly well. They belonged to the North Carolina Cavalry regiment, once prisoners and paroled on the field. Undoubtedly appreciating their former treatment said to us, as long as we remained in their charge, we should not be ill-treated; adding, however, that after getting into prison we might expect "tough times". Oh! Most fortunately for us we could not realize the full meaning of those two words, "tough times". Most happily there was no-one to tell us that five-sixths would not live to ever see the Stars and Stripes again; that in less than one month we would begin to realize the horrors of continued exposure, hunger and starvation; loathsome scurvy, the hideous gangrene, studied brutality, and the heart-sickness of hope deferred, would find an end, and rest from pain and suffering the barren sands of that hungry southern soil.

"Many wounded, other than those mentioned, requesting the same consideration were refused, being told they would be taken care of in the city. Reaching Petersburg at night-fall, weary and tired – in fact, completely exhausted – we were crowded into the city jail, a stone structure similar to many others in southern cities, used to confine criminals. Entering the portals the detachment we were marched into one room, soon realizing that there, we must remain at least for the night. No rations were issued, most everyone being provided, having well-filled haversacks.

"That night, in Petersburg jail, its horrors, its suffering, the agony, groans, shrieks, moans of sick and wounded men, crowded so thick together that there was not room for all to lie down upon the floor, in one corner of which there were two buckets for use to answer nature's calls, many suffering from diarrhea. All those men in the early morning of that day answered the bugle's call to arms, fought in the ranks and marched in the hot sun to be cast like felons in a dungeon, treated like beasts, is an experience so thoroughly impressed upon the memory, the recollection of which should the age of Methuselah be reached, will recall of the time thought, can it be? Is such a thing possible for a Christian and enlightened country? And the horrible reality of that night answers, aye! It is even so.

"Some of the worst among the sick and wounded were sent to a hospital; all were taken to an adjoining room and searched for valuables, knives and money; their name, rank, Company and regiment recorded, being told that all taken from us was entered on the register to our credit, and would be returned to us when released. During the search those who were suspected of trying to conceal anything, were stripped naked and every particle of clothing thoroughly inspected; under the arms, in the hair, shoes and stockings, or where suspicion might dictate that a stay greenback was allowed. Those who freely produced their little store of wealth when requested were passed easily. It was not our good fortune to witness unobserved some of this before our turn came. Profiting by knowledge thus gained, a large dirk-knife was hidden amongst the broken hard-tack and meat in our haversack. Coat and blouse were unbuttoned, shoes were untied, in fact, and our whole attire and appearance was made to simulate slovenly simplicity. A small pearl handled penknife slipped into one shoe, money secreted else ware, we unhesitantly limped with a badly swollen foot in the presence of the searchers, saying, "Can I go to the hospital to have my wound washed and dressed?"

"Well, we'll see about that. Have you any money or anything about you?" "Yes, sire." And producing a pocket-book saying there is only a little money in this, which I would like to keep buying grub. It was taken counted and pretense of record made. "Now, what else, young fellow? Come let's see what you have got? Knives, papers or letters?" Producing a black-handled three-bladed pocket knife, I said "I want to keep this to eat my rations with" It was taken. "Is that all?" "Yes, sir." Clothing and haversack are shaken a little; we are passed on and returned to former quarters. With all the care taken by our custodians many of the prisoners had succeeded in secreting money and other valuables. One scheme we learned was in taking the caps off the brass buttons on the uniform and putting bills in the cavity, replacing the cap. Hence Yankee cunning in many instances was more than a match for the Johnny rebs. That day several embraced the opportunity to pencil short letters to the dear ones at home, trusting that they would reach them and relieve their anxiety regarding our fate. Then follows another night in jail, to some the suffering worse than the previous night. The next day we were transferred from the jail to more commodious quarters in a tobacco warehouse nearby. Suffering from the wound in my foot and diarrhea for several days following, I was too ill to note passing events.

"Those not sick began to feel that pangs of hunger; the allowance given once in twenty-four hours not being enough for half a decent meal. At the end of the week we were glad to get orders to be ready to move, any kind of change being agreeable. En route the rebels said we were going to a large prison camp located in a healthy part of the State of Georgia; that a fine stream of water ran through it, and we should get plenty to eat; the country was rich, producing plenty for all. On the first day of June the train arrived at Andersonville. Leaving the rail road station, fifteen hundred prisoners from Richmond and Petersburg were marched to the headquarters of the commandant of the prison, Capt. Wirtz. Our names, rank, Company and Regiment taken, and a search for valuables was commenced but soon abandoned, all having been searched at Richmond or Petersburg. While standing in the ranks a very heavy shower of rain poured down upon us, and being in the front rank we stepped to the rear that a comrade might receive part protection from the rain by sharing our piece of oil cloth blanket. Wirtz, passing at the time, observed the movement, and with a string of blasphemous language and a revolver pointed in our face he said "If you are not in your place in half a minute I'll settle your hash". The first impulse was to resent such bullying, but calm judgment said a drunken man is not responsible for what he does, and it is well that calm judgment prevailed, for we soon learned that had we so much as said a word, the brute would have fired his pistol. Aye, with our own eyes we were soon to see men shot in cold blood for less offences. Our names being taken we were marched into the prison camp, or stockade as it was called. The walls were formed of large hewn pine logs, planted in the ground, side by side, about twenty feet high above ground and enclosing a square of about twelve to fourteen acres. Passing through the gate men from every state were gathered about the entrance anxious to see if any of the new-comers were from their regiments or were acquaintances. The sight there spreads out before our eyes was horrible beyond description – hundreds, and it seemed to us thousands of men appeared to us as if they were walking skeletons arisen from the grave. To know that among the human beings before us there was represented the young blood and flower of our Northern soldiers, called forth the expression from several, "Is this hell?" No, it is worse. There can not be a worse hell than this. Routine of prison existence begins. Those that entered the stockade the night previous, are called together and divided into detachments of 270 men each, being numbered in rotation with former entries. Detachments were divided into three squads of ninety men each, and a Sergeant placed in charge whose duty it was to get his men in line each morning for count and roll call, and to draw rations. Squads were further subdivided into messes of thirty; men were then numbered in the mess from one to thirty; messes numbered one, two, and three in squad, and squads one, two and three in each detachment.

"When rations were brought into the stockade the chief in charge of the detachment would take three men and proceed with them near the entrance, where the so-called rations were brought in by an army wagon drawn by four mules. The number of each detachment was called by an officer on the wagon, and the Sergeant of the detachment given his allotment. This was carried to the quarters where the detachment was located, and divided as near as possible into three parts, that no unfairness or favoritism might be changed. Each day alternatively a man was selected from one of the squads, stationed with his back to the three subdivisions or so he could not seen them, and the person in charge pointing to say one of the sub-divisions that his fancy would dictate to him to point at, he would say, "Who has this?" The one with his back turned would say "squad three," "one" or "two" and the sergeant in charge of the squad would take his allotment and go through the same process in dividing to the messes, and finally, the one in charge of each mess would divided thirty mites by the same process. Our rations for the first day were two ounces of maggoty bacon and one pint of raw corn meal.

"Frequently a shot from a sentry on post would cause a little excitement for a few moments, and on inquiry, it would be found that another poor fellow had been "exchanged." Shortly after our entry into the stockade four of us, as was the case with many others, believing that "in union there is strength," came to a mutual understanding to stand by each other, sick or well, whatever fate might have in store for us. Our group was composed of James G. Pixley, Thomas L. Russell, Albert Tombers and Alfred Lyth, all of Company H. Early in June, Tombers, when outside one day with a dead body, secured four saplings with which, with our old rubber blanket and another piece of blanket for which Pixley had given his watch, we erected a shelter, or awning, to protect us from the burning rays of the sun. It was a mansion compared to what some poor fellows had, though it was very little use to protect us from the frequent and excessive rainstorms. Regarding the rations issued to us, if anyone had been told that they could exist upon such food for one short month, they would have believed it impossible. At first, it was either a small piece of corn-bread, about the size of half a small brick, or a pint of coarse corn-meal, raw, and about two ounces of rusty, maggoty bacon, which, later on, disappeared altogether; once in a while a half pint of boiled rice or beans were substituted for the corn meal, frequently half cooked and sour. It seemed to be the policy of the Reb authorities to unfit as many as possible for future service, hence the continual reduction in quantity. We have seen men reduced to the last stages of starvation through insufficiency, badness and coarseness of their food; suffering from diarrhea and dysentery; having scurvy and body sores from lying exposed on the hot sand and wet ground, with hunger gnawing at their vitals, reject the coarse corn bread or meal, and turn from it with loathing; again we have seen them glad to trade it for two tablespoonfuls of half boiled beans with some one who had received that kind of food, and worst of all, we have seen men, along the edge of the swamp gathering undigested beans there deposited, washing and cooking them to stay hunger while they were actually starving to death.

"With such scenes as these daily before our eyes, no wonder we sometimes thought, and still believe, the rebel authorities were designedly trying to kill us off, especially when we knew the country for miles around us was producing green corn, sweet potatoes and all manner of green vegetables in abundance.

"The frequent rumors of parole and exchange seemed to reconcile many to the horrors about them, and the constant hope and longing for again seeing 'God's Country', with a determination not to look on the gloomy side of fate aided, with courage and determination, to carry many through the trying ordeal. Frequent disappointment on the other hand would cause many to give up all hope, and yielding to the influence of the horrors about them, a speedy death would surely end their sufferings. It seemed strange, with all the cruelty, horrors and suffering inflicted upon the prisoners by the rebel authorities, and with all the afflictions they had to contend, caused by neglect, that among our own number there were those who, lost all sense of honor and justice, formed a band of marauders to prey upon the weak and defenseless, to steal, plunder, and even murder when resistance to their unlawful methods was met.

"A tunnel traitor was caught at one time, and the letter T pricked with India ink in his forehead. Wirtz, on hearing of it, stopped the rations for one day.

"Toward the latter part of July the increasing number of prisoners must have made the prison authorities apprehensive of an outbreak. They raised a line of white flags on poles through the prison from north to south near the west side of the stockade and orders were issued for us not to collect in groups between the flags and the gates. Some said the flags were set up to give the batteries the range of certain points. Forts and rifle pits were built and all the appliances of defensive warfare got ready in anticipation of an outbreak. Notwithstanding all this, some know there was a plot hatching and many felt that an outbreak would be attempted; hoped to be among the successful ones to get away. Another expedient adopted by the authorities to pacify us was the frequent information sent into the prison that an exchange was agreed upon. On August 1, a priest, sent by Gen. Winder gave us the news; many believed it and were in high glee.

"Speculations as to the future, and what fate had in store for us, were with many a daily subject for consideration. Following the recital of some atrocious act on the part of those in charge over us, these thoughts would arise. Not a day passed but some new outrage was the talk of the camp. One day it would be the shooting of a crazy prisoner, who had wandered over the dead line; another, the punishment meted out to some poor unfortunate for having failed to make good his escape; next, the stoppage of rations for punishing a traitor. Two incidents that came to our knowledge September 1st, having procured two or three days previous, will illustrate in part the inhumanities to which we were compelled to submit. There was a strict order against any of the prisoners purchasing vegetables from any of the rebel Sergeants who came into the stockade to call the roll, or, in fact, from any one but the sutler in the prison. That said sutler was supplied by Wirtz and Winder, who made an enormous profit on what they offered for sale. Duncan, the rebel quartermaster, coming into the stockade with the ration wagons, observed a poor scurvy-stricken prisoner lying near the gate, moaning and calling in his weariness and distress for his mother, and begging her for something to eat. He had on an overcoat much better than was usual to be found in the prison. Duncan inquired what he wanted. He replied he wanted some onions, Duncan told him he would bring him some the following day when he came in with rations if he would give him his overcoat, which offer the poor fellow eagerly accepted. The next day when he came he threw him some unions, saying: "There are your onions; I've done my part." Wirtz, who came in with Duncan, stepped up and took the onions away, and had the poor fellow taken out and put in the stocks for twelve hours in the broiling hot sun, where he went crazy and died in a few hours afterward. Another of the brutal acts of the brute incarnate, Duncan, was perpetrated on a poor, half-witted fellow, who was standing near by when he was issuing bread. Duncan, observing him said: "You d____ Yankee. What do you want here?" He replied, "Nothing." "Well, here's something for you," said the brute, whereupon he knocked him down, kicked him and threw him over the dead line, when a sentinel shot and killed him.

"On the 15th all the sick that could walk to the station were told to get ready. I determined to make a grand determined effort. Having reserved our tent saplings, I got some men to make me a couple of rough crutches. By this aid I got through the gate, pass the guard, where I sank to the ground, completely exhausted and unable to maintain an upright position any longer. Determined not to give up, however, I propelled myself to the cars, crab fashion, and being assisted into an old baggage car by comrades my spirits soared to the skies, and the happy blissful contemplation of being homeward bound, seemed to fill the world with sweetness, and for the time being made me forgetful of pain and hunger.

"Before proceeding further, and in order to give you a better idea of Andersonville, we will look over the records a little, and see what we are leaving behind. During the month of July, the deaths were 1,817, and the number left in the prison at the end of the month was 31,678. Think of all those human beings existing, cooped up on thirteen acres of ground. The scorching sun, baking the hot sand, burning and blistering the skin, blisters becoming bleeding wounds - breeding ground in the sick and helpless for maggots, or for the still more deadly gangrene. The number of deaths in August was 3,076. In all there were 45,613 taken to Andersonville. Twenty-nine percent of the "boys" who as much as set foot in Andersonville, died there. This record does not tell the many who died after leaving for other prisons or for parole.

"Comrade Hartman Yox, who is with us today, was an inmate at the hospital at Andersonville and has furnished me with memoranda of his experience there, and its condition; but we will take rebel testimony for fear some of you may think we exaggerate. Here is what a rebel physician, sent to examine and report upon the condition of the prison and the hospital says – speaking of the hospital - -"The entire grounds are surrounded by a frail board fence, and are strictly guarded by Confederate soldiers. The patients and attendants, nearly 2,000 in number are crowded into this confined space and are in but poorly supplied with old and ragged tents. Large numbers of them were without bunks, and lay upon the ground, off-times without even a blanket. No beds or straw appeared to have been furnished. The tents extend to within a few yards of a small stream, the eastern portion of which, as we have before said, is used as a privy, and is loaded with excrements, and I observed a large pile of corn-bread, bones and filth of all kinds, thirty feet in diameter, and several feet high, swarming with myriads of flies, in a vacant place near the pots used for cooking. Millions of flies swarmed over everything and covered the faces of sleeping patients, and crawled down their open mouths and deposited their maggots in the gangrenous wounds of the living, and in the mouths of the dead. Mosquitoes in great numbers also infest the tents, and many of the patients were so stung by these pestiferous insects that they resembled those suffering from a slight attack of measles. The police and the hygiene of the hospital were defective in the extreme; many of the sick were literally encrusted with dirt and filth and covered with vermin. When a gangrenous wound needed washing, the limb was thrust out a little from the blanket, or board or rages, upon which the patient was lying, and water poured over it and all the putrescent matter allowed to soak into the ground floor of the tent. The supply of rags for dressing wounds was said to be very scant, and I saw the filthiest rags which had been applied several times and imperfectly washed, used in dressing wounds. Where hospital gangrene was prevailing it was impossible for any such wound to escape contagion under the circumstances. The result of the treatment of wounds in the hospital were of the most unsatisfactory character from this neglect in cleanliness, and in the dressings and wounds themselves, as well as from various other causes, which will be more fully considered. I saw several gangrenous wounds filled with maggots; the air of the tents was foul and disagreeable in the extreme and, in fact, the entire grounds emitted a most nauseous and disgusting smell. The persons and clothing in most instances, and especially those suffering with gangrene and scorbutic ulcers, were filthy in the extreme, and covered with vermin. It was too often the case that patients were received from the stockade in a dying condition, begrimed from head to foot with their own excrements, and so black from smoke and filth that they resembled Negros rather than white men". The death rate of the prison hospital when we entered was: In June, one in every twenty-two died; in July, one in every eighteen; in August, one in every eleven; in September, and one in every three. The average daily deaths in the stockade for June was forty; for July, fifty-six, for August, ninety-nine, and for September, ninety. The greatest number of deaths in one day is reported to have occurred on the 23rd of August, when one hundred and twenty-seven died, or, one man every eleven minutes.

"Owing to the closely packed condition of the stockades during July and August, there was monotony in our misery, and the temptation to sit still in one's own quarters became very great. The ground was so densely crowded with holes and contrivances for shelter, that it was quite a task to move about the camp. There were not regularly laid out paths, go where you would, the same unwelcome sights met the view. Men with swelled limbs, gangrenous wounds, scurvy, dropsy, diarrhea, dysentery, dying men, aye, men literally rotting to death. Take a position anywhere and look in any direction, the same view would meet the eye. There would be men in the last stages of scurvy and diarrhea, wasting away, skin clinging to bones of the face, arms, hands, ribs and thighs, with their feet and legs swollen and distended with gallons of water matter, livid gums and teeth dropping out; near by would belying some poor wretch with sores on the body caused by exposure to the hot sun; the sores full of maggots, and long before death the maggots would be crawling in the eyes, nose, ears and mouth. Go anywhere in the prison these sights were all about you. Crazy men were to be seen all over the camp. It may seem to many that under such conditions it is a wonder how so many survived the terrible ordeal, but let me tell you, comrades, that many thousands lives were saved by the generous devotion to each other of chums, who, realizing what their future was likely to be in such a place, agreed to stand by one another to the last, and I am happy to say the little family of four to which I was attached are to-day all living, and I wish I could say well and hearty. None of that family of four but at different times surely needed the comfort and assistance rendered freely by the others. Thus there were thousands of instances where the nursing and care of noble and true-hearted comrades helped many to again see that oft-mentioned place, 'God's country'.

"One of the incidents of Andersonville should not be passed without mention, and that is the sudden breaking out, one night, on the north side of the creek, near the summit of the sandy ridge of a large spring of pure water. Many looked upon it with awe and wonder. Believing truly a miracle had been wrought in our midst, and that Providence has surely provided this fountain for the benefit of the perishing thousands in the prison. It was named Providence Spring.

"I have the good fortune to form a very agreeable acquaintance with some comrades in the hospital which soon ripened into intimate friendships. One of them became well enough to assist in the hospital, and getting a parole he one day managed to get off from the camp about a mile and secured a chicken by trading dead men's shoes for it. The next day we had chicken soup and a piece of the bird. Under these occasional pleasant opportunities and the reaction of the previously nearly fatal despondency, my condition began to improve, and having a pair of crutches made, I was under parole allowed one day to leave the hospital camp to go to a small creek near by to wash and bathe. I exceeded the permission by wandering and crawling off about a mile in the woods, and when so far away from those hateful surroundings began to seriously consider the chances of getting away, and to contemplate not going back unless captured and brought back. There were two great obstacles in the way, however; first, the pledge to return, and, second, my enfeebled condition. Towards the later end of the month the hospital, with all the sick was removed inside the stockade, one corner of which, was fenced off somewhat similar to the dead line, and guards with beats along the fence line to prevent those located in the stockade from flanking into the hospital department. For while we were entirely without shelter, but early in November, rude shelters, sheds or awnings were constructed for our accommodation; we had to lie upon the base ground, however, unless we were fortunate enough to possess an old piece of blanket or coat.

"The suffering, disease, hunger and all the horrors experienced at Andersonville stockade were much worse at Florence. Lieut. Barrett was in charge of the prison; his disposition might be compared to Wirtz, being subject to the same insane fits of rage. I have seen him walk into the stockade with a loaded revolver in each hand, pointed directly in front firing promiscuously into the crowd, simply for devilment and to see the "d—d Yankees" scatter. He was one of the most foul-mouthed persons that ever drew a breath. I have seen him standing on the railing in the morning while the dead were being carried from the hospital to the dead line near the prison gate to be carted away, gloating over the spectacle with drawn saber pointed at each corpse and as it was carried past he would utter the most blasphemous, vulgar, indecent, horrible tirade, interspersed with remarks such as "there goes another dam'ed dirty Yankee, just look at the lice crawling all over the _____. Oh that's the way to get rid of the dirty dogs" etc, etc. I could not, if I wished, repeat the foul-mouthed epithets used by this worse than brute. Once he stopped all rations for the camp because he suspected a tunnel, and I am informed that to satisfy him, and for the purpose of appeasing the hunger of starving thousands in the camp a lot of noble fellows got together and decided by lot, who should be reported as tunnel instigators, and actually a tunnel was started and four or five men delivered Barrett for punishment whereupon rations were issued.

"In the hospital department we escaped this experience. Those that we given up were sent to the guard-house outside during the night, and the next morning were suspended by the thumbs with their feet from the ground, and when the poor fellows suffering, would cry: "For God's sake, kill me! Kill me! Shoot me if you want to, but let me down from here." He would stand by laughing and say, "jest hear 'em squeal, won't ye," and then would follow a lot of abusive language. This was the regular punishment for those who tried to escape and were caught." *[Ed. -Alfred was finally paroled in November, 1864 and, under a flag of truce, left Charleston harbor for Parole Camp in Annapolis, Maryland to recover.]*

"At the conclusion of the above concise description of prison life, Comrade Lyth was heartily applauded. During the reading of the paper many were moved to tears, and some ladies, who have dear ones reposing in cemeteries of these prisons, were observed sobbing aloud as they listened to the horrible sufferings and tortures to which they were subjected." [51]

Veterans Association of the 100th Regiment N.Y. State Vol. – Proceedings of the Sixth Annual Reunion held at Buffalo, N. Y. on July 17, 1892

"… as a brotherhood of reunited veterans and comrades of a regiment conspicuous for its fighting qualities, and looking into each others' faces this day, calling to mind the scenes, trials and sufferings during the dark days of the rebellion, and making them an actual present life through memory, we must not forget the preservative forces of our national life, and that it is the supreme lesson of the hour to teach the millions born since the great Civil War, loyalty to country and reverence for the Old Flag. Teach them who these men are, called veterans and comrades of the Grand Army of the Republic, and why they are called; why they are unlike any other body of men or organization. Teach them that these men are the saved from ore than two thousand battlefields; from hospitals and prisons. Teach them that the save the Union it cost over 400,000 human lives – fathers, sons, husbands and brothers – and four billions of dollars. That 3,000,000 men were called for by President Lincoln, and 2,700,000 were obtained; that more than 2,500 battles were fought, and 1,000,000 casualties are recorded; that 200,000 died from disease, and 100,000 from other causes, and are buried in graves under the head of that dread word "unknown"; that it left 1,000,000 widows and orphans, and 3000,000 men were made cripples for life.

"Teach the youth of this land the history and significance of the flag and its several baptisms in blood form 1776 to the present hour, and that in these wars those stripes and stars were never allowed to trail in the dust while a life was needed to bear them aloft amid the fire and smoke of battle. Then, let the millions now, and to be, possess this culture, and the Union for which Washington was so solicitous and Lincoln's martyr, will stand forever. Yes, Mr. President, that as individual survivors of that sanguinary struggle for national life, and at how great a cost have been purchased the blessings we enjoy, we should often refresh our minds with the record in detail of blood and treasure, that we may fully appreciate the inevitable privilege with which the people are crowned – the result of that warfare for the life of the Republic.

"We live in the past to-day, made glorious by the deeds of sublime heroism of our dead and living comrades, that the millions multiplied generations, as they rise and fall throughout the land, may read and know the history of this people as written in blood by the wages of battle; that in the future war may be averted – sad, calamitous and bloody – even to save the unity of government.

"We should rehearse repeatedly to ourselves the glaring facts of our great Civil War; that to save the union of these States cost 400,000 lives and 4,000,000,000 of dollars. Four hundred thousand dead! An obligation upon the altar of country, the magnitude of which seems beyond estimation; a tribute of blood, freely offered by self- immolated patriots, with no other known thought save the nation's thanks and world's remembrance. Sublime offering; immortal dead! Fortunate is any country blessed with sons like these! What would have been the spectacle in our land to-day had not these dead and living heroes thrown themselves into the breach at the supreme moment of the nation's peril and risked their lives to preserve it from destruction? With humiliation and shame we would have witnessed the result! The government revolutionized; the constitution subverted; slavery established a corner-stone of the so-called Southern Confederacy; the Stars and Stripes obliterated and a strange flag floating from the Capital that Washington established; the experiment of free government's failure on this continent; the Great Republic gone out in darkness and in blood and despotism, and throughout the world rejoicing."[52]

Charles Walbridge then spoke:

"Grave fears were felt that men who had so long been free from the restraints of home. Accustomed to the rough features of camp life, would when discharged and turned loose upon the country, prove to bee a lawless element which would be difficult to control, and reference was made to scenes of violence which followed the disbanding of the armies of Europe in former times. The end of the came and the armies were disbanded, and with what results. They melted away quietly and almost imperceptivity, the veterans merged themselves into the ranks of civil life, and speedily earned character and standing as mechanics, farmers, merchants and professional men. The discipline and training, the courage and perseverance which they exhibited in their soldier day has stood them in good stead in civil life and today there is no more, loyal, law abiding, enterprising, and successful class of citizens, than those who went to the front in the days of the rebellion."[53]

"The following poem was composed by comrade Jonathan E. Head of Paris Station, N. Y. and ordered printed in these proceedings:

How grandly glad I'm here today
Though somewhat wrinkled, a little grey
And not as full of fun and play
As thirty years ago.

Still comrades I'm glad that I am here,
To help make this day a day of cheer
To grasp the hands of comrades dear
Whom I've not seen for many a year
Near thirty years have passed.

Comrades brave, comrades true.
Comrades who once wore the blue,
Comrades who their duty know
And did it too with royal will.
And do it now, could do it still,
As thirty years ago

Your every thought was loyal, brave,
The Union boys, we must save.
Strike the shackles from the slave
Or in the trenches find our grave
Most thirty years ago.

Hark! The fight is on, who will it spare
Our flag is waiving in the air.
Comrades following every where
The 100th. Ah! T'was always there
Some thirty years ago.

However fierce the fight might be
The 100th's flag you'd always see.
Wave old banners, proudly well,
Hundreds round you fought and fell
Most thirty years ago.

We thought of home, of loved ones fair,
Would we home's comforts ever share.
Or would there be a vacant chair,
God in mercy heard our prayer
Most thirty years ago." [54]

Veterans Association of the 100th Regiment N.Y. State Vol. – Proceedings of the Fourteenth Annual Reunion held at Buffalo, N. Y. on August 16, 1900

"A business meeting was held and the record of the proceedings includes the following poems and songs: Words written by Madeline Welcome of this city with slight changes are very appropriate to this occasion:

You have shared the cruel war of years ago,
You have borne the mid-day heat;
Your hands are clasped together now,
And you are disclaiming defeat.
Your hearts may cling together
As your loving glances meet
Your burdens are not hard to share,
Though your cup is bitter sweet.
Comrades silently have gone to sleep,
You gave them smiles and tears,
Your once fair brows are furrowed now,
Your locks are streaked with gray.
The glowing cheek, the sparkling eyes,
Will soon have passed away.
Oh, what a joy, a privilege,
To see prosperity in our land,
To hear from all the world such praise.
Yes, you are proud, and grateful, too,
As you rejoice with hearts aglow
To see our loved, "Red, White and Blue,"
Floating aloft where'er we go."[55]

A Song
By Capt. Jonathan E. Head

How grand it is to meet as Comrades once again,
In these autumn months, so cool, so fair,
To talk about the days we fought the Dixie Grays,
And we, as soldier boys, were camping there.

Chorus – Sing with me my Comrades,
Be cheerful, blithe and gay,
While we tell o'ver again the tales of long ago
Of our life in Dixie and far away.

We fought as Comrades true when we wore our country's blue,
And thousands fought and fell as we know.
But Treason's flag went down – the Stars and stripes they won,
On Appomattox's plains long ago.

Chorus - Shout aloud my Comrades;
Let your cheers be heard afar –
While we tell o'er again the tales of long ago,
Of our life in Dixie's land.

Be cheerful then, old men, your duty was well done,
Old Glory is respected far and near –
For we are now united, as a nation we are one;
Be cautious, foreign lands, when we cheer.

Chorus – Hip! Hip! Hurrah! My Comrades
The war is past, we know,
For we were loyal sons and were standing by our guns
On Dixie's gory fields years ago.

We now are getting old, our numbers growing less,
Other boys will take our place, that we know –
But that Old Glory ne'er we will boast of a truer, loyal host,
Than defended her in Dixie long ago.

Chorus – Join with me my Comrades
We dare to think – we know -
That Old Glory ne'er will boast of a truer, loyal host
Than defended her in Dixie long ago.[56]

HE WAS THE ONLY SON

By S.A. Bass, Co "C"

He was an every-day sort of boy, in eighteen sixty-one;
His country called and off he went, though he was an only son.

His father was vexed – but his mother prayed, and his little sister too;

He talked of a dozen battles and of the "Grand review"

He was one of the fighting regiments that lost two hundred killed;
But in Sixty-Five he returned again and the vacant chair he filled.

With health impaired for thirty years, at Washington he applied for aid,
But, for some "red tape" reason, was many years delayed.

He often to the office went, to learn about his claim;
It must have been his heart gave out, for after he died it came.

He served in the "Eastern Army," his comrades we all know –
T'was Colonel Brown's old regiment that went from Buffalo.[57]

Veterans Association of the 100ᵗʰ Regiment N.Y. State Vol. – Proceedings of the Sixteenth Annual Reunion held at Buffalo, N. Y. on August 16, 1902

"A business meeting was held and included in the proceedings was this poem.

"The following poem was written March 7, 1902 and dedicated to this Association by the Author to commemorate the anniversary of this Regiment's departure from Buffalo for the seat of war."

1862 The Hundredth Regt. N.Y.S. Vols. – 1902
(By Madeline Welcome)

It seems long ago, since Sixty-One
When our boys marched far away
The cruel war had just begun -
We remember that day
Our dear ones in their youth went forth.
And linked their fate with war;
To slay their traitor, who would deface
That flag we adore.

The gallant ones who bravely led,
Were foremost in the fight -
Lie groaning, dying, even dead –
At Fair Oaks – fiercest strife – some fell;
Their gaping ranks showed plain,
That this mighty host had fought so well,
But they filled each space again.

When peace and victory came at last
To God we gave our thanks.
As tears of joy and grief fell last-
We missed some from the ranks.
We thought of those we left behind
And sadly felt our loss,
"Cypress" and "Laurel" were entwined
As the "Crown" surrounds the "Cross."

How like old days! To meet this way,
Though "Taps" sounds now and then,
And Roll-call shorter day by day
Of officers and men.
  Yes! They eyes grow dim, the locks turn grey
While furrows seam the brow –
We'll cling together while we stay –
We're but a few left now.[58]

Veterans Association of the 100th Regiment N.Y. State Vol. – Proceedings of the Twentieth Annual Reunion held at Buffalo, N. Y. on July 18, 1906

"A business meeting was held and included in the proceedings was this poem:

MORE'N FORTY YEARS AGO

is the title of an original poem, read at the joint entertainment, by Capt. Jonathan E. Head of Co "A", 100ths, which was greatly enjoyed and applauded. It was unanimously voted to print same in the "Proceedings." Here it is:

Comrades of the 100th and 116th of the New York Association,
Who made many a square meal of hard tack as ration?
And grumbled not at our sad lot or station;
But accepted gladly a soldier's perilous vocation,
Each soldier doing his part to save the nation
More'n forty years ago.

On April twelfth in sixty-one
A sound like the boom of a distant gun,
Rolled North o'er valley plain and hill
O'er river brook and babbling rill,
Through out the North it sent a thrill
More'n forty years ago.

Secession's lamp shone bright and far
Which betokened dire civil war?
At Charleston, that city by the sea,
Treason was rocked in infancy.
More'n forty years ago.

For four long years the strike went on,
Sorrow entered many a home,
The cause was just, right must prevail;
We couldn't spoil that short word "fail,"
More'n forty years ago.

Hark! The fight is on – who will it spare?
Sulphurous smoke is in the air;
Comrades are falling everywhere,
But Old Glory was waiving there.
More'n forty years ago.

However fierce the fight may be,
Our starry flag you'd always see,
You waved old banner proudly well,
Many 'round you fought and fell.
More'n forty years ago.

Governor Dix, the flag unfurled,
Then spoke the words which shook the world,
More'n forty years ago.

How oft we heard that Rebel yell,
How oft a gallant comrade fell
Fighting bravely, fighting well;
Who the sad story cares to tell
Of forty years ago.

Sickening smoke, war's dire flame,
Carnage fiendish, how oft it came;
But New York boys they cast no shame,

On our loved State's most honored name.
More'n forty years ago.

Oh, the hearts were racked with pain,
How many fields had crimson stain?
How oft our boys there fell like rain,
Thousands were 'mong the missing slain,
More'n forty years ago.

Of home we thought, of loved ones there,
Would we home comforts ever share.
Or would there be a "vacant chair"?
God in mercy, heard our prayer,
Some forty years ago.

Comrades, patriots, brave and true,
Comrades who once wore the blue
And did it, too, with loyal will;
Can do it now, would do it still,
As forty years ago.

Your every thought was truly brave,
The Union, boys we fought to save,
Or in the trenches find our grave.
More'n forty years ago.

On April ninth in Sixty-five,
Secession's lamp was just alive,
T'was burning low, with hurrah about;
The Union boys just blew it out;
More'n forty years ago.

That vast host of all hope shorn,
Laid down their arms that April morn,
Glad that the end at last had come.
Glad to sing: "Johnnie comes marching home."
More'n forty years ago.

Four years of war, the tale's too sad,
The end did come, we all were glad;
War's black horrors all have passed
Appomattox – it came at last.
More'n forty years ago.

This reunion is "jubilee day."
So let's be happy, jolly and gay,
Though we are wrinkled, pretty gray,
And not as full of fun and play
As forty years ago.

Let each feel glad that he is here,
Make it a day of social cheer,
This grandest one of all the year;
Grasp the hand of comrades dear;
Talk o'er the past, through sad and drear
Of forty years ago.

Now comrades,
Where e'er you go, on land or sea,
Our flag is waving, peacefully, free,
It war's sad music often faced
We brought it home, and not disgraced,
More'n forty years ago.

We are now getting old, our members growing less
Other boys will take our place that we know,
Bur Old Glory ne'er will boast of a truer, loyal host,
Than defended her in Dixie.
More'n forty years ago."[59]

Thomas Maharg visited Morris Island and offered the following comments to his comrades:

April, 1905 "Comrades – I had the pleasure this spring of spending nine days on Morris Island. The government maintains a light-house on the south end of the island and I arranged by letter for board with the keeper. There are three buildings on the island, not including the light-house, all belonging to the government. The largest is occupied by the keeper and his two assistance (sp), the other two are used as a charity school for orphaned children, established and maintained by a Charleston church society, all of these buildings are located on the south end of the island.

"There is very little satisfaction to be gained by a visit to the island further than feeling that you are on the old camping ground where many anxious and pleasant hours were spent by us forty two years ago.

"The island has changed so much in appearance, by the growth of vegetation, shifting of the sand hills and the encroachment of the ocean, that locating the different places we are most interested in is largely a guess.

"Standing on the beach at the south end, and looking across the inlet to Folly Island, the scene is as familiar as when we were there, excepting the stone houses connected with the army. Standing there brought to mind very clearly the morning we charged through the battery at the north end of Folly, and the boats that carried us across the inlet to Morris Island.

"The camp ground, to us is the next important spot on our way to the upper end of the island, but I could not locate it to my full satisfaction. However, judging the distance as I remember it, from our camp site to the landing and also that it was south of the sand hills, I think I got pretty close to it.

"Next comes the sand hills that separated the camp from the trenches, they are there. I think they are not so high, leaving the sand hills to the south at a place where the diagonals began, there is a series of low ridges at varying intervals running from beach to swamp which I concluded was all that we left of the trenches.

"About ½ the distance from the sand hills to the place where in my judgment I located Fort Wagner. There is a well defined ridge extending straight across the island from the beach to swamp and overgrown with Palmetto and other trees, which I can not recall as being any part of our works.

"After passing this ridge, the low ridges continues more or less distinct up the ridge I judged to be all that was left of Fort Wagner, for this point to the other end of the island is simply low irregular sand hills.

" I need not tell you that the beach, Ocean and swamp appear the same as when we were there, marching the beach from camp to trenches, keeping tab on our fleet in the offing, doing picket duty along the swamp and building the battery for the swamp angle which by the way is to be plainly seen from the edge of the march.

Notes of Thomas Maharg

Permission of the War Department was granted March, 18, 1905 by the Secretary of War "to permit this old soldier to visit Forts Sumter and Moultrie, subject to the usual restrictions as to photographs, etc"60

December 1, 1906 – Taps has sounded. Lights are out. This soldier, George H. Stowits sleeps.

Veterans Association of the 100th Regiment N. Y. State Vol. – Proceedings of the Twenty-Second Annual Reunion held at Buffalo, N.Y. on June 17, 1908

A business meeting was held and included in the proceedings was the following:

"Among us few survivors, of the 100th, is there one who does not remember Saturday night, July 18th, 1863? That carnage, that carnival of death, that slaughter of loved ones, that hell of terror and fire, that thunderstorm of heavy ordinance, and din of small arms, mingled with appalling storms of thunder and lightening, when the faces of your comrades as they advanced, could only be seen only by the lurid glare of Heaven's lightning; that charge of brave men over a smooth surface, flanked by sea and swamp, with not a tree, stump, shrub or hillock to cover for a moment. That assault has been described by imaginary observers, but all fail in the true reality. We few remember. It was a dance with death; no romance, but groping by the side of torn and mangled comrades; no fight with winged steeds from the scene of blood and pain, but an hourly living at the mouth of a tomb, with no requiem save the moaning surf along the sandy shore." [61]

Veterans Association of the 100th Regiment N.Y. State Vol. – Proceedings of the Twenty Sixth Annual Reunion held at Buffalo, N. Y. on March 7, 1912

A business meeting was held and the local newspapers reported on the proceedings:

"Forty-nine grizzled, gray haired veterans of the 100th N. Y. Voluntary Infantry responded to their names when the roll of the regiment was called at the reunion this morning at the 74th Regiment Armory. Fifty years ago today the regiment marched away to the Civil War, and to commemorate the event this reunion was held. Of the 960 who marched through Buffalo's streets a half century ago, only 187 remain.

"About eleven o'clock the veterans gather in the headquarters room of the armory. Reminiscences flowed freely. Surprising was the number of upright, hearty men. It was apparent that many enlisted in the regiment while they were yet of tender age. And every one of the veterans was proud to be there. There was a perceptive stiffness, a throwing out of shoulders as the heroes of many hard-fought battle stalked about the room, stopping here and there to greet comrades.

"One man seemed to want company. He approached a reporter for the Commercial and engaged him in conversation. His talk was interesting.

"I tell you," said he, "this occasion makes me feel grievous – rather an unexpected word. I haven't seen some of these men for forty years. But I find no difficulty in recalling them, as soon as they tell me who they are. From the time I entered this regiment until I was discharged I never was out a day. And I served three years and over.

"Pathetic indeed was the calling of the roll. This was done by Adam J. Wagner, corresponding secretary. It stirred one's blood to see the way in which the veterans sat stiffly upright waiting for the sound of their names. All tried to answer in gruff tones as if to do away with any idea that age had overtaken them. And too many of the names there could never come any answer. "Dead." was the laconic reply that greeted the calling of several of the names. The veterans had passed away since the last reunion.

"Letters from many of the veterans, regretting their inability to be present, were read. Most of these were pathetic in character.

"When all business was finished, they marched, headed by the 74th Drum Corps., to Fort Porter, where at the castle, Col and Mrs. Tuitt had a delicious repast for them. The south entrance of the castle was covered with a huge flag, and on the terrace in the front of this veterans posed for their photographs. This accomplished they were whirled in automobiles preceded by the drummers and fifers to pay their respect to their faithful brigade quartermaster, Col. Charles E, Walbridge, at no. 120 Oakland Place. A group of children waving flags greeted the veterans and Col. Walbridge was in an upper room. Comrade Maharg entered with a huge bouquet, bearing the greetings of the assembled comrades. From there they went down Richmond to Porter and over to Front Avenue."[62]

"Comrade Wagner spoke feelingly of the "boys" who fifty years ago today – their faces flushed in youth, filled with patriotism, eager to get to the front to do battle for the preservation of the Union and Old Glory – marched over the same route we did this afternoon, who never returned to their loved ones but gave their life's blood that the nation might live. He recalled some of the names of those who fell, and concluded by suggesting that the assemblage rise and stand one-half minute to honor the memory of those comrades of the regiment who have gone to their eternal camping ground.

"The Toast-master rapped up those present and all stood one-half minute in memory of their honored dead.

"After the exercises were concluded, the boys just simply visited as only comrades, whose ties welded in the fire of battle can visit. They were seated in little groups in the banquet hall and in different parts of the hotel, hastily relating their walks in life, but when the time for departure approached cheerful countenances changed to sad ones, voices became horse and tears glistened on the cheeks of many as the "good-byes and "God bless you" "Hope we'll meet again" were said realizing that in the majority of the cases it was the last leave-taking here below".[63]

The following touching anniversary poem to the 100th Regiment was written by Mrs. Inis L. Corbett, a daughter of Comrade Andrew Lyth of Company B.

To the 100th Regiment New York Volunteers
1862March 71912

When the first guns stormed Fort Sumter
In our Nation's darkest hour
When the haters of the Union
Strove to overflow our power.

O'er the land the call came ringing
For the volunteers so brave,
Who would face the battle's fury?
That their country's peace might save.

From each hamlet came the answer
Of the youth so sturdy, strong,

Giving health and life, if need be,
To our country's life prolong.

Of the suffering and danger
Such as we can never know,
Indescribable privations
Never heroes suffered so,

From the fair Queen City members
Came a Regiment brave and true,
Enthusiasm strong among them
As they proudly donned the blue.

Fifty years have come and gone
And their ranks are thinning fast,
But the patriotic spirit
Will remain until the last.

March the seventh 1912
O'er the route they trod before
Marched the veterans brave and true
But as soldiers, go no more.

Bent with suffering, grey with years
Come the "boys" with stead tread
To the strains of march through Georgia
As of yore, with lifted head.

As the people crowded near them
Banners waved and hats were raised,
Dimmed were many eyes with tears
As upon these men they gazed.

May our youth be taught to honor
The bronze button proudly worn
By these men, our noble heroes
And their comrades who have gone.

When the reveille is sounded
In the land beyond the sky,
They will answer to the roll-call
Jesus, captain, here am I.

Inis L. Corbett.[64]

Echoes from Absentees - 1912

EDWARD L. COOK – *Dear Adam – On account of sickness in my family, it will be impossible for me to get away for the 50ᵗʰ anniversary of the departure of the 100ᵗʰ N. Y. Vols. from Buffalo on March 7ᵗʰ. It is a great disappointment. I could not reply to your post card sooner as I have been hoping for a favorable change in conditions that would enable me to meet with my old comrades. I wish you would remember me kindly to all of them. This will probably be the last occasion when so many of the survivors will be together. I shall be with you in thought. I hope that it may be a delightful day and a joyous occasion. For the members of my old company H, my heart beats with love. To the brave boys of the model Company F who shared the contents of their haversacks with me on the march to Appomattox I send my kindest remembrances. Please hand the enclosed check to Comrade Chamberlain and especially remember me to our old executive committee who served together for so many years without ever a misunderstanding or disagreement.* [65]

Veterans Association of the 100ᵗʰ Regiment N. Y. State Vol. – Proceedings of the Twenty-Eighth Annual Reunion held at Buffalo, N. Y. on August 15, 1914

Echoes from Absentees – 1914

GEORGE G. BARNUM, *Duluth, Minn. July 18, 1914 – "I regret that your reunions always come at the time of the year that I find it impossible to leave my home or business. . . I am sure that you will have a good time at the present reunion and in the course of nature, while there will be reunions, the number attending them will gradually grow less. I envoy the ones who live nearby and have the privilege of attending these annual meetings."[66]*

EDWARD L. COOK, *Oakland, N. Y., Aug. 14, 1914 - I had hoped to meet with the old comrades tomorrow but I am feeling so weak and poorly this afternoon that I may not deem it wise to leave home, and therefore enclose a P. O. order of $5.00 for my 1914 dues. If I feel strong enough to walk two and a half miles to the railroad station early tomorrow morning, I shall make the start and try to be with you, probably for the time. If I shall not answer the roll call, please give my love and best wishes to all who may be present and tell them I shall not be seeing them on this occasion as long as I live. To yourself and the other members of the old executive committee, I would wish to be remembered. To the members of Companies H and F, with whom I served as comrade and often in camp, marches and battle line, I send greetings and hope that they may live many more years to enjoy the fruits of their services that made our country what it is today. Kindest regards to yourself and all others present.[67]*

Veterans Association of the 100th Regiment N.Y. State Vol. – Proceedings of the Twenty-Ninth Annual Reunion held at Buffalo, N. Y. on August 28, 1915

"I now take great pleasure in presenting your well known comrade, Adam J. Wagner of Company I, who will give a sketch of the Fighting 100th, which he knows so well how to do."

"Mr. chairman, ladies and gentlemen and comrades: Words cannot express the great honor conferred upon me, and the great blessing from Almighty God to be privileged to address my own comrades on so important and patriotic occasion as this – Comrades with who I have touched elbows to make the history that we so substantially memorialize today by dedicating and unveiling this lasting boulder and tablets. Fifty five years ago this date I was mustered into Company "I" of the 100th regiment and three years later received an honorable discharge there from out of the trenches in front of Petersburg, Va. – of which record I feel justly proud....

"Comrades and friends – The miniature history inscribed upon these tablets just dedicated, to be unveiled, is fraught with intense hardships and sufferings from hunger, thirst, and exposures in the numerous campaigns in which this regiment participated. Approximately 400 of our comrades, fathers, sons, brothers and lovers, freely gave their lives for freedom and a United Country. Some died between the contending lines, unable to move or obtain medical aid; others died in prison pens, but no tongue can ever tell what they endured. Others were pierced by bullets in the fury of battle, or torn by shells in the trenches.

"This boulder and tablets are placed here by the survivors and relatives of the Regiment who stood shoulder to shoulder with them in the fierce struggle for the life of the nation, as a lasting testimonial of their undying love, to commemorate the valorous deeds and sacrifices, and as an object lesson for future generations to emulate: to defend the honor of our glorious flag and the principles it represents; to see to it that the work of George Washington – the father of our country, and his patriots, and that of Abraham Lincoln – the savior of the union, and the 400,000 loyal lives, shall not have been sacrificed in vain thus demonstrating to the world that a government of the people, by the people and for the people can, and shall endure until the trumpet shall sound and life's shadows fell away forever.

"The address was attentively listened to and liberally applauded."[68]

Report of the Treasurer

"Alfred Lyth, treasurer of the memorial fund, then told of the unanimity with which the boulder marker had been placed at the Front, and that it was paid for, and money left in the treasury. By a recent gift from George. G. Barnum of Duluth, of a check for $100 following a previous gift they were able to add to the boulder by surrounding it with granite coping within which would be flower beds. Comrade Lyth's report was cheered."[69]

Veterans Association of the 100ᵗʰ Regiment N.Y. State Vol. – Proceedings of the Thirtieth Second Annual Reunion held at Buffalo, N. Y. on July 18, 1918

Echoes of the Absentees

ED. L. COOK, Oakland, N. Y. – *Dear Friend and Comrade: It is my great disappointment to be unable to meet with you and all my other comrades last Thursday. I made all the arrangements to be there, but on the previous Sunday had a severe attack of rheumatism in the head, eyes, ears and neck, which put me on my back and under the doctor's care. I am sitting up and dressed for the first time in ten days and on the way to speedy recovery. I enclose a check for one dollar for dues. Hope for better luck next year and for an enjoyable meeting for all present. . . .*[70]

GEORGE G. BARNUM, *Duluth, Minn. – Dear Comrade: I have been under the weather for the last few months and have been away from home; I have just received your letter of the 29ᵗʰ of June, announcing a meeting of the Regiment, it being the 55ᵗʰ Anniversary of the Charge on Fort Wagner. Would like very much to have participated in this meeting with you.*[71]

Veterans Association of the 100ᵗʰ Regiment N.Y. State Vol. – Proceedings of the Thirty Seventh Annual Reunion held at Buffalo, N. Y. on July 18, 1923

"...President Lyth produced a letter, written by him to Comrade Thomas Maharg, of his company, while in Andersonville (Ga.) prison, 56 years ago, and which he, as was his custom, enclosed in a letter to his parents, for them to mail to the regiment. The letter with the enclosure did not reach its destination until after Comrade Lyth returned home, and he himself found it among the mail in their letter box at the post office. He put it with some of his other letters and papers, forgetting about the enclosure. Last summer, while looking over old books and papers, he found the letter, still sealed, and upon opening it found Comrade Maharg's letter. He occupied a seat in front of President Lyth and, after relating the above incident, he delivered the letter to

Comrade Maharg unopened. The relating of the incident was very interesting and enjoyed by all present. Comrade Maharg prizes it very highly."[72]

> *Camp Sumter, Andersonville*
> *Sept. 3rd, 1864*

> *Dear Friend Tom*
> *I send you these few lines to let you know that Jim Pixley and myself are in good health; also that Tom Russell is doing well. When we first came to this prison there was about 130 of the Regt but 15 of them have died since. There was 12 from our Co. mainly T. Russell, C.R. Mojo, C. Toner A. P. Cushman, T. B. Reynolds, W. Bishop, A. Tomes and myself and Jim. We are also doing well except W. Phillips who is in the hospital with the scurvy. We oft wish we were with you and the old Salt Junk again. Give my best respects to all the boys. Sergt Maj. Jones is well. Jim sends his regards to you all.*
> *From your old friend,*
> *Alfred Lyth*

Echoes from the Absentees

GEORGE G. BARNUM, *Duluth, Minn – Dear Adam: Yours received. Please to hear from you and hope to for years to come . . . Your annual meetings come in the heat and the summer and in my vacation time. I would very much like to meet with you. Our comrades are passing away, and we will soon only be a memory to those who come after us. I hope that you will have a well attended meeting of all those who live near Buffalo and also hope they will be continued until the last man. I hope to be in Buffalo in the season, and will have the pleasure of seeing you and the rest of the "boys" who live in your city.*[73]

Veterans Association of the 100ᵗʰ Regiment N. Y. State Vol. – Proceedings of the Thirty-eight Annual Reunion held at Buffalo N. Y. on August 18, 1924

December 15, 1924 – Taps has sounded. Lights are out. This soldier, Alfred Lyth, sleeps.

August 13, 1925 - Taps has sounded. Lights are out. This soldier, Thomas Wharton, sleeps.

Veterans Association of the 100ᵗʰ Regiment N. Y. State Vol. – Proceedings of the Fortieth Annual Reunion held at Buffalo, N.Y. on August 16, 1926

Echoes from Absentees

THOMAS MAHARG, Buffalo, N. Y. August 16, 1926 - *Dear Adam: I herewith send to you my dues for 1926, by my nurse; regret I am not well enough to attend the meeting Remember me to all the "girls" and "boys". Maybe next time. Best Wishes*[74]

Veterans Association of the 100ᵗʰ Regiment N.Y. State Vol. – Proceedings of the Forty Second Annual Reunion held at Buffalo, N. Y. on July 18, 1928

Echoes from the Absentees

GEORGE G. BARNUM, *Duluth, Minn, July 31ˢᵗ, 1928 - Dear Comrade: I am enclosing a check for $25.00 which I understand takes care of the perpetual dues. I was in hope that I might have joined you this year at Buffalo at the various reunion but various things prevent it. Of the members now living, I think you and Tom are about the only ones that I know and I guess Tom is confined to the house. He has a brave heart but a cowardly pair of legs. I think you would enjoy a trip up this way. There is a fine line of steamers leaving Buffalo two or three times a week. . .*[75]

Veterans Association of the 100ᵗʰ Regiment N.Y. State Vol. – Proceedings of the Forty-Fifth Annual Reunion held at Buffalo, N. Y. on July 16, 1931

A business meeting was held and the proceedings included this poem:

STAND TOGETHER

While our ranks are growing thinner,
   Comrades falling, one by one
Let us closer stand together
   Till life's battles shall be done.

Stand together, touching elbows,
   As we stood in days of yore
When we brave the hall of battle,
   Heard the cannon's awful roar.

Comrades, we have glorious memories,
   By no others understood –
Memories of a mighty struggle,
   A nation saved by loyal blood.

Keep those memories ever sacred
   In the heart, as days go by;
Let them be as rays of sunshine
   While shadows heavy lie.

Let us keep the fires fraternal
   Burning brightly in each breast,
Till for us the "taps" are sounded
   And we take our final rest.

When our last discharge is given,
   And service here is o'ver,
May we be prepared for muster
   Over on the other Shore.

Our lips shall tell it to our sons,
   And they, in turn, to theirs,
Till generations yet unborn
   Shall tell it to their heirs.[76]

Echoes from the Absentees

THOMAS MAHARG, Buffalo, N.Y. July 13, 1931 – *"President Alfred Lyth, Jr. Secretary Inis L. Corbett and Comrades All: Greetings! I had notice that the 100th Regt. Ass'n. Will hold its annual reunion on the 16th instance. Enclosed please find five dollars ($5.00) for my dues to date, residue, if any, to our worthy secretary for services rendered. I am unable to attend. All I can do is to wish you a jolly good time and a successful meeting".77*

November 26, 1931 -Taps has sounded. Lights are out. This soldier, Thomas Maharg, sleeps

"This chum [Tom Maharg] and I were very close friends all during the war. It was only a short time ago that I received a telegram from his people in Buffalo that he had died over 89 years old. At this present writing, I am nearly 89 myself. At the last reunion of my regiment in July there were only about 16 of the regiment left. Out of about 35 commissioned officers in the regiment, I am the only one left."78

ROLL CALL

Some of the "Boys"
100ᵗʰ Regiment, New York State Volunteers
"Taps have sounded. Lights are out. The soldier sleeps."
Company H

George Clark – George Clark was never seen again after the assault of Fort Wagner on July 18, 1863, and was presumed lost.

George Barnum – George Barnum died on August 2, 1936, in Duluth, Minnesota, at the age of ninety-two. After the war, he moved to Duluth to help survey the land for the railroad. In 1894, he organized the Barnum Grain Company and remained as president of the firm until he died. He won fame for his benefactions to charity and welfare benefit organizations, especially for the benefit of orphaned children. The town of Barnum, Minnesota was named in his honor. Never active in the GAR, he always turned over his monthly civil war pension check to the Children's Home. He would occasionally attend the Veterans Association reunion meetings of his old regiment in Buffalo, New York

Edward Cook – Edward Cook died in his home in Oakland, New York, on November 1, 1919, at the age of eighty-one years. He was a resident of Buffalo for many years, and he was engaged in the plumbing and heating business. He was treasurer of the Veterans Association for a number of years and was a regular attendant at the meetings until unable to do so. He was a gentleman of the old school and had countless friends.

Alfred Lyth – Alfred Lyth passed away on December 15, 1924, at the age of eighty-one years. He was mustered into the 100ᵗʰ Regiment in August 30, 1862, and was captured on May 16, 1864, and confined to Andersonville Prison. He was one of the most faithful, active, and dependable members of the Veterans Association from its organization to the day he expired; he even served as its president. In civil life, he was a member of the firm of John Lyth and Sons, brick and tile business. He became director of several Buffalo banks.

Thomas Maharg – Thomas Maharg died in his home on November 26, 1931, at the age of eighty-nine. He was the last Buffalo survivor of the 100th Regiment New York Infantry, and his death reduced the number of the 100th Regiment survivors to less than a score. Apparently in good health and recovered from a serious illness two years prior, Mr. Maharg was entertaining a group of friends Wednesday night in his home when he suffered a heart attack. He was assisted to bed then collapsed into a coma during the night and did not rally.

Returning to Buffalo at the close of the war, he went to work for his uncle, Hugh Thompson, who operated a soap factory at Chicago and Perry Street. Entering the real estate business in the 1880s, he was successful almost from the beginning and in 1895 built the James Street residence near Elmwood Avenue that he occupied until his death. He retired from active business a short time after building his residence.

At the age of nineteen, Mr. Maharg enlisted in Company H of the famous regiment in 1861 as a private and was promoted to sergeant shortly before the Battle of Appomattox. Until five years prior to his death, Mr. Maharg had never missed a reunion of his regiment. Among his war buddies at these gatherings, he was known as "Sarge Maharg." Accepting his role as the last man in a philosophical manner, Mr. Maharg had only one complaint in later years: "I can take care of my own affairs each day," he once told an interviewer, "but it is rather lonely to have nearly all of your old friends gone. I feel sort of left behind."

Relics that he brought back upon his return as a sergeant indicated the active service he took part in, and after his death, they were kept in his "souvenir box." Strangest of these mementoes is a small piece of shell fastened to the facsimile of the regimental insignia engraved on a copper plate. The piece of shell was taken from Mr. Maharg's lip in 1922 after the metal had protruded through the flesh. To the best of his memory, this wound was suffered sixty years before in the attack on

Fort Wagner at Charleston, South Carolina. He was unaware that the piece of shell had lodged in the "slight cut" he suffered at that time. In later years, Mr. Maharg described the attack of Fort Wagner as one of the most vigorous of the four-year campaign. He recalled vividly the futile attempt to land on Morris Island, which was balked by the bitter fire from the fort. Another cherished relic was the remnant of a quilt that Mr. Maharg confiscated after the capture of a blockade runner.

Edwin Nichols – Edwin Nichols returned to Buffalo, New York, after the war but had left Buffalo by 1867. He wrote a detailed journal during the war. He became a farmer in Leland, Washington, and died in 1891. He didn't participate in the activities of the Veterans Association.

George N. Stoddard – After the war, George Stoddard became a druggist and pharmacist in Buffalo, New York, and did not participate in the activities of the Veterans Association. On the cover of his diary, it indicated that his brother was a member of the Third Missouri Cavalry in the Confederate Army. In later life, he moved to Wilson, New York, and remained there until his death in 1926.

George H. Stowits – George Stowits died in Buffalo, New York, on December 11, 1906, at the age of eighty-four years. He was one of the most popular officers of the 100th Regiment, New York State Volunteers, and one of the most earnest and faithful members of the Veterans Association since its organization in 1887. His forceful addresses to the comrades, their friends, and especially the young—teeming with patriotism and teaching them the lesson of the awful cost of blood and treasure to keep the United States intact—will be heard no more. He was also the author of the regimental history. He served as an orator at numerous reunions as well as its president. He was a principal for many years in the public schools of Buffalo, New York, and was one of the first to inaugurate the salute of the flag by the pupils upon entering the school.

Charles E. Walbridge – Charles Walbridge died on February 13, 1913. He was an active member of the Veterans Association. He was a clerk at Pratt and Company Hardware Store prior to enlisting in the 100th

Regiment. When he returned to Buffalo, he was hired as a buyer by the same company. He ultimately went into business for himself as Walbridge and Company. He was the president of the board of trustees of North Presbyterian Church, president of Buffalo Seminary, and a bank trustee.

Thomas Wharton – Thomas Wharton passed away August 13, 1925. Comrade Wharton was an enthusiastic member of the Veterans Association from the beginning. He always looked forward to the reunion of his regiment. He was janitor of the old Seventy Fourth Regiment Armory—now Elmwood Music Hall building—for many years, but failing health compelled him to retire. For the last ten years of his life, he had no use of his limbs, but he would be brought to the hall on the day of the reunions, and he would remain to the end. He enlisted December 2, 1861, at Buffalo, New York, to serve three years in Company H. He was accidentally wounded at Gloucester Point, Virginia, and in September 1862 was wounded in action at Morris Island, South Carolina on July 18, 1863. He mustered out with detachment January 30, 1865, at Buffalo, New York.

Epilogue

The 100th Regiment, New York State Volunteers was mustered into service from between September, 1861 to January, 1862 and mustered out of service on August 28, 1865. During its service the regiment lost by death, killed in action, 9 officers, and 115 enlisted men and lost by wounds received in action, 2 officers, 68 enlisted men. The regiment also lost by disease and other causes 3 officers, and 20 enlisted men. Furthermore, 19 officers and 417 men were wounded but recovered from their wounds.

In aggregate, of the 2021 men that joined the 100th regiment, a total of 398 men or almost 20% of the regiment died, of whom 1 officer and 79 enlisted men died in the hands of the enemy. In addition, 11 officers and 253 enlisted men were missing, a total of 274, which would bring the total of dead soldiers and missing soldiers to 652 men or 32% of the total regiment! [79]

In the History of the One-Hundredth, New York State Volunteers, the soldiers who authored this book chose to reflect upon the war and express their hope for the future of their young republic. It is fitting to close with their words as well.

"The task is done. The marches, battles and sieges in which the one Hundredth took a prominent and honorable part are recorded . . . . The battles have been refought. During the past year by night and by day, have we stood by the side of dead and wounded comrades, and felt, oh! how intensely, the great sacrifice of human life for the restoration of the Union.

"We have stood by the side of open graves on Morris Island, and before Richmond and Petersburg, with an acute anguish, as deeply felt in imagery, as when the gloom of the hour enthralled us. *Now* we hope to push the *fact* and *thought* far into the mists of memory, and come up as cheerfully as we may have to the consideration of the fruits and blessing of that great, grand and glorious struggle for the life and existence of the nation.

"In the whirl of the age, this great civil war has passed into the shadow-land of history. So recent, that the grass has barely grown over the graves of thousands of the fallen. As a soldier, we were taught to love our country more. The sky, the green earth, the blue waters, *all,* are dearer to us now, than when we had no this bitter lesson of sanguinary war. We were pleased to veil from memory most of the events that attend our thoughts; but they are ever present as the tuition for the practical lessen we have learned, to value the country beyond compare, and daily teach the children under our care to love it beyond words to express.

"The "*unmarked graves*" throughout all the South appeal to us: at Gettysburg, Fortress Monroe, Andersonville, Morris Island and the Southwest, speaking in tones of thrilling import:-we died that you might live. Their bones are bleaching on the Isles, and along the streams, to be remembered as the sacrifice for the existence of the best and freest government the world has every seen. Their forms are ever present, and their deeds are held in grateful remembrances. Our fates might have been reversed. They might have stood where we stand, while we would have been known only as they are known, in praise, in story and in song. Let us not think lightly, not undervalue the martyred dead, who have been sacrificed in a war to save and perpetuate the Union and every star in the "Dear Old Flag". Thank God, they are all there; and those of us, who have survived the crimsoned ordeal, will ever cherish this symbol of our national unity; knowing, that when kissed by the breezes of all lands, the nations will feel and know, that the flag is the emblem of unity and freedom, baptized in the blood of heroes, for its protection and perpetuity, while government lasts and the living millions are shadowed with its folds of stripes and stars.

"As a soldiery, we are not forgotten. In the battle and strife of material life, the soldier may feel that he is neglected, but reflection will speak to him the truth; that it cannot be, as long as memory lasts and government exists, and these waters of the lakes rest in their cradled basins, and the Niagara's current moves swiftly along to the cataract's verge, where rising mists an incense offered to the Giver of all blessings, of a nation's gratitude for the preservation of its unity, peace and power forever.

"To live the life of a soldier does not occur to the citizen but rarely in the course of a century, or in the life of a nation. As soldiers, we tried to do our duty; as citizens, we rejoice. Should foreign foes, or factious one at home, seek again the life of the nation in our day, and then the military culture acquired will serve us, as in the days of the rebellion.

"As a people may we know war no more. May neither our children nor our children's children every act its bloody drama; but in its growth, enterprise, power and vitality, may this youthful republic enjoy peace and freedom evermore.

Hosannas for a land redeemed
The bayonet sheathed, the cannons dumb;
Passed, as some horror, we have dreamed
The fiery meters that have streamed
Threat'ning within our homes to come.

Again, our Banner floats abroad,
Gone the one stain, that on it fell;
And battered by His chast'nigh rod,
With streaming eyes uplift to God,
We say: 'He doeth all things well'"[80].

Footnotes

Part 1

The Organization and Service of the Initial Recruits in the 100th Regiment section and the chapter introductions from chapters two through eleven were excerpts from Lt. Col Charles E, Walbridge's address at the first Annual Reunion of the Veterans Association of the 100th Regiment New York State Volunteers, pages 5-22.

1. George Barnum, Personal Notes, March 7, 1932, page 2.
2. *Ibid.,* page 2.
3. *Ibid., page 3.*
4. George Stoddard, *The 100th Regiment on Folly Island from the Diary of George Stoddard* (Buffalo, New York, Niagara Frontier, v. 1. Winter, 1953-Winter, 1954), page 77. "A Memorandum of Events Passing in the Company and Regt. Of Interest only to George N. Stoddard. Should this fall into the hands of the enemy, I would request of some one of them to do me the kindness to forward it to my Brother, a soldier in the Confederate Army. Direct thus: Henry E. Stoddard, Co. E, Capt. Lotspich, 3rd Mo. Cavalry, Major Samuels, Commanding."
5. *Ibid.* page 78.
6. *Ibid.,* pages 78-79.
7. *Ibid.,* pages 79-80.
8. *Ibid.,* pages 114.
9. *Ibid.,* page 115.
10. *Ibid.,* pages 80-81.
11. Clara Barton, *Letter to Elvira Stone, July 11, 1863,* Clara Barton papers, Manuscript Division, Library of

Congress, Box 1.

12. Clara Barton. *Letter to Dear Friends, December 8. 1863,* Clara Barton papers, Manuscript Division, Library of Congress, Box 1.

13. Diary of E. Nichols, *Veterans Association of the 100th Regiment, N. Y. State Volunteers – Proceedings of the Thirty-Seventh Annual Reunion held at Buffalo, at Buffalo, New York on July 18, 1923*, pages 14-15.

14. Clara Barton, *Letter to Brown and Duer, March 13, 1864,* Clara Barton papers, Manuscript Division, Library of Congress, Box 2.

15. Clara Barton, *Letter to Mr. Parker, December 9, 1863,* Clara Barton papers Manuscript Division, Library of Congress, Box 1.

16. *National Tribune:* A Memorial Charge – Fort Wagner, January 10, 1884.

17. *Harpers Weekly,* The Attack on Fort Wagner, August 8, 1863, page 510.

18. Lt. Henry F. W. Little, *The 7th New Hampshire Volunteers in the War of the Rebellion* (Concord, New Hampshire, Ira. C. Evans, 1896) page 122.

19. *Ibid.,* page 123.

20. W.C. King and W. P. Derby of the 27th Maine, *Camp-Fire Sketches and Battlefield Echoes* (Springfield, Massachusetts, King, Richardson and Co, 1886) page 247.

21. Barnum, page 10.

22. *Veterans Association, 100th Regiment-Proceedings of the Third Annual Reunion, July 4, 1889* (Buffalo, New York, 1892) pages 16-17.

23. *Ibid.,* pages 21-24.

24. *Ibid.,* pages 25-26.

25. *Ibid.,* page 28.

26. *Ibid.,* pages 25-26.

27. *Ibid.,* pages 34-35.

28. *Ibid.,* page 37.

29. *Ibid.,* pages 42-46.

30. *Ibid.,* pages 47-48.

31. *Ibid.,* page 46.

32. *Ibid.,* pages 49-50.

33. Thomas Maharg, *Personal Notes,* 1929.

34. Barnum, page 11.

35. *Ibid.,* page 13.

36. *Ibid.,* page 12.

37. George H. Stowits, *History of the One Hundredth Regiment of New York State Volunteers* (Buffalo, New York: Printing House of Matthews & Warren, 1870), pages 348-349.

38. *Ibid.,* pages 348-351.

39. *Ibid.,* pages 347-348.

40. *Ibid.,* page 353.

41. *Ibid.,* page 355.

42. *Ibid.,* page 356.

43. Barnum, page 14.

44. *Veterans Association, 100th Regiment-Proceedings of the First Annual Reunion. July 1, 1887* (Buffalo, New York, Sunday Truth, 192 to 200 Washington Street, 1887), page 4.

45. *Ibid.,* page 33.

46. Veterans Association, *100th Regiment-Proceedings of the Second Annual Reunion, July 18, 1887* (Buffalo, New York, 1888) page 6

47. *Ibid.,* pages 6-7.

48. *Ibid.,* pages 24-27.

49. *Veteran's Association, 100th Regiment-Proceedings of the Third Annual Reunion, July 4, 1889* (Buffalo, New York, 1889) pages 14-15.

50. *Ibid.,* page 15.

51. *Ibid.,* pages 15-50.

52. *Ibid.,* page 50.

53. *Veterans Association, 100th Regiment-Proceedings of the Sixth Annual Reunion, July17, 1882* (Buffalo, New York, 1892) pages 7-9.

54. *IIbid.,* page 10.

55. *Ibid.*, page 13.
56. *Veterans Association, 100ᵗʰ Regiment-Proceedings of the Fourteenth Annual Reunion, August 16, 1900* (Buffalo, New York, 1901) pages 22-23.
57. *Ibid.*, page 24.
58. *Ibid.*, page 24.
59. *Veterans Association, 100ᵗʰ Regiment-Proceedings of the Sixteenth Annual Reunion, August16, 1902* (Buffalo, New York, 1903) page 24.
60. Thomas Maharg, *Personal Notes, Visit to Morris Island, April, 1905.*
61. *Veterans Association, 100ᵗʰ Regiment-Proceedings of the Twenty Second Annual Reunions, June 17, 1908* (Buffalo, New York, 1906) pages 16-18.
62. *Ibid.*, page 20.
63. *Veterans Association, 100ᵗʰ Regiment-Proceedings of the Twenty Sixth Annual Reunions, July 7, 1912* (Buffalo, New York, 1912) pages 40-42.
64. *Ibid.*, pages 46-48.
65. *Ibid.*, pages 58-59.
66. *Veterans Association, 100ᵗʰ Regiment-Proceedings of the Twenty Eighth Annual Reunion, August 15, 1914* (Buffalo, New York) page 31.
67. *Ibid.*, page 33.
68. *Veterans Association, 100ᵗʰ Regiment-Proceedings of the Twenty-ninth Annual Reunion, August 28, 1915* (Buffalo, New York, 1919), pages 26-30.
69. *Ibid.*, page 31.
70. *Veterans Association, 100ᵗʰ Regiment-Proceedings of the Thirty Second Annual Reunion, July 18, 1918 (Buffalo, New York, 1924) page 20.*
71. *Ibid.*, page 18.
72. *Veterans Association of the 100ᵗʰ Regiment – Proceedings of the Thirty Third Annual Reunion, August 16, 1919 (Buffalo, New York) pages 10-11.*
73. *Veterans Association, 100ᵗʰ Regiment-Proceedings of the Thirty Seventh Annual Reunion, July 18, 1923*(Buffalo,

New York, 1928) page 26.

74. *Veterans Association of the 100th Regiment – Proceedings of the Thirty Eighth Annual Reunion, August 18, 1924 (Buffalo, New York)* page 12.

75. *Veterans Association, 100th Regiment-Proceedings of the Fortieth AnnualReunion, August 16, 1926* (Buffalo, New York, 1932) page 16.

76. *Veterans Association of the 100th Regiment – Proceedings of the Forty-First Annual Reunion, August 16, 1927, page 20.*

77. *Veterans Association of the 100th Regiment – Proceedings of the Forty Second Annual Reunion, July 18, 1928,* pages 30-31.

78. *Veterans Association of the 100th Regiment – Proceedings of the Forty-Fifth   Annual Reunion, July 16, 1931,* page 31.

79. Barnum, page 2.

Epilogue

80. Frederick Phisterer, *New York in the War of the Rebellion, (*Albany, New York: 3rd ed. (Albany, New York, J. B. Lyon Company, 1912).

81. Stowits, page 359-362.

Bibliography

Books:

Blight David W. *Race and Reunion.* Cambridge, Massachusetts: The Belknap Press of Harvard University Press, 2001

Bradshaw, Timothy E. Jr. *Battery Wagner.* Columbia, South Carolina: Palmetto Historical Works. 1993

Bryan, Charles F. Jr. and Nelson D. Lankford, ed. *Eye of the Storm.* New York, New York: The Free Press, 2000

Burton E. Milby. *The Siege of Charleston 1861-1865.* Columbia, South Carolina: University of South Carolina Press, 1970

Child, William. *Letters from a Civil War Surgeon.* Solon, Maine: Polar Bear & Company, 1995

Galloway, Richard P. *One Battle Too Many – The Writings of Simon Boliver Hulbert, Private, Company E, 100th Regiment, New York State Volunteers 1861-1864.* Gaithersburg, Maryland: Olde Soldier Books, Inc, 1987

Horn, John. *The Petersburg Campaign June 1864 – April, 1865.* Conshohocken, Pennsylvania: Combined Publishing Company, 2000

King, W. C. and W. P. Derby. *Camp-Fire Sketches and Battlefield Echoes.*
Springfield, Massachusetts: King, Richardson and Co., 1886

Lankford, Nelson. *Richmond Burning.* New York, New York: Penguin
Books, 2002

Little, Henry F. W. *The 7ᵗʰ New Hampshire Volunteers in the War of the
Rebellion.* Concord, New Hampshire: Ira C. Evans, 1896

Longacre, Edward G. *Army of Amateurs.* Mechanicsburg,
Pennsylvania: Stackpole Books, 1997

Logue, Larry L. *To Appomattox and Beyond.* Chicago, Illinois: Ivan R.
Dee, Inc, 1996

Marvel, William. *Andersonville, The Last Depo.t* Chapel Hill, North
Carolina: The University of North Carolina Press, 1994

McConnell, Stuart. *Glorious Contentment The Grand Army of the
Republic* – 1865-1900. Chapel Hill, North Carolina: University
of North Carolina Press, 1992)
Oates, Stephen B. *A Woman of Valor Clara Barton and the Civil War.*
New York, New York: The Free Press, 1994

Phisterer, Frederick. *New York in the War of the Rebellion, 3ʳᵈ Ed.*
Albany, New York: J. B. Lyon Company, 1912

Ray, Jean R. *The Diary of a Dead Man 1862-1864.* New York, New
York: Eastern Acorn Press, 1981

Robertson, William Glenn. *Back Door to Richmond.* Baton Rouge,
(Louisiana; Louisiana State University Press, 1987

Stoddard, George. *The 100ᵗʰ Regiment on Folly Island from the Dairy of
George Stoddard.* Niagara Frontier, Vol. 1, Winter 1953, Winter, 1954.

Stowits, George H. *History of the One Hundredth Regiment of New
York State Volunteers.* Buffalo, New York: Printing House of
Matthews & Warren, 1870

Geoffrey C. Ward,. *The Civil War.* New York, New York: Alfred A. Knopf, Inc., 1990

Wheeler, Richard. *Voices of the Civil War.* New York, New York: Thomas Y. Cronell Company, 1976

Winik, Jay. *April, 1865, The Month that Saved America.* New York, New York: Harper Collins Publishing Co., 2001

White, Otis. F. R. *New Hampshire in the Great Rebellion.* Claremont, New Hampshire: Tracy Crabe & Company, 1870

Wise, Stephen R. *Gate of Hell.* Columbia, South Carolina: University of South Carolinas Press, 1994

Woodhead, Henry. *Voices of the Civil War.* Alexandria, Virginia: Time-Life Books, 1997

Periodicals, Diaries and other Publications:

Personal Notes, George Barnum, March 7, 1932.

Personal Notes, Thomas Maharg, 1929.

The Attack on Fort Wagner. August 8, 1863 *Harper's Weekly* page 510.

Veterans Association – Proceedings of Annual Reunions of the 100th Regiment New York Volunteers, Vols. I –LV, 1887-1941

Index

Breinigsville, PA USA
01 December 2009

228449BV00005B/1/P